LANDSCAPING WITH NATIVE TREES

LANDSCAPING WITH NATIVE TREES

THE NORTHEAST, MIDWEST, MIDSOUTH & SOUTHEAST EDITION

GUY STERNBERG & JIM WILSON

CHAPTERS PUBLISHING LTD., SHELBURNE, VERMONT 05482

Published by
Chapters Publishing Ltd.
2031 Shelburne Road
Shelburne, Vermont 05482

Library of Congress Cataloging-in-Publication Data

Sternberg, Guy.
Landscaping with native trees : Northeast, Midwest, Midsouth & Southeast edition / by Guy Sternberg and Jim Wilson.
p. cm.
Includes bibliographical references (p.) and index.
ISBN 1-881527-65-4: $34.95. —ISBN 1-881527-66-2: $24.95
1. Ornamental trees—United States. 2. Trees—United States. 3. Landscape gardening—United States. 4. Ornamental trees—United States—Pictorial works. 5. Trees—United States—Pictorial works. I. Wilson, Jim. II. Title.
SB435.5.W54 1995
635.9'5173—dc20 94-25253

Trade distribution by
Firefly Books Ltd.
250 Sparks Avenue
Willowdale, Ontario
Canada M2H 2S4

Printed and bound in Canada by Metropole Litho, Inc.
St. Bruno de Montarville, Quebec

Designed by Eugenie Seidenberg Delaney

Front Cover: photograph by Larry Lefever/Grant Heilman Photography, Inc.
Back Cover: background photograph by Richard W. Brown;
author photograph by McJunkin Photography
Tree & Leaf Silhouettes: illustrations by Adelaide Murphy
USDA Hardiness Zone Map: illustration by Jean Carlson Masseau

We dedicate this work to Edie Sternberg and Jane Wilson (our patient tree-widows), and to our parents, who opened early doors to appreciation of the natural world. We also respectfully acknowledge some wise mentors from decades past who taught us about woody plants, natural ecosystems and the virtues of native-species use before that concept became popular.

—G.S. & J. W.

CONTENTS

PART ONE

INTRODUCTION

MANY OF OUR COMMON NATIVE TREES would be the cream of any ornamental crop. They are beautiful and they belong. They reinforce our sense of place, evoking childhood memories and reassuring us that this, indeed, is home. When their basic needs are respected, they give us a landscape that makes few demands yet bestows the aesthetic benefits and seasonal nuances that only the most well-adapted plants—the natives—can provide.

Throughout our history, we in North America have sought the unusual and exotic: Old World crystal for our tables, tropical birds for pets and the most rare or flamboyant of foreign plants for our gardens. However, there is a movement afoot to reassess our horticultural preferences. We are beginning to appreciate our native trees and other plants and to recognize some faults among the exotics. There is a decided trend to use more native plants in residential and commercial landscapes.

What exactly is a "native plant"? This depends on the context in which the term is used. Most plants, except those developed through human tinkering and hybridization, are natives of somewhere. Because, over time, species adjust their ranges with evolutionary adaptations and environmental changes, the definition of "native" must be flexible. Some plants now considered native to the southern United States, for example, might have evolved in Canada during a warm climate period millions of years ago.

In this sense, the only purely native trees are the ones that still grow where they originated. Scientists call such species autochthonous. Some plants are considered endemic to a particular area because they are not found elsewhere at present. Others might be pandemic and distributed across a vast natural range, usually with geographic races adapted to local habitats, or provenance. In a more general sense, we could define a native plant as one that is truly a plant in its natural place.

Fox squirrels and other animals depend upon native trees. Previous page: dogwoods.

For the purpose of discussion in this book, a native tree is considered to be a species that existed in what is now eastern North America prior to the arrival of European settlers (as opposed to a naturalized tree, which has escaped into a new habitat because of human influence). More precisely, a native tree, for you, is one that has proven its adaptability to your climate and soil conditions over the past several thousand years! Each of us can make a contribution to our environment by helping to preserve such native trees and by using them in our landscapes.

What is so wrong with nonnative plants? Sometimes, nothing at all. Anyone with a genuine interest in horticulture must admit a certain fascination with a favorite Asian flower or European shrub. And our meals would be quite dull, indeed, without some of the exotic food crops from our gardens or farms. Even some of what we think of as native plants become nonnative when we cultivate them beyond their natural ranges or habitat types or modify them by breeding.

Many native plants have been "improved" for horticultural purposes by the infusion of a stray gene here and there from a foreign relative. This genetic manipulation is usually done to increase a plant's ornamental value. But the widespread cloning of such genetically engineered individuals can narrow the gene pool, with potentially disastrous results. Occasionally, genetic manipulation is undertaken to give some native plant resistance to a disease that it caught from an imported species. Ironically, the resistant gene is often extracted from the newcomer to fight the very disease it introduced. We thus find ourselves responsible for the adverse effects of carelessly moving plants from one part of the world to another.

Many exotic plants have been moved into environments that present few limits to their reproductive or competitive ability. Some of these species are becoming the starlings of the plant kingdom: multiplying out of control, displacing beneficial native species, overwhelming nature preserves and causing general ecological havoc.

Most biologists, and quite a few gardeners, are aware of some of the environmental problems caused by punk tree, Australian-pine, kudzu, Japanese honeysuckle, multiflora rose, autumn olive, purple loosestrife and on and on through a litany of ecological nightmares brought about by myopic meddlings. We humans have been slow to learn. In fact, some of these weedy species are still propagated and sold in parts of the United States and Canada. But a backlash against some imported species has begun.

The majority of exotic plants we cultivate might never become such ecological pests, but they still could have some surprises in store. The "super" exotic plants, the ones that thrive here in the absence of their native predators and parasites, can eventually begin to languish as those debilitating organisms gradually find their way here. Even in the absence of these controls, many aggressively marketed aliens simply don't live up to their glowing reputations as "wonder trees" except under ideal conditions.

Other exotic plants require a lot of care in our conditions, and many of them may not be worth the effort. Some have very beautiful flowers, which might last for a few days each year if the buds aren't killed by a late frost, for which they are not adapted. Many lack significant fall color or have little resistance to leaf mildews and other problems. Some will die back every few years as the extremes of our climate take their toll. Some are conspicuously out of place because of silvery foliage or other qualities developed in response to their own habitats—characteristics that may clash with your garden or with the native plants best suited to it.

While annual flowers from China or Africa might be pretty, they are small, inexpensive, temporary condiments for the landscape. They are replaced easily, so their loss to winter cold or summer drought is of no great consequence. Trees, however, can live for many decades and are dominant features in any landscape setting. Tree-planting is a lifetime investment, and such investments should always be made with prudence.

OUR NATIVE SPECIES HAVE EVOLVED WITH our climate, soils and pathogens and with each other over thousands of years. Not so with exotic imports. Many of them have been grown here for only a few decades or less (sometimes *much* less). They have not been tested by the same climatological uncertainties as our native plants. The next weather extreme—next month or next year—could eliminate some of them from the landscape.

Scientists know from tree-ring analyses, fossil records, glacier ice cores and other data that our prehistory was marked by frequent environmental upheavals and that only the most adaptable species survived. Presumably, such ecological changes will continue and, from time to time, will topple some of the short-term foreign pretenders from the thrones of our landscape. Some of your expensive exotic trees could be among the casualties.

Considering the threats to our environment—ozone holes, global warming, air pollution, soil disruption, habitat destruction and the introduction of exotic pests to new habitats—nothing is certain. We live in an evolving system, and our actions—demographic and environmental—are accelerating the spiral of change. Thus it makes increasing sense to rely on our native plants, the survivors that have adapted to the changes in our regional environment and that continue to grace our wild lands, unaided by (or in spite of) human intervention.

In this book, we present a cross-section of native trees. Some are readily available at local nurseries. Others can be found in mail-order catalogs or easily propagated from seeds or cuttings. Some may be difficult to find or to start, but they are suggested for selective preservation if they are already growing on your land or sprout as volunteers in some appropriate place. Some are recommended simply for you to protect and admire in a park or forest. Like wild animals, they are best untamed. Their value to wildlife, and to the entire ecological web in which they have evolved and persevered, commends them to you as much as their visual quality.

If you are considering digging native plants from wild populations, please think again. Such collecting involves ethical, legal and scientific considerations, which we will address later. Authorized plant rescues conducted one step ahead of a bulldozer might be commendable (although not always successful), and minor collecting of common species from disturbed sites may be harmless. But your first choice should always be to preserve existing trees or to purchase well-grown, nursery-propagated native species.

Such plants have been cultivated and managed to assure successful transplanting. They are worth a fair price in the long run. In addition, purchasing natives from a nursery will encourage the production and sale of more native plants. You could be the first gardener, landscape architect or conservationist in your area to reach beyond the selection of exotic plants that most nurseries stock in such great numbers. You might have to insist that your nursery special-order native trees, but do persist. You may start a trend toward greater availability and appreciation of native plants in your area.

Join the growing vanguard of modern, responsible landscape design and management—learn from nature, plant and preserve native trees and then take pride in a job well done. Your accomplishments will benefit garden design, our environment and your spirit.

AT HOME IN THE FOREST

NATURE IS A SYSTEM OF OVERLAPPING parts, with edges that are constantly changing. Each piece or species follows certain strategies for success in a competitive world, where the occupation of every space is contested by myriad organisms. Over time, the competing flora sort themselves into a predictable assemblage for specific soil and climatic conditions.

Superior trees and other organisms equally suited to a particular set of soil, temperature, moisture, light and air quality conditions form a natural community that can be found wherever those conditions prevail. The balance of species can be so finely tuned that subtle changes in growing conditions result in different species dominating in different areas or in some species being entirely replaced by others.

The minimum winter temperature in your area will dictate which trees are hardy there. Some southern species drop out of the

A mixed conifer-deciduous forest in Vermont. Limitations to tree growth here include acidic soils and winter cold. Previous page: Montezuma cypress.

picture at the first hard frost. Others are eliminated progressively as one travels northward, in a pattern reflected by the zones shown on the USDA Hardiness Zone Map (see page 287). Many species are able to protect their sap from freezing at temperatures well below those that turn water to ice. This process, and the trees that use it, will fail precisely at 40 degrees below zero, which is the northern limit of USDA zone 3. Other trees tolerate even greater cold, but many will wither in the heat of a southern summer or be unprepared for a late killing frost in spring.

Local conditions, or the microclimate, can explain a tree's ability to survive in certain portions of your site but not in others. This selective survival is increased by factors such as protection from drying winds, soil-temperature moderation on north-facing slopes (or under mulch) and shade from the hot afternoon sun. It can be adversely affected by summer heat that builds up in urban areas with their expanses of pavement and concrete and by the cumulative impact of our vehicles, our pets and our daily activities. The genetic pattern of an individual tree also plays a part, with trees of local origin frequently having an edge over trees of the same species from a distant area.

Some species that are native to one area may succeed in adjacent areas where only some of the conditions are the same, as long as their most prominent limiting factors—drought, perhaps, or deep shade—remain unchanged. Such species are often ecological generalists, capable of surviving reasonably well under varied conditions. Other species will specialize, becoming perfectly adapted to a narrow habitat at the expense of their adaptability to other niches. These specialists are indicator species. Their occurrence on your site is strong evidence of certain specific growing conditions. Such specialists are often found on marginal sites where their competitors cannot thrive, but some will do fine under cultivation on more productive land, if competition is controlled.

Many trees prefer acidic soil; others grow in limestone areas. Some require ample moisture, while others can compete under drier conditions. Either type might be tolerant, or intolerant, of flooding or of the poor drainage that accompanies tight, com-

A grove of paper (canoe) birch adds a singular beauty to the deep woods or landscape of the North.

pact soils. Some trees resist damage from fire, wind, ice, insects or ocean salt spray better than others. Some will take charge on ideal growing sites that offer everything in moderation but will fail under less-than-perfect conditions. And some, called climax species, will succeed in displacing others over the long term as local conditions are changed by the growth of the pioneer trees.

Such changes can be caused by the shade or leaf litter cast by the pioneers, which can suppress weedy herbaceous plants or reduce evaporation from the soil. Other changes occur with the establishment of forest-inhabiting mycorrhizal fungi, important to the survival of the trees that follow the pioneers. There also might be changes in wildlife influence, because of habitat development, that affect seed dispersal. Many plants are allelopathic, releasing chemicals that selectively retard certain competitors. Usually, changes affecting germination and seedling establishment are the most important, because a tree is most vulnerable at the seedling stage.

By learning what types of trees are growing on your land and what types are not, you can make some reasonable judgments about your overall growing conditions. Some of these can be changed. Pulling weeds or providing irrigation, even for a short time, might allow a desired species to become established. On the other hand, some conditions, such as soil acidity or summer heat, can be difficult or impossible to alter.

As you read about the needs of the various trees in this book, you will notice certain patterns beginning to emerge. You can look at the trees in your neighborhood and assume that you can plant those same species and have them flourish. As you become more familiar with forest guilds, or groups of trees, you can begin to make reasonable assessments of which other uncultivated native plants will also succeed.

Why aren't these other species already growing on your property? The trees may have been cut for timber or killed by livestock grazing. There might be increased road salt leaching into the ground or more exhaust fumes in the air. Fire control could have eliminated the necessary conditions for some seeds to germinate.

Development brings changes to the environment, and the consequences can be felt by trees as much as by more delicate-looking flora.

If these changes persist, select trees that are adapted to some of these new or stressful conditions. Many swamp trees, for instance, tolerate compacted urban soil. Trees from floodplains are resistant to the soggy state of heavily irrigated lawns. Prairie species are more tolerant than forest types to the competition and allelopathic effects of turf roots.

Trees that are the first to establish in a sunny field, so-called early-successional species, may be able to

The rocky soils of the Northeast can present problems for tree planters, but species such as maple and birch respond surprisingly well to such conditions.

handle the heat near a south-facing brick wall or a city sidewalk. Those accustomed to hardpan might best adapt where the natural soil profile has been destroyed by a careless contractor. If you are lucky enough to have great soil and are careful to limit the encroachment of turf or pavement in your planting area, by all means put in some of the magnificent classic tree species that require optimum conditions.

When you begin to draw up a list of trees for your landscape, you may want to include a favorite native or an exotic species that is not ideal for your site. That would be understandable; this is what turns landscapes into gardens. However, remember that the farther you reach for special trees to achieve a certain effect, the more you will be burdened with site preparation and maintenance. This stands in contrast to the premise of native-plant landscaping. Pick adaptable natives and you will be on a path toward a beautiful and varied landscape that makes comparatively few demands.

GETTING STARTED

THERE ARE PERHAPS FIVE OPTIONS, OR PATHS, you can choose when beginning to work with a site. They include: propagation, purchase, natural regeneration, wild collection and preservation. If you are fortunate enough to own a forested tract, your first option will be preservation. But if you start with a cleared piece of land (or wish to enlarge or diversify your existing forest) you may choose from among the remaining options. Each has its advantages and drawbacks.

PROPAGATION: If you are bringing in new trees, you may want to consider propagating them yourself from seed or by using cuttings or grafting. Many of us remember the first acorn we planted as a child, and we feel a special relationship with the tree that grew from it. Growing trees from known sources is a good way to guarantee that they are from quality stock adapted to your area. As we discuss each species in this book, we will provide information on propagating and transplanting.

PURCHASE: If you lack a green thumb or the time required to grow trees from scratch, buy native stock from a reliable nursery, where you can evaluate characteristics like form, fall color, and perhaps flowers, before you bring it home. You may want a cultivar (cultivated variety) that promises a predictable form, color and vigor.

In general, nursery-grown stock up to 2 inches (5 cm) in diameter is a good value. Larger trees become proportionately more expensive and increasingly hard to handle. If you have enough money and an open, accessible planting site, there is almost no limit to the size of the tree you can transplant. But bear in mind that smaller trees become established more quickly than larger ones.

Site preparation and maintenance will govern the success of any planting. A favorite nurseryman's proverb is "Don't put a dollar tree in a dime hole." The entire area should be loosened over a distance of several times the diameter of the rootball you are transplanting, at least to spade depth. If the soil needs to be amended or the drainage improved, do it before you set in the tree. Once the tree is lowered into its new home, keep foot traffic and turf out of the root zone. Grass may seem inconsequential, but its roots can steal valuable nutrients and water.

NATURAL REGENERATION: Instead of shopping at a nursery, you may want to encourage natural regeneration. If you have the space, prepare a seedbed of a few hundred square feet or several acres. Remove the turf, clear out the accumulated duff and let the wind blow in seed. Let squirrels bury nuts. Let nature take its course. There is no better way to achieve a random pattern of species and spacing. Plan to thin

Throughout the seasons, trees interpret nature's magic. A glaze of ice can turn a field of nursery stock to crystal. Previous page: Silver maple seedlings dot the forest floor.

When transplanting trees, remember the proverb "Don't put a dollar tree in a dime hole."

A mechanical tree-mover can make short work of saving a good tree that was growing in a bad spot.

seedlings as they develop, with a careful eye toward the potential size of the young trees you leave in. Remember that a forest is a dense community of tall trees reaching for a piece of the sky, whereas a savanna is a scattering of full-crowned shade trees. Decide at the beginning what type of grove you desire.

WILD COLLECTION: An option we must discuss with some reservation is collecting wild trees. Most trees are so easy to propagate or buy that wild collection should generally be disdained as a form of piracy. Yet, there are circumstances when it is a viable, and even noble, option—with the owner's permission and with any applicable permits in hand.

Some trees reproduce on disturbed sites in such numbers that most seedlings will die in a year or two. Other seedlings take root in pastures and fields that are periodically cultivated. Hence, without relocation, the trees are doomed. Still other species send up suckers, or new stems, that are extraneous, or even detrimental, to the parent plant. Under such conditions, it can be appropriate to relocate some of the surplus material.

Any native plant collecting should be governed by etiquette and ecological sensitivity. Remember to fill any excavation. You want to maintain the goodwill of the landowner and ensure that no one stumbles into the hole. You might be liable. Take the time to explain your collecting to anyone who might be watching. You want to educate others by explanation and example. To the extent possible, apply these additional guidelines: Never take the biggest or the best or any colorful species from a prominent spot. Collect in the dormant season. Disturb as little of the site as possible. Never take plants from designated natural areas. Be aware of what species locally are protected by the Endangered Species Act of 1973 or by similar state or provincial legislation. And don't try to move trees from shady to sunny areas. In sum, never allow

Many native-plant nurseries grow a surprising array of species in small sizes and at reasonable prices.

With professional care, priceless specimens like this enormous bur oak can be preserved during construction, adding value to the property and comfort to the home.

Sometimes, even fairly large trees can be dug by hand from construction sites and moved to where they can be saved and appreciated.

exuberance to overcome restraint. If you do proceed, remove a large ball of soil around the tree to minimize damage to its roots. Wild trees have not been root-pruned by a nursery.

There is an exception to the collector's caveat, one that landscape restorationists call a "rescue operation." If all attempts to save a forest or a tree have failed and the bulldozer is on its way, break out the spades, wheelbarrows and horticultural skill. If endangered species are involved, consult with your state or provincial resource-management agency. Your best efforts may fail. You may be scoffed at by developers. But you may succeed and, thereby, preserve not only a rare or beautiful tree but much of the complex web of life dependent on it.

PRESERVATION: If your property is graced with a varied stand of trees, you are fortunate but perhaps not free of difficult decisions. You can choose the preservationist path and draft a landscape plan that incorporates the prominent trees already on your site. However, there may be tension between your plans and your trees—which may stay and which may have to go—as you build a house or realize a landscape design. Let the trees influence the process.

Inventory the trees with a certified arborist and landscape architect to identify the "keepers" before you settle on any construction plans. Then monitor all construction activities to prevent damage. You may want to preserve specific trees for a number of reasons. Some trees may be rare locally and will maintain the biological diversity of your site. Some may have particular aesthetic or wildlife value. Some may be more healthy and vigorous than their neighbors. Some may be resilient species, best able to cope with construction disturbances that may lie ahead.

Indian-trail marker trees, such as this old white oak, represent a precious living connection with the unwritten history of North America.

Your land may be home to some endangered tree species or to commanding, picturesque specimens. There may be giants (possibly national champions for their species) or commemorative and historic trees. These are irreplaceable and should not be treated as simply, in the parlance of forestry, "renewable resources." The rights of ownership carry social responsibility.

Site preparation and maintenance can be rewarded by spectacular spring displays, such as the one offered by these flowering dogwoods.

Historic trees may have shaded important tribal gatherings or provided a backdrop for great orations. Their towering height may have been a landmark for competing armies. As living, growing organisms, they denote the passage of time and give the perspective of age to a place or event. The size and condition of a particular tree may have been recorded in a historical photograph or drawing, making it a visual part of war or peace. As arboreal archives, trees speak not only of the human past but of the history of the natural world. Within their layers lies a chronological record of the slow but unceasing changes of our climate and of the land.

As a landowner, you are a temporary steward of the soil and the plants. When the time comes to pass this responsibility on, do it with the positive feeling that, to the extent possible, you preserved the important living connections to the past.

The responsibility for preservation, however, is not limited to landowners on their property. Vast tracts of land under public ownership are home to thousands of commanding and historically significant trees. Too many public agencies have no legal mandate, no budget and little inclination to conserve these trees that happen to grow within their domain. Too few have any understanding of arboriculture. All of us must try to help each new generation of public land managers appreciate the venerable living resources that have been placed under their care. With preservation, there are no compromises. If a tree or a forest is to be saved, it must stay in its present location and in its present environment.

Preservation involves being faithful to the past. The other options for expanding or restoring woodland diversity—propagation, purchase, natural regeneration and wild collection—are all undertaken with an eye to the future. Your efforts will take time to bring rewards. But your achievements will grant future generations the opportunity, and the challenge, of preserving what you have begun.

BUILDING AROUND YOUR TREES

This is a book about native trees more than a work on tree protection and maintenance. However, care for one often involves concern about the others. We expect that many people who own a woodland or share our broad curiosity and love for trees may also be considering the construction of a house, an addition, a garage, a patio or a pond and that you might welcome advice on how to protect your trees during the process.

Trees grow so large, change so gradually and live so long that we sometimes forget how easily they can be killed or injured. Part of that misunderstanding is due to the slow, resolute physiology of the tree itself. Unlike vegetables or herbaceous ornamentals, trees do not immediately show the effects of drought, illness or injury, in part because they accumulate enormous food reserves while healthy. Girdle a peony and it keels over in a day. Girdle a tree in the summer and it may live out the season, apparently unaffected. But most likely it will slowly die.

Above left: Prominent protection can spare trees inadvertent damage from heavy equipment. Above right: Tree roots are often damaged during construction by excessive cutting and filling, compacting soil and improperly installing utility lines. Previous page: A stately sugar maple graces a house in Maine.

Though slower to take their toll, injuries to a tree reverberate through your landscape with far more resonance than damage to your "lesser" plants. The trauma takes so much longer to undo. Once a mature tree dies, it cannot be replaced in one season or five seasons, or sometimes even in a human lifetime. Prevention, then, is critical because too often there is no cure.

If you are embarking on a construction project, conducting an inventory of your trees should be your first step. That should be followed with a site analysis and the assignment of priorities to individual trees, or groups of trees, and patches of smaller, understory vegetation. Engage a landscape architect, who will help you realize a design that is in harmony with your site analysis. The landscape architect and your arborist should address concerns such as grade changes from excavating or soil compaction from heavy equipment before these issues become a problem for your trees. Certain trees might be pruned or transplanted before they get "in the way" of construction vehicles.

The primary root area of each tree, within approximately 15 feet (5 m) of the trunk (this measurement will vary depending on the tree's size), should be protected from trenches for pipes or utility lines. However, where there is no alternative, the trench should run directly under the tree, rather than a few feet from it and across the spoke-like pattern of the roots. Boring under the trunk or root flare by hand or with small power tools and sliding pipes or wire under the exposed roots will minimize injury.

Where fill must be dumped, incorporate porous material or inexpensive tile aeration systems to reduce soil compaction and loss of oxygen to the tree roots. If an excavation for a footing would cut major roots, consider posts or piers to bridge the critical area. Your design team of landscape architect and arborist may come up with a number of creative and inexpensive solutions to spare the trees that you will want to en-

Landscape trees in your yard deserve protection: they cannot be replaced in a season, or sometimes even in a lifetime.

joy long after the construction is completed.

When choosing a contractor, ask for references from owners of other wooded sites. It often takes several years for tree damage to become apparent, so don't be content to look only at the job he finished last month. Try to draft an agreement that includes a bonus for taking precautions to preserve your trees and a penalty clause for damage in accordance with standard tree-appraisal procedures adopted by the International Society of Arboriculture.

Ask your arborist to review the measures intended to protect trees during construction. These may include fencing to limit traffic and restrict the stockpiling of material to specific areas, away from the roots of your most important or sensitive trees. Construction workers may need to be reminded that a tree is more than a post with leaves, that spilled fuel, concrete slurry, mortar and paint can be toxic to its roots. They might not realize that minor branches should be pruned with a saw, not a backhoe, or that a shallow root pruning with a trencher should be done before any excavation in the root zone. They may not know that backhoe work should be done from a radial position, (facing the tree) with a vertical slicing motion, so that any unpruned roots are not wrenched laterally. Broken or torn roots should be neatly trimmed with a saw and kept from drying or freezing while the excavation is open.

All of this might seem like a lot of trouble, but remember, you only have to take these precautions once. If you do, the minor wounds inflicted on the landscape will quickly heal. If you do not, the consequences may be impossible to rectify.

Protecting your trees from construction disturbances is only part of this discussion. Protecting your house from trees is another. A picturesque old specimen with craggy limbs and a few dead branches high in its crown can become a hazard if a house is built, a car is parked or a sidewalk is laid out beneath its canopy. If one of those "widow maker" branches falls, someone could be hurt, and assuming it is someone else, you could be liable. Even young healthy trees pose problems if buildings or utility lines are too near. Branches that normally arch above a roof or an overhead wire on a calm day can sag several feet under a load of fruit, ice or wet foliage. Have these overhanging branches pruned before they sweep off your shingles or knock out your electric service.

Tree roots, too, present potential problems. Spreading out like inquisitive fingers, roots can invade drainpipes, heave sidewalks and even crack thick concrete foundations. Many headaches and much expense can be spared by keeping young trees at least 10 feet (3 m) away from buildings, pipes and walkways. If, for some reason, a tree grows within that 10-foot zone, consider installing a commercially fabricated barrier to keep the roots out of your basement or your plumbing.

Trees that appear to have survived the rigors of construction in fine health may still have been weakened. It can take several years for them to adjust to their new environment and for some injuries to become apparent. Prior to construction, the trees might have been in a forest area; those that remain may now be receiving more sun and may be surrounded by a

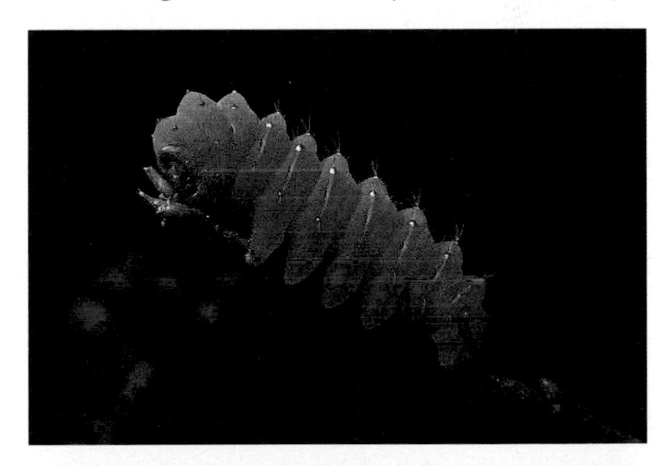

Top: Solitary caterpillars, such as this polyphemus larva, do very little damage to established trees and become some of our most spectacular moths and butterflies. Above: Working from within, a variety of borers—sometimes the most damaging of insects—weakened and ultimately killed this honey locust.

Topping is never a sound practice unless the tree is being removed.

new lawn. Turf roots can steal their nutrients and compete for precious water. Mulch any soil that has become compacted, and try to be restrained in watering your new lawn. Tree roots may decay and die in ground that is soggy and starved of oxygen because of excessive irrigation.

If some of your young trees were transplanted or suddenly exposed to the wind by the removal of their neighbors, you might have to carefully tie them to a stake for a season. Staking is not ideal. Trees need to flex in order to develop the strength to support themselves. Tying should be done without constricting the trunk, as Sir Francis Bacon noted more than 350 years ago in his epic tree book *Sylva Sylvarum*. "Binding," he wrote "doth hinder the natural swelling of the tree." However, supporting a few trees may be a necessary part of post-construction care.

Closely monitor all your prized trees for signs of weakness, insect infestation, drought and disease. These might be minor concerns for vigorous trees, but they pose a serious threat to those recovering from stress. You may have planned your entire design around certain specimens, and you will want to keep them as fixtures in the landscape.

The best indications that your trees have made it through the post-construction period are: no branches dying in the upper part of the canopy; no fungi on or around the base and an annual growth increment at the ends of the twigs similar to that prior to construction. Once you are satisfied that your trees have recovered, you can relax somewhat and slip into more casual, long-term management. This can involve deep-watering during severe droughts and mulching.

Mulching was another technique praised as early as 1627 by Sir Francis Bacon: "for that it retaineth the moisture which falleth at any time upon the tree, and suffereth it not to be exhaled by the Sunne." Establishing a broad, shallow mulched area around a tree remains one of the most effective things a landowner can do to moderate weather extremes, control weeds and simulate natural, woodsy soil conditions.

You might consider lightning protection as well, if you have a valuable specimen (or any tall tree on an exposed hill), and cabling and bracing, if your tree has a structural weakness. These should not be considered do-it-yourself measures but should be contracted to a qualified arborist. You might also ask the arborist to

The bark of young trees may need protection to prevent this type of damage from browsing rodents and larger mammals.

Mulching provides a favorable rooting environment and keeps fallen fruit and leaves off lawns.

handle any pruning needs that are beyond your capability. Don't ask him to "top" the tree, however. Topping destroys the tree's appearance and its structural integrity, leading to its premature death. There is never a legitimate excuse to top a tree.

Young trees should be pruned when they are still small to remove double leaders, suckers and parallel or clustered limbs and to encourage a strong, aesthetic structure. Pruning recommendations have changed over the past few years, based upon new research, so read one of the many current books or seek knowledgeable advice.

Techniques for managing insects and disease have evolved in stages over the years as well. A few decades ago, North America was wallowing in the age of "modern" chemicals, and the accepted practice was to saturate the environment with the most deadly sprays available. Then we entered the period of *Silent Spring* and chemical backlash, and organic procedures were in vogue. Certain aspects of chemical and organic strategies were later combined in what is called Integrated Pest Management, or IPM. Pest levels are monitored and action is taken, starting with the least toxic approach, if an economic or biological threshold of damage is reached. Now, we are entering the age of Plant Health Care, or PHC. We don't wait for a problem to develop but try to maintain healthy, vigorous trees to discourage disease and harmful insects from ever becoming a threat. IPM, organic methods and selected chemicals remain important, but fertilizing, watering, mulching, correct pruning and special treatments, such as lightning protection and bracing, play a more central role in maintaining tree health.

Regular inspection of your trees is a good way to identify problems before they become serious. We will mention specific ailments and weaknesses when we discuss each species, but, in general, look for the following: reduced growth rate, thin or pale foliage, fungi, infestations of mistletoe, sprouts along the trunk, cracks and splits, holes from borers, caterpillars, wilting branches and loose or cankered patches of bark. Look for splits and broken limbs after ice storms or high winds. Look for insects when the critters are likely to be present but before they have had time to do much damage. If you notice such troubling signs, treat them quickly yourself or hire a professional. If your inspection shows that your trees are healthy, the time will not have been wasted. You will have become better acquainted with your environment and probably a little more appreciative of the trees that do so much to improve it.

In areas where deer are abundant, trees may need to be protected by electric fencing.

PART TWO

DEPENDABLE, ORNAMENTAL NATIVES

LET US FIRST PUT FORWARD THE DEFINITION of a tree that served us in the preparation of this book. Trees are woody plants that, under favorable conditions, will be tall enough for you to stand back and look up at, large enough for you to sit under and, barring injury, will retain one dominant stem throughout life (or sometimes a few dominant stems, as in the case of paper birch). We have included some native species that others might consider large shrubs, but we were guided in our decision by their form as mature plants.

Remember that a native tree is a a species that has established itself and grows naturally, without human influence, in a particular location. The location can be as broadly defined as the planet, or the eastern half of North America (which is the area we cover); more precisely, it is a narrowly described habitat in a particular locality. A plant is "native to" an area with a certain set of climate, moisture and soil conditions. The word "native" means little without the associated "to"

Native trees like redbud are as beautiful in the garden as any exotic species. Previous page: dogwoods and redbuds.

and a description of the geographic limits of those conditions. The trees we speak of are native to eastern North America, west to the High Plains and south to the Gulf of Mexico.

HOW TO USE THIS BOOK: The trees we have chosen are arranged alphabetically, by scientific name (genus and species), and these names are repeated at the bottom of each right-hand page, for quick reference. The common name is the headline for each entry, but the scientific name is used as the organizing principle because it is much more uniform from region to region. In a few cases, the correct scientific name has changed recently and is not found in older reference books, so we include some synonyms for cross-reference.

The information within each species entry is given in the same sequence. We begin with a **general description** of the tree, including its potential size and special characteristics. United States national champion trees of record at the time the text was written are mentioned. **Leaf descriptions** follow. All leaves are assumed to be simple, deciduous and alternately arranged along the twig unless otherwise indicated. **Flowers and fruits** are described next. Some trees have special flowering characteristics, such as dioecious species with separate male and female plants, and these are noted.

We then become subjective and rate the tree through the various **seasons** on its landscape value. Your own viewpoint may differ from ours if, for example, you consider edible fruit more important than beautiful spring flowers. But we give you our opinion just the same, and the reasons for it.

The overall natural **range** of every tree species is described, along with the additional area where it might grow successfully under cultivation. Once again, remember that provenance and habitat conditions influence the presence or performance of individual trees in specific locations. We use the plant hardiness zones of the United States Department of Agriculture as a beginning (see page 287), because they are a widely accepted, uniform system, but we realize that there is much more to plant adaptability than tolerance of winter cold. So, we offer suggestions regarding soils, moisture, exposure and other factors that can make or break a tree. Along with recommendations on culture, we offer information based on our experiences with transplanting and propagation.

Every tree has **problems**, and the next section of each entry discusses a few of the main ones. We include scientific names for insect pests and diseases so that you will be able to look up more detailed information in other sources, but our pest lists are not intended to be comprehensive. Physiological weaknesses inherent within each species of tree, and any serious problems caused by the tree itself, are mentioned, as are sensitivities to environmental stresses.

In the next section, we discuss some specific selections. Selected **cultivars** of some native species are available from nurseries. Cultivars are chosen for special virtues, such as form, spectacular flowers or fall color. Some cultivars, however, do not grow well outside their region of origin. And because every plant of the same clonal cultivar is genetically identical, their wide use narrows the genetic diversity that can protect trees from fast-spreading diseases.

Strict reliance upon cultivars also eliminates the individuality of plants. With "natural" trees, grown from seed, one never knows exactly what a specific tree will look like until it has grown past adolescence. If you need uniformity or predictability, select an appropriate cultivar, if one is available. If not, choose natural trees grown by reliable nurseries from a locally adapted seed source. As a compromise, propagate your own seedlings or cuttings from selected local parent trees that have characteristics you admire.

If you choose a named cultivar, remember that true cultivar names (the ones that can be registered legally for plant patents) and trade names (the ones that can be registered as trademarks and copyrighted) are usually not the same. Some so-called cultivars are propagated by seed from selected individuals and retain some genetic variability. Most popular horticultural reference books don't differentiate properly among these categories, and various name categories are used interchangeably even at many botanic gardens.

So, with sincere apologies to horticultural nomenclaturists everywhere, we have decided to use the names most recognizable in the trade, in order to make it easier for you to find the specific plants you want. The names of all of these selections, whether true cultivar names, trade names or some other name category, are enclosed in single quotes (the form used officially only for true cultivars) so they will be recognizable as designating specific plants. Remember, though, that not all are true cultivar names.

Once you have read those sections about your tree, you should know quite a lot about it. We then extend this information to other **related species**, describing the main characteristics that distinguish them. Some of these related species are common in our area and are similar to those already described, some originated from other parts of North America but are well known or often seen in cultivation and some are shrubby relatives of the larger trees, but all are native to North America. We will recommend some species for planting and that others just be preserved and admired for their beauty or their value to wildlife. We try to provide a little information on each tree's familial relationships as well.

The final **comments** on each species are intended to spark your interest. Wildlife values or historical associations are discussed, and we include some of our personal experiences with a few of the trees.

TREE & LEAF SILHOUETTES

Tree silhouettes are of a mature specimen with leaves and are drawn to scale.
Leaf silhouettes are not to scale and are for shape reference only.

125 ft. / 100 ft. / 75 ft. / 50 ft. / 25 ft. SCALE: 6.5 MM = 25 FEET	*Aesculus glabra* Ohio Buckeye, p. 48	*Aesculus pavia* Red Buckeye, p. 50	*Amelanchier arborea* Downy Serviceberry, p. 52	*Asimina triloba* Pawpaw, p. 54
Betula alleghaniensis Yellow Birch, p. 56	*Betula nigra* River Birch, p. 58	*Betula papyrifera* Paper Birch, p. 62	*Carpinus caroliniana* Hornbeam, p. 64	*Carya cordiformis* Bitternut Hickory, p. 66
Carya illinoensis Pecan, p. 68	*Carya ovata* Shagbark Hickory, p. 70	*Carya tomentosa* Mockernut, p. 72	*Castanea dentata* Chestnut, p. 74	*Catalpa speciosa* Northern Catalpa, p. 78
Celtis occidentalis Common Hackberry, p. 80	*Cercis canadensis* Redbud, p. 83	*Chionanthus virginicus* Fringe Tree, p. 85	*Cladrastis kentuckea* Yellowwood, p. 87	*Cornus drummondii* Roughleaf Dogwood, p. 89

Cornus florida Flowering Dogwood, p. 91	*Cotinus obovatus* Smoke Tree, p. 96	*Crataegus mollis* Red Haw, p. 98	*Diospyros virginiana* Persimmon, p. 102	*Euonymus atropurpureus* Wahoo, p. 104
Fagus grandifolia Beech, p. 106	*Forestiera acuminata* Swamp Privet, p. 110	*Fraxinus americana* White Ash, p. 112	*Fraxinus pennsylvanica* Green Ash, p. 114	*Gleditsia triacanthos* Honey Locust, p. 116
Gordonia lasianthus Gordonia, p. 118	*Gymnocladus dioicus* Kentucky Coffee Tree, p. 120	*Halesia carolina* Silverbell, p. 122	*Hamamelis virginiana* Autumn Witch Hazel, p. 124	*Ilex opaca* American Holly, p. 127
Juglans nigra Black Walnut, p. 130	*Juniperus virginiana* Red Cedar, p. 133	*Larix laricina* Tamarack, p. 135	*Leitneria floridana* Corkwood, p. 138	*Liquidambar styraciflua* Sweet Gum, p. 140

125 ft. / 100 ft. / 75 ft. / 50 ft. / 25 ft. SCALE: 6.5 MM = 25 FEET	*Liriodendron tulipifera* Tulip Tree, p. 142	*Maclura pomifera* Osage Orange, p. 144	*Magnolia acuminata* Cucumber Tree, p. 147	*Magnolia grandiflora* Southern Magnolia, p. 150
Malus ioensis Prairie Crab, p. 153	*Morus rubra* Red Mulberry, p. 156	*Nyssa sylvatica* Black Gum, p. 158	*Ostrya virginiana* Ironwood, p. 162	*Oxydendrum arboreum* Sourwood, p. 164
Picea glauca White Spruce, p. 166	*Pinckneya bracteata* Pinckneya, p. 169	*Pinus banksiana* Jack Pine, p. 171	*Pinus echinata* Shortleaf Pine, p. 174	*Pinus resinosa* Red Pine, p. 177
Pinus strobus White Pine, p. 179	*Platanus occidentalis* Sycamore, p. 182	*Populus deltoides* Cottonwood, p. 186	*Populus tremuloides* Quaking Aspen, p. 190	*Prunus americana* Wild Plum, p. 194

Prunus serotina Wild Cherry, p. 196	*Quercus alba* White Oak, p. 199	*Quercus macrocarpa* Bur Oak, p. 203	*Quercus muhlenbergii* Chinkapin Oak, p. 205	*Quercus phellos* Willow Oak, p. 208
Quercus rubra Red Oak, p. 211	*Quercus shumardii* Shumard Oak, p. 214	*Quercus virginiana* Live Oak, p. 217	*Rhus typhina* Staghorn Sumac, p. 222	*Robinia pseudoacacia* Black Locust, p. 225
Sabal palmetto Cabbage Palm, p. 228	*Salix lucida* Shining Willow, p. 230	*Sapindus drummondii* Soapberry, p. 233	*Sassafras albidum* Sassafras, p. 235	*Sorbus americana* Mountain Ash, p. 237
Taxodium distichum Bald Cypress, p. 239	*Thuja occidentalis* Arborvitae, p. 242	*Tilia americana* Basswood, p. 244	*Tsuga canadensis* Hemlock, p. 247	*Ulmus americana* American Elm, p. 250

BALSAM FIR

Abies balsamea

DESCRIPTION: Balsam fir is one of our most hardy and aromatic conifers. It thrives in cold, moist climates throughout most of Canada, yet it can be grown successfully through the mid-latitude United States in Iowa, Illinois and eastward as far south as Virginia, from sea level to the highest elevations that can support tree growth. With its dense, pointed silhouette, balsam fir is a common component of our boreal forests, and it has been named the provincial tree of New Brunswick.

The largest balsam on record in the United States is in Fairfield, Pennsylvania. It stands 100 feet (30 m) tall and is almost 4 feet (1.2 m) in diameter. Even larger specimens may exist in Canada, but most balsams are medium-sized. Balsam fir often retains its attractive, dense habit and full, symmetrical, spire-shaped crown throughout its life.

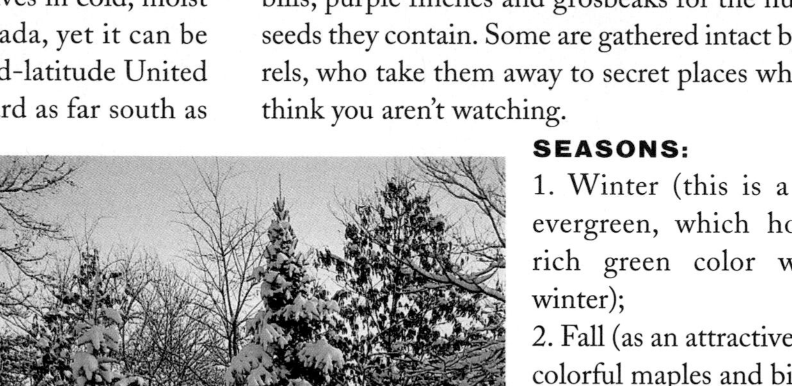

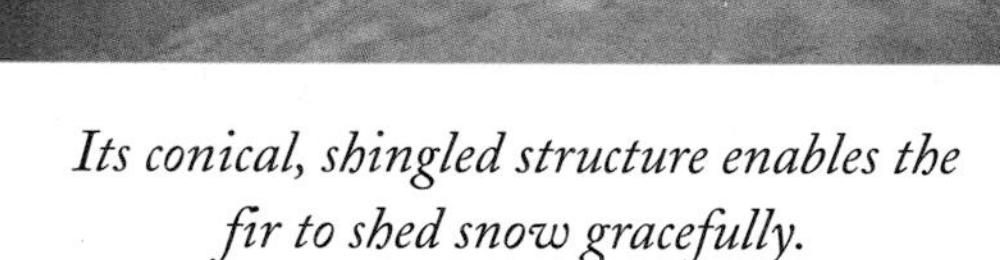

Its conical, shingled structure enables the fir to shed snow gracefully.

LEAVES: Balsam needles are flattened and soft to the touch, less than 1 inch (2.5 cm) long, dark with contrasting undersides, and arranged in horizontal ranks on the lateral branches. They are pleasantly aromatic when broken or scraped and make this tree a good selection for fragrance gardens. Its scent and its persistent, relatively soft foliage also make balsam a favorite Christmas tree.

FLOWERS AND FRUIT: The flowers are inconspicuous, even for conifers. Staminate (male) flowers, or strobiles, sometimes show to advantage as they release their greenish yellow pollen. The female strobiles, or cones, stand erect on the upper branches and are about 3 inches (8 cm) long and sticky with resin. As with other true firs, the cones disintegrate on the tree when ripe and don't pose a significant litter problem. Many of them are opened by chickadees, crossbills, purple finches and grosbeaks for the nutritious seeds they contain. Some are gathered intact by squirrels, who take them away to secret places when they think you aren't watching.

SEASONS:
1. Winter (this is a classic evergreen, which holds its rich green color well all winter);
2. Fall (as an attractive foil for colorful maples and birches);
3. Spring (the light green new growth contrasts well with mature foliage from the previous year);
4. Summer (balsam is always good as a background plant or as an isolated specimen where an accent form is desired).

NATIVE AND ADAPTIVE RANGE: In Canada, balsam fir's range extends to the Peace River in northern Alberta, around James Bay and across Quebec to the coast of Labrador. To the south, it grows into the Great Lake states and New England. It can be planted successfully from USDA zone 2 south, wherever summers are cool and moist. It does not perform well below USDA zone 5, though, unless given a cool north-facing slope or a lakeshore site. Its natural range is a good indication of the area where it will thrive under cultivation without special attention.

CULTURE: Balsam can do well in shade or on wet soil, both of which are fatal to many other conifers. It prefers acidic, organic, friable soil and likes to be kept cool and moist during the growing season. If possible, southern plantings should be located next to cool springs, caves or other features that provide a moderating microclimate.

Balsam is very easy to grow from stratified seed and to transplant. We once transplanted a 15-foot (5 m) tree by hand, with no reduction in growth rate after the first season. Where its requirements for a cool, moist environment can be met, balsam is one of our most smog-tolerant conifers. It is very resistant to attack by gypsy moth (*Lymantria dispar*), which frequently defoliates much of the surrounding forest in the East.

PROBLEMS: This tree can develop a ragged appearance with age, especially if planted south of its natural range in areas with hot summers. It is one of our most susceptible conifers to deer and moose damage (by browsing and rubbing). It can be damaged or killed by heavy infestations of the spruce budworm, *Choristoneura fumiferana*, or the balsam woolly adelgid, *Adelges piceae* (introduced into Maine from Europe in 1908) and by late-spring freezes. In naturalized or wild stands, its low branches, abundant resin blisters and thin bark make it very sensitive to wildfires.

CULTIVARS: No tree-form cultivars are commonly available, although named globe and prostrate forms can be found in botanic gardens and dwarf conifer collections. Balsam is easy to graft, and attractive individuals can be propagated readily.

RELATED SPECIES: Many beautiful firs can be found in the western states and provinces and elsewhere worldwide, but only one other minor species occurs in our area. The Fraser fir (*Abies fraseri*) is confined in the wild to high altitudes in the Appalachians. Like balsam fir, it is commonly planted at lower elevations as an ornamental or for Christmas trees. It is more southerly and alpine in distribution, with more contrasting foliage. It requires better drainage but is less susceptible to spring freeze damage. Fraser fir is becoming an endangered species in the mountains of its natural habitat because of acid rain and the woolly adelgid.

A reported hybrid between the two species, called Canaan fir, is grown for Christmas trees. Some selections of the concolor fir (*Abies concolor*) of the Rocky Mountains also grow well in the East, but this tree is not truly native anywhere in our area. Several exotic fir species are also common in cultivation.

COMMENTS: Many of us can remember the sticky, fragrant substance called "Canada balsam" that we used to attach cover slips to microscope slides in science class. It was a natural product: the resin of the balsam fir tree. Trimmings of balsam fir also make comfortable, fragrant beds for campers, attractive holiday decorations and great winter mulch for tender perennials.

Balsam fir is an important wildlife tree. We once stood silently in a fir forest until the local red squirrels, emboldened by our quiet, began to bombard us with the cones they were harvesting for winter. The fragrant, flat boughs of balsam and Fraser firs also host a variety of rare mosses and liverworts, and they are preferred nesting sites for many birds.

Top left: The soft, fragrant foliage of balsam is borne in flat sprays. Above: Dark green spires of balsam fir contrast with the autumn hues of their deciduous neighbors.

RED MAPLE

Acer rubrum

DESCRIPTION: Maples as a genus have been designated the official arboreal emblems of Canada. The red maple has also merited official status in the United States, being the state tree of Rhode Island. The red maple is one of our finest ornamentals, a tree for all seasons that develops into an attractive yard specimen in a great range of soils and climates.

It grows fairly quickly in favorable conditions, and it occurs naturally in habitats from boreal forests to southern swamps in full sun or shade. It can be found on shallow, rocky, upland forest soils, in wet interdunal areas along lakeshores, on old strip mine spoil banks and on floating logs in the swamps and bayous of the South. Red maple generally develops a uniform crown of ascending limbs and can attain a very large size. The record tree in the United States is 179 feet (55 m) tall and nearly 6 feet (2 m) in diameter. Its canopy shades a considerable area in St. Clair County, Michigan. Typically, however, this is a medium-large tree.

One of our finest ornamentals, red maple is a tree for all seasons.

Although one of the "soft maples" (taxonomic section *Rubra*), red maple is not as prone to storm damage as some of the other, more brittle species. Red maples selected from northern areas are extremely winter-hardy, and those from southern areas are very heat-resistant. The reverse, though, is not always true. Likewise, upland and swamp types are not always at home in each others' habitats.

LEAVES: The opposite foliage of this species is variable from tree to tree, ranging from 2 to 6 inches (5-15 cm) long, from three- to five-lobed and from light green to woolly white underneath. The emerging spring and vivid fall color can be exceptional, but these characteristics also vary considerably.

FLOWERS AND FRUIT: True harbingers of spring, the flowers of red maple appear to cast a scarlet mist in the forest very early in the year. Red maple is one of the more uniformly dioecious maples, having male and female flowers on separate trees. However, some trees may be partly female and predominantly male or vice versa, and some may change their dominant gender from year to year in response to stress.

Both staminate and pistillate trees are attractive in bloom. Some of the most brilliant-flowered selections include 'Autumn Spire', 'Embers', 'Festival', 'October Glory', 'Red Sunset', 'September Song' and 'Shade King'. Most of these selections are functionally females, except 'September Song'. The immature fruits of the females, hanging in bright clusters, continue the vibrant color display of the flowers.

SEASONS:

1. Fall (for the majority of individual trees, which display the magnificent scarlet color for which the entire species has become known);
2. Early spring (for those with the best flower color);
3. Winter (for vigorous young trees, which have smooth, silvery gray bark);
4. Summer (especially for those varieties with contrasting leaf surfaces that shimmer in the wind).

NATIVE AND ADAPTIVE RANGE: Red maple grows from Lake of the Woods in southeastern Manitoba, across southern Canada to Lake St. John and the Gaspé Peninsula in Quebec and southward throughout the eastern United States. Its western limit is closely linked to the boundary of the Prairie Peninsula, the eastern extension of tallgrass prairie into Illinois and Indiana. Red maples can be transplanted to almost any location with a comparable climate and soil. However, none seem to enjoy dry heat, exposed Midwestern prairie sites or soils with a pH above about 7.0.

CULTURE: This tree can be transplanted very easily. Plant seeds in spring, as soon as they fall. Make sure you give the new tree enough water, protect its thin bark from strong sun and watch out for manganese-deficiency chlorosis on high pH (basic) soils. Wild red maples are very sensitive to fire, because of their smooth, thin bark, but they will resprout vigorously. If you prefer a seedling tree over a cultivar yet want bright autumn foliage, select your tree at the nursery in the fall when it shows its "true colors." Standard precautions about provenance apply to this species. Always try to use locally adapted trees.

PROBLEMS: Red maple can be damaged by sunscald, ice glazing, insufficient soil acidity, wilt disease (from *Verticillium albo-atrum* or *Verticillium dahliae*) and drought. Leafhopper insects (*Alebra albostriella*) sometimes cause considerable injury. Most red maple trees are not very resistant to decay and begin to decline following any substantial structural damage or bark injury. They are a preferred species for browsing deer and moose.

Although red maple casts a relatively open shade that permits turf growth under the crown, its shallow roots can cause problems in neatly groomed lawns. Failure due to graft incompatibility (similar to organ-transplant rejection in humans) can be a serious concern with some cultivars, unless they are grown from cuttings or tissue culture.

CULTIVARS: A naturally occurring variety, Drummond red maple, has large leaves with whitened woolly undersides and grows in southern swamps. Cultivar selections are numerous. Some are upright, or fastigiate, like 'Bowhall', 'Columnare', 'Autumn Spire' and 'Karpick'. Others have exceptionally good fall color, like 'October Glory', 'Autumn Flame', 'Embers', 'Firedance' and 'Red Sunset'.

Above: The smooth gray bark of red maple is a decorative feature in the dormant season. Below left: Red maple flowers, especially on male trees such as this one, add color to the spring landscape.

A few like 'Northwood', 'Olson', 'Landsburg' and 'Phipps Farm' were introduced as colorful trees with tough foliage for extreme hardiness. 'Burgundy Belle', propagated from a female tree found in northeastern Kansas, is one of the finest, with dramatic fall color and superior stress resistance. 'Autumn Spire', a product of the hardy plant research program managed by our friend Harold Pellett in Minnesota, is a cold-tolerant columnar selection. 'Autumn Flame', 'Karpick', 'September Song' and some others are seedless males. Refer also to the Freeman hybrid maple selections listed under silver maple (*Acer saccharinum*).

RELATED SPECIES: The tree most closely related to the red maple in our area is the silver maple, which crosses with red maple to produce *Acer* x *freemanii*. Maple genetics are not neat and precise; some speculate that Drummond red maple originated in the wild as a Freeman maple crossed back to red. Several allied species can be found in Asia.

COMMENTS: Red maple, as a species, includes some of our most intensely colorful and widely adapted landscape trees. Young red maples are preferred by prairie warblers as nesting trees, and the twigs furnish valuable winter food for rabbits, porcupine, deer and moose.

SILVER MAPLE

Acer saccharinum

DESCRIPTION: Many people know silver maple, somewhat unfairly, as a large, fast-growing shade tree with invasive roots, messy seeds, brittle branches and a weak crown structure. It is also viewed with disdain as one of the "poor folks' trees," frequently planted in lieu of some of the more expensive "quality" trees.

Silver maples can attain great size very rapidly, often exceeding 100 feet (30 m) in height and 3 feet (1 m) in diameter. The former United States record tree, located in Columbia County, Wisconsin, is 115 feet (35 m) tall and almost 8 feet (2.3 m) in diameter. It grows as a clump, like most of its neighbors. Another tree in Polk County, Iowa, is only 61 feet (19 m) tall, but has a 10-foot (3 m) trunk. Because of its tremendous girth, it was recognized in 1993 as the new record silver maple.

Above: The shimmering foliage of a silver maple graces the historic Illinois home of Abraham Lincoln. Left: Silver maples can attain great size very rapidly.

The branches of this species develop a characteristic sweeping pattern, with upturned ends, which can give such large old trees a graceful outline. Young silver maple seedlings frequently form dense "dog-hair" stands in abandoned bottomland fields, where the red color of their twigs *en masse* over the silver-gray bark of the lower stems can make an otherwise stark floodplain glow warmly on sunny winter days.

LEAVES: The leaves are 3 to 6 inches (7-15 cm) long, opposite, deeply incised and whitened beneath, giving the tree a silvery appearance as the leaves flash in the wind. They can turn a good, clear yellow in the fall, with some specimens being brighter than others.

FLOWERS AND FRUIT: One of this tree's most valuable ornamental assets comes not from extreme beauty, but from timing. Its red flower clusters are the first sign, along with male pussy willow (*Salix discolor*) catkins, that winter is losing its grip on the cold northland. They offer us hope for spring. Beauty is a comparative perception, and during the time when silver maples bloom, frequently glowing through coats of ice, they are the belles of the ball. Silver maple can be dioecious, with separate male and female trees, but unlike the red maple, it is not predominantly so.

The whirling airborne seeds add dynamic life to the landscape, but they can be a real nuisance if they fall on patios or germinate (as they love to do) in flower gardens. Where this is objectionable, seedless male selections may be used.

SEASONS:

1. Late winter (when the red twigs and flowers contrast so well with the silver-gray bark of young stems);
2. Fall (for the yellow foliage);
3. Summer (for the shimmering leaves).

NATIVE AND ADAPTIVE RANGE: Silver maple is a very hardy species, growing from Trois-Rivières in Quebec, south throughout the eastern and central United States to the coastal plains. Under cultivation, it performs well into USDA zone 3. It actually does better in cold climates than it does in milder ones for two reasons: cold areas have more snow, rather than freezing rain, which causes glazing damage, and cold winters satisfy the dormancy requirements of the terminal buds. Sometimes without sufficient dormancy, these end buds don't grow in the spring and are overtopped by growth from pairs of lateral buds, resulting in the V-shaped limb junctions that make this tree more susceptible to damage from wind and ice.

CULTURE: Professor William Chaney, a tree physiologist at Purdue University, refers to silver maple as "the coyote of trees" because of its adaptability.

Silver maple germinates freely, transplants readily and grows rapidly in any decent soil. It is somewhat more difficult to grow one well. This requires protection from damage and attention to corrective pruning and training to develop a strong branching pattern with a single central leader. This is important, because the tree is not very resistant to decay once damaged.

Silver maples produce great quantities of winged seeds each May.

Although many books recommend these trees for difficult or low-maintenance sites, they will perform better with reasonable care. Silver maple prefers floodplains and seasonally wet areas with rich, porous soil; it will germinate quickly and become a majestic tree under such conditions. It can develop a good limb structure if careful attention is given to developmental pruning to remove multiple leaders formed when the terminal bud fails to grow.

PROBLEMS: Seed and twig litter can be significant problems if these trees are grown in manicured landscapes. The roots are shallow and invasive and can lift sidewalks and cause other problems if the trees aren't sited properly. Wilt diseases such as *Verticillium*, decay at points of injury, manganese-deficiency chlorosis on very basic soils and a plethora of minor insect pests can all affect this species. Cottony maple scale insects (*Pulvinaria acericola*) are especially conspicuous on silver maple but are usually not serious.

Recent studies indicate that storm breakage is not as severe as was once thought if the trees are properly trained and maintained. Individual branches may snap off, but long, destructive tearing injuries and splits are not as common with well-pruned silver maples as they are with many of our exotic shade trees.

CULTIVARS: Several cultivars have been selected for a variety of traits. 'Northline' is a very hardy selection from Canada that grows more slowly than others. 'Silver Queen' is a fruitless form for those who wish to avoid seed litter. There are also weeping and cutleaf selections, selections with pyramidal or columnar growth and selections with golden or crinkled leaves. Many of them are horticultural curiosities with little practical value, but the cutleaf forms ('Wieri', 'Skinner' and 'Beebe') are graceful specimens when well grown.

Some of the most exciting horticultural developments involving silver maple have come from its hybrids with the closely related red maple (*Acer rubrum*), resulting in the Freeman maple, *Acer* x *freemanii*. Freeman maple selections 'Autumn Fantasy', 'Marmo' and 'Scarlet Sentinel' all have brilliant spring flowers as well as great fall color. 'Armstrong' and 'Scarlet Sentinel' develop fastigiate forms, while 'Autumn Blaze' and 'Celebration' have luminous fall color ('Celebration' is two-toned, red-around-yellow). 'Marmo' and 'Celebration', and perhaps some others as well, are claimed to be seedless.

RELATED SPECIES: Red maple and some of the Oriental maple species are closely related to silver maple. They are collectively known as the "soft maples" (taxonomic section *Rubra*).

COMMENTS: Because of its rapid growth, silver maple is the subject of biomass energy research funded by Oak Ridge National Laboratory. It is useful for controlling erosion on streambanks, and it contributes to wildlife habitat.

Silver maple seeds have a nostalgic value for those of us whose introduction to horticulture involved sitting in our childhood sandbox watching the magic maple "whirlybirds" rain down and begin to sprout almost immediately into little trees. We, and probably many other tree people as well, might not have become fascinated by the works of nature at such an early age were it not for watching, growing and delighting in those maple seeds. Later, in grade school, we came to welcome the aerial assault of ripe maple seeds as a harbinger of summer vacation.

Why not plant or preserve a silver maple at some appropriate location, such as a day-care center or a schoolyard, to give another generation the same source of inspiration?

SUGAR MAPLE

Acer saccharum

DESCRIPTION: The sugar maple's foliage sets the standard by which all other trees are measured in the fall. Found in the mesic forests of most of eastern North America, it thrives in dense shade as a tall, clear-boled, dominant tree. In open areas, it becomes large, dense and full-crowned. The sugar maple leaf graces the flag of Canada.

A sugar maple in Norwich, Connecticut, is 93 feet (28 m) tall and over 7 feet (2 m) in diameter. In the deep woods, many become even taller but more slender. This slow-growing, strong species, one of the "hard maples" (taxonomic section *Acer*), is quite variable but always attractive. It is deservedly popular as a shade tree on any good site, and it has been designated the state tree of New York, Vermont, West Virginia and Wisconsin.

Sugar maple bark is dark and deeply textured.

LEAVES: The opposite leaves are coarsely toothed, 4 to 7 inches (10-18 cm) wide by slightly less in length, and they vary in thickness and toughness depending upon provenance. Trees originating in milder climates might grow faster but have thinner foliage that is more susceptible to tatter and scorch. Trees from harsher, drier areas usually grow more slowly and develop smaller, tougher foliage. Autumn colors are never disappointing and range from golden through orange to carmine.

FLOWERS AND FRUIT: Sugar maples tend eventually to dominate where they grow. Their pendulous, pale spring flowers create a soft yellow haze in the leafless woods and are most visible when viewed against the dark bark or against a clear blue sky. The winged fruits are not particularly conspicuous but feed many birds in the fall.

SEASONS:

1. Fall (any sugar maple can outperform almost any other tree for color duration and intensity);
2. Spring (the flowers, emerging before the leaves, are fine-textured and can light up the woods);
3. Summer (a shapely tree that casts a dense, cool shade).

NATIVE AND ADAPTIVE RANGE: Sugar maple dominates mesic forests from northern New Brunswick and southeastern Manitoba, down through the southern Appalachians. Provenance is important with this species, but with careful selection, it or its close relatives can be grown in almost every climatic zone.

Some authorities recognize three ecotypes, or regional genetic groups, within this species. Northern trees are very resistant to winter injury but sensitive to drought and leaf damage if grown in warm areas. Those from central latitudes exhibit adequate cold resistance and better drought tolerance, while southern trees resist drought and leaf scorch but are less winter-hardy. The adaptable central tree group also shows increasing toughness but decreasing fall brilliance from east to west, with test trees from parts of Illinois, Missouri and Iowa performing best over a broad planting range.

Sugar maple should generally be considered hardy north through USDA zone 3. Its southern and western relatives are best planted in their respective areas.

CULTURE: Sugar maple thrives in a reasonably clean atmosphere and moist, well-drained soil. Given those requirements, this maple is easy to transplant and grow, and it can be coaxed into moderately fast growth with a little attention to water, mulch and fer-

A young sugar maple in bloom.

tilizer. It thrives in full sun or deep shade, yet it suffers from salt, compacted soil and hot, dry locations.

PROBLEMS: Sugar maple is prone to a little understood decline disease in certain locations. It may be caused by road salt, air pollution, periodic drought or localized manifestations of global warming or acid rain. Trees on poor sites, or selections not adapted to local conditions, are susceptible to scorch, sunscald, leaf tatter and other stresses. Sugar maples are great for rural or suburban areas, but they often suffer in downtown locations.

Maple wilt, caused by the ubiquitous vascular fungi *Verticillium dahliae* and *Verticillium albo-atrum*, is a systemic, fatal disease that attacks some trees. Many sugar maples are predisposed to develop narrow branch crotches that weaken their structure, but their strong, hard wood compensates for this to some degree. In test plantings in Pennsylvania, sugar maple cultivars were not injured by rabbits, but the closely related black maple (*Acer nigrum*) and canyon maple (*Acer grandidentatum*) were decimated.

The dense shade and shallow roots of sugar maple may preclude growing lush grass under its canopy. Where it is locally adapted, sugar maple can dominate the forest through a combination of reproductive success and allelopathy, outcompeting every other tree over time.

CULTIVARS: Many selections of this species are available in the nursery trade. 'Bonfire' and 'Commemoration' are early-coloring and heat-tolerant. Both have bright red-orange fall color. 'Goldspire', 'Monumentale', 'Endowment' and 'Columnare' develop narrow crown forms. 'Green Mountain', 'Adirondack' and 'Legacy' are colorful selections recommended for harsh summers, when resistance to leaf scorch and tatter are necessary. 'Majesty' is a fast-growing selection with exceptional cold resistance.

'Caddo' is, aesthetically, a rather average selection from outlying groves in Oklahoma, but it demonstrates the strongest tolerance to adverse conditions. It becomes a narrow, upright tree and colors late in the fall. 'Sweet Shadow' is a very graceful, fine-textured tree with deeply incised leaves. Other selections are available. Researchers looking for superior qualities continue to introduce new ones.

RELATED SPECIES: There are several other native hard maples similar to sugar maple. Some of them are considered varieties rather than separate species by many taxonomists, but they do display distinctive horticultural qualities.

Black maple is a large-growing mimic of sugar maple. It usually lacks the red fall colors displayed by some sugar maples, but it may perform better at the western edge of the species range and on floodplains. The selection 'Green Column' is a narrowly upright form. Southern sugar maple (*Acer barbatum*) is a smaller tree that is more tolerant of southern summers but still winter-hardy. It lacks, however, the brilliant red fall color of sugar maple, turning yellow to rust-colored.

Chalk maple (*Acer leucoderme*) is a very similar small species of mid-southern latitudes. It often has good red fall color and attractive, chalky bark. Canyon maple is another small look-alike native to the Rocky Mountains and Mexico that is sometimes planted in our area.

COMMENTS: Sugar maple is expected to have trouble adapting throughout much of the southern portion of its range over the next century, if predictions about global warming are borne out. This tree is the source of maple sugar and syrup and of some of the world's best fall colors. Where it can be grown under favorable conditions, it is a superior ornamental shade tree. Its decline would be tragic.

Sugar maples show consistently outstanding and long-lasting autumn color.

OTHER MAPLES

Acer species

Several other native maples are very useful in certain situations. The boxelder (*Acer negundo*) is our only compound-leaved native maple, and it is the only one that is consistently dioecious. Also known as Manitoba maple, it has an expansive natural range covering most of our area. It is able to survive more adverse conditions than any of our other maple species, but it is notorious as a weedy, short-lived, insect- and decay-prone seed-machine with weak wood.

Unlike most boxelders, this compact, variegated selection is suited to a refined landscape.

Its fast growth and subsequent tendency toward structural damage and decay do help boxelder provide many cavity homes for wildlife in riparian agricultural areas previously cleared of forest habitat. Although it usually attains only a modest size, boxelder can grow into a large tree. One in Lenawee County, Michigan, is 110 feet (33 m) tall and over 5 feet (1.6 m) in diameter. And although this species usually lives a hard and sometimes short life, we know of some old specimens such as one standing at Cannonball House in St. Michaels, Maryland. Lanterns were hung from its branches to confuse British gunners during the War of 1812.

A well-grown boxelder can be an attractive shade tree, and its early flowers add a pleasant froth of yellow-green above the banks of prairie creeks. Several variegated selections are useful even in some of the most refined landscapes. The cultivar 'Sensation' is unusual in developing bright red fall color. In general, though, this species is most appreciated in those harsh areas of the High Plains where it is almost the only tree that can survive. It was cited in a Canadian conference on xeriscaping (landscaping for water conservation) as one of the best trees for drought tolerance.

The flowers of female boxelders are the primary food of the detested but harmless *Leptocoris trivittatus*—red and black bugs that invade houses each fall. This problem, as well as unwanted seed litter, can be minimized by planting or saving only male trees. Nature sometimes does this for us on harsh sites. Boxelders growing along streams in such areas are often female, while those surviving on adjacent uplands are usually male. This is due to complex and fascinating gender-biased, competitive evolutionary processes that we only partially understand, relating to the metabolic costs associated with seed production for females and the effects of location upon optimum pollen distribution for males.

Two other native maples, shrubby species that sometimes become small trees, are among the most beautiful of our ornamental native plants. The striped maple (*Acer pensylvanicum*) and the mountain maple (*Acer spicatum*) are understory species that cannot be established easily in hot, sunny locations or very far outside of their natural ranges. They occupy the opposite end of the adaptability scale from boxelder. But as native trees by the strictest of definitions (they exist as natural components of the local forest), these trees are spectacular ornamentals and are especially cold-hardy. Striped maple will survive north into USDA zone 3, and mountain maple grows north to USDA zone 2.

Striped maple is slightly larger than mountain maple and more often grows as a graceful, arching small tree; mountain maple usually exists as a large, erect shrub or small, multiple-stemmed tree. The largest striped maple on record grows in Nassau County, New York, at the Bailey Arboretum. It is more than 75 feet (23 m) tall and 15 inches (38 cm) in diameter. The biggest mountain maple is in

Top: Mountain maple holds its flowers in upright spikes. Above: Striped maple flowers resemble cascades of green bells.

Houghton County, Michigan, and is about 60 feet (18 m) in height and 10 inches (25 cm) in diameter. These trees are exceptional; most are much smaller.

Striped maple leaves turn a bright, clear yellow in the fall, while mountain maple turns a brilliant mottled orange. Both species have textured, rugose opposite leaves that are ornamental in spring and summer; and both have attractive flower clusters—those of striped maple are pendulous, while those of mountain maple develop as erect spikes. These two small maples are among the most resistant of all to attack by the voracious gypsy moth (*Lymantria dispar*) and should be used where that pest is prevalent.

Striped maple flowers are fascinating. In any given year, on any given tree, they may all be female, depending on local environmental conditions. Their sex is not determined until they begin to expand in the spring. Dormant branches cut for forcing will be female. You can bring them indoors and be confident they will not litter the room with pollen, while the branches left on the same tree might produce copious amounts of the stuff.

These two small maples are best adapted to cool, moist areas and rocky soils in Canada, the northern Great Lake states and the Appalachians. We have admired beautiful masses of mountain maple along shorelines in Quetico Provincial Park and along some of the northeastern tributary streams of Lake Superior in western Ontario. Equally impressive striped maples can be seen in the Adirondacks of upstate New York and east to Mount Desert Island, Maine. Where they can be grown, and especially where they occur in the wild, they rival the best of the Oriental maples for fall color, bark, graceful form and bloom.

Mountain maple's fall color is rich and mottled.

OHIO BUCKEYE

Aesculus glabra

DESCRIPTION: The Ohio buckeye is typically a medium-sized tree of rich mesic habitats and stream valleys, which seldom emerges from the shade of its taller associates. Although this is the state tree of Ohio, the largest known Ohio buckeye grows in Liberty, Kentucky, standing 144 feet (45 m) tall with a trunk more than 3 feet (1.1 m) in diameter. But the species seldom reaches such proportions. It usually grows as a small tree or, on drier sites, a large shrub, seldom dominating any forest stand.

Ohio buckeye is representative of several of the buckeyes that can grow into medium or large trees. All are coarse-branching with opposite, palmately compound leaves, which give them an almost tropical appearance. Most species are unique among our native trees in that they imitate the spring woodland wildflowers by leafing out extremely early, taking advantage of the sunlight penetrating the otherwise leafless forest. They become dormant in late summer, as soon as their annual growth matures.

Buckeyes are among the first trees to leaf out in spring.

LEAVES: The buckeyes are among the first of our native woody plants to green up in the spring, and their frost-resistant new leaves herald the end of winter. A hard freeze will cause the expanding leaves to droop, as though frost-killed, but they usually recover as the temperature rises. The leaves of Ohio buckeye are typically composed of five leaflets, joined at a single point on the leafstalk, and are bright green. They may scorch during hot summers. Toward the end of the season, buckeyes are usually the first of our trees to turn color (yellow, orange or tan) and lose their foliage.

FLOWERS AND FRUIT: All buckeyes are known for their showy flowers and for the hummingbirds they attract. The Ohio buckeye has greenish yellow flowers in panicles up to 12 inches (30 cm) tall at the ends of branches. Of those trees that bloom on the current season's growth, they are among the earliest, but the flowers do not expand until after the foliage has developed.

Buckeyes are named for their nuts, brown with a light eyespot like the eyes of deer. Buckeye fruit clusters are ornamental in early fall and remain on the tree after the leaves fall. The purplish brown nuts of Ohio buckeye occur singly or in clusters of two or three. The nuts are enclosed in bright tan leathery pods or husks covered with a scattering of weak prickles. While toxic to humans and cattle, the nuts are a great food for squirrels.

SEASONS:

1. Early spring (when they unfold bright new leaves in an otherwise dormant deciduous forest);
2. Late spring (the flowers can show surprisingly well against the backdrop of new foliage);
3. Fall (for the ripe nuts or if you need a tree that drops its leaves early, simplifying cleanup, and opens its canopy to early fall sun).

NATIVE AND ADAPTIVE RANGE: Ohio buckeye grows in suitably moist habitats throughout the central United States, and it is reliably hardy at least through USDA zone 3 in Minnesota and those similar areas of Canada. It is the most widespread and northerly member of the genus.

CULTURE: Buckeyes are simple to propagate from stratified seed and can be transplanted easily if moved in the early spring while still dormant or in late summer following natural defoliation. In Illinois, we hand-dug and moved trees up to 6 inches (15 cm) in diameter with no signs of transplanting stress. The trees prefer decent, moist, well-drained soil. In hot, dry conditions, they may lose their leaves prematurely unless they are mulched and watered.

Ohio buckeye flowers develop in tall spikes on new growth.

PROBLEMS: Ohio buckeye is not affected significantly by insects or disease. However, when grown under poor conditions or infected by the leaf fungus *Guignardia aesculi*, its leaves may be scorched or blotched. Its loss of foliage in late summer might be considered unattractive, and the toxic nuts are a concern for children, pets and livestock. The foliage, too, is somewhat toxic, an apparent defense against animals that would feed on it in early spring while other trees are still dormant.

CULTIVARS: Ohio buckeyes seem to show little variation from tree to tree, thus they have not lent themselves to horticultural selection. There is an interesting natural dwarf (variety *nana*) with bristly little seedpods that remains a low shrub.

RELATED SPECIES: The yellow buckeye, *Aesculus octandra* (syn. *A. flava*), resembles Ohio buckeye, but it is larger in almost every feature. It has a more restricted southeastern range, but it can be planted successfully almost anywhere the Ohio buckeye grows. It is one of the dominant canopy trees in some cove hardwood forests of the eastern mountains, where individual trees can exceed 5 feet (1.5 m) in diameter. Its fruit husks are smooth, and its flowers are often brighter yellow than those of Ohio buckeye. The flowers are an attractive feature on open-grown landscape trees that have retained their lower branches.

The Texas buckeye (*Aesculus arguta*) is a smaller version of Ohio buckeye (sometimes listed as a variety) better adapted to hot, dry conditions. Painted buckeye (*Aesculus sylvatica*) is a southeastern species similar in size to Texas buckeye. Its yellow flowers often appear to be painted with red. 'Autumn Splendor' is a cultivar that originated from the seed of painted buckeye, but now, after several hybrid generations, it no longer resembles that species.

Most of these species hybridize readily, and reliable identification can be difficult. They are nearly interchangeable in landscaping. There are additional species in California, Europe and Asia. The European horse chestnut (*Aesculus hippocastanum*) is common in cultivation.

COMMENTS: Aesculin, the toxic substance in buckeye nuts, makes them inedible to humans. Native Americans boiled and leached out the aesculin to make the nuts edible when acorns or other foods were scarce. The smooth nuts are pleasant to handle, and "lucky buckeyes" travel in the pockets of many schoolchildren each fall.

Yellow buckeye has deeper-colored blooms than Ohio buckeye and grows larger.

RED BUCKEYE

Aesculus pavia

DESCRIPTION: Red buckeye is a small tree or large shrub that grows under taller trees in rich woodlands. It and its close relatives (the other small buckeyes) are spread throughout the southeastern United States, and they can dominate the understory on favorable sites. The largest recorded red buckeye is located well beyond the species' natural range, in Kalamazoo County, Michigan. It is 64 feet (20 m) tall with a diameter of 2 feet 5 inches (75 cm). In general, any specimen more than 25 feet (8 m) tall or 1 foot (30 cm) thick is a big tree for this species.

LEAVES: Red buckeye leaves are dark, lustrous and early to emerge in the spring. All buckeyes have similar distinctive, opposite, compound foliage and, except for the bottlebrush buckeye (*Aesculus parviflora*), they drop their leaves early in the fall. As a defense against browsers searching for the first foliage of spring, buckeye leaves are toxic.

FLOWERS AND FRUIT: The carmine flower panicles of this species are among the most beautiful of any temperate-zone tree. On specimens that have grown in full sun and have a dense crown, the blooming period is almost theatrical in brilliance. Plant breeders are attempting to incorporate the superior color of red buckeye flowers into other buckeye species. The nuts are similar to those of Ohio buckeye (*Aesculus glabra*) but are more of an orange-brown color and are encased in smooth husks.

SEASONS:

1. Late spring (during the blooming period);
2. Early spring (when new leaves emerge long before those of other associated trees).

Top: Red buckeye develops beautiful crinkled foliage in very early spring while the rest of the forest sleeps. Above: The rich crimson flowers of red buckeye.

NATIVE AND ADAPTIVE RANGE: Red buckeye ranges throughout the southeastern United States, from North Carolina through eastern Texas and north to Illinois. It is hardy north into USDA zone 4.

CULTURE: Grow this species from stratified seed and give it good, rich soil for best results. Transplant it in very early spring with care for its fleshy roots. It tolerates heavy shade but becomes more dense in full sun. Plants growing in the sun should be mulched and watered to maintain a cool, moist root zone.

PROBLEMS: Red buckeye has no serious pests, although squirrels occasionally will strip sections of bark and girdle branches. If its recommended habitat requirements are met, and the habitual but harmless early defoliation can be tolerated, this small tree is one of our most trouble-free species. Toxicity of the nuts (a characteristic of other buckeyes as well) should be considered in any landscape design to minimize risk to children and pets.

CULTIVARS: Naturally compact and dwarf forms or varieties of red buckeye and one yellow-flowering type (var. *flavescens*) are offered by some nurseries. There is sufficient variation within the species to support cultivar selection, but no true cultivars are commonly available.

As a species, red buckeye is a 1995 winner of the coveted Pennsylvania Horticulture Society Gold Medal Plant award.

RELATED SPECIES: Differentiation of the small buckeye species can be confusing. Some authorities recognize the parti-colored buckeye (*Aesculus discolor*)

Never a large tree, red buckeye has dark, lustrous leaves. In full sun, its blooms are almost theatrical in brilliance.

as a distinct species. It is usually a shrub with large panicles of flowers that are sometimes two-toned—red and yellow. Several other nearly identical taxa are occasionally recognized by various authorities under various names, including the splendid *Aesculus splendens*. A hybrid with the European horse chestnut is the popular red-flowering ruby horse chestnut (*Aesculus* x *carnea*) which has several named selections.

Bottlebrush buckeye was named for its large spikes of tiny white flowers.

The most significant and distinct of the other small buckeyes is *Aesculus parviflora*, the bottlebrush. It usually remains a shrub, spreading into large clonal thickets over time, but occasionally some of its stems reach tree size. One tree in the Blue Ridge Mountains at Cashiers, North Carolina, is 20 feet (6 m) in height. It has very tall panicles of feathery snow-white flowers, and it blooms in the heat of early summer long after the other eastern buckeyes have finished their displays.

The bottlebrush is unique among the hardy buckeyes for retaining its foliage, in good condition, into fall. The leaves develop a glowing yellow color. Its natural range is confined to Alabama and adjacent areas, but it can be grown northward through USDA zone 4. One selection, 'Rogers', which was introduced by an old friend, Professor Joe McDaniel at the University of Illinois, blooms even later than the species.

COMMENTS: The small buckeye trees, along with their larger relatives (covered under Ohio buckeye, *Aesculus glabra*), are some of our most attractive woody plants when in bloom, and, with their early foliage, they are among our most welcome harbingers of spring. They are attractive to hummingbirds and to a broad array of butterflies.

DOWNY SERVICEBERRY

Amelanchier arborea

DESCRIPTION: Serviceberries are small ornamental trees and shrubs that bloom with clouds of white flowers in the early-spring woods. We have chosen to describe the downy serviceberry, one of the most tree-like, as an example of this ornamental but taxonomically confusing genus. Other species are very similar, differing mostly in size and in their tendency to form clumps. Most of them will hybridize and reproduce from unfertilized seeds by a process called apomixis. Such reproductive variability can make identification of a particular plant difficult.

While many serviceberry species and hybrids are low, suckering shrubs, several become attractive small trees. A few will reach into the forest canopy. A downy serviceberry in Burkes Garden, Virginia, is 60 feet (18 m) tall and nearly 3 feet (1 m) in diameter. The closely related smooth serviceberry (*Amelanchier laevis*) can grow even taller but not as stout. We have seen smooth serviceberries 70 feet (21 m) tall in the Finger Lakes region of New York. Typically, serviceberries grow as understory, but in the sun on bluff ledges or clearings, their dense flowering branches and smooth reflective bark make them visually arresting.

The bright white flowers of serviceberry light up the early-spring woods.

LEAVES: Serviceberry leaves resemble those of their close relative, the apple. True to their names, downy serviceberry leaves usually emerge downy on the lower surface while smooth serviceberry leaves are always smooth. Fall color seems to vary within each species. Some authorities hold that smooth serviceberry has the best fall color, ranging from orange to purple. We have found, among the plants in our collection in Illinois, that downy serviceberry develops a wine-red color, while most of the other species turn yellow or light orange. Soil conditions might influence fall colors, as they do with some other trees.

FLOWERS AND FRUIT: While various authorities disagree about the timing of leaf and bloom, we have found with the eight species we grow that all bloom within a week of one another, just as the leaf buds begin to open. Downy serviceberry is among the earliest.

Serviceberry flowers are a spectacular clear white, except for the occasional tree with light pink blossoms. The flowers, which hang in elegant clusters, are at their peak for only a few days. They fade just as redbud (*Cercis canadensis*) steps forward to change the predominant color of the woods from white to rose. The flowers of smooth serviceberry and its hybrids tend to be larger than those of most of the other serviceberry species.

The purple fruits are small pomes, like miniature apples. Smooth serviceberries taste great. Downy serviceberries are less filling. Birds and other wildlife love them both, but many birds seem to prefer the drier fruits of downy serviceberry, which leaves more of the juicy fruits of smooth serviceberries for us.

SEASONS:

1. Early spring (for those few days when the flowers dominate the landscape);
2. Fall (most serviceberries develop good color, whether purple, orange, red or yellow);
3. Summer (for the fruit);
4. Winter (the smooth gray bark and artistic branching patterns enhance the landscape and show up well when sunlit from the side against a dark or evergreen background).

NATIVE AND ADAPTIVE RANGE: Downy serviceberry is native from the Gulf Coast, north to Thunder Bay in Ontario and Lake St. John in Quebec, and it is reliably hardy through USDA zone 4. Smooth serviceberry is nearly as widespread and is equally hardy. Several other species occasionally reach tree size. They have more restricted ranges but are nearly as hardy.

CULTURE: All serviceberries prefer well-drained soil but tolerate a wide variety of conditions and thrive in full sun to fairly dense shade. They can be propagated from seed or by dividing clumping types, and are very easy to transplant.

PROBLEMS: Serviceberries suffer from many of the same insects and diseases that affect orchard trees, particularly trunk borers and various leaf rusts and blights. They are quite susceptible to cedar-apple rust (*Gymnosporangium juniperi-virginianae*) and are favorite targets of defoliating insects, especially the gypsy moth (*Lymantria dispar*). Rabbits seem to prefer serviceberries to almost any other woody browse, and they destroy many seedlings and small trees.

'Forest Prince' is an apple serviceberry distinguished by brilliant fall color.

Another problem with serviceberries is taxonomic—you seldom get what you ask for if you request a particular species. Species identification can be so confusing that names are used interchangeably. But acquiring a particular species may be unimportant if you find one with the form you want. All serviceberries are ornamental.

CULTIVARS: Regardless of the confusion with species, most cultivars are consistent and predictable. Many of the best have been selected from the apple serviceberry (*Amelanchier* x *grandiflora*). This is sometimes confused with *Amelanchier* x *lamarckii*, which is a hybrid with *Amelanchier canadensis* as one parent. Apple serviceberry is a natural cross between downy and smooth serviceberries. It has large, ornamental flowers and usually has its peak blooming period just prior to smooth serviceberry. Selections such as 'Autumn Brilliance', 'Cole's Select', 'Cumulus', 'Forest Prince', 'Princess Diana', 'Robin Hill' and 'Rubescens' all seem to have been derived from apple serviceberry.

'Spring Glory' and 'Tradition' reportedly were selected from thicket serviceberry (*Amelanchier canadensis*) although they behave more like smooth serviceberry selections. We have been unable to confirm the species origin of 'Robin Hill Pink', a tree-sized selection with pink flowers, but we suspect it was derived from apple serviceberry. 'Strata' is a superb apple serviceberry shown to us by Professor Ed Hasselkus, the serviceberry expert from the University of Wisconsin. It displays the superior blooming and stratified, layered branching typical of this hybrid at its finest.

The Agriculture Canada Research Station at Kentville, Nova Scotia, has introduced a variety of smooth serviceberry from eastern Canada called 'R.J. Hilton', a prolific bloomer with unusually sweet fruit.

RELATED SPECIES: Besides the downy and smooth serviceberries and their hybrid, apple serviceberry, other species occasionally reach tree size. *Amelanchier canadensis*, frequently confused with the downy serviceberry, usually remains a large, suckering shrub. *A. bartramiana*, *A. interior*, *A. neglecta*, *A. sanguinea* and *A. spicata* all grow as large shrubs or small trees in portions of our area. Running shadbush, (*A. stolonifera*) is a low, spreading species popular in landscape plantings. A few species from western North America and Europe are also found in cultivation, including cultivars such as 'Regent' (from *A. alnifolia*, the western Saskatoon).

COMMENTS: Regardless of the confusion over names and identities, most of the serviceberries make fine ornamental and wildlife plants. The fruits of smooth serviceberry and some of the shrubby species (particularly *A. stolonifera*) are attractive and delicious. This was appreciated by early pioneers and Native Americans, who planted serviceberries and used them with dried meat to flavor pemmican cakes. Serviceberries furnish valuable food for nesting birds, deer, bear and many other animals.

PAWPAW

Asimina triloba

DESCRIPTION: The pawpaw is the nonconformist of its family. It looks like a tropical tree, and indeed all of the other members of its taxonomic family (the Annonaceae) are subtropical or tropical.

Most pawpaw trees are less than 30 feet (10 m) tall, but a specimen in Newton County, Mississippi, measures twice that height, with a trunk 2 feet 5 inches (75 cm) in diameter. Trees that are allowed to send up multiple sprouts never attain such respectable proportions, but they are attractive *en masse*. This is an understory tree of rich woods and high stream terraces. Pawpaw frequently forms thickets of small stems in its favorite habitats, but it can be grown in the landscape as a small ornamental tree with one or several stems.

In the woods, pawpaw is often an understory tree, but in the home landscape, it can be an attractive ornamental.

LEAVES: Pawpaw has such a tropical appearance, in part, because of its foliage. Up to 1 foot (30 cm) long and half as wide, the leaves make it look like an avocado tree. The fall color is usually a good clear yellow, which is very appealing if the tree has escaped damage or drought during the growing season.

FLOWERS AND FRUIT: The three-lobed flowers, like inverted trilliums, give the tree its specific name, *triloba*. They mature to a handsome claret-brown color but are not very visible from a distance because the developing foliage overpowers them. The flowers are best viewed up close, from beneath.

The yellow, bean-shaped fruits ripen into soft, fragrant, custard-like berries, somewhat similar to ripe bananas in taste and consistency. They are the largest berries produced by any of our native trees, sometimes reaching 6 inches (15 cm) in length. Each encloses a few large seeds, which contain an alkaloid and are not edible. The fleshy part of the fruit, though, is so tasty that many selections have been made for the home orchard. Fruits with orange-yellow flesh, as opposed to pale yellow or white, are reported to taste the best. Pawpaws require cross-pollination for good fruit set.

SEASONS:
1. Fall (the foliage texture and color is eye-catching, and the ripe fruits are appealing to any animal with two or more legs);
2. Spring (for the emerging new foliage, with the structure of the tree still visible, and later for the flowers if they can be viewed closely);
3. Summer (for the avocado effect of the leaves).

NATIVE AND ADAPTIVE RANGE: Pawpaw grows in rich soils throughout most of the eastern United States, from the Gulf to the southern Great Lakes and extreme southern Ontario, Canada. It can be planted successfully from USDA zone 5 southward.

CULTURE: Pawpaw is one of those clonal grouping trees, like sassafras, that are sometimes difficult to transplant from the wild because any stems derived from suckers are deeply rooted. Even seedlings can be a little tricky to move. But container-grown plants present no problems, as long as you select a suitably moist planting location with rich soil. The flexible lower branches of shrubby specimens can be rooted by layering.

Pawpaws are also easy to propagate from seed, which should be squeezed from the soft fruit pulp and sown in the fall. Young seedlings are especially sensitive to ultraviolet light and should be grown in the shade for the first year. This may be the factor that limits pawpaw reproduction to shady areas in the wild; however, older specimens thrive in full sun when planted there or when surrounding canopy trees are removed.

Once established, pawpaw requires little attention. It grows fast if mulched well and watered during droughts. It will develop an open crown in dense shade and a more compact, uniform crown in full sun.
PROBLEMS: Most complaints about pawpaw concern the messiness of its fruit on sidewalks or patios. This can be minimized by planting only one tree, because pawpaws seldom set much fruit without cross-pollination. The occasional suckers that pop up from the root system should be hand-pulled when small, if unwanted. Mowing or pruning them simply encourages sprouting from basal buds on the suckers. This tree has very few cultural problems that adequate moisture and fertilizer won't eliminate.
CULTIVARS: We are unaware of any ornamental pawpaw cultivars currently available in the nursery trade. However, many selections have been made for the tree's edible fruit by hobbyists, fruit growers and researchers, and some might be found through local horticultural or permacultural societies.

Pawpaw displays three-part deep red flowers.

The large, pendent leaves of pawpaw are resistant to deer browsing and turn pale yellow in fall.

RELATED SPECIES: No other pawpaw species grow in our climate, although some authorities list a dwarf southern form, *Asimina parviflora*, as a distinct species.
COMMENTS: Pawpaw provides food for the striking zebra swallowtail butterfly, a welcome visitor to any ornamental landscape. It is not surprising, though, that few other insects bother this plant. Pawpaw has been making horticultural headlines recently as a source of biological (organic) insecticide. In studies conducted at Purdue University, powdered pawpaw twigs have been shown to be effective against a wide variety of harmful insects and mites.

Pawpaw extract is also being used experimentally in cancer therapy and has been rated 300 times as potent as the other, more famous, plant extract, taxol. The extract works by overcoming the ability of some cancer cells to reject chemotherapy.

Pawpaw fruits were a favorite food of Native Americans, and they helped to feed the conquistadors of Hernando DeSoto during their discovery of the Mississippi River more than 400 years ago. They have been relished ever since and are a treat for those who can beat the wildlife to them. Many mammals eat the fruits whole. The seeds pass through them scarified but undigested, germinating readily the following spring.

YELLOW BIRCH

Betula alleghaniensis (B. lutea)

DESCRIPTION: We have chosen the yellow birch to illustrate the group of species we call the dark-barked northern birches. Yellow birch, unlike the other birches, is a climax forest species that is shade tolerant and relatively long-lived. It grows larger than any of our other birches and is a dominant canopy tree in the cove hardwoods of the Appalachians and the mixed forests of the Great Lake states. Although much taller individuals can be found, there is a tree in Deer Island, Maine, that is 76 feet (23 m) tall and 6 feet 8 inches (2 m) in diameter. Open-grown specimens develop a massive candelabra form, with heavy limbs arching skyward from a short trunk, while forest trees are taller and more slender.

Yellow birch bark peels in papery curls.

This species has a silvery yellow, shredded, curly bark that looks like that of some Oriental tree lilacs and smells like wintergreen. While not as striking as the white bark of some other birches, yellow birch bark is very handsome. In its preferred cool-climate habitats, this species is relatively resistant to *Agrilus anxius*, the borer that attacks most of the exotic white-barked birches.

LEAVES: Yellow birch's paper-thin leaves are 3 to 5 inches (7-12 cm) long and turn a nice yellow in the fall. The fall color is especially effective when the leaves, along with the papery bark, are backlit and viewed against a dark background.

FLOWERS AND FRUIT: All birch catkins are similar, expanding in the spring just before the leaves emerge. The staminate catkins are about 3 inches (8 cm) long and hang in clusters like bundles of pale green icicles from the slender twigs. Moved by the slightest breeze, they offer a delicate and impressive display. The seed clusters of yellow birch are shorter and broader than those of our other birches, and the seeds are dispersed by wind throughout the fall and winter.

SEASONS:
1. Fall (the combination of papery bark and yellow leaves brightens the dark forests where this species commonly grows);
2. Winter (the bark, like that of most birches, is a primary ornamental feature);
3. Spring (the catkins add a soft, delicate touch).

NATIVE AND ADAPTIVE RANGE: Yellow birch grows abundantly around the Great Lakes, eastward through Newfoundland and south along the Appalachian Mountains, with scattered populations in favorable habitats well outside the primary range. It is adapted to cool climates and moist, well-drained soils north through USDA zone 3.

CULTURE: This is one of the only birches that will do well in semishade. It prefers cool, moist, well-drained soil, is easy to transplant in the early spring and can be propagated from seed sown on bare soil in the fall. Open-grown trees tend to develop massive lower branches, while those in the forest maintain slender, erect stems up to the foliage canopy.

PROBLEMS: The northern birches all demand cool, moist soil in the summer, otherwise they may fall victim to the bronze birch borer beetle (*Agrilus anxius*). They can be attacked by leaf miners and other leaf-feeding insects, although yellow birch and the related sweet birch (*Betula lenta*) are more resistant to gypsy moth (*Lymantria dispar*) than other birches. Birches are subject to stem cankers, decay organisms and browsing deer, moose, porcupines and rabbits. All birches, and particularly yellow birch, are extremely sensitive to fire, and mature trees are not found in a burned-over forest.

CULTIVARS: No cultivars of this species are available.

RELATED SPECIES: Sweet birch is a medium-sized tree with rich, dark reddish bark like that of an Oriental cherry tree. This is the source of birch beer, a popular libation in some areas. Sweet birch needs more sun than yellow birch but less than the white-barked birches. This species probably has the best fall color of any birch. Its vibrant gold leaves form an eye-catching combination with its cherry-colored bark. Like yellow birch, it is somewhat resistant to the bronze birch borer, depending on the tree's vigor. Sweet birch has an even stronger aroma than yellow birch, and it was once exploited commercially for making wintergreen oil.

The round-leaf birch (*Betula uber*) is very closely related to sweet birch. Like yellow birch and sweet birch, it does best with its leaves in half sun but its roots in deep shade. It grows naturally only in a single isolated location in Virginia, and it is classified as a federally endangered species. Therefore, it cannot be collected or sold without a permit. It was considered extinct until 1975, when a few trees were discovered. Several cooperators, including one of the authors, are assisting under permit with *ex situ* recovery efforts for this rare species.

Shade tolerant and long-lived, yellow birch can become a dominant tree in the hardwood forests of the Appalachians.

Birches are closely related to alders (*Alnus* spp.), a mostly shrubby genus of water-loving species. Alders have a symbiotic relationship with soil bacteria capable of fixing atmospheric nitrogen in nodules on their roots. They frequently grow in sandy areas and old mine tailings, where the lack of soil nitrogen stunts other plants. The hazel alder (*Alnus serrulata*) occasionally reaches tree size and looks much like a small, dark-barked birch with stiff little seed cones. Other alders, mostly exotic, are common in cultivation for ornamental and conservation purposes.

COMMENTS: Yellow birch loves to grow on old logs and rotting stumps in the forest. As these "nurse logs" decay, the birches are left on stilted roots that can be several feet high and resemble legs. Young children have been known to come running back to a campsite in a panic, having seen their first yellow birch tree "walking" through the dimly lit woods.

RIVER BIRCH

Betula nigra

DESCRIPTION: People who live in the southern two-thirds of our area, from about USDA zone 5 south, have found it difficult to grow birch trees because of the bronze birch borer (*Agrilus anxius*), a small, metallic-colored beetle that attacks and eventually kills any birch under summer stress. Researchers have traveled to Japan, Russia and China in search of a magic birch that can resist this pest. But, to date, the best resistance has been found close to home. A tree must be so well adapted to its climate that hot summer weather will not cause the stress that allows the insect to prevail.

Our native river birch is such a tree. Unlike other birches, this species grows naturally as far south as Florida and shrugs off summer. It can become almost as large as yellow birch (*Betula alleghaniensis*). A tree in Alabama is 111 feet (34 m) tall and more than 4 feet (1.3 m) in diameter. Most river birch trees eventually reach at least two-thirds that size, even on a poor site. The tree develops a pinkish tan peeling bark and a spreading crown of several large, ascending limbs that support slightly weeping branches.

The rough bark of river birch offers rich textural contrast.

LEAVES: River birch leaves are more triangular than those of yellow birch and grow from 2 to 5 inches (5-12 cm) long. They develop the yellow fall color typical of most birch species, although they are not always as bright as some of the other species.

FLOWERS AND FRUIT: The catkins resemble those of the other birches. The tiny seeds grow in clusters called strobiles, like those of yellow birch, and are dispersed gradually by the winds of winter. In the wild, they quickly colonize newly exposed mud flats or sandbars, but they cannot establish easily on areas already occupied by other plants.

SEASONS:
1. Winter (the bark of many individual trees is outstanding and is most visible after leaf abscission);
2. Fall (as the leaves prepare to drop, they can turn from an average green to a fairly nice yellow);
3. Spring (as with the other birches, the delicate expanding catkins provide landscape interest).

NATIVE AND ADAPTIVE RANGE: This tree is native in wet sites from Minnesota and New Hampshire to Florida and Texas. It is rated hardy north at least through USDA zone 4.

CULTURE: River birch loves water but does not require excessive amounts. The tree can survive in low areas that remain flooded for months, but we have grown it on fairly dry sites in Illinois without irrigation, once it establishes a deep root system. It is perhaps the only birch that accepts tight clay soils without complaint, as long as those soils are not so high in pH that they trigger iron chlorosis. It is easily transplanted and can be propagated from seed or softwood cuttings. Unlike the yellow birch, this—and most other birch—species will not survive in the shade.

PROBLEMS: Various leaf miners and aphids bother river birch, but its freedom from borers makes all other insect problems seem inconsequential. The tree prefers full sun and acidic soil (below pH 6.5) for best growth and good leaf color.

CULTIVARS: This plant will probably yield several good selections as more tree researchers realize its adaptability to hot summers. An interesting new dwarf selection, 'Little King', is being introduced by

Chicagoland Grows and marketed under the trademark name 'Fox Valley River Birch'. It has a compact form and grows only about one-fourth as fast as other river birches. Strongly weeping forms of river birch can be found occasionally, and nurseries will likely begin selling one before long.

The most impressive cultivar, released by our friend and associate Earl Cully after years of testing, is 'Heritage'. This selection won the Pennsylvania Horticultural Society Gold Medal in 1990. It has disease-resistant leaves, good form and hardiness and buff-colored bark that peels in large sheets to reveal an inner bark nearly as light as that of the white-barked birches. No genetic link to paper birch (*Betula papyrifera*) has been established, but 'Heritage' river birch is a heat-loving tree with superior cultural adaptability that has many of the aesthetic qualities of paper birch. An even whiter-barked improved selection, possibly a mutation of 'Heritage', is currently under production.

RELATED SPECIES: The trees that resemble river birch most closely, aesthetically and horticulturally, are all Asian species. Some are equally attractive, but none of them can match river birch for its adaptability to our climate. The western water birch (*Betula fontinalis*) is a shrubby species of Rocky Mountain streams that grows well in our test planting in Illinois.

COMMENTS: Most birches are known for their beautiful bark, which can dominate any landscape in the dormant season. Whichever species you select, it will be most striking if planted in groupings against a dark background of foliage or shadow. Fortunately, that is the way birches prefer to grow. They seem to enjoy the company of others of their own kind, providing collective shade for their roots and acting together to create a microenvironment to suit this need.

During the past two decades, Guy and Edie Sternberg have tested 29 birch varieties, both native and exotic, in central Illinois. None outperformed river birch in our hostile continental climate of hot summers, cold winters, droughts, floods, ice storms and unpredictable spring and fall freezes.

A 'Heritage' river birch grove decorates the edge of a pond.

PAPER BIRCH

Betula papyrifera

DESCRIPTION: The most conspicuous and characteristic deciduous tree of the North Woods surely must be the paper birch. This extremely cold-hardy transcontinental birch, with its many varieties and geographic races, is the primary white-barked birch that lights up the forest. It is a pioneer of disturbed habitats, reproducing in spectacular, densely packed groves following logging or forest fires. Paper birch is highly sensitive to fire yet well adapted to it; if the top is killed or damaged, it seeds profusely and develops a basal root collar from which protected dormant buds send up clusters of new shoots. Many wild trees grow as clumps for this reason, and nature's idea has caught on in the landscape trade as well, with attractive clumps of birch being planted in many northeastern towns. Paper birch is the state tree of New Hampshire and the provincial tree of Saskatchewan.

Above: The bark of paper birch peels and curls like ribbon. Previous page: Densely packed groves of this species light up the North Woods.

Paper birch grows rapidly and becomes one of our largest birches. The United States record tree, in Cheboygan County, Michigan, is 93 feet (28 m) tall, with a clump of trunks arising from a base 5 feet 8 inches (1.7 m) in diameter. Most trees in the forest or the residential landscape are juvenile specimens of much more modest stature. And those that cling to the barren rock of high mountains seldom become more than shrubs.

LEAVES: Much of the considerable geographic variability exhibited within this species is apparent in the leaves. They average 3 inches (8 cm) long, are usually hairy below and are rounded or heart-shaped at the base. They turn bright yellow in the fall.

FLOWERS AND FRUIT: Birch catkins are similar from species to species, but those of paper birch seem more ornamental because of the background of peeling white bark and the dark twigs from which they are suspended in spring. Unopened male catkins, formed in late summer, stand out from the ends of twigs like gatherings of small brown worms. The minute seeds spread in profusion every year and quickly colonize bare soils, exposed rocky slopes, sandy lakeshores and peaty bog margins.

SEASONS:

1. Winter (because of its bark, this tree is the king of winter, just as sugar maple is the king of autumn, throughout its range);
2. Fall (the yellow foliage partially hides yet highlights the white bark);
3. Early spring (the hanging catkins accent the dark twigs and white branches).

NATIVE AND ADAPTIVE RANGE: Paper birch and some of its shrubby relatives will grow nearly to the tree line in northern Canada but disappear from the woods to the south, where the average July temperature exceeds 70°F (21°C). White-barked birches, especially some related exotic species, are often planted beyond their preferred ranges because of their spectacular bark. They cannot maintain their vigor and resistance to insects in areas with hot summers and must be pampered and sprayed with insecticides to have much chance for long-term survival.

While this intensive management and risk may be acceptable to some gardeners or plant collectors, it violates the basic concepts of native tree use that are the premise of this book. By all means, grow the beautiful paper birches if they are adapted to your area; but look

Above: The paper birch and the covered bridge stand together as symbols of New England. Below right: Like other birches, paper birch develops pendent catkins in the spring.

for other fine native trees to grow if you live in the Southeast or the lower Midwest.

CULTURE: We have found in provenance trials in Illinois that selecting a source keyed to local climate and soil conditions is critical for success with this variable species in marginal habitats. Paper birches grow easily from seed and can be transplanted with a soil ball in spring without difficulty. Give this tree full sun, but keep the roots cool and moist in a slightly acidic soil and treat the bark with a recommended insecticide to prevent borers, unless you live in ideal birch habitat.

PROBLEMS: Paper birch is a favorite browse of deer and moose, which can limit natural reproduction. It can be very sensitive to the bronze birch borer (*Agrilus anxius*) under unfavorable growing conditions, though less so than some of its cousins from Europe and Asia. Paper birches do show considerable borer resistance, however, in cold climates. Where they can be grown, no other tree displays more spectacular bark. Although the bark does peel, it does not shed in heavy plates like that of some other trees and is not a major litter problem.

CULTIVARS: Surprisingly, cultivar selections of paper birch are not known in the horticultural trade. Perhaps no one has presumed to improve upon the tremendous degree of geographic variation shown by the natural varieties. We are trying one selection at Starhill Forest, the Sternbergs' arboretum in Illinois, from the Niobrara River of Nebraska. Art Ode (former director of the Nebraska Arboretum) provided the seed and believes that this selection may be resistant to borers. Horticultural selections are much more abundant in the similar but inferior (for North America) European species.

RELATED SPECIES: The faster-growing but smaller gray birch (*Betula populifolia*) is abundant on poor, open sites, and several shrub birch species can be found, mostly around bogs and on mountaintops. Birches also hybridize freely, and the paper birch will cross with the shrubby species. Some interesting selections could be expected from such crosses, but none are on the market yet. Many of the white-barked birches seen on suburban lawns are European or Asian species.

COMMENTS: The bark of paper birch reaches its maximum ornamental value in natural stands with a dark background of pine, spruce and fir. This bark was the campfire tinder of early woodsmen and the material of the aboriginal bark canoe, sewn with larch roots and caulked with balsam resin (hence the tree's alternate name, canoe birch). The bark is so durable that we have seen intact shells of trees on the Canadian forest floor long after the wood inside has vanished.

The specter of global warming raises concerns about the future of the paper birch throughout most of the United States. Heat waves and drought are expected to increase with the rise of human-induced greenhouse gases that trap radiant heat. The loss of paper birch will be one of the early signs that humans have fouled their nest.

HORNBEAM

Carpinus caroliniana

DESCRIPTION: Also called blue beech because of its smooth, blue-gray bark, the hornbeam is a fine-textured, graceful understory tree with strong wood and sinewy fluted stems that give it yet another name: musclewood. Its trunk and major limbs develop a pronounced taper and a spiraling, serpentine growth that can give the tree a bonsai-like appearance, looking older and more venerable than it is.

It typically grows no bigger than a semidwarf fruit tree, but some ancient hornbeams can become medium-sized trees. The United States record tree stands in Ulster County, New York. It is 69 feet (21 m) tall and has a trunk 2 feet 6 inches (75 cm) in diameter. Similar to its namesake, beech (*Fagus grandifolia*), the hornbeam can spread by sending up occasional root suckers some distance from the parent plant, but most reproduction is from seed.

LEAVES: The paper-thin leaves grow up to 5 inches (12 cm) long and about half as wide. They have pointed tips and finely toothed margins. The fine texture of the tree is the result of the leaves and the intricate branches that support them. The claret-colored new foliage, which develops in sunlit locations, contrasts beautifully with the bright green older leaves.

Top: The bark of hornbeam is smooth and sinewy to the touch. Above: In a reversal of its autumnal hues, the spring foliage turns from crimson to green.

The foliage on most trees turns a clear yellow or orange in the fall, but sometimes it is a luminous scarlet. This variation may be genetic, but it could be influenced by environmental factors affecting leaf-sugar synthesis and transport. The dried leaves sometimes persist in winter but not as often as those of some closely related European and Asian hornbeam species.

FLOWERS AND FRUIT: Hornbeam is related to the birches (*Betula* spp.), and it has similar staminate catkins in the spring as the leaves are unfolding. The catkins are not spectacular, but they do enhance the overall aspect of the tree. The fruits are tiny winged nuts suspended in small clusters, and they blend in with the foliage. They are particularly favored by ruffed grouse and are sought by finches and wild turkeys as well.

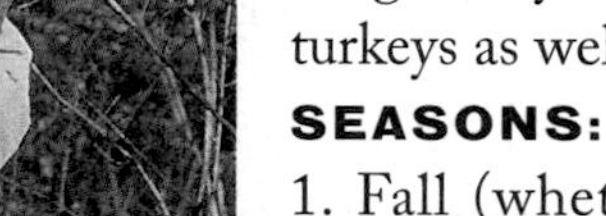

SEASONS:

1. Fall (whether red, orange or yellow, this tree gives a nice display, especially when backlighting silhouettes the branching structure);
2. Spring (when the flowers and foliage begin to emerge, adding a colorful cast to the tracery of the fine branches);
3. Winter (the bark, sinewy growth and graceful structure are best viewed during the dormant season, with low sidelighting against a dark background).

NATIVE AND ADAPTIVE RANGE: Hornbeam spans an incredible range of latitude, from the northeastern shore of Georgian Bay in southern Ontario, east to the vicinity of Quebec City and down the entire eastern United States to northern Florida and eastern Texas. Its range extends through the mountains of Mexico and Guatemala to Honduras. Trees selected from northern sources will survive at least as far north as USDA zone 3, making this one of the most broadly adapted of all our native trees.

CULTURE: This species is occasionally reported to be difficult to transplant. We have moved many

Hornbeam is a slender, trouble-free tree that prefers shady conditions.

This propagated hornbeam displays a distinctive fastigiate (narrowly upright) form.

medium-sized trees in Indiana and Illinois—from both seedling and sprout origin, with soil and without and in both spring and fall—and we have never lost one. The roots are usually shallow and spreading, so dig the tree with a wide, shallow rootball. Hornbeam loves shade, but it will become more dense and uniform in a sunny but cool and moist location. Mulching and selecting an appropriate planting site will help keep the roots moist. Seed should be collected when semi-ripe and planted outdoors immediately, to germinate the next year.

PROBLEMS: This tree is notable for its freedom from insect and disease problems. A few minor leaf-spot diseases and cankers strike occasionally, but they are generally insignificant. The smooth bark of hornbeam can be blemished by careless use of turf equipment, and the roots are sensitive to soil disturbance. The tree develops narrow branching angles, but its strong wood makes it resistant to breaking under a coat of ice. When given moist soil, it is carefree.

CULTIVARS: One old columnar selection, 'Ascendens', is listed but not commonly available. Other upright-growing specimens are seen occasionally, suggesting that selections could be made for growth form. Selections could also be made for provenance (regional adaptability) and fall color.

RELATED SPECIES: This is the only native representative of a widespread genus of ornamental American, European and Asian trees. They are members of the birch family and are closely related to the similar, stringy-barked ironwood or hop-hornbeam (genus *Ostrya*).

COMMENTS: Hornbeam enjoys shady conditions at the base of north-facing slopes and in the well-drained floodplains of brooks in our area, but we have seen it in the cool, moist, mountainous cloud forests of Mexico. The hornbeam is a clean ornamental with no off-season, and it makes an excellent little shade tree for small yards or intimate landscapes. It brings additional beauty to any setting by attracting songbirds to nest in its branch forks and dense crown and to feed on its seeds.

BITTERNUT HICKORY

Carya cordiformis

DESCRIPTION: Bitternut hickory is one of the so-called "pecan hickories" (taxonomic section *Apocarya*) distinguished by winter buds that are not covered with overlapping scales. The buds of bitternut are bright sulfur-yellow, giving the tree its alternate name, yellowbud hickory. This species is, by a narrow margin, the northernmost and most widespread of the hickories, and it is one of the fastest growing.

Bitternut is also one of the largest of the hickories, frequently exceeding 100 feet (30 m) in height on the rich sites where it prefers to grow. Trees at Lake Accotink, Virginia, and LaGrange, Tennessee, are more than 115 feet (35 m) tall and 4 feet 6 inches (1.4 m) in diameter. One in Cass County, Michigan, is 137 feet (42 m) tall and nearly 4 feet (1.2 m) in diameter. Bitternut typically develops several primary ascending limbs, forming an arched shape. Its bark is tight and relatively smooth and occasionally develops scattered horizontal fissures, like the scars of old wire on fencerow trees.

Bitternut hickory shows its bright fall color early in the season.

LEAVES: Bitternut leaves are narrower than those of most other common hickories and are pinnately compound with seven to nine leaflets. They attain a lighter autumn hue than the leaves of other hickories and turn a bright, clear yellow. Hickories are among the first of our major forest trees to display fall color, and their tall, yellow crowns can be seen from a distance.

FLOWERS AND FRUIT: The flowers appear as the leaves are reaching full size. The pendent male catkins hang like tinsel from the branches and are visible below the leaves, like miniature festoons of moss.

The nuts develop from the smaller, pistillate flower spikes. Unlike most hickory nuts, those of the bitternut seem useful only as ammunition for little boys' slingshots. They are too bitter to interest even squirrels, although they probably serve as emergency rations.

SEASONS:

1. Fall (the clear yellow of bitternut combines well with the somber greens and earliest reds of the surrounding hardwood forest);
2. Late spring (the staminate catkins embellish this species, already one of the finest-textured of the hickories);
3. Summer and winter (a fine tree for lawn or forest in all seasons).

NATIVE AND ADAPTIVE RANGE: Hickories are almost exclusively North American natives, and bitternut is the most common and widespread hickory through most of the area covered by this book. It grows naturally on mesic sites and bottomlands from central Minnesota, east to Trois-Rivières in Quebec and south to northern Florida and eastern Texas. In protected valleys, it can grow well north through USDA zone 3.

CULTURE: This is one of the easiest of the hickories to transplant, but that distinction is barely meaningful since all hickories are difficult to move. It is best to transplant them when they are very small or to simply plant the seed where you want the tree to grow. Even mature trees can be injured by soil compaction, so protect the root zone as you would the trunk from construction equipment or piles of material. With adequate water and fertility, this species will grow better than some of the other hickories, but it can survive under a wide range of less favorable conditions.

The small nuts of bitternut hickory are easy to crack but inedible.

Long, graceful staminate catkins adorn the bitternut hickory.

PROBLEMS: Hickory wood may be stronger, pound for pound, than steel, but that of the pecan types, including bitternut, is less so than that of many of their relatives. Also, the frame of this species is weakened by its branching structure, frequently divided into several ascending primary limbs. Nonetheless, it remains one of our stronger shade trees.

In manicured lawns, the small nuts of bitternut hickory can be a nuisance. Sapsuckers seem to prefer the sap of bitternut over that of other species, and they occasionally damage the bark. In spite of the hard, dense wood, stressed or damaged hickories are attacked and sometimes killed by the painted hickory borer (*Megacyllene caryae*), the hickory bark beetle (*Scolytus quadrispinosus*) and other borers.

CULTIVARS: There are no named cultivars of bitternut hickory, but its large natural range should yield regionally adapted ornamental selections.

RELATED SPECIES: Other members of the pecan-type hickories, besides the pecan (*Carya illinoensis*), are the water hickory (*Carya aquatica*) and the nutmeg hickory (*Carya myristicaeformis*). The water hickory is remarkable for its tolerance of wet soils, yet it can flourish on well-drained sites. It and bitternut hybridize with pecan, producing trees called bitter pecans.

Nutmeg hickory is an uncommon species whose leaves are attractively whitened underneath. It grows on upper terraces of floodplains along the Red River in Texas and in a few other isolated locations. It is more tolerant of shade than other hickories. Water hickory and nutmeg hickory are restricted in nature to limited habitats in the southern United States.

COMMENTS: Bitternut is among the best of all of our common trees as a forest soil builder because of the mineral content of its leaves. It casts a relatively light, open shade compared to other hickories, which allows turf or ornamental plants to thrive under its canopy.

Along with other hickories, it serves as primary host for some magnificent and relatively harmless moths, including the beautiful luna moth, several colorful underwing moths and the scary-sounding little funeral dagger wing. But the most impressive tenant of the hickories is the giant regal moth, with its 6-inch (15 cm) wingspan and its unforgettable larva, the hickory horned devil, our largest North American caterpillar.

PECAN

Carya illinoensis (C. illinoinensis)

DESCRIPTION: The pecan is our largest and most commercially valuable hickory as well as the state tree of Texas. Many people who love its tasty nuts don't realize it is a hickory. In fact, it is most closely related to those hickories with some of the bitterest fruits, and it shares many characteristics with bitternut hickory (*Carya cordiformis*). It is a tree of river bottoms, and in the rich, moist soil of its fertile habitat, it grows faster than any other hickory.

While grafted orchard pecans sometimes stay small, wild trees can be immense. One in Cocke County, Tennessee, is 143 feet (43 m) tall and has a trunk over 6 feet (1.8 m) in diameter. Several huge old pecans growing in Maryland and Virginia were planted by such gardeners as Thomas Jefferson and George Washington. Old trees in open, sunny locations can have limbs that span more than 100 feet (30 m), and even forest-grown trees will form broad crowns of long, arching primary limbs.

Top: The stately pecan is our largest hickory.
Above: Large, old pecans stand beside Mount Vernon, George Washington's Virginia homestead.

LEAVES: Pecan leaves are pinnately compound, like all hickories, and can have 15 or more narrow leaflets. The foliage has a dark, brownish green cast when seen from a distance, so this species is easy to distinguish from its bottomland associates. It turns yellow in the fall, but not as impressively as other hickories.

FLOWERS AND FRUIT: Pecans have catkins similar to all other hickories. The fruits, however, are in a class by themselves. They are so thin-shelled that many kinds can be cracked barehanded to yield large kernels of superior meat. Most, if not all, horticultural selections of pecan were chosen for the size, taste, abundance, hardiness, ease of shelling or annual bearing of the nuts.

SEASONS:
1. Fall (when the nuts ripen);
2. Winter (the brown, shaggy countenance of the pecan is interesting in the landscape);
3. Summer (an old, spreading pecan will offer dappled shade in hot southern backyards).

NATIVE AND ADAPTIVE RANGE: Pecan is restricted in the wild to the valleys of the lower Mississippi and Ohio rivers and their larger tributaries. Its range extends along the Mississippi River corridor, from the Gulf Coast north through Illinois, and reaches westward well into eastern Texas and Oklahoma, bypassing the highlands of the Ozark Plateau. Not originally native to many areas east of the Mississippi Valley, it is now widely planted throughout the southeastern United States. Although not critical for survival (some southern forms may live as far north as USDA zone 5), provenance is crucial for fruit production. Northern forms, which have very small nuts, require a winter chilling period, while southern forms

need a long growing season to mature their crop.
CULTURE: Like bitternut, this is among the easiest of the hickories to transplant, which isn't saying much. The taproots of seedlings can grow 5 feet (1.5 m) in two years, unless they are pruned or contained. It grows easily from seed and can be grafted to propagate good nut-producing trees. The pecan likes rich, moist soil and can tolerate short-term flooding.
PROBLEMS: In very humid regions, the nuts are sometimes ruined by sprouting while still on the tree. Like all hickories, pecan is affected by various borers, cankers and decay organisms, but most of these are secondary problems, serious only on already weakened trees.
CULTIVARS: The numerous pecan selections have been chosen almost exclusively for fruiting. Most commercial nuts are grown on the old standby 'Stuart' or the newer 'Schley'. 'Mahan' and its improved offspring 'Mohawk' bear huge, long nuts, easily the size of a Vienna sausage. Northern growers frequently plant 'Colby' or 'Major' because they offer hardiness and relatively early maturity. Some of the commercial selections develop into trees of predictable form and vigor and therefore have horticultural value.
RELATED SPECIES: See listings under bitternut hickory. Pecan can cross with other pecan-type hickories (taxonomic section *Apocarya*) but to little advantage, producing bitter-fruited "hican" hybrids like 'Pleas'. Pecan will also cross with some "hard" hickories (section *Carya*), producing more tasty hicans.
COMMENTS: Giant pecan trees once grew in the flatlands along the Mississippi River, in Missouri and southern Illinois. Family members who harvested the wild nuts each fall during the Great Depression have told us how the navigation dams built by the Federal government in the 1930s raised the water table in the flats, even behind the levees, and slowly drowned the great pecans and other hardwoods. Environmental assessments were not required in those days. No one had a forum to speak for the ancient trees.

The first pecan cultivar, 'Centennial', was propagated by a Louisiana slave in 1848. Since then, more than 500 selections have been made. Many of these are adapted to specific areas. In older neighborhoods across the South, pecans are often the principal shade trees. In any setting, forest or landscape, feeding the wildlife should be a prime consideration when planting or managing pecans.

The pecan's great, spreading form is stark and captivating beneath a winter sky.

Wild pecans have small but very tasty nuts.

SHAGBARK HICKORY

Carya ovata

DESCRIPTION: This is the tree most of us think of as "hickory," with shaggy bark that peels in long, tough curls along its trunk, usually starting about waist height. It is a tall, narrow-crowned tree found in moist to relatively dry uplands. Shagbark hickory is one of the "hard" hickories (taxonomic section *Carya*), with buds covered by overlapping scales. Compared with the pecan-type hickories (section *Apocarya*), the hard hickories generally maintain a single central stem higher into the crown, with shorter, horizontal side limbs.

Along with bitternut hickory (*Carya cordiformis*) this species is one of the most northern and widespread of the hickories. It generally grows slowly, but after many years it can reach a large size. The record specimen is located in the Sumter National Forest in South Carolina and is 153 feet (46 m) tall. This United States champion is 3 feet 6 inches (1 m) in diameter, remarkable for this relatively slender species. We have counted more than 150 annual growth rings on shagbark hickory stumps less than 18 inches (45 cm) across.

Warm bronze fall color is typical of shagbark hickory.

LEAVES: The compound leaves of the shagbark usually have five leaflets; each is proportionately wider than those of its frequent associate, the bitternut hickory. The heavy, substantial leaflets are about 5 inches (13 cm) long and very striking when they emerge from the expanding, pastel buds in spring. Many people mistake these tulip-like leaf buds for blossoms. Indeed, their appearance is much superior to the tree's actual flowers. The foliage turns bright gold relatively early in the fall, as is typical of the genus. The leaves eventually dry to a warm bronze.

FLOWERS AND FRUIT: The flowers of the shagbark and all other hickories occur as separate male and female catkins on the same tree. The pistillate catkins develop into the delicious but thick-shelled hickory nuts used for cake and bread. They are a favorite of squirrels and chipmunks, which seem singularly capable of cracking them. If you do the cracking and scatter the nuts in your bird feeder, you will soon attract an appreciative following of cardinals, chickadees, nuthatches, titmice and other songbirds.

SEASONS:
1. Fall (shagbark hickory is an erect, golden torch in the early fall woods, and the concurrent nut harvest is as valued by humans as it is by wildlife);
2. Spring (the emerging foliage and swelling inner bud scales provide a "blooming" more splendid than the actual flowers of many trees);
3. Winter (the gray, shaggy bark adds a picturesque texture to the dormant season);
4. Summer (a nice, upright shade tree).

NATIVE AND ADAPTIVE RANGE: Shagbark hickory can be found from southeastern Minnesota, east to Trois-Rivières in Quebec and south throughout the eastern United States, except for the Atlantic coastal plain and the lower Mississippi Valley. We have seen attractive specimens in the mountains of eastern Mexico as well. It is dependably hardy from USDA zone 4 south.

CULTURE: Shagbark hickory, like all of the hard hickories, is one of the most difficult of our native trees to transplant. In digging seedlings only a few feet tall, we invariably encounter taproots that actually seem to increase in diameter with depth to a point beyond the reach of our spade or our patience. They can be moved if the taproots were undercut during their first growing season or if the deep roots can be severed below the point where they begin to branch.

But until more nurseries grow hickories in root-controlling containers, it is best to plant hickory nuts in the fall in their planned permanent locations.

Shagbark hickory is very tolerant of most well-drained soils, but it grows slowly on all but the best. Most of the other hard hickories, except shellbark hickory (*Carya laciniosa*), grow even more slowly.

PROBLEMS: Tough to transplant and slow to grow, shagbark hickory is also sensitive to disturbance once it does become established. Undamaged trees are quite disease-resistant, but the hard hickories, in general, are among the first to show stress when wooded sites are burned or built upon. Weakened trees are frequently attacked by the hickory bark beetle (*Scolytus quadrispinosus*).

Shagbark hickories generate considerable quantities of litter from their bark plates, leafstalks and nut husks, and the falling nuts can be hazardous to an unprotected head—especially if carefully aimed by a spiteful squirrel. This species is a beautiful shade tree when planted or preserved in a visible, open setting. Often, though, it is best grown in a pasture, the open woods or a landscape border away from lawns, patios or possible root damage from construction.

CULTIVARS: Selections have been made for trees with large, sweet, easy-to-crack nuts but not specifically for landscape planting. Most of these selections are very limited in distribution and best grown in their home region, such as 'Wilcox' in Ohio, 'Porter' in Pennsylvania, 'Harold' in Wisconsin and 'Grainger' in Tennessee.

'Burton' and 'Pixley' are selections of hican, a cross between shagbark hickory and pecan (*Carya illinoensis*). Both have tasty nuts and are adapted to colder climates than the pecan. 'Pixley', from Illinois, is also known as an attractive landscape tree. Many other selections can be found locally.

RELATED SPECIES: The shellbark or "big shagbark" hickory is a bottomland species with a more central distribution. It is almost identical to the shagbark but larger in all proportions. Its leaves, with their seven (or nine) leaflets, are the largest of any hickory. Its nuts, also the largest, are edible, especially from selections such as 'Keystone' and from such hybrid (hican) selections as 'Bergman' and 'Underwood'. Its bark generally peels in longer, but fewer, strips than that of shagbark, and it tends to maintain smooth bark farther up its base. The largest known shellbark hickory grows in Rixeyville, Virginia, near the eastern edge of the species' range, and is 105 feet (32 m) tall and 4 feet 7 inches (1.4 m) in diameter. Shellbark hickories from northern provenances are hardy through USDA zone 5, but they can be injured by spring frosts. Other hard hickories are described under mockernut hickory (*Carya tomentosa*).

Above: The opening leaf buds of shagbark hickory are as attractive as many flowers.
Below left: Shagbark hickory was named for its curled plates of bark.

COMMENTS: Where there were no sugar maples, shagbark hickory furnished a sweet sap to Native Americans, who also made cooking oil by boiling the nuts. Its green wood imparts the familiar hickory-smoked flavor to fish and meat, and the rare hickory hairstreak butterfly can be found only where shagbarks grow.

From these trees, Andrew Jackson, the battle-hardened seventh President of the United States, took his nickname "Old Hickory." He planted some of the trees in 1830 at the Hermitage, his Tennessee home. They have survived to shade his grave.

MOCKERNUT

Carya tomentosa

DESCRIPTION: The "hard" hickories (taxonomic section *Carya*) other than shagbark (*Carya ovata*) and shellbark (*Carya laciniosa*) can be difficult to distinguish from one another. We will describe mockernut hickory as a representative of the remaining species. This tree is a tall, stately component of dry upland forests. Its dark bark is rough but does not peel like that of shagbark hickory.

Mockernut can survive on some pretty inhospitable sites, where it tends to be small and slow-growing. On good soil, it can outgrow shagbark hickory. The largest known specimen is in Humphreys County, Mississippi, and measures 156 feet (48 m) tall and 3 feet 8 inches (1 m) in diameter. While this height is exceptional, many others exceed 100 feet (30 m).

LEAVES: The compound leaves of this species are intermediate between those of shagbark and shellbark hickories. They generally have seven leaflets, but occasionally only five, and are pleasantly aromatic when crushed. As the species name *tomentosa* implies, the leafstalks of this species are covered with a fuzzy tomentum. They are very attractive when the buds begin to swell in the spring.

Tall and stately, with dark, unpeeling bark, mockernut is arguably the best fall hickory.

The tree's fall foliage color equals or exceeds that of any other hickory. Indeed, as long as it has not suffered severe drought, its golden color will rival the display of any tree.

FLOWERS AND FRUIT: Mockernut hickory flowers consist of separate male and female catkins similar to those of other hickories. The nuts resemble those of shagbark hickory but are more rounded, have thinner, more aromatic husks and are generally larger. Their size, though, mocks those who would gather these nuts for food. The extra mass is all shell. Mockernuts have the toughest shells in the business. The kernels are usually passably sweet but very small and inextricably entwined in the deep convolutions of the shell. Crushing the nuts between bricks and putting the pieces, shells and all, into your bird feeder might be their best use.

SEASONS:

1. Fall (possibly the best of the hickories for color);
2. Spring (during budbreak, when the tree looks almost tropical);
3. Winter (presents a rugged silhouette);
4. Summer (a stately shade tree).

NATIVE AND ADAPTIVE RANGE: Mockernut hickory is common on uplands throughout the eastern United States, except for the northern Great Lakes area and Maine, and reaches into southern Canada around Lake St. Clair and Niagara Falls. It is very common in the southern portions of this range and along the southern Atlantic coast, becoming increasingly rare toward the north. This is the hickory commonly associated with oaks (*Quercus* spp.) or pines (*Pinus* spp.) in dry or sandy forests over much of the southeastern United States. It does best when planted in suitable areas within its natural range, which extends north through most of USDA zone 5.

CULTURE: Mockernut hickory is similar to the other hard hickories in that it is a challenge to transplant. It must be grown in the nursery with root-control techniques or seeded directly into its permanent location. Husking the seeds for planting is always a

Mockernut bark is tight and rough to the touch.

pleasure because of the spicy aroma of the husks.

Mockernut responds to good soil and reasonable moisture, but it can survive with meager allotments of each. It is not as tolerant of shade as shagbark and shellbark hickories, but on sunny, fertile sites, it exhibits stout, vigorous growth as a young sapling.

PROBLEMS: Like all hickories, this species is sensitive to fires, especially when small. But hickories resprout readily, and many of the straight, vigorous young stems or clumps that can be seen in woods that burn occasionally have grown from the root collars of fire-damaged young trees. Mockernut hickory is attacked by most of the same insect pests as shagbark hickory, and the nuts present similar litter problems in manicured landscapes.

CULTIVARS: No selections are known, but we have seen considerable regional variation.

RELATED SPECIES: Authorities disagree on exactly how many other species of hard hickories exist. The variable pignut (*Carya glabra*) has small leaves and nuts, but the tree can reach considerable size on good sites. One pignut tree in Robbinsville, North Carolina, is 190 feet (58 m) tall. Frequently, though, the pignut is stunted by the rigorous ridgetop sites it seems to favor.

A closely related species, the sweet pignut (*Carya ovalis*), has more palatable nuts and shaggier bark than the pignut. Some authorities suspect it might be a cross between pignut and shagbark (*Carya ovata*) hickories, and some others classify it as a variety of pignut, *Carya glabra* var. *odorata*. Both pignut and sweet pignut occupy ranges similar to that of mockernut hickory.

Black hickory (*Carya texana*) and pale hickory (*Carya pallida*) are smaller, southern species that grow on dry, rocky or sandy uplands. Black hickory is limited mostly to west of the Mississippi River, while pale hickory grows from the Mississippi east to the Atlantic Coast.

COMMENTS: Mockernut hickory has a rich historical tradition. It was the first of the hickories encountered by European settlers in Virginia and was mentioned in literature dating from 1640. Native Americans made a juice from the crushed nuts that they called *Pocohicora*, which later was corrupted to *Hicoria* (an early scientific name for all hickories) and finally to *Carya*, the current name for the genus. *Carya* may also be traced to *Kapva*, an old Greek name for nut trees.

The aesthetic combination of its rich fall color and its aromatic, spicy-scented fruits make this tree one of the standout species of the harvest season. Each autumn, several magnificent old mockernut hickory trees light up the vicinity of Abraham Lincoln's Tomb at Oak Ridge Cemetery in Springfield, Illinois, with their golden foliage.

Mockernut hickory is celebrated for its fall leaves.

CHESTNUT

Castanea dentata

DESCRIPTION: Our North American chestnut is a magnificent tree, but it has been excluded from planting recommendations for decades because of its susceptibility to the Asian blight fungus, *Cryphonectria parasitica* (formerly *Endothia parasitica*). The fungus, which was introduced to North America in about 1904 on nonnative chestnut trees, illustrates the botanical risks of importing exotic species. Within a few decades, the alien fungus, which kills the bark and girdles the tree, had largely exterminated the American chestnut from its native range. That tragic past, however, may be about to change.

Native chestnuts now exist mostly as stump sprouts from fungus-blighted trees, but these patriarchs once ranked among our largest forest trees. Chestnut trunks of more than 10 feet (3 m) in diameter were reported from virgin hardwood cove forests. The largest remaining trees were planted years ago outside their natural range, where their isolation saved them from the blight. One, planted in Washington State, is already 106 feet (31 m) tall with a 6-foot 3-inch (1.9 m) trunk. Open-grown trees such as that one are massive and spreading, while forest trees develop long, clear trunks. The characteristic bark is smooth on young trees and deeply furrowed on larger ones.

Young chestnuts begin to fruit when only a few years old if they have cross-pollination.

LEAVES: Unlike the leaves of the commonly planted Chinese chestnut (*Castanea mollissima*), those of our native tree are smooth and narrowly tapered at both ends. They grow to about 9 inches (23 cm) long and turn golden in the fall.

FLOWERS AND FRUIT: The staminate catkins expand after the leaves, and a grove of blooming chestnuts swaying in the wind looks like a pale green sea with creamy whitecaps. The nuts grow in spiny burs and mature in the fall. They usually require cross-pollination because of protogynous blooming (timing differences between male and female flowers on the same tree), so isolated trees produce many empty burs. Chestnuts are not periodic bearers like many other nut trees. Trees that receive adequate pollination produce dependable nut crops almost every year. They also begin to bear nuts when only a few years old, unlike most other nut trees.

SEASONS:

1. Fall (for the gold color and the nut harvest);
2. Early summer (during the blooming period);
3. Winter (for the rugged branching pattern and deeply corrugated, spiraling bark on mature trees).

NATIVE AND ADAPTIVE RANGE: Chestnut is native to southern Ontario, from Niagara Falls west to the southern tip of Lake Huron, and it is listed as a threatened species by the Canadian government. It ranges southward throughout the mountainous areas of the eastern United States to the southern end of the Appalachians. However, since the blight, chestnut has the best chance of succeeding when planted anywhere outside of its native range (north through USDA zone 4), although no tree is completely safe. This recommendation will change dramatically once the blight is conquered, and that goal is within sight.

The delicious nuts of our native chestnut come packaged in a prickly bur.

CULTURE: Chestnut is among the most adaptable of trees, succeeding on almost any well-drained site. Research has shown that chestnut ranks higher than almost any other tree in competitive ability over a broad range of combinations of light and nutrient resource levels. Nursery-grown trees are not difficult to transplant in the early spring, and the seeds are very easy to grow as long as they are not allowed to dehydrate. This species grows best in full sun on rich, well-drained, slightly acidic soil.

Of course, the fungus is the chestnut's limiting factor. It survives harmlessly on other trees, such as oaks (*Quercus* spp.), until the next chestnut grows large enough to develop the furrowed bark that expedites infection.

Gathering nuts under a native chestnut tree.

PROBLEMS: Besides the fungus, the main drawback with chestnut is the presence of vicious spines on the bur that encloses the nut.

CULTIVARS: Most chestnut cultivars are selections from one of the Asian species, chiefly Chinese chestnut. A few Asian-American hybrid selections have been named, and they vary widely in their growth form, nut quality and blight resistance. 'Clapper', 'Sleeping Giant', 'Douglas' and the 'Dunstan' series were some of the earliest and best-known hybrid selections to show promise, but they are being left behind by the current backcrossing programs. Once chestnut blight is brought under control, we can begin to select from the pool of disease-resistant trees for growth form, hardiness and other features.

RELATED SPECIES: There are several European and Asian chestnut species, plus three smaller North American chestnuts known as chinkapins. The nearly identical European chestnut (*Castanea sativa*) was traditionally called *castaneo* in parts of Europe, and the nuts were *castaneas*—hence the genus name.

The rare Ozark chinkapin (*Castanea ozarkensis*) reaches about 50 feet (15 m) on good sites in the Ozark Plateau. Allegheny chinkapin (*Castanea pumila*) usually grows as a shrub or very small tree, ranging as a scattered understory species throughout the southeastern United States. Florida chinkapin (*Castanea alnifolia*) is a shrubby species of northern Florida and adjacent areas. All are susceptible to chestnut blight. The European horse chestnut (*Aesculus hippocastanum*) is a buckeye and not related to the true chestnuts.

COMMENTS: Chestnuts were once the preferred food of wood ducks, ruffed grouse, nuthatches and many other birds, as well as a favorite of wild mammals and humans. We all begrudge what has been taken from us by the blight fungus. But there is a biological war in progress, and the formerly invincible blight is beginning to stagger.

This disease cannot act in contact with the soil because of antagonistic soil fungi, and this is why chestnut roots can resprout after infection. Employing this fungal antagonism, mudpacks of soil from around the base of infected trees have been used successfully to treat individual fungus cankers.

Some offspring of trees grown from irradiated seed—an old research technique that has been on the back burner until recently—are beginning to display

Unless the native chestnut tree has cross-pollination, most of the burs that develop each year may not be filled.

some blight resistance. A few wild trees have also survived, despite the fungus, and progeny testing is continuing to select for modest levels of natural resistance and to identify the genetic combinations responsible.

Hypovirulence, a condition in which the fungus itself is diseased with a virus, is showing great promise in Europe, and it has the potential to save North American trees. Researchers are looking for ways to encourage the natural spread of this virus. Meanwhile, scientists in New Jersey have reportedly synthesized it.

Genetic engineering is also being used against the fungus. Molecular biologists are attempting to introduce a gene in susceptible trees that would enable them to produce a biochemical peptide compound that may inhibit the blight.

Controlled hybridization programs, involving successive generations of backcrossing the Asian genes that impart disease resistance into our native trees, are expected to produce, within a few years, resistant trees that are 98 percent *Castanea dentata*. Some of these hybrid lines are already only a single generation away from the final backcross, and resistant backcrossed trees that are almost pure *Castanea dentata* could be available in the near future. It will take longer, of course, to develop the multiple lines of disease-resistant trees to preserve genetic diversity within the entire backcross program, but the progress is exciting.

These various strategies bring the day closer when we can reintroduce the North American chestnut to its former range. Most of this fascinating work is being coordinated by several state university research programs and by the American Chestnut Foundation, a nonprofit research organization headquartered at 469 Main Street, P.O. Box 4044, Bennington, Vermont 05201-4044. We are ACF members and support these efforts. We encourage other native tree enthusiasts to join us. The magnificent chestnut was the dominant tree of our eastern forests once, and it is coming back.

NORTHERN CATALPA

Catalpa speciosa

DESCRIPTION: Northern catalpa is the northernmost representative of a genus of trees and shrubs native to primarily the south-central United States and portions of China. Unlike the other species, this catalpa can become an imposing specimen. A slingshot-shaped catalpa on the state capitol grounds in Michigan is 107 feet (32 m) tall with a trunk 6 feet 5 inches (2 m) in diameter, and we have seen many other weathered old monarchs that approach such dimensions. They typically develop massive trunks, supporting uneven crowns of several large, curving, ascending limbs with few twigs.

The wood is decay-resistant but brittle, so these trees sometimes don't age gracefully. Neglected old trees with craggy crowns become picturesque, in a stark way, and would look very much at home towering over Boot Hill on Halloween. However, pruned and maintained with care, these trees make an impressive visual statement in parks or rural settings, where their size and texture are appropriate to their surroundings.

Catalpa matures as an open, irregular tree and blooms in early summer.

LEAVES: Catalpa leaves are heart-shaped and 12 inches (30 cm) or more in length. They are arranged in pairs or, frequently, in whorls of three. Fall color generally does not develop, and most leaves simply turn brown and drop after the first hard frost.

FLOWERS AND FRUIT: Individual trumpet-shaped white flowers about 2 inches (5 cm) across, with yellow stripes and purple spots inside, develop in large clusters during early summer. From a distance, the huge flower clusters of catalpas rival those of any other tree. Up close, they are as impressive as orchids.

Seedpods, or "catalpa beans" ("cigars" as they are known to foolish boys who try to smoke them), follow the flowers. The clusters of 15-inch (40 cm) pods frequently remain attached throughout the winter, hanging in visually powerful vertical lines like brown icicles from the thick twigs.

SEASONS:
1. Early summer (the flowers are spectacular);
2. Winter (for the picturesque form and interesting seedpods);
3. Summer (if the large leaves fit the landscape setting).

NATIVE AND ADAPTIVE RANGE: Northern catalpa is surprisingly adaptable for a tree with an original range that covered only a small portion of the bottomlands around the confluences of the Wabash, Ohio and Mississippi rivers, down to about Memphis, Tennessee, and north to Lawrence County in southeastern Illinois. A few outlying populations were reported, but their extent is difficult to determine because this tree has been so successfully established in forestry plantings throughout the eastern and midwestern United States. It is fully hardy when planted in USDA zone 4.

CULTURE: This species can survive under very diverse conditions, including rich or poor soils, alternate flood and drought, full sun or partial shade and basic or acidic soils. It even resists salt spray. Like other adaptable trees, it performs much better when properly tended, but it can persist despite total neglect. It grows naturally in the deep, alluvial soils of large river valleys, and providing similar conditions in cultivation will yield surprising dividends. It is very easy to transplant or to grow from seed.

PROBLEMS: Catalpas are major litter producers, continuously shedding seedpods, large leaves and small branches, and they should be located with future yard grooming in mind. They require corrective pruning when young and dead-branch removal when older, if they are to grow into well-formed trees.

Although relatively disease-resistant, some trees become infected by *Verticillium* wilt disease. They serve as hosts for voracious feeding groups of the large, spotted caterpillars of catalpa sphinx moth (*Ceratomia catalpae*). The large leaves can become bronzed from ozone pollution. The wood is brittle, but because of their coarse branching structure, catalpas do not accumulate much ice during glaze storms and so are considered highly resistant to breakage.

Above: Catalpa flowers are among the most beautiful on any tree.
Below left: The dry seedpods of catalpa add interest to the winter landscape.

CULTIVARS: Northern catalpa is very consistent in growth habit across its limited natural range. No cultivars of this species are available, although one or two old selections with spotted foliage have been listed. Other catalpa species have yielded more selections.

RELATED SPECIES: The southern catalpa (*Catalpa bignonioides*) is a smaller tree with a more southerly natural range. More variable than northern catalpa, it has given rise to several cultivars and hybrids. The most distinctive and commonly seen of these is 'Nana', a densely branching dwarf that frequently was grafted on a tall stem to make the so-called umbrella-tree catalpas popular in garish Victorian landscapes. A pink-flowered intergeneric hybrid of southern catalpa with the southwestern desert-willow (*Chilopsis linearis*) is available for planting in the South, and one of the Asian species, *Catalpa ovata*, can also be seen occasionally in the United States.

COMMENTS: Some people in the southern United States grow catalpas solely as fodder for sphinx moth larvae. They use these "catalpa worms" as a convenient bait that requires no digging, thus the colloquial name for southern catalpa, "fishbait tree." This verbal insult only hints at the problem with this practice. As the fishermen hit the trees with sticks to shake loose their bait, they break branches and tear the bark. Fungus cankers frequently invade the tree through the wounds. Whenever we begin to presume that reverence, or at least respect, for trees surely must be an innate part of the human intellect, we need only think about the poor "fishbait tree" to revisit reality.

COMMON HACKBERRY

Celtis occidentalis

DESCRIPTION: This is one of our most versatile shade trees. Hackberry is related to the elms (*Ulmus* spp.) and looks very elm-like in form and foliage. The tree has attractive bark that develops layered, warty bumps or plates over a smooth gray background. The bark of some trees is much smoother than others.

Hackberries on good bottomland soils of the Midwest prairies grow fast and tall. The record is held by a tree in Mason City, Illinois, just minutes from Guy and Edie Sternbergs' research arboretum, Starhill Forest. This specimen is 94 feet (29 m) tall and more than 6 feet (2 m) in diameter.

This hackberry shows the species' typical spreading form and bronzy yellow fall color.

Similar giants can be found throughout the midwestern United States. More often, hackberries are medium-sized trees that grow on less ideal sites. They are very tolerant of rocky ridgetops, high pH soil, drought, air pollution, salt spray and short-term flooding, but they grow more slowly under such limitations.

LEAVES: The finely toothed leaves are about 4 inches (10 cm) long with wide, asymmetrical bases that taper to a long point. They look much like those of stinging nettle, and hackberry is occasionally called nettle-tree. The fall color, a variable greenish yellow, is usually not impressive.

FLOWERS AND FRUIT: Inconspicuous greenish flowers appear in spring, with both sexes on the same tree. The small drupes that follow the flowers turn orange-brown and finally purplish black as they ripen in late summer and ultimately reach the size of a garden pea. The thin, leathery layer of flesh that surrounds the hard seed has a pleasant raisin-like taste and is relished by birds. Some of these fruits persist into late winter, providing food for many northward-migrating birds, unless a greedy flock of cedar waxwings finds them first. The fruits are consumed whole and the seeds pass through the birds, providing the primary means of seed dispersal and propagation for all species of hackberries. Hackberry fruits can float and sometimes drift on a swamp or stream to a suitable growing spot.

SEASONS:

1. Winter (the interesting bark and fine-textured branching are most apparent during the dormant season);
2. Summer (a good general-purpose shade tree that attracts many butterflies).

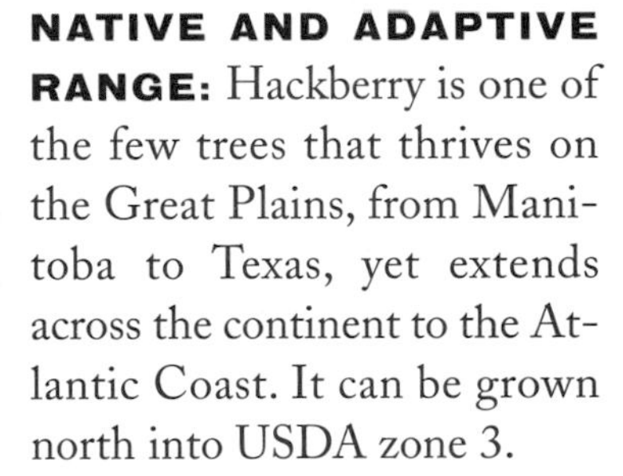

NATIVE AND ADAPTIVE RANGE: Hackberry is one of the few trees that thrives on the Great Plains, from Manitoba to Texas, yet extends across the continent to the Atlantic Coast. It can be grown north into USDA zone 3.

CULTURE: Although this tree will adjust to almost any reasonable cultural situation, the best hackberry sites are rich, deep, alluvial soils with neutral to basic pH, adequate moisture and sun; such conditions often stimulate very rapid growth. Sow seeds in the fall. Hackberry is easy to transplant but will take a year or two to recover.

PROBLEMS: Many authors refer immediately to the occasional rosetting of small twigs into witches'-brooms (caused by *Eriophid* mites and *Sphaerotheca phytophila* mildew) as the tree's primary problem, but this is usually nothing more than a blemish that actually can provide some winter interest. Hackberry is subject to leaf galls and mosaics, but nothing serious. Several hackberry species are reported to be strongly allelopathic and may adversely affect the growth of some other plants within their root zones.

Probably the most important problem we have observed is susceptibility to decay, which frequently begins after damage from storms, fires or improper pruning. The bark is prone to fire injury, and the tree's forking, arching architecture can lead to weak branch unions and splitting. These characteristics are compounded by the tree's generally poor decay resistance. Damaged hackberries don't age gracefully.

CULTIVARS: One might think that many selections of this variable species would be available, but few individual trees have shown a decided advantage over random seedlings, so few cultivars have been named. 'Prairie Pride' is one of them, selected from a tree in Illinois. It has dark, tough foliage and develops a strong central stem that resists storm damage. 'Chicagoland' and 'Windy City', introduced by our friend Roy Klehm, also of Illinois, are strong, upright trees with central stems.

RELATED SPECIES: There are more than 50 other hackberry species in the world, and several of the finest for landscape use are North American natives. One that makes an excellent shade tree from USDA zone 5 south is sugarberry (*Celtis laevigata*). It has smoother bark and narrower leaves than common hackberry, and it can tolerate extensive flooding and soil compaction. Sugarberry is not seriously bothered by witches'-brooms or some of the leaf galls that attack common hackberry. However, it seems more prone to decline following damage from ice, wind, lawn mowers or playful children climbing its branches.

Sugarberry is one of the predominant trees of the Cumberland Plateau in Tennessee, the Ozark Plateau, the southern coastal plain and down the lower Mississippi River Valley. Its range extends into Mexico, where it is called *palo blanco* ("white tree") for its soft white wood. Its branching pattern is frequently more graceful and sinuous than that of other hackberry species, and its light gray bark can be as smooth as beech (*Fagus grandifolia*). 'All Seasons' hackberry is a selection of sugarberry.

The fruits of dwarf hackberry are colorful and attract migrating birds in the fall.

Grooved and warty, hackberry bark is distinctive.

Dwarf hackberry (*Celtis tenuifolia*) is one of our finest small trees. It resembles a common hackberry in miniature, with colorful orange-brown fruits, and makes a picturesque specimen for the yard or terrace. It grows slowly under cultivation, and given that its natural habitat includes dry cliffs and stony ridges, it should be one of the most suitable and decorative trees for raised planters. Dwarf hackberry grows widely in the United States and is occasionally seen at the edge of its range in southern Ontario. It can be cultivated at least as far north as USDA zone 5.

Additional hackberry species can be found in the southwestern United States and Mexico. One of these, *Celtis reticulata*, is a tough little tree, occasionally cultivated in the East. Other hackberries grow in Europe and Asia.

COMMENTS: Hackberries are among the best food and shelter trees for wildlife. Their persistent fruits provide birds and mammals with sustenance over a long season. The narrow limb crotches and numerous spur branches of some species attract many nesting birds. The cavities in decaying old branch stubs can offer cozy spots for both nesting and hibernation. Wonderful butterflies come to dine on the foliage, including the snout butterfly, the question mark, the mourning cloak, the tawny emperor and the friendly hackberry butterfly, which will often land on a human shoulder to say hello.

REDBUD

Cercis canadensis

DESCRIPTION: Redbud has neither red buds nor red flowers, but it is nonetheless one of our most outstanding ornamental trees. While in full bloom, it dominates the landscape. Lesser beauty would be lost amid the spectacle of the season. Its arching branches are covered with rose-pink blossoms in early spring, as colorful as those of any flowering Oriental tree.

Redbuds always remain relatively small. The two largest on record grow in Nashville, Tennessee, and Roanoke County, Virginia, and both are about 40 feet (12 m) in height and 3 feet (1 m) in diameter. Often this species will develop as a clump, becoming little more than a large shrub, but old specimens develop that certain "bonsai" quality and appear larger and more ancient than they are.

Redbud becomes a small, full-crowned tree and takes on a soft yellow hue in early fall.

LEAVES: The smooth, heart-shaped leaves of redbud can reach 6 inches (15 cm) in length and width. Those in harsher climates, in the southwestern portion of the tree's natural range, are smaller, thicker and glossier. The leaves are reddish when they emerge and turn green as they expand. Leaf color is influenced in the same manner as the tone of the flowers. Plants on which the young leaves do not exhibit much red have pale pink or even white flowers. On others, the spring foliage is unusually red. The selection 'Forest Pansy' carries this crimson hue into summer. Fall color is a nice but not brilliant yellow.

FLOWERS AND FRUIT: At their prime, the rose-pink flowers of redbud are one of the most impressive woodland sights. They reach their peak between the very early white flowers of serviceberry (*Amelanchier* spp.) and wild plum (*Prunus americana*) and the overlapping and subsequent blooming of white dogwood (*Cornus florida*). The pea-like blooms of redbud provide subtle contrast and tonal variation on the otherwise virtually unbroken sequence of white in the early-spring deciduous forest. Redbuds stand out with particular clarity on days when the white flowers on these other plants fade into a background of bleak sky.

The pink of redbud is highlighted by white flowering dogwood in the spring forest.

Occasionally, a white-flowered redbud (*Cercis canadensis* var. *alba*) can be seen, but its graceful, arching form still sets it apart from other whites. The flowers are not restricted to the one-year twigs or spur branches, as they can be on other blooming trees. Flower buds push through the bark of all but the very oldest and largest limbs. The dry, brown seedpods develop in clusters and remain through the winter.

SEASONS:

1. Early spring (for the flower display);
2. Winter (the arching limbs with clinging seedpods add interest).

NATIVE AND ADAPTIVE RANGE: Despite its species name, *canadensis*, redbud is a rare tree in Canada. We have found isolated specimens near Point Pelee in southeastern Ontario, and a few have been reported on Pelee Island in Lake Erie and around Lake St. Clair. The breadth of its range to the south, however, is impressive. It is common from Iowa east to Pennsylvania, south throughout the eastern United States and westward into the Great Plains. It has been named the state tree of Oklahoma. We have even seen varieties in the majestic mountains of northern Mexico.

This tree's hardiness is known to vary with its provenance. Redbud has served countless graduate students as a textbook example of how cold tolerance

Picturesque redbuds grace many old Victorian homes.

is linked to a plant's geographic roots. It is very important to select landscape trees that are adapted to your conditions. There is a very hardy selection growing at Starhill Forest in central Illinois from seed collected at the northwestern limit of the species' range along the Iowa River. The Minnesota Landscape Arboretum near Minneapolis, in the northern part of USDA zone 4, also has some potentially hardy seedlings in trial plantings.

CULTURE: Redbud needs well-drained soil yet can tolerate the short-term flooding that occurs along small streams. The tree does equally well in acidic or basic soils. It grows well in fairly dense shade but becomes more dense and blooms more heavily in sunny locations as long as it has adequate moisture. Sow seeds in early fall, before they dry out. Seedlings frequently sprout up around mature trees. These can be moved easily when very small. Larger plants, however, develop coarse and extensive roots making them trickier to transplant.

PROBLEMS: Redbuds have three primary health problems: *Botryosphaeria* stem cankers, *Verticillium* wilt and sensitivity to chlorinated phenoxy weed killers, such as 2,4-D. Each can be serious, but most redbud trees are not affected. Redbud can be bothered by leaf maladies, such as anthracnose. Its arching form makes it somewhat prone to damage from ice storms, and the volunteer seedlings can be a minor nuisance in manicured landscapes.

CULTIVARS: The white-flowered variety has yielded at least one selection, 'Royal White', with larger flowers and a more compact form than wild trees. It was found growing in Scott County, Illinois, by Professor Joe McDaniel. White-flowering redbuds ("whitebuds") often come true from seed. Sometimes a seedling's blossom color can be predicted by the hue of its new leaves. Muted foliage suggests pale flowers.

At the other end of the color scale, 'Forest Pansy' has unusually dark flowers. It retains its reddish leaf color even after the foliage matures. It is one of the most refined of red-leaved trees, and it presents an acceptable native alternative to red-leaved Oriental maples and European beech trees, where tasteful colored foliage is appropriate. But any tree with such pronounced foliage color has the potential to appear contrived or gaudy in most landscapes. 'Silver Cloud' is a variegated selection, again useful only for those limited situations in which colored summer foliage is desirable. Neither of these selections seems as robust as local wild trees.

'Pinkbud' and 'Withers Pink Charm' both have flowers that are true pink, without the rose-colored pigment. This makes them easier to place among other flowering plants. 'Flame' is a double-pink selection.

RELATED SPECIES: Redbuds from Texas and Mexico have very small, glossy leaves and a compact form. Selections are being introduced from these provenances for cultivation in southern regions, perhaps north through USDA zone 7. They include the varieties *mexicana* and *texensis* as well as the related species *Cercis reniformis* (considered a synonym of variety *texensis* by some authorities) and its selections 'Oklahoma' and 'Texas White'. Other redbud species can be found in California, Europe and Asia.

COMMENTS: People in parts of Mexico pick redbud blossoms for food, as did the early settlers in North Carolina, who used them in salads. The flowers are visited for nectar by a broad spectrum of early-season butterflies, and the petals are the primary food for the larvae of one of our unusual spring ephemeral butterflies, Henry's elfin. This interesting little insect is seen only when redbuds are blooming.

FRINGE TREE

Chionanthus virginicus

DESCRIPTION: The scientific name of fringe tree, which translates to "snow flower," hints at the beauty of this small tree. Old fringe trees typically form irregular, spreading crowns supported by clumps of stems. Essentially, they are shrubs that just don't know when to stop growing. They can be cultivated as single-stem trees or maintained as large shrubs by periodic pruning.

A fringe tree growing at Mount Vernon, near George Washington's former home in Fairfax County, Virginia, is 32 feet (10 m) tall with a trunk 17 inches (38 cm) in diameter. A venerable specimen of comparable girth grows at Spring Grove Cemetery in Cincinnati, Ohio, and even taller ones have been found in moist areas of open woods, reaching for the shafts of light that penetrate the crowns of adjacent trees. But fringe trees grown in semishade seldom achieve stem diameters more than half as large as the old ones at Mount Vernon and Spring Grove.

The fringe tree's scientific name means "snow flower" and hints at the late-spring beauty of this small ornamental.

LEAVES: The thick, opposite dark green leaves grow 5 to 9 inches (12-23 cm) long and have a waxy appearance. They emerge very late in the spring, barely in time to serve as a foil for the earlier flowers, and turn yellow in the fall, usually dropping early. They look impressive in the fall when viewed against stark architectural elements such as concrete or brick retaining walls. Occasionally, some fringe trees will maintain their green foliage well beyond the first hard frost. The heavy leaves and thick twigs give small fringe trees a strong, coarse texture when not in bloom.

FLOWERS AND FRUIT: Fringe tree begins flowering when very young. The fragrant, late-spring blossoms signal the closure of spring and the onset of summer. The flowers are cloud-like, pure white and brilliant when viewed *en masse* against the expanding green foliage. Many people call fringe tree "old man's beard" or "granddaddy graybeard" because of the wispy flowers.

Fringe trees are dioecious, with staminate and pistillate flowers on separate plants. The male plants are more impressive in bloom, but the females bear clusters of date-like fruits that ripen to a dark blue. They are ornamental in late summer and fall and are attractive to wildlife.

SEASONS:

1. Late spring (during the blooming period);
2. Early fall (when the fruits ripen and when the more colorful specimens achieve their peak foliage).

NATIVE AND ADAPTIVE RANGE: Fringe trees can be found scattered in moist woods and swamp borders from eastern Texas and southern Missouri, eastward to the Atlantic Coast and north to Ohio and Pennsylvania. The restricted northern limit of this natural range is a mystery of the plant world since these little trees thrive under cultivation north through USDA zone 4 into southern Quebec and Ontario.

CULTURE: Transplant fringe tree as a container plant or dig it with enough soil to protect a large amount of its coarse root system. It prefers loose, moist, sandy soils but will grow in silty clay and can tolerate urban conditions. Fringe trees are found in open shade in the wild, but they become denser in the landscape with full sun as long as they receive enough water.

Fringe tree flowers reflect the warm color of evening light.

The fruits of female fringe trees will mature to an attractive dark blue.

This species is easy to grow from seed, but be patient because the seed sometimes remains dormant until the second year after planting. Cracking the seed coat before planting and seeding outdoors in late fall or stratifying over the winter helps ensure quicker and more uniform germination. The gender of seedlings cannot be determined until the plants begin to bloom. Since this is a dioecious species, the sexes are separate. For fruit production, plant enough seedlings to ensure inclusion of both genders. Plants of known gender can be propagated by grafting onto ash (*Fraxinus* spp.) understock.

PROBLEMS: Fringe trees sometimes become infested with rose scale (*Aulacaspis rosae*), but not much else bothers them. Given a suitable site and protection from excessive deer browsing, this is among the most trouble-free of small trees.

CULTIVARS: No cultivars are listed for this species, although natural variation is significant enough that some authors recognize several natural botanical varieties. They include forms with narrow leaves, broad leaves and pubescent leaves, none of which is sufficiently distinct for ornamental purposes to merit individual evaluation here.

RELATED SPECIES: A rare, shrubby *Chionanthus* known as pygmy fringe tree (*Chionanthus pygmaeus*) grows locally in central Florida, but it is surprisingly hardy much farther north under cultivation. Healthy specimens can be found in Michigan and at the Mt. Cuba Center in Greenville, Delaware. We are testing it in Illinois but have not grown it long enough to evaluate its hardiness. It is an endangered species and cannot be collected or sold without a permit. Bok Tower Gardens, at Lake Wales, Florida, grows this rare tree as part of its endangered species conservation program.

The Chinese fringe tree (*Chionanthus retusus*) is sometimes cultivated in the southeastern United States. It is similar to our native tree but more shrubby, with smaller leaves and flower clusters. Fringe tree is in the same botanical family as ash (*Fraxinus* spp.) and swamp privet (*Forestiera acuminata*).

COMMENTS: Fringe tree fruits are among the favorite foods of wild turkeys and many other birds. Tea made from the boiled bark holds an esteemed place in traditional medicine as a tonic and a topical treatment for skin irritations. But its beautiful flowers outshine its utilitarian values. This species looks especially stunning, almost ethereal, at peak bloom at night, illuminated by your car's headlights as you enter your driveway. It is even more dramatic along a wooded creek, lit only by the cool light of a full moon, its image reflected in the dark water.

In herbal medicine, fringe tree bark is boiled for a medicinal tea.

YELLOWWOOD

Cladrastis kentukea (C. lutea)

DESCRIPTION: Yellowwood combines the smooth gray bark of beech (*Fagus grandifolia*), the vase-like form of elm (*Ulmus americana*) and the snow-white flowers of locust (*Robinia pseudoacacia*) in a single, handsome tree. It usually forks repeatedly into a spreading outline in cultivation or on open hillsides exposed to full sunlight. In dense forest, it maintains a single tall stem and a much narrower form. Yellowwood is a medium-sized tree that is part of the subcanopy in Ozark and Appalachian cove forests and limestone ridges.

The largest known specimen, a stout but declining old tree that grows along the edge of Spring Grove Cemetery in Cincinnati, Ohio, is more than 7 feet (2.2 m) in diameter but only 72 feet (22 m) tall because of storm damage. Most yellowwoods are more slender. Many of the finest specimens have been cultivated in sheltered spots. Several beautiful trees grow on university campuses in the Midwest, planted decades ago by wise horticulturists who appreciated their refined beauty.

LEAVES: The leaves are pinnately compound, usually with about seven leaflets, each about 4 inches (10 cm) long and half as wide. The leafstalks cover the buds, so it can be tricky to determine where the compound leaf stops and the twig begins. In fall, the foliage can be a clear yellow or sometimes a warm gold-orange. In either case, it contrasts handsomely with the smooth gray bark.

FLOWERS AND FRUIT: Yellowwood doesn't bloom every year, but when it does, it is spectacular. Fragrant, white pea-like flowers hang from the twigs in late spring in chains more than 12 inches (30 cm) long that densely cover the tree. The small, dry pods that follow the flowers ripen in the fall and remain into winter.

Top: The refined beauty of yellowwood is particularly apparent in fall. Above: Harmless, decorative lichens grow on the smooth bark.

SEASONS:
1. Late spring (during the blooming period);
2. Winter (when the smooth bark and elegant branching pattern show to best advantage, especially in morning sun against an approaching stormy sky);
3. Fall (for those trees that exhibit colorful foliage);
4. Summer (a pleasant, graceful shade tree).

NATIVE AND ADAPTIVE RANGE: This tree is confined to isolated locations across the southeastern United States and is rarely found in any number. Its range appears to be shrinking. Yet under cultivation, yellowwood is healthy throughout the eastern United States, north from Minnesota to Maine and into southern Canada to USDA zone 3.

CULTURE: Yellowwood is usually recommended for sunny areas, where its crown becomes full and dense, but it is very happy and quite stunning when naturalized on the north-facing slope of a forest. It can be transplanted easily in the spring with a soil ball, and it grows readily from stratified seed. The pH of the soil is not critical, but the tree should have good drainage. Corrective pruning is important when the tree is young to eliminate weak branch forks (the scientific name of the yellowwood genus means "brit-

Most yellowwoods are slender. Few achieve the stature of this national champion in Cincinnati, Ohio.

tle branch"). Pruning should be done in early fall rather than in spring to minimize sap loss from cuts.

PROBLEMS: Yellowwood grows relatively slowly and takes a long time to reach blooming age. Its wood is strong, but without early training, its branching structure can be weak, inviting storm damage and ultimately decay. The thin bark is easily damaged and sometimes attracts some of the same vandals who carve their initials on beech. Curiously, while some wild yellowwood populations seem to be declining, cultivated trees in the same area are doing fine.

Long racemes of white flowers hang from the branches of a yellowwood tree.

CULTIVARS: Yellowwood as a species is a 1994 winner of the prestigious Pennsylvania Horticultural Society Gold Award. 'Rosea' is a pink-flowering form that has been propagated by seed from a single tree in Massachusetts. The seedlings are being tested by several cooperating researchers to find one with even deeper pink flowers. Considering the wide separation of wild populations, it seems likely that additional distinct forms have evolved and could be propagated.

RELATED SPECIES: We have only one yellowwood species in North America. Others can be found in Asia, and some of those are cultivated here. Yellowwood is a member of the vast legume family, along with many other beautiful flowering trees and shrubs.

COMMENTS: The root bark of yellowwood was a primary dye for early settlers in the southern Appalachians, and the wood was once prized for gunstocks. Today, the chief value of this tree is ornamental.

Yellowwood is so uncommon in the wild that when we happen upon a mature specimen in full bloom, we feel a deep aesthetic appreciation and an explorer's sense of discovery. This certainly must have been the reaction of botanist André Michaux, who found the species in the winter of 1796. Even though it was dormant, the tree captured his attention and he returned to propagate it.

ROUGHLEAF DOGWOOD

Cornus drummondii (C. asperifolia)

DESCRIPTION: Several shrubby dogwood species become small trees in portions of eastern North America, and roughleaf dogwood is probably the most resilient of the lot. It is a clumping shrub or small tree of the prairie border that exists on that harsh ecological fringe where most woody plants yield to the herbaceous flora of the plains. Exceptional tree-like specimens were seldom found in such habitats. Fires destroyed woody plants in the grasslands. Dogwoods and a few others persisted by sprouting from unburned roots and growing in thickets until the next fire pruned them back.

But because prairie fires are increasingly rare, roughleaf dogwoods can rise above their shrubby nature to become attractive small trees. One in Mississippi is 18 feet (5.5 m) tall with a 2-foot 3-inch (70 cm) stem. We frequently see this species as a small tree if its central-stem growth has not been stunted by suckering from the roots. It occupies its old haunts, at the edges of former prairie.

Roughleaf dogwood can be grown as a small flowering tree or a shrub.

LEAVES: The leaves of most of the small dogwoods are similar, being arranged in pairs and growing about 4 inches (10 cm) long, with veins that curve to parallel the leaf margin. They are rough to the touch, as the name implies, and turn a deep purplish red in early fall; the exact timing is somewhat dependent on the vigor of the plant.

FLOWERS AND FRUIT: The tiny white flowers of the small dogwood species are displayed in clusters but without the colorful bracts that surround those of some of the larger species. The flat-topped flower clusters of this species are among the largest, and can be quite showy when seen from above against the newly expanded foliage. The white fruits of roughleaf dogwood, with their bright red stalks, tend to be even more attractive because they mature as the leaves are developing fall color. Dogwood fruits generally cling to the trees until harvested by hungry birds. These trees and shrubs are some of our most valuable plants for wildlife. Bluebirds, cardinals, kingbirds and several woodpeckers feed on their fruits.

SEASONS:
1. Fall (for the combination of foliage color and fruit);
2. Late spring (during the blooming period).

NATIVE AND ADAPTIVE RANGE: Roughleaf dogwood grows naturally from southernmost Ontario, west to South Dakota and south into Texas, Louisiana and Mississippi. It is reliably hardy north into USDA zone 4.

CULTURE: This species does well on open, dry sites, while most of the other small dogwoods prefer more moisture. All are easy to transplant and can tolerate a wide range of soil textures. Sow the fresh seed in early fall for best results.

PROBLEMS: Although resistant to the gypsy moth (*Lymantria dispar*), most of the dogwoods can be stripped of foliage in a few days by the dogwood sawfly (*Macremphytus tarsatus*), which should be controlled promptly in ornamental plantings. Dogwoods can be afflicted with borers, stem cankers, scale insects and twig blight, but most of these problems are not serious if the trees are kept in good health.

The small dogwoods, including roughleaf, naturally form clumps or thickets. You can allow them to do that or maintain them as trees or solitary shrubs by mowing or pulling the surplus shoots.

Top: Roughleaf dogwood, with its small white flowers, is often planted as wildlife habitat. Above: Dogwood fruits feed a variety of birds in fall and winter.

CULTIVARS: A few variegated selections of this and similar species have been cultivated. A wild plant growing at Starhill Forest Arboretum in central Illinois develops variegated foliage on certain branches each year. This phenomenon occurs in other dogwood species as well. Such curious patterns are often due to virus mosaics, but the virus seems harmless and the visual effect can be interesting in the right setting. Some of the other small dogwood species have yielded cultivars with brilliant red or yellow winter bark, but the best color is on the vigorous young shoots of those plants pruned as shrubs.

RELATED SPECIES: There are many small dogwoods. Their identification can be very confusing, and their taxonomy and nomenclature are widely disputed. Many of them are identical, except for minor taxonomic distinctions irrelevant to their landscape value. Gray dogwood (*Cornus racemosa*) is a tough upland species similar to roughleaf dogwood but with smoother leaves and smaller, more pyramidal flower clusters. Willow dogwood (*Cornus amomum*), stiff dogwood (*Cornus foemina*) and silky dogwood (*Cornus obliqua*) are usually shrubby, have blue-tinted fruits and prefer wetter sites, along with the grex (closely related group) of extremely cold-hardy red osier dogwoods, such as *Cornus sericea.*

The USDA Soil Conservation Service has been evaluating several of the shrubby dogwoods for conservation use to stabilize soil and to provide windbreaks and wildlife habitat. In 1982, a silky dogwood from Michigan called 'Indigo' was released. It was followed in 1986 by 'Ruby', a red osier dogwood from New York. 'Indigo' is recommended for conservation planting throughout the eastern United States. 'Ruby' does well in New York and New England.

Pagoda dogwood (*Cornus alternifolia*) is a small tree unique among the dogwoods for its alternate leaf arrangement. It develops what botanists call a sympodial branching pattern, similar to sassafras (*Sassafras albidum*). Lateral twigs grow from current-season lateral buds and give the branches a stepped appearance, like the roof of a pagoda. Pagoda dogwood is occasionally subject to *Cryptodiaporthe* canker, a host-specific twig disease. But it is very winter-hardy and grows in woodlands from southern Manitoba, east to Newfoundland and south in mesic habitats throughout the southeastern United States. It does not do well in hot, sunny exposures, but it thrives in any cool, moist location with afternoon shade. We have encountered some beautiful specimens along the Finger Lakes Hiking Trail in New York.

COMMENTS: Many of the small dogwoods are cultivated as ornamental shrubs by pruning out old stems. The vigorous shoots that resprout can develop intense bark color on some species, which provides the dominant ornamental feature in a winter landscape. Dogwood fruits feed a large variety of birds in the fall and winter, and their foliage is host to several interesting creatures. Among these are the buttercup moth and the friendly probole moth, one of the most inquisitive and sociable of garden insects.

FLOWERING DOGWOOD

Cornus florida

DESCRIPTION: The king of spring in the eastern United States and southern Ontario, flowering dogwood may be the most spectacular of our flowering trees. It grows slowly into a multilayered pagoda of color—its symmetrical branching pattern provides a crown of horizontal tiers similar to that of pagoda dogwood (*Cornus alternifolia*). Understory trees can reach 40 feet (12 m) or so into the forest canopy and have supple, wispy stems. But at the woodland edge, exposed to sunlight, the trees are shorter and develop a compact crown. This shows their dense blossoms to advantage along rural roadsides.

Native flowering dogwood is the "king of spring" in the eastern United States and southern Ontario.

The largest known flowering dogwood is an old tree in Norfolk, Virginia, that is 33 feet (10 m) tall with a trunk about 3 feet (90 cm) in diameter. In general, flowering dogwoods more than 1 foot (30 cm) in diameter are considered large specimens.

LEAVES: The leaves of this species resemble those of other dogwoods, but they can grow up to 6 inches (15 cm) long on vigorous young shoots. If the flowers were not so impressive, this tree would be more famous for its radiant red fall color. The litter from flowering dogwood leaves, which are rich in calcium, enriches the topsoil for associated plants.

FLOWERS AND FRUIT: The small flower clusters are surrounded by four leafy bracts that turn white as they expand; this enhances the blooms like the pink sepals enhance the flowers of pinckneya (*Pinckneya bracteata*). The bracts initially emerge greenish white, sometimes showing a pinkish touch when partially expanded. They become visually effective when they reach a span of about 2 inches (5 cm) and attain their full brilliance several weeks later when they grow to almost double that size. On some popular selections, the color can be pink or red. The long blooming period overlaps with redbud (*Cercis canadensis*). The two species are often found together and provide a spring flowering spectacle that, once seen, is never forgotten.

The small clusters of fruit are a glossy, bright red and add sparkling highlights to the rich red fall foliage. Some fruits usually persist after the leaves have fallen, unless migrating birds find them first. They are an important food for overwintering birds, especially bluebirds, in the South.

SEASONS:
1. Spring (during the blooming period);
2. Fall (when the colored foliage and fruit are nearly as impressive as the flowers);
3. Winter (with violet-tinted, layered branches punctuated by points of light from the turban-shaped flower buds).

NATIVE AND ADAPTIVE RANGE: Flowering dogwood can be found from Toronto, Ontario, south to the Gulf Coast and from southern Maine to eastern Texas. It has been named the state tree of both Virginia and Missouri. This broad range can be misleading. Flowering dogwood provides a classic example of the influence of provenance. Individual trees may not be reliably hardy or may not bloom well if transplanted far in any direction from their ancestral region. Always try to acquire planting stock that thas been grown from a lineage adapted to your climate and soil. Keeping this fact in mind, one can say that flowering dogwood is hardy north through USDA zone 5.

CULTURE: This tree grows readily from seed but is not very easy to transplant. Move it with a soil ball in early spring, and be sure to set it a little high in

Previous page: A venerable dogwood in flower lends grace to all the other elements of a landscape design.

the planting hole. Although wild dogwoods seem to survive in rather exposed locations, cultivated ones do best in a birch-type setting: leaves in the sun, roots in the cool shade. A breezy location will add some motion to the flowers and will discourage the *Discula destructiva* anthracnose disease. Trees in fairly deep shade will thrive but will become leggy and not bloom as profusely.

PROBLEMS: The red-tinted cultivars are generally not as hardy or as vigorous as most white-blooming forms and must be grafted because their seedlings usually have white flowers unless pollinated by another red tree and selected for color. Many minor leaf diseases and insects attack flowering dogwood. Healthy trees are far less susceptible than those that are poorly planted, infrequently watered or otherwise abused. Dogwood borer, *Synanthedon scitula* (a clearwing moth resembling a slender bee), is attracted to weakened trees, pruning cuts and sunscald-damaged bark. Despite its reputation as a delicate tree, however, flowering dogwood seems unaffected by smog and is impervious to the notorious gypsy moth (*Lymantria dispar*).

Dogwood anthracnose (*Discula destructiva*) is a newly described disease that first gained notoriety about 1980. Although it is very destructive in some mountain forests in the southeastern United States, most pathologists do not believe it will be as widespread or deadly as chestnut blight or Dutch elm disease. Anthracnose apparently cannot survive intense summer heat and cannot spread on dry foliage. In sunny areas, well-maintained landscape trees with good air circulation and soil moisture are rarely killed. New trees should be purchased from a disease-free nursery, not transplanted from an infected forest.

CULTIVARS: Many selections of flowering dogwood have been recorded since the species was discovered more than 300 years ago. Most of them may be grouped into one of the following categories: large-flowered, pink-flowered, red-flowered, heavy-blooming, fragrant-flowered, double-flowered, variegated-leaved, dwarf or weeping. Most of them originated from plants in the southern portion of the species' range, and they are generally more cold-sensitive than local wild dogwoods.

Of particular interest to us are those selections made for winter hardiness. 'Ozark Spring', introduced by our friend John Pair in Kansas, is one such plant, and 'New Hampshire' (from Atkinson, New Hampshire) is another. More commonly available selections include 'Cherokee Princess', 'Cloud Nine' and 'White Cloud', which have white flowers; 'Cherokee Chief', 'Royal Red' and variety *rubra*, which have pink or red flowers; and 'Rainbow' and 'Welchii', which have colored foliage.

Guy and Edie Sternberg are testing the variety *urbiniana* in Illinois, grown from seed that Guy collected in the mountains of Nuevo Leon, Mexico. Its flowers are unusual in that the bracts remain attached at the ends, giving them the appearance of Chinese lanterns. If it proves fully hardy in the north, this high-elevation variety will greatly add to the diversity of the cultivated species.

Some of the newest dogwood selections on the market are hybrids with other large-bracted species. 'Eddie's White Wonder' was derived from a

The small, glossy red fruit clusters of flowering dogwood are attractive to hungry birds, as well as to the human eye.

Most pink-flowering dogwoods are more cold-sensitive than white-flowering types of local provenance.

cross with the Pacific dogwood (*Cornus nuttalli*). Crosses with the Asian *Cornus kousa* have yielded 'Stardust', 'Galaxy', 'Aurora', 'Constellation', 'Ruth Ellen' and 'Stellar Pink'. These selections do have some "native blood" and incorporate some of the best qualities of each parent, but in a strict sense, they are not native or even natural.

RELATED SPECIES: Flowering dogwood is closely related to the other dogwoods covered in this book and to the tiny ground cover bunchberry (*Cornus canadensis*). It is most similar, however, to the giant Pacific dogwood of western North America and to the Asian *Cornus kousa*.

COMMENTS: This ornamental tree has been admired by horticultural writers at least since the publication of Ray's "Historia Plantarum" in 1680. More than a century later, in 1791, the famous naturalist William Bartram wrote at length in his "Travels in Georgia and Florida" of the beauty of an exceptional grove of "dog-woods" that "continued nine or ten miles unaltered." During that same period, Washington and Jefferson initiated a trend by planting dogwood at Mount Vernon and Monticello. Venerable landscape specimens can surely be magnificent, but we prefer to imagine the unbroken spectacle of Bartram's "dog-woods" in peak bloom.

SMOKE TREE

Cotinus obovatus (C. americanus)

DESCRIPTION: Only two species of smoke tree are known. One, *Cotinus coggygria*, is a large shrub from Europe and parts of Asia that is frequently cultivated. The other, *Cotinus obovatus*, is rarely seen although it is native to North America. Of the two, the North American native is certainly the superior plant. It becomes a small tree, sometimes with multiple stems that sprout from stumps. If allowed to grow in its own style and if undamaged by storms or careless pruning, it becomes a striking specimen.

If undamaged by storms and careless pruning, smoke trees become striking specimens.

As with many trees, *Cotinus obovatus* grows larger in cultivation than it does in the wild. The smoke trees on the limestone highlands of the Edwards Plateau in Texas are shrubby, while those in other parts of the range become small trees. We have admired a particularly fine old smoke tree for several decades. It grows in West Lafayette, Indiana, many miles from its natural range, and is a former national champion. This specimen stands nearly 40 feet (12 m) tall and has a single stem 2 feet 6 inches (75 cm) thick. The current champion, shown on page 97, is shorter but broader, with a multiple stem, and grows even farther from the tree's natural range.

LEAVES: The leaves of our native smoke tree grow almost twice as large as those of its exotic cousin. They are nearly round and about 4 inches (10 cm) long. Few other trees can rival their brilliant orange fall color.

FLOWERS AND FRUIT: The misty flower sprays of our native smoke tree are smaller but no less attractive than those of the exotic species. They resemble puffs of smoke on the ends of the branches, hence the common name "smoke tree." All smoke trees are dioecious, so each plant is either male or female. Male trees have larger, showier flower clusters—up to about 6 inches (15 cm) long—than females.

The beautiful flower structures develop in late spring and remain attractive into the fall as fruit panicles. The actual seeds are inconspicuous and sparse (many panicles have no seeds) but are a choice food of some of our native finches.

SEASONS:

1. Fall (its fiery yellow-orange color against a dark background of ledge rock or evergreens is unsurpassed);
2. Spring and summer (for the smoke effect of the panicles, especially striking when in front of a white house or backlit before a shadowy background).

NATIVE AND ADAPTIVE RANGE: Smoke trees occur in isolated stands on limestone soils in Alabama, Arkansas and Texas; a few scattered trees range north to Kentucky and Missouri. Like many trees from these harsh habitats, it grows vigorously in cultivation well beyond its natural range—north at least through USDA zone 5.

CULTURE: Most of the usual suggestions for growing the exotic species apply to our native one, including a sunny exposure on well-drained soil. It is easy to transplant, but propagation from seed can be frustrating because so few seeds form and they take so long to germinate. Smoke tree sprouts readily from the stump and may be grown as a shrub by cutting old stems out periodically. The species is so impressive as a small tree, though, that renewal pruning might better be reserved for the exotic Asian smokebush.

PROBLEMS: Basically, this tree can be planted and forgotten. Once established, it thrives on neglect. Its only weakness might be its fragile wood, typical of many members of the cashew family. If the stems are broken by a storm, prune them back to a crotch or cut them to the ground and allow them to start over.

CULTIVARS: Several smoke tree cultivars can be found in nurseries, but almost every one is a selection from the Asian species. 'Red Leaf' is described by some authors as a native selection with very good fall color. The native smoke tree is so stunning and uniform that cultivar selection may be unnecessary.

RELATED SPECIES: *Cotinus coggygria*, the Asian or European smokebush, is the only other member of the genus. Its cultivars are very common in the landscape trade. Some of them maintain a raucous purple leaf color throughout the growing season, making them a challenge to fit in any discreet, noncommercial landscape. We believe that too many people accept this challenge and fail.

COMMENTS: Smoke tree has a white inner bark that turns orange when it is peeled. This bark and the yellow wood were early sources of dyes. The range of smoke tree is scattered and skips over entire states, so it would seem logical that distinct wild forms could be located. A few nurseries in the southeastern United States are beginning to consider this possibility, and we expect eventually to see some selections marketed. If these really are improvements over the species, they will be special, indeed.

The feathery fruit clusters of our native smoke tree are more subdued than those of the common exotic species.

The national champion smoke tree in Willimantic, Connecticut, has a crown spread of 44 feet (13 m).

RED HAW

Crataegus mollis

DESCRIPTION: If we attempted to discuss all the hawthorns, this book would need a companion volume. Canada has at least 25 hawthorn species, and perhaps several hundred more can be found in the United States. Of them all, red haw is probably encountered most often and over the broadest range, and it might be the easiest to identify. It is a tough little flowering tree with a short ashen-gray trunk and a dense crown of spreading, thorny branches.

Red haw is one of the largest of the hawthorns. One tree in Grosse Ile, Michigan, is 52 feet (16 m) tall and has a trunk 2 feet 9 inches (85 cm) in diameter. But most red haws, and most hawthorns in general, seldom exceed 30 feet (9 m) in height or 18 inches (45 cm) in diameter.

LEAVES: Red haw is sometimes known as downy haw because of its fuzzy leaves. For hawthorn leaves, they are large, reaching up to 5 inches (12 cm) in length. Most hawthorns are susceptible to a number of leaf diseases, and red haw may be the most prone of all to early defoliation from leaf blight (*Fabraea thuemenii*), scab (*Venturia inaequalis*) and several rusts (*Gymnosporangium* species). Its fall color is usually aborted when the leaves drop in late summer due to these infections, but by then, they have done most of their work for the year. This particular species is not known for great fall foliage color anyway, so little harm is done.

Top: A red haw spreads its blooming branches over the prairie soil of a Midwest farm. Above: Premature but relatively harmless defoliation from leaf diseases offers an early display of the colorful fruit.

FLOWERS AND FRUIT: All hawthorns are attractive in bloom. The native species have clusters of white blossoms that develop in spring, and red haw is among the earliest to bloom. The fruits, known to schoolchildren as thornapples, are also the first to ripen, and they drop to the ground as school begins each fall. But before they drop, leaf diseases sometimes remove the foliage and fully display the bright scarlet fruit. The fruits are edible, as most young children discover, but they are not especially attractive to wildlife until long after they have fallen. When they soften, they become forage for ruffed grouse.

SEASONS:

1. Spring (during the blooming period);
2. Late summer (when the fruit ripens);
3. Winter (most hawthorns are interesting in the dormant season because of their dense, intricate branching, and many have reflective gray bark).

NATIVE AND ADAPTIVE RANGE: This species is found from southeastern North Dakota, east through southern Ontario to Nova Scotia and southwest to northwestern Alabama and eastern Texas. It grows in the forest and savanna understory and along the prairie border, and it is fully hardy in USDA zone 4.

CULTURE: Hawthorns will survive conditions that thwart most other flowering trees. They are indifferent to soils, tolerate full sun or considerable shade and

Above: The white flowers of red haw are borne in baseball-sized clusters. Below left: The scaly gray outer bark of old hawthorns sometimes flakes away to reveal a colorful inner layer.

resist drought. Many will endure wetter conditions than most other trees in their family. Yet, hawthorns are highly recommended for xeriscaping. They are not as easy to transplant as their close relatives, the crabapples (*Malus* spp.), but they are not particularly difficult either. Seeds should be planted in the fall, and they may not germinate until the second year.

PROBLEMS: If you expect any fall foliage, you have to spray this species with an orchard fungicide. It can survive just fine without treatment, however, and as mentioned previously, early leaf abscission enhances the fruit display. One of the primary leaf diseases of red haw, cedar-hawthorn rust (*Gymnosporangium globosum*), is not a serious problem except where junipers (*Juniperus* spp.), the alternate host of the disease, grow within a few city blocks. Hawthorns as a genus are defoliated quickly during outbreaks of the gypsy moth (*Lymantria dispar*).

The other serious problems with this species are inherent. It has long, sharp thorns that are hazardous at eye level. Its fruits, which fall with abandon in autumn, can make walks and driveways slippery at this time of year.

CULTIVARS: Several hawthorn cultivars are common in the nursery trade, but none are derived from red haw.

RELATED SPECIES: Authorities differ on the worldwide number of true, distinct hawthorn species, with estimates ranging from about 200 to 1,200. Hawthorns are in the rose family, together with many of our most popular ornamental and orchard trees.

COMMENTS: Because of their conspicuous fruits, hawthorns are assumed to provide valuable food for wildlife, and they are known to have been planted for fruit by Native Americans. Many animals do snack on them, especially during winter when food is scarce, but the real value of this genus to wildlife is for nesting and roosting cover. Their dense, thorny branches and habit of growing in thickets and fencerows rank the hawthorns among the most useful of all woody plants for wildlife habitat.

OTHER HAWTHORNS

Crataegus species

Many of our hawthorns are superior ornamental and conservation plants. A few of the most common and decorative are discussed here.

Washington haw (*Crataegus phaenopyrum*) is an upright-growing, densely thorny species. Its small, glossy leaves turn red in the fall, and the small, bright fruits remain through most of the winter or until eaten by hungry wildlife. It grows in scattered locations from southern Illinois to the Gulf Coast, but it is hardy north through USDA zone 4 in southern Canada. Seedling selections have been made for more columnar growth, which is useful in narrow planting areas. This species seems very resistant to the leaf diseases that attack some of the other hawthorns.

The long-lasting fruit display of a mature Washington haw.

Cockspur haw (*Crataegus crus-galli*) develops a spreading, flattened crown of long, layered limbs that, on mature specimens, sometimes sweep the ground. Its narrow, glossy leaves turn orange to red in the fall, and its dull red fruits persist into winter. This tree has some of the longest thorns of any hawthorn, but a thornless variety, *inermis*, is available. Cockspur haw has a broad natural range, from the Florida panhandle to Montreal, Quebec, and it can be grown north through USDA zone 3. 'Crusader' is a thornless cultivar of this species, and the heavily fruiting cultivar 'Vaughn' is reported to be a hybrid with Washington haw. The colorful hybrid *Crataegus x lavallei* is also a descendent of cockspur haw.

The similar but slightly smaller dotted hawthorn (*Crataegus punctata*) is a dense-branching floriferous species with marble-sized red fruits and heavily veined small leaves. This hardy little tree can be found growing north into southern Newfoundland. The Secrest Arboretum has introduced a hybrid selection, 'Ohio Pioneer', that is substantially thornless and quite ornamental.

Green hawthorn (*Crataegus viridis*) is a species of broad southern river bottomlands and coastal plains, known primarily by its Indiana cultivar 'Winter King'. Among the outstanding ornamental fruiting trees of this genus, this might be the most impressive. It doesn't bear heavily every year, but in good years, no tree's winter display is more brilliant. The fruits are persistent and retain their substance and color until early spring, unless they are discovered by flocks of hungry cedar waxwings. Green hawthorn can be grown north into USDA zone 4.

Fleshy hawthorn (*Crataegus succulenta*) is a species with glossy leaves, a profusion of bright red fruit and waxy blossoms that look like porcelain. Its ornamental value merits more cultivation. Fleshy hawthorn has a wide natural distribution, from the southeastern corner of Saskatchewan and southern Manitoba, east through southern Quebec to Cape Breton Island and south to Tennessee and North Carolina. 'Toba' is a hybrid of this species with the European cultivar 'Pauls Scarlet'.

Another hardy northern species, *Crataegus arnoldiana*, has given us the seed-propagated selection 'Homestead'. It originated at the Agriculture Canada Experiment Station in Morden, Manitoba, and is rated hardy north through USDA zone 3. 'Homestead' Arnold hawthorn has pale yellow flowers and bright red fruit that ripens early, like that of red haw.

Frosted haw (*Crataegus pruinosa*) resembles a small red haw. Its waxy foliage is a deep blue-green in summer, and its purplish fruits grow almost as large as those of red haw. The frosted haw is commonly en-

Through most of the winter, green hawthorn holds its bright fruit, which combines nicely with its silvery bark.

Cockspur haw has lustrous foliage and some of the most forbidding thorns of any hawthorn.

countered in thickets from Newfoundland southwest to eastern Oklahoma.

May haw (*Crataegus aestivalis*) is a popular ornamental tree in the southern United States. In the wild, it grows throughout the lower Atlantic coastal plain from North Carolina south in seasonal swamps, borrow pits or ditches that dry up in late summer. Horticultural selections such as 'Big Red' (from Mississippi), 'Super Berry' (from Texas) and 'Lindsey' (from Georgia) can be grown in regular garden soil and should be mulched to retard evaporation. We have gathered the fruits of wild may haws in swamps, where the trees grew about 15 feet (4 m) high, by skimming the water for them as if harvesting cranberries. May haw jelly and wine are highly regarded.

Green hawthorn, with its showy white flowers, is a species of southern bottomlands and coastal plains.

Another small southern species, parsley hawthorn (*Crataegus marshallii*), shares the general flower and fruit qualities of other hawthorns but might have the most ornamental foliage of all. The leaves are deeply dissected and look like garden parsley. The very tiny red fruits contribute to the fine appearance of this tree. Parsley hawthorn grows in low woods and wet areas, but it is adaptable to average garden soil.

Many hawthorns seen in cultivation are cultivars of one of the European species. Both *Crataegus monogyna*, the European hawthorn, and *Crataegus laevigata (C. oxyacantha)*, the English May hawthorn, are well represented in ornamental horticulture.

PERSIMMON

Diospyros virginiana

DESCRIPTION: Most people know persimmon as a shrubby tree of old fields and fence lines. It is found in such habitats with sassafras (*Sassafras albidum*) and sumacs (*Rhus* spp.) and, like them, forms thickets of root suckers. However, in bottomland forests with good soil and moisture, persimmon can become a large tree. Specimens more than 100 feet (30 m) tall and 3 feet (1 m) in diameter grow in nearly every southeastern state, and United States co-champions of that size exist in Tennessee, Georgia, Texas, Missouri, Mississippi and Arkansas.

Persimmon is an attractive tree when well grown; it is symmetrical in youth and, with maturity, develops a picturesque, wild branching pattern and dark, charcoal-checkered bark. A member of the ebony tree family, its hard black heartwood closely resembles that of its tropical cousins. It is quite adaptable and tolerates dry sites, sterile soils, flooding, heat, shade, wind and almost any other factor that might overwhelm a weaker species. It grows best in rich, organic soil with abundant moisture and full sun.

Top: Persimmon flowers, both staminate (shown here) and pistillate, form beautiful waxy bells but are hidden by the foliage unless viewed from up close. Above: The attractive but messy fruits borne by female persimmon trees are not palatable until fully ripe.

LEAVES: Persimmon leaves emerge in late spring and eventually reach up to 6 inches (15 cm) in length. They tend to hang from the twigs when mature, giving the tree a soft appearance. Its fall foliage is variable in color. Individual trees can be quite impressive, while others appear drab.

FLOWERS AND FRUIT: Persimmon flowers are usually dioecious. Staminate trees bear small flowers in clusters of three. Pistillate trees have larger, solitary flowers up to ¾ inch (2 cm) wide that are yellowish white, powerfully fragrant and provide excellent nectar for honeybees.

The 1-inch (3 cm) orange fruits give the genus its name. *Diospyros* has been interpreted as "God's fruit" or "God's fire," and either name can be appropriate, depending on whether the berry is eaten when completely ripe or while still firm and "puckery" to the taste. In late fall, wildlife compete with humans for ripe persimmons, which can be made into pudding, bread, beer, brandy and preserves. After the leaves drop in the fall, the clinging orange fruits on female trees stand out like Christmas ornaments until they are removed by wildlife or by winter winds. Mockingbirds are especially fond of them, and wild turkeys and deer pick them from the ground as they fall.

SEASONS:

1. Fall (especially if your tree has good color or is a female loaded with fruit);
2. Winter (for the bark and picturesque branching).

NATIVE AND ADAPTIVE RANGE: Persimmon trees can be found at lower elevations from southern Connecticut to eastern Kansas and south to the Gulf Coast. Under cultivation, it does well in the north at least through USDA zone 5.

CULTURE: This is among the most difficult of our native trees to transplant successfully in large sizes due to its coarse, deep root system. Once established, though, that same root system virtually guarantees the tree's survival. Persimmon seeds germinate easily, but the hardy seedlings grow slowly unless given ideal conditions. Persimmon trees survive neglect but thrive with attentive watering and on enriched soil. They tolerate shade but grow faster in full sun. Wild trees sprout freely from the roots if damaged by fire. Persimmons are deep-rooted, good soil-building trees, so males make excellent lawn trees where quality turf is desired.

PROBLEMS: The overripe fruit falling from female trees can be a nuisance if the trees are planted near paths and driveways. Otherwise, persimmon is usually trouble-free, except for possible infection by persimmon wilt (*Cephalosporium diospyri*), a systemic disease that has killed many wild trees in Tennessee. We have also seen entire fence lines of persimmons defoliated by a twig-girdling insect, *Oncideres cingulata*, but the trees seem to recover fully.

CULTIVARS: Seedless forms are known, and many tasty selections have been named since Captain John Smith of Jamestown first sampled the fruit almost 400 years ago. Among the favorites for table fare are 'Craggs', 'Florence', 'Garretson', 'John Rick', 'Killen', 'Meader', 'Morris Burton', 'Penland', 'Pieper' and 'Wabash'.

The branching form of a large, old persimmon tree is picturesque in any season.

Professor Joe McDaniel gave us some seed in 1972 from his favorite 'Woolbright' persimmon, which was selected for its superior red fall foliage. The two resulting male seedlings, growing at the Sternbergs' home in Illinois, have performed brilliantly, although with some surprises: each fall, one turns violet and the other bright gold. Fall color is difficult to predict, even from superior parent stock, unless trees are asexually propagated.

Both of these unnamed 'Woolbright' offspring merit further study as ornamentals that produce minimal fruit litter. We expect to see other male selections become available in the trade as nurseries learn how to transplant persimmon and as the public becomes more aware of its ornamental and resilient qualities.

RELATED SPECIES: Many ebonies are found in the Tropics, and several half-hardy species from Asia and Europe are grown in mild-temperate climates. One other native species, the Texas persimmon (*Diospyros texana*), occurs in southern Texas and Mexico; it is not hardy in the north.

COMMENTS: Persimmon is one of our most diversely useful trees. It has obvious landscape value, and its fruit is important to wildlife and humans. Native Americans relied on the bark as a cure for fevers and the roots as a treatment for dropsy. The rock-hard wood has been used for many specialty products, such as golf clubs and loom shuttles. Persimmon trees attract two of our most spectacular garden moths: the regal moth, which can be 6 inches (15 cm) across, and the ethereal swallow-tailed luna moth.

WAHOO

Euonymus atropurpureus

DESCRIPTION: Many people are familiar with the winged burning bush (*Euonymus alatus*), which was introduced here and has escaped from cultivation to become a serious weed species in many forests. Some also know the exotic wintercreeper (*Euonymus fortunei*), which can overtop trees and crowd out native wildflowers. Few, however, are aware of several attractive native species of *Euonymus*, including one that can become a small tree.

The wahoo, or strawberry tree, is an understory species of rich woods and stream valleys throughout most of eastern North America. It sprouts from the roots and commonly forms loose clonal thickets under favorable conditions in shady forests, but it can become a dense, symmetrical, flat-topped small tree when cultivated in the open. The largest known wahoo tree grows in Michigan and stands 32 feet (10 m) tall with a stem 7 inches (18 cm) in diameter.

The wahoo's fruit display is long-lasting, persisting into winter.

LEAVES: All *Euonymus* leaves are arranged in pairs along the twigs. Those of our native wahoo become larger than most, reaching 5 inches (13 cm) or more in length. They seem one with the fresh lime-colored twigs, as though molded from the same green plastic in a single pour. The red fall color is similar to that of the exotic winged burning bush, except that its foliage is free of the clashing magenta overtones that can make winged burning bush so difficult to place in the landscape.

FLOWERS AND FRUIT: In early summer, wahoo flowers hang in branching clusters from the new twigs. They are mostly hidden by the leaves but add a fine texture and are visually effective when you can look up into the canopy. Each tiny purple flower has four petals and develops into the four-parted fruits, which are the best ornamental feature of this plant and explain its common name, strawberry tree.

In late summer, the fruit capsules color gradually to white, then to rosy pink. Later they split open to expose shiny red-skinned seeds similar to those of magnolias (*Magnolia* spp.). Wahoo usually fruits annually, and some individuals bear very heavily. The seeds are released gradually through early winter, remaining ornamental for an extended period because birds, particularly bluebirds and mockingbirds, use them only for emergency rations.

SEASONS:

1. Fall (for the dependable, long-lasting fruit display and red foliage);
2. Winter (for the bright green twigs).

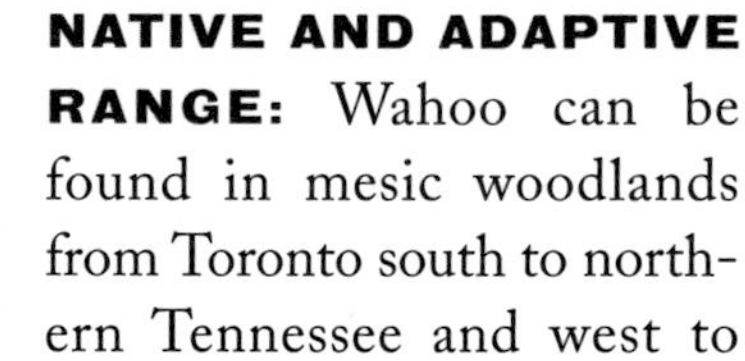

NATIVE AND ADAPTIVE RANGE: Wahoo can be found in mesic woodlands from Toronto south to northern Tennessee and west to central Kansas, with outlying groups extending into southeastern North Dakota, central Texas and almost to Florida. It seems most at home in the Midwest and can be grown under cultivation north into USDA zone 3.

CULTURE: This is one of our most shade-tolerant woody plants, yet it grows well and becomes an attractive, dense specimen in full sun. It prefers a rich forest soil but has no special drainage or pH requirements as long as it gets sufficient moisture during the growing season. Its dense, shallow mass of roots makes it very easy to transplant when dormant. Propagate it from suckers or from seeds sown in the fall.

Above: The fruits of wahoo are initially light green and gradually reach their brilliant color in late summer. Below right: Wahoo flowers are inconspicuous from a distance but merit a close inspection.

PROBLEMS: Wahoo is not immune to the Asian scale insect (*Unaspis euonymi*) that plagues other members of the genus. It also attracts browsing deer and rabbits and should be protected until it outgrows their reach. The seeds are reported to be poisonous to humans but are eaten by wildlife. Wahoo is one of our few native understory trees that endure high levels of ozone pollution without foliar damage.

Occasional root suckers may be pulled off as they occur if a single-stemmed tree is desired, or the plant may be allowed to form a clump. Suckering seems to be less prevalent on cultivated wahoos in open settings than on those growing in the forest.

CULTIVARS: No cultivars are listed for this species. Selections probably should be made for superior fruit displays, since this characteristic seems to vary from tree to tree.

RELATED SPECIES: Our other native *Euonymus* species are low or running shrubs. There are Asian and European species that develop into small trees similar to wahoo, and many popular horticultural selections have been derived from some of the exotic species.

COMMENTS: The pink popcorn fruit capsules of wahoo, reminiscent of bittersweet (*Celastrus* spp.), are distinctive in the fall and are sufficient reason to give this small tree a place in the ornamental landscape. They are especially attractive after the leaves have fallen and are a decorative, rustic touch in floral arrangements. When planted with witch hazel (*Hamamelis virginiana*), the late fall combination of yellow flowers and red popcorn fruit makes a brilliant display, from the Canadian Thanksgiving in early October through the late November Thanksgiving celebrated in the United States.

For a horticulturist, the root system of wahoo is a delight to behold. A small specimen dug from silty forest soil and rinsed off in a bucket or nearby brook reveals a fine, luxuriant, fibrous white root mass that any plant propagator would admire.

BEECH

Fagus grandifolia

DESCRIPTION: With its combination of expansive range and distinctive appearance, the gray-barked beech is one of the most familiar forest trees of eastern North America. Its common name is related to the Anglo-Saxon word for letter (*boc*), since centuries ago, messages were often carved on the smooth bark of the European species, *Fagus sylvatica*. Beech competes with sugar maple (*Acer saccharum*) over a vast range as the climax species of the hardwood forest—the tree that eventually dominates in the absence of such disturbances as fire or logging. Both trees are very tolerant of shade and can develop under the canopies of other trees, but they differ in their reproductive strategies.

While maple produces great quantities of seedlings, some of which invariably survive, beech cannot be so dependent upon seedlings, because most of its seeds are eaten by wildlife. So, once it becomes established, beech develops suckers from its vast system of surface roots. Many supposed beech "seedlings" in the forest are connected by such a root system. They have a significant competitive advantage over true seedlings and are able to dominate drier sites than the maple. Entire beech groves have grown from the roots of a single tree.

Beech becomes a large, fine-textured tree with a dense canopy and a graceful, spreading form. It is highly phototropic, meaning it responds to shade patterns by leaning toward the strongest light. The United States national champion is located in the northeast corner of Ohio and measures 130 feet (40 m) in height with a trunk nearly 6 feet (1.8 m) in diameter. Equally impressive specimens might be found in Canada, given the large Canadian range of the species.

With its distinctive appearance, the gray-barked beech is one of the most familiar forest trees of eastern North America.

LEAVES: Seen against the background of smooth gray bark, bright new beech leaves emerging from the long pointed buds are a sight not quickly forgotten. The leaves expand to 5 inches (13 cm) in length and remain attractive throughout the growing season. In fall, they turn yellow and then golden bronze. Like those of some of their close relatives, the oaks (*Quercus* spp.), beech leaves are marcescent, meaning that some of them usually cling to the tree each winter, bleaching in the sun and rattling in the cold wind.

FLOWERS AND FRUIT: The staminate flowers hang from long stalks in marble-sized round clusters; the pistillate flowers are arranged in pairs on shorter stalks at the ends of the branches. They develop into triangular beechnuts, which are among the most important foods for wildlife ranging from wild turkeys to squirrels. Studies have shown them to be a primary food for more than 30 wildlife species. In season, they can make up half of a black bear's diet.

Beechnuts were the primary fall food for passenger pigeons that once graced this continent by the millions. Enormous flocks feeding in beech groves have been described as one of the most impressive sights in nature. However, because of their indiscriminate slaughter and human impacts upon their habitat, passenger pigeons are now extinct.

In the open, beech trees can become beautifully symmetrical and develop an enormous branch spread.

SEASONS:
1. Early spring (when the long sharp buds expand and fresh new leaves emerge a spectacular green after a long hard winter);
2. Winter (for the silvery smooth bark and intricate twig structure, most visible in the dormant season, accented by some clinging leaves);
3. Fall (the yellow foliage is modest compared to adjacent maples and some of the oaks, but the combination of leaves and bark is quietly elegant);
4. Summer (a stately tree that casts a cool but luminous shade).

NATIVE AND ADAPTIVE RANGE: Beech can be found in rich mesic forests between wet bottomlands and dry hills from Sudbury, Ontario, Cape Breton Island and Quebec City down the eastern United States to northern Florida and eastern Texas. As with other trees with such a broad range, local seed usually produces the best-adapted trees. Northern beech ecotypes can be grown north to USDA zone 3.

CULTURE: This tree is extremely intolerant of root-zone disturbance, drought and wildfire. It should be preserved in natural forest settings or planted in evenly moist sites where it can be left alone. It has the undeserved reputation of being difficult to transplant, probably because many people have tried to collect wild "seedlings" that actually were root suckers, or because it will not survive if planted too deeply. We have successfully moved wild trees of seedling origin and even a few small sprouts. Nursery-grown specimens can be transplanted in large sizes.

Beech can be grown easily from seed, which must be protected from rodents and birds throughout the first growing season, or by layering (rooting the tips of low branches and then cutting them from the mother plant).

PROBLEMS: The most immediate concern with beech is a serious bark-fungus disease, *Nectria coccinea* variety *faginata*. The fungus seems to be fatal most often when it invades trees after they have been at-

Top: The long-pointed buds of beech burst into feathery tassels of new foliage in spring. Above: The lush foliage of beech is adapted to the shade of the deep woods.

Another common pest peculiar to beech is the woolly beech aphid (*Phyllaphis fagi*). This insect does not kill the tree, but it litters the ground (or patio) below with a sticky honeydew.

Beech is also intolerant of drought and poor soil drainage. Newly planted trees (or those recently exposed by adjacent clearing) are prone to sunscald. Beech trees in the forest are easily killed by fires. Damaged trees are very prone to decay.

The shallow surface roots make it difficult to establish and maintain turf under beech. On the other hand, grass roots and whirling lawn mower blades can hurt the roots. The best solution, for your mower and your beech, is to let a natural duff or mulch accumulate under the canopy and allow the lower limbs to sweep the ground or encourage native wildflowers to fill in beneath.

CULTIVARS: The European beech has given rise to more horticultural selections than almost any other forest tree, but this is not so with our native species. Two selections from Indiana, 'Abrams' and 'Abundance', were made in 1926 for nut quality, and another, 'Jenner', was added more recently from New York.

There are natural geographic races, known locally as red beech, gray beech and white beech, and some authorities recognize a variety or two. We have not yet seen the dawn of cultivar development in native beech, perhaps because any seedling will dependably produce a tree of superior ornamental value or perhaps because our native species is more site-demanding than most trees, including its European cousin. Cultivar development may also be limited because the European beech had been tinkered with for centuries before

tacked by the beech scale insect (*Cryptococcus fagisuga*), which was introduced to Nova Scotia from Europe around 1890. Researchers hope the disease will run its course and that the most resistant trees will survive to contribute their genes to future beech forests.

botanists discovered our native tree, and no one perceived the need for more beech cultivars. However, once the day of native cultivar introductions arrives, it should be a dawn to behold.

RELATED SPECIES: There are about 10 species of beech worldwide, all in the northern hemisphere, but only our native tree and the European species are hardy in most of eastern North America. European beech may be slightly more heat-tolerant, while our native species is more cold-hardy. A similar species from the mountains of Mexico might be hardy in the southern United States. The beech trees of the southern hemisphere actually belong to *Nothofagus*, a related genus.

COMMENTS: Two of the more interesting organisms associated with beech are a small, quick, brown-over-blue butterfly called the early hairstreak and beechdrops (*Epifagus virginiana*), a parasitic plant that grows beneath beech canopies. Beech bark, especially where it is naturally sculpted around unions where low limbs join the stem, is a tactile as well as visual masterpiece. It should be part of all interpretive trails for the visually impaired. Old trees, under a gray sky in winter, appear to have been cast from molten pewter.

Everyone interested in woodslore probably has heard about Daniel Boone recording his hunting success by carving on the smooth bark of beech trees "D. Boone cilled a bar." Unfortunately, this backwoods graffiti has been widely imitated. It is increasingly difficult to find elegant old beech trees with smooth, lichen-mottled bark that has not been thoughtlessly disfigured.

Beech cannot be grown outside of its undisturbed natural habitat without careful attention to its precise requirements, but it is a prize well worth the cost for those who want to grow or preserve one of the world's most beautiful trees. It can serve as the "canary in the coal mine" for those who hope to build their houses in the forest without damaging the surrounding trees. When the beech in your wooded lot starts to die, you will know that your construction was not benign and that other trees may also die.

Many scientists predict that beech will fall victim to environmental degradation in the United States based upon current projections of global warming and acid precipitation. Beech's uptake of calcium is inhibited by the unnatural aluminum concentrations in soils affected by acid rain. While global warming might not kill trees in managed landscapes or in the coolest woodland ravines, the warming, drying effect of "greenhouse gases" may, within the next century, eliminate most of the beech from many of our forests. We all should work to reverse such ominous ecological destruction—for the noble beech and for our own species.

The fall color of beech is conspicuous in the understory of Jim Wilson's woods.

SWAMP PRIVET

Forestiera acuminata

DESCRIPTION: The wild privets are represented here by swamp privet, the hardiest member of the genus and the only one adaptable to much of our area. They are an obscure group of small trees and shrubs, almost unknown in cultivation, except where they have been transplanted from nearby swamps or in the special gardens of plant collectors. Generally shrubby in the wild, swamp privet can be grown as a small tree. The largest specimen known is 42 feet (13 m) tall with a main stem 10 inches (25 cm) in diameter. It was found growing in Richland County, South Carolina. Larger individuals probably exist in some inaccessible bayou.

Swamp privet is related to olives (*Olea* spp.), and a mature specimen looks similar to an olive tree: it has smooth gray bark, stone fruits about the size and shape of a small Mission olive, opposite leaves and a picturesque crown. Unlike olives, though, it shares a special ability with buttonbush (*Cephalanthus occidentalis*) and water tupelo (*Nyssa aquatica*) to survive in swampy soils that may be underwater for nearly the entire growing season.

Swamp privet, a floodplain species, is at home at the edge of a lake.

LEAVES: The leaves are arranged in pairs on bright green new twigs, which contrast with the ivory-gray bark of the older branches. The foliage is very smooth, and individual leaves generally do not exceed about 3 inches (8 cm) in length by less than half as wide. They drop in the fall without showing any significant color.

FLOWERS AND FRUIT: The swamp privet is usually dioecious, but occasionally some fruits can be found on predominantly male plants. Flowers emerge without petals in early spring, before the leaves, and the staminate flowers are one of the best-kept secrets of ornamental horticulture. The plants become a mass of pale yellow, similar to the misty-yellow of male spicebush (*Lindera benzoin*), and they can illuminate the most dismal swamps.

Female trees bear clusters of reddish purple olive-like drupes, which ripen in early summer and fill an important food need for nesting waterfowl and songbirds. The fruits are lightly textured and reach the size and consistency of large raisins.

SEASONS:
1. Early spring (during the blooming period, especially for staminate trees);
2. Winter (for the smooth bark and the branching character of large, well-grown specimens);
3. Summer (for pistillate specimens loaded with fruit).

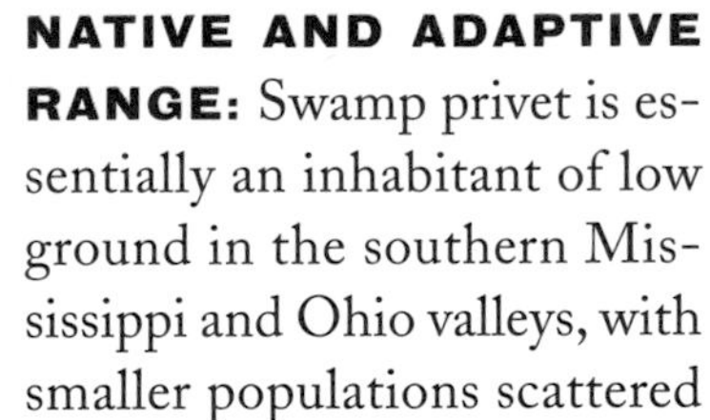

NATIVE AND ADAPTIVE RANGE: Swamp privet is essentially an inhabitant of low ground in the southern Mississippi and Ohio valleys, with smaller populations scattered east to South Carolina and west to central Texas and eastern Kansas. Its range reaches up the Mississippi and Illinois rivers into central Illinois and up the Wabash River into southwestern Indiana. This species is so rarely seen in cultivation that its full hardiness is probably not known, but we have seen landscape plantings doing quite well through USDA zone 5.

CULTURE: Swamp privet is not a very demanding species, but it does best in rich, moist soil. It is very useful for planting in wet areas, where almost no other small tree can survive. Part of its competitive strength lies in its ability to grow where many other

plants would drown or be washed away by floods. It is tolerant of shade but, like many other species, forms a more dense, uniform crown in full sun.

Fresh, ripe fruits may be sown with their pulp intact as soon as they fall, and they will germinate within days. The resulting seedlings should be given fertile soil and plenty of sunlight and water to help them grow large enough to withstand their first winter; the smaller ones will benefit from winter protection in the north. (This protection is not needed after the first year.) Trees of known gender can be propagated by layering their lower branches. This way, fruiting females and flowering males may be planted together to produce fruit for wildlife. A purely ornamental planting can be established with males alone.

PROBLEMS: Fruits can be messy if they fall on paved surfaces before the birds find them; however, they will disappear into mulch or turf without notice.

We have found damage from the ash borer (*Podosesia syringae* var. *fraxini*) on this species, which seems logical because ash trees (*Fraxinus* spp.) are close relatives of swamp privet. Deer and rabbits can injure young plants by browsing, and wild plants are occasionally tilted or smothered by heavy siltation from severe flooding in their natural habitats.

CULTIVARS: No cultivars are listed for any wild privet species.

RELATED SPECIES: Several similar species are restricted to extreme southern portions of the United States and parts of Mexico. The Florida privet (*Forestiera segregata*) is a species from the Atlantic coastal plain that extends north only to the Savannah River in Georgia. Narrow-leaved privet (*Forestiera angustifolia*) is a dry-land species of southern Texas and eastern Mexico, and desert-olive (*Forestiera phillyreoides*) is restricted to dry, rocky areas in southern Arizona and western Mexico.

Some authorities follow a different taxonomy and recognize a different species, *Forestiera neomexicana*, as desert-olive and *Forestiera ligustrina* as a distinct southeastern species. Swamp privet is obscure enough without such additional confusion. In any event, none of these other species is very hardy within the geographic scope of this book. The closest familiar native relatives of swamp privet are fringe tree (*Chionanthus virginicus*) and ash. The introduced and frequently invasive common privets (*Ligustrum* spp.) are also related, as are lilacs (*Syringa* spp.) and olives.

COMMENTS: Sometimes gardeners and conservationists wisely accept the biological premise that diversity within communities of native species is healthy for its own sake and that rare or unusual plants frequently have ecological value that escapes casual notice. If for no other reason, swamp privet is worthy of consideration. In addition, its early flower display, colorful summer fruit clusters and ability to thrive on exposed riverbanks and in wet sites that would be fatal to most other trees should earn swamp privet wider use in conservation plantings and specialty landscapes, and greater preservation and appreciation in the wild wetland forests it calls home.

Above left: The showy flowers of male swamp privets brighten wetlands and riverbanks in very early spring. Below: Swamp privet fruits ripen to a deep purple in early summer.

WHITE ASH

Fraxinus americana

DESCRIPTION: The ashes are among the most common and widespread of our native forest trees, and white ash is the largest and most impressive species. It shows strong apical dominance whether grown in an open field or under the dense competition in a cove hardwood forest. With great age, however, ash increases in spread as far as its neighbors will permit.

The corduroy-textured bark of a mature white ash invites close inspection.

The largest, though certainly not the tallest, white ash tree known grows next to a restaurant in Palisades, New York. It stands 95 feet (30 m) tall with a massive trunk more than 8 feet (2.5 m) in diameter. Forest-grown white ash trees can become half again as tall but seldom more than half as thick as this stout old witness to the Revolutionary War.

Most ash species prefer wet soil, but white ash is a tree of mesic uplands and the well-drained valleys of small streams. It tolerates short-term flooding in order to gain the mineral-rich alluvial sediments, and it makes its best growth in such seasonally enriched soil.

LEAVES: Most native ash leaves are similar. White ash develops opposite, pinnately compound leaves composed of about seven leaflets arranged in pairs along the twigs. The leaflets are 2 to 5 inches (5-13 cm) long by slightly less than half as wide. They are held on short petiolules, or stalks, and are whitened underneath. Fall color is variable, depending upon genetics and perhaps soil acidity. It is always impressive, whether it is the gold that predominates in the South or the orange-purple so prevalent in the North.

FLOWERS AND FRUIT: Ash trees are dioecious. Male trees bloom annually; in early spring, clustered purplish bronze flowers appear. Most female trees bloom heavily only once every several years. The female flowers have reddish purple pistils that develop into loose clusters of greenish yellow winged seeds. On some trees (forma *iodocarpa*), the red color is retained as the seeds expand. This form was found in Maine in 1911 and described by Merritt Fernald. It is very striking in summer as the fruits mature. This is good reason to plant female trees, which are often avoided during cultivar selection because of the fruit litter. The ripe seeds are tan, winged samaras about 2 inches (5 cm) long and are a favorite food of grosbeaks and finches.

SEASONS:

1. Fall (white ash generally has the best color of any ash, especially on trees that turn an iridescent orange-violet, and it is among the first of our large trees to color);
2. Late spring (for those select female trees that have colorful immature fruit).

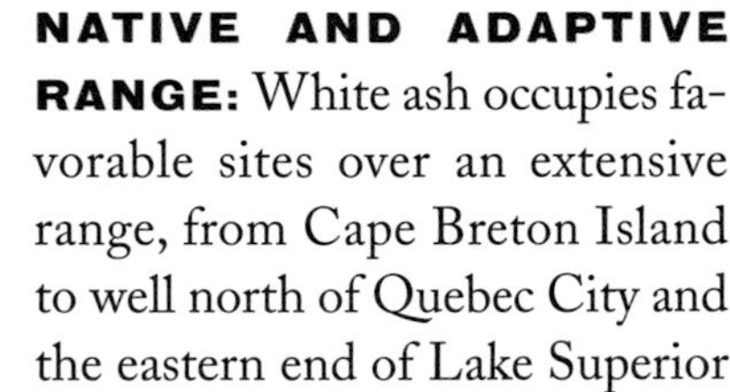

NATIVE AND ADAPTIVE RANGE: White ash occupies favorable sites over an extensive range, from Cape Breton Island to well north of Quebec City and the eastern end of Lake Superior and south through almost the entire United States east of Omaha and Dallas. It misses only southern Florida and the coastal plains of the adjacent southeastern states. Trees of properly selected provenance are hardy under cultivation throughout the East up to USDA zone 3.

CULTURE: This species does well in a wide range of moderate conditions, but it will not tolerate extremes. It is easy to transplant when dormant, and it can be propagated from seed or by budding selected trees onto the rootstock of seedlings. White ash is relatively resistant to smog. Wild trees can stand quite a bit of shade when young, but if you want them to develop a full crown, you have to clear away competing trees to give them a generous share of sun.

PROBLEMS: The most critical insect problem on white ash is the ash-lilac borer (*Podosesia syringae* var.

fraxini), which also attacks swamp privet (*Forestiera* spp.) and other related plants. Ash trees are less likely to be damaged if they are healthy and vigorous, but borers can become a serious concern on weak specimens. The adult borer moths are active during the morning, and their populations may be monitored with inexpensive pheromone traps to determine when (or if) spraying is worthwhile. Oystershell scale insects (*Lepidosaphes ulmi*) can also be serious pests on ash. All of the ashes are very resistant to the gypsy moth (*Lymantria dispar*), which defoliates so many other trees.

Ash yellows is a poorly understood, frequently fatal disease caused by a mycoplasma-like organism (MLO). It results in lost vigor, dead branches, the sprouting of multiple leaders (loss of apical dominance) and the growth of congested witches'-broom on the trunk. It may be transmitted by insect vectors or by dodder (a parasitic vine).

Ash trees are disfigured by anthracnose (*Gnomoniella fraxini*) in years with wet spring weather, but the disease is not a serious health threat. Fall color is occasionally lost due to premature defoliation by leaf spot (*Mycosphaerella effigurata* or *Mycosphaerella fraxinicola*).

Seed litter can be a problem in some landscapes. Heavy seed crops probably weaken female trees, which makes them vulnerable to insect and disease damage. Trees that develop more than one stem with narrow forks can be subject to ice damage, but white ash is generally considered a strong tree.

CULTIVARS: White ash selections have been made for seedlessness (male trees) and superior fall color. 'Autumn Applause' and 'Autumn Purple' are two of the most popular. 'Chicago Regal', 'Elk Grove', 'Autumn Blaze', 'Fall Festival' and 'Royal Purple' are excellent new selections with outstanding color. 'Rosehill' and 'Champaign County' are more adapted to southern areas. 'Manitoo' and 'Skyline' are narrow upright forms.

RELATED SPECIES: There are more than a dozen ash species in North America; several are treated individually in the following pages. The one most likely to be confused with white ash is Biltmore ash, considered a separate species (*Fraxinus biltmoreana*) by some authorities and a variety of white ash by others. Blue ash (*Fraxinus quadrangulata*) is a similar upland species restricted to a much smaller natural range. It has ridges, or wings, on its twigs, which can make the twigs look square in cross section. Blue

Fruits of the rare white ash form iodacarpa are pendent and a striking purple-red.

ash is a medium to large tree, unique among the hardy species of ash for its exceptional tolerance of drought and alkaline soil; this makes it suitable for prairie areas. It develops a dense crown and clear yellow fall color and is hardy under cultivation in USDA zone 4. Although some authorities list this species as monoecious, all of the trees we have seen are either male or female, just like most other ashes.

COMMENTS: Many people think of white ash in terms of the baseball bats made from its sapwood, but we prefer to admire the tree as a living organism. It is one of the fastest growing of our strong-wooded shade trees, and it has outstanding early fall color. It casts a bright, inviting shade because of the light color of the undersides of its leaves, and it is a choice host for the tiger swallowtail butterfly.

White ash is intermediate in tolerance to nearly every growing condition. It does well under a wide range of "average" circumstances but poorly on extreme sites, so it is an excellent choice for the "average" landscape.

GREEN ASH

Fraxinus pennsylvanica

DESCRIPTION: While white ash (*Fraxinus americana*) may be the most impressive member of the genus, green ash is certainly the most widespread and adaptable. We incorporate all of its variations, including the taxonomically distinct form called red ash, in this discussion.

Green ash is probably the most commonly seen of our ash species, both in the wild (in bottomland forests and along prairie streams) and under cultivation. It develops massive limbs, exhibiting less apical dominance than white ash, and can reach impressive proportions in favorable habitats. The United States national champion, located at a country crossroads in Cass County, Michigan, is 131 feet (40 m) tall and has a trunk more than 6 feet (2 m) in diameter. The species has an extensive Canadian range as well, so there may be even larger green ash trees in Canada.

By planting male selections of green ash, the heavy litter of seeds can be avoided.

LEAVES: Green ash leaves are opposite and pinnately compound. They resemble white ash leaves in size and shape, but the leaflets are usually narrower than those of white ash and their stalks are slightly winged. Green ash leaves are uniformly green on both sides during the growing season and turn bright yellow in the fall.

FLOWERS AND FRUIT: Like most ash species, this tree is dioecious. The flowers and fruits resemble those of white ash. Female trees are prolific annual seeders, so they provide much food for wildlife and much litter in the domestic landscape.

SEASONS:

1. Fall (for the bright foliage color).

NATIVE AND ADAPTIVE RANGE: Green ash is successful over a broad and challenging range that essentially matches that of white ash but which expands northeast through the Gaspé Peninsula and around Lake St. John in Quebec, northwest to central Alberta and west to central Wyoming. Over much of this range, it is one of the only deciduous trees tough enough to survive. Selected trees are reliably hardy north to USDA zone 2.

CULTURE: The term "culture" seems almost foreign to green ash. As long as the tree is planted "green side up," it seems capable of surviving. Yet, like other trees with reputations for toughness, this species will respond noticeably to good treatment. Moist, fertile soil will stimulate amazingly fast growth. Careful attention to pruning during its early years will minimize the poor form and weak branch unions for which it is notorious. And selections of locally adapted provenance will be less affected than unadapted ecotypes to drought, cold, heat and other debilitating factors.

PROBLEMS: Green ash is subject to the same insect and disease problems as white ash. Although less influenced by marginal environmental conditions, its characteristic poor form makes it prone to structural damage from wind and ice. As mentioned, proper pruning of young trees will enhance and strengthen the primary limb structure. Seed-bearing female trees are terribly litter-prone, so males should be planted in areas where seeds would be a nuisance.

CULTIVARS: There is a standard caution that any cultivar you plant should be from a geographic provenance adapted to your area and that you should not create a large monoculture of a single cultivar in any landscape. That said, green ash perfectly illustrates the advantage of cultivars over random seedlings. Many named selections exist, some so superior to average seedlings that they look like different species.

'Marshall Seedless', introduced in 1946, was one of the first modern tree cultivars, and it remains popular today. 'Aerial', 'Bergeson', 'Dakota Centennial', 'Emerald', 'King Richard', 'Newport', 'Patmore', 'Prairie Spire', 'Robinhood', 'Sherwood Glen' and 'Summit' are among the many highly recommended new male selections. Each of these cultivars develops a stronger branch structure than the average green ash, and most have attractive foliage and good vigor.

'Cimmaron', 'Urbanite' and 'Skyward' are also listed as improved new selections of green ash, but they display foliage characteristics and reddish fall color that suggest they might have been derived from hybrids. 'Patmore' originated in Manitoba and may be the hardiest selection for northern regions. Since 1985, the Prairie Farm Rehabilitation Administration of Canada has been testing other green ash selections as windbreaks at their research station near Indianhead, Saskatchewan. The USDA Soil Conservation Service is also testing provenance selections of green ash.

Above: Each of the many outstanding cultivars of green ash offers predictable uniformity with a characteristic shape and fall color. Below left: A colonnade of pop ash, water-loving trees of the Southeast.

RELATED SPECIES: Most authorities now incorporate red ash under the taxonomic umbrella of green ash, which had formerly been considered a variety (*subintegerrima*) of red ash.

Pumpkin ash (*Fraxinus tomentosa*) is intermediate between the red ash and white ash types, and it possibly originated as a stabilized hybrid between the green ash and the white ash. It has a spotty distribution and is found mostly in wetland areas of the Atlantic coastal plain and Ohio and Mississippi river valleys. It can be grown through USDA zone 5. Pop ash (*Fraxinus caroliniana*) is a similar swamp tree, but it is more southerly in distribution and smaller in stature. Black ash (*Fraxinus nigra*) is usually a small tree, but it can exceed 100 feet (30 m) on good sites. It occupies wetland habitat in the boreal forests of the northern states and Canada and even survives in peat bogs. Its one cultivar, 'Fallgold', is a superior male selection with long-lasting fall color that was introduced by the Morden Experimental Station in Manitoba. There are several additional western and southwestern species that are neither native nor well adapted to cultivation in eastern North America. Several European and Asian ash species are also common landscape trees.

COMMENTS: Green ash could be considered the junkyard dog of the genus. Left to its own devices, it is a survivor but not much more. However, when taken into cultivation, selectively propagated and properly trained, it becomes a respectable shade tree for the most refined landscapes.

We all have been fascinated by the Journey of Discovery undertaken by Lewis and Clark from 1804-1806. Green ash might have kindled their campfires and those of the nomadic Native Americans they encountered over much of the upper Missouri River Valley. Unlike its prairie associates, cottonwood (*Populus* spp.) and boxelder (*Acer negundo*), it burns well without being seasoned. Had it not been for green ash, those famous explorers might not have survived their first winter on the Great Plains and gone on to chart a route to the Pacific.

HONEY LOCUST

Gleditsia triacanthos

DESCRIPTION: Honey locust is one of our most adaptable and graceful trees. Its cultivars have brought shade and beauty to our streets for several decades. A critical distinction must be made, however, between the typical wild form of this species and its cultivars. While most *Gleditsia* cultivars are seedless and virtually all are thornless, many wild trees are neither. The seedpods are merely inconvenient because they litter the landscape, but the long, needle-sharp thorns are the most dangerous spears carried by any temperate-zone tree and are capable of puncturing shoes, tractor tires and anything else without armor plate. The thorns emerge on new twigs with the leaves, but even larger ones—up to 2 feet (60 cm) long with multiple points—sprout annually in red clusters directly from the lower trunk and form downward-pointing pickets that convincingly discourage squirrels and other tree-climbers. Old thorns turn brown then weather to gray, but they persist for decades.

Thornless cultivars of honey locust make safe and desirable lawn trees.

The arching form and fern-like foliage of honey locust would make it appear at home with the acacias of tropical Africa, to which it is related. But in the temperate forests of North America, it has no aesthetic equivalent. The loftiest specimens usually grow in floodplain forests. One in Wayne County, Michigan, stands 115 feet (35 m) tall and has a trunk nearly 6 feet (1.8 m) in diameter.

LEAVES: The feathery compound leaves of this species and its close relatives are unlike those of any other native tree. The slender leaflets are about 1 inch (3 cm) long and are usually simply compound, or pinnate, on old trees but doubly compound, or bipinnate, on vigorous young trees. They turn a clear yellow in the fall.

FLOWERS AND FRUIT: Staminate and pistillate flowers generally develop separately but on the same tree, and they are not conspicuous. Pistillate flowers grow into curved brown legume pods sometimes 18 inches (45 cm) in length with hard seeds embedded in a sweet, sticky matrix that is eaten by foxes, squirrels and livestock. Seedless trees can be grown by grafting or rooting branches that bear only male flowers, even if the branches are from a tree with both male and female flowers.

SEASONS:

1. Summer (the feathery grace and filtered shade of this tree is unique in our area);
2. Fall (the yellow color of some selections shows well against the dark bark, and the maturing pods of fruitful forms are conspicuous and attractive);
3. Winter (for wild trees with thorns and seedpods, which combine to make a bristly silhouette).

NATIVE AND ADAPTIVE RANGE: Honey locust is commonly found from central Pennsylvania and southeastern South Dakota down to New Orleans and Dallas. We have seen natural populations near London, Ontario, and in the Sierra Chiquita mountains in Tamaulipas, Mexico. Provenance is critical with such a wide-ranging species, especially one with the broad genetic variation of honey locust; Mexican seed should certainly not be planted in Canada or vice versa. But with proper attention to seed source, honey locust can be grown in suitable sites throughout our area, north into USDA zone 3.

CULTURE: Honey locust grows well under a variety of conditions, but it prefers moist, deep, well-drained soil. It must have full sun, but it is remarkably tolerant of urban conditions, alkaline soil, drought, road salt, heat and compacted soils. On marginal sites, this species sometimes remains a large shrub.

Thorny wild trees are obviously impervious to grazing animals (and climbing children). They frequently are the first trees to appear in an overgrazed pasture—they are spread by the cattle that eat the fallen pods but pass the seeds. Under heavy browsing pressure, nature selects the most forbiddingly thorny seedlings to survive, and an old pasture full of such trees becomes impenetrable.

It is very easy to transplant honey locust at any size, and it can be propagated from seed (thornless forms come true about half of the time) or by grafting (use scionwood from a male branch of a thornless tree). It casts a light shade, which does not inhibit turf growth, and it does not deplete the soil, so it is generally a desirable lawn tree. But sometimes it forms knobby surface roots that can fracture pavement or interfere with mowing.

PROBLEMS: Thorny trees, and to a lesser extent seed-bearing trees, are inappropriate for the domestic landscape, although they can be picturesque in rural settings. Many cultivars have been selected to eliminate these concerns.

Honey locust is resistant to many of our most troublesome defoliating insects, including the gypsy moth (*Lymantria dispar*), but the mimosa webworm (*Homadaula albizziae*) is a voracious pest in the South that sometimes strips away almost every morsel of foliage. A fungus canker, *Thyronectria austro-americana*, is a serious problem on some trees. The same fungus causes a vascular wilt disease in the related Japanese honey locust (*Gleditsia japonica*).

CULTIVARS: Honey locust trees vary in the size and number of their thorns. Cultivars selected from thornless trees make safe and desirable lawn trees. Some of the most useful are 'Bujotii' (a weeping form), 'Elegantissima' (a compact form), 'Emerald Lace', 'Fairview', 'Green Glory' (a large, tough tree with a central leader), 'Halka' (a strong, vigorous tree, but not seedless), 'Imperial' (a small, erect form with a few seeds), 'Majestic', 'Maxwell' (an artistic form and very cold-hardy), 'Moraine' (the first popular selection and still one of the best), 'Rubylace' (with red young foliage but poor form), 'Shademaster' (another old, reliable selection), 'Skyline' (an erect pyramidal form with great fall color), 'Summer Lace', 'Sunburst' (with yellow early foliage, not as vigorous as some others), 'True-Shade' and 'Perfection'.

Top: An avenue of honey locust in fall. Above: Not all honey locusts sport vicious thorns; some are thornless.

RELATED SPECIES: Water locust (*Gleditsia aquatica*) is a smaller, swamp-loving species. It has smaller leaves, with miniature seedpods and shorter, but even more numerous, thorns. The two species will occasionally interbreed, forming Texas honey locust (*Gleditsia* x *texana*). Water locust offers little advantage over honey locust except for genetic diversity, but it would make a formidable hedge plant.

At least ten other species of honey locust occur in other parts of the world; some are hardy in North America, but many are not common. They all look very much like our native species.

COMMENTS: Honey locust has been so popular during the past several decades that many people have grown bored with it. This is unfortunate because it remains one of our most attractive and adaptable shade trees. Wild, thorny trees are used by shrikes to hold their prey. The tree attracts many colorful butterflies including the silver-spotted skipper, the iridescent honey locust moth, the moon-lined moth and the tiny orange-wing. New thorns formed on the trunk each year are blood-red, as if to warn those who come too close. The ripening seedpods add color and, later, winter interest as they rattle and clack in the wind.

GORDONIA

Gordonia lasianthus

DESCRIPTION: The gordonia, or loblolly-bay, is a splendid, slender, flowering tree with evergreen leaves. Its ultimate size depends upon soil moisture. It usually grows rather slowly, but it can reach well into the forest canopy on favorable soils when crowded by surrounding trees. The largest gordonia on record is found in the Ocala National Forest in Florida. It is 94 feet (30 m) tall and has a 30-inch (75 cm) trunk. We have admired smaller but striking specimens, clothed to the base with leaves and flowers, growing on swamp hummocks around the eastern edge of Okefenokee National Wildlife Refuge in southern Georgia.

LEAVES: The evergreen leaves are leathery and deep green, approximately 5 inches (12 cm) long by less than half as wide. The upper surfaces are textured with indented veins. At the northern limit of its range, gordonia becomes partially deciduous, like the sweet bay magnolia (*Magnolia virginiana*) that it resembles and with which it often grows.

The clear white flowers of gordonia show well against the backdrop of its dark foliage.

FLOWERS AND FRUIT: Gordonia bears silky white flowers that resemble those of its close relative, the camellia. They reach 3 inches (8 cm) across and are very fragrant. The flowers occur singly in leaf axils but are concentrated at the branch tips, giving the appearance of clusters. The individual cup-shaped flowers on each twig open one at a time, which prolongs the attractive blooming period.

The woody fruits, which appear later, are shaped like little green tulips with sharp-pointed divisions. They turn brown in the fall and split open gradually throughout the winter to release small winged seeds.

SEASONS:
1. Summer (as the fat, erect flower buds swell and open progressively through each cluster);
2. Winter (trees are very conspicuous after nearby deciduous trees drop their own leaves; the evergreen foliage is especially handsome on windy days, when the pale undersides turn up).

NATIVE AND ADAPTIVE RANGE: Gordonia is a southern coastal tree of swamps, bays and bayous. It ranges from southern Mississippi, around the southeastern fringe of the United States, up to Albemarle Sound in North Carolina and extends inland as far as Augusta, Georgia. It is hardier than many other broadleaf evergreen trees and can be grown in protected areas with suitable soil into USDA zone 7.

CULTURE: For a swamp tree, gordonia can be surprisingly tolerant of dry, sandy soil, in which it grows in the wild as a large shrub. It does best under cultivation in full sun with ample moisture. A high water table with occasional standing water suits it just fine, and in the wild, acidic, infertile, sandy soil is its substrate of choice.

Few gardeners can offer wetland habitats, but gordonia can be grown under mesic conditions if mulched heavily with pulverized pine bark and watered during dry spells. It should be protected from wind and direct sun during the winter along its northern limits. To keep its evergreen leaves from dehydrating in cold climates, it might be planted over a warm utility tunnel or near a heated basement, where the soil will not freeze.

This tree is not particularly easy to transplant,

but new plants may be propagated from seed or, with luck, from softwood cuttings. Gather seedpods in late summer, when the capsules show signs of splitting down the sutures. Dry the capsules in a paper bag until they open, and sow the seeds outdoors in sandy potting soil. Some seedlings will begin to emerge the following year, and the remaining seeds will sprout a year or more later. Small container-grown plants are easy to establish if watered frequently during the first year. Stump-sprouts will develop readily to replace cut or broken stems.

PROBLEMS: Gordonia has few insect or disease problems, but it can be finicky and short-lived under cultivation unless its natural habitat is closely duplicated. Its leaves can become scorched and discolored if the tree is planted in full sun without adequate mulch to keep its roots cool and moist. Prior to planting, amend clay soils with a generous amount of gritty sand, pine bark and sphagnum peat moss to prevent root problems. A significant limitation of gordonia in the North is its lack of winter hardiness, but it will grow farther north than many broadleaf evergreens.

CULTIVARS: No cultivars of this species are recorded. It seems to vary in size and shape due more to habitat conditions than to its genetic makeup. We suspect that, like sweet bay and other similar southern trees, provenance might influence winter hardiness.

RELATED SPECIES: Gordonia has been upstaged in nurseries by its closest relative, the deciduous Franklin tree (*Franklinia alatamaha*). Franklin tree is fascinating in that it became extinct in the wild shortly after it was brought into cultivation in 1770. It does not grow as large as gordonia and is not evergreen, but it has similar flowers and good fall color and can be grown north through USDA zone 6. Hybrids of the two species have been produced, and more breeding work might lead to improved hardiness or other horticultural qualities.

Old gordonia trees develop rough-textured bark.

Gordonias, such as this one in Georgia, can reach more than 70 feet in height.

Stewartias are similar and also related, as are the Asiatic gardenias and camellias. A close Asiatic relative, *Camellia sinensis*, is the commercial source of tea. There are two shrubby native stewartias, the mountain stewartia (*Stewartia ovata*), which can become a small tree and is hardy to USDA zone 5, and the silky stewartia (*Stewartia malacodendron*), which is not much hardier than gordonia.

COMMENTS: Gordonia frequently grows with swamp cyrilla (*Cyrilla racemiflora*) and pond pine (*Pinus serotina*) near water and with sweet bay magnolia on slightly drier soils. Seed can be gathered in such areas, but we don't recommend trying to collect seedlings of this tree from wild populations. Nurseries seldom seem to stock it, although it can be found as a small container plant at some firms that specialize in native plants. Those who are too impatient to begin with small plants or seed or whose thumbs are not sufficiently green to satisfy gordonia's rather precise growing requirements would do well to visit it in its native habitat. The trip will be memorable for anyone who appreciates beautiful trees.

KENTUCKY COFFEE TREE

Gymnocladus dioicus (G. dioica)

DESCRIPTION: This tree has a wide range but nowhere is it common. It has been designated the state tree of Kentucky, more because of its name than its predominance in the landscape. Appropriately, the champion tree grows in West Liberty, Kentucky. Although not particularly tall, at 78 feet (22 m), it has a trunk almost 6 feet (1.7 m) in diameter.

Most often, Kentucky coffee trees grow alone or in small clonal groups, all connected as sprouts to a common root system. They can be found occasionally on rocky hillsides and coves or in limestone woods with blue ash (*Fraxinus quadrangulata*), but more commonly they are scattered in river valleys and floodplain terraces.

Coffee tree matures into a graceful, rounded specimen with an open, airy crown.

LEAVES: The leaves of this tree are bipinnate. While the leaflets seldom exceed 2 inches (5 cm) in length, a complete compound leaf assembly can grow to 3 feet (90 cm), which gives the tree a fern-like demeanor when in full foliage. Leaves of this tree are among the very last to emerge in the spring; this allows the warming spring sun to reach wildflowers on the ground below.

Even when fully developed, the leaves of this tree cast a very light shade. They emerge reddish, fade to green as they enlarge and usually turn a nice yellow early in the fall. Some trees develop scarlet rachises, which cling longer than the leaflets and so offer two stages of fall color.

FLOWERS AND FRUIT: Kentucky coffee tree is typically dioecious. Where clonal groves have developed, an entire grove will be the same sex.

The flowers occur in long terminal clusters in late spring. The clusters, or panicles, of male trees are about 3 inches (8 cm) long, but those on female trees reach nearly 1 foot (30 cm) in length and become pleasantly fragrant as they open. The flowers are not conspicuous because they become lost amid the fine texture of the new foliage.

Female trees bear the seedpods (although not every year), which mark them as members of the legume family. Some pods will already be forming while other flowers on the same panicles are still blooming. The pods are stouter but shorter and straighter than those of honey locust (*Gleditsia triacanthos*). They are heavy and hard, almost woody, and are filled with a gooey pulp that surrounds several smooth, stony, marble-sized seeds. Many pods persist through the winter and add interest to the dormant landscape. The seeds have been roasted as a coffee substitute, hence the name, but they contain cytisine and are toxic when raw. Animals must sense this, or perhaps they are thwarted by the hard seed coat, because few of them seem to feast on Kentucky coffee beans.

SEASONS:

1. Fall (when the gray bark, yellow leaflets, red leafstalks and dark purple fruit are visible together);
2. Winter (with snow dusting the coarse, dramatic branching and shaggy bark and pods clinging to female trees);
3. Spring (when the pinkish leaves begin to emerge);
4. Summer (the fine-textured foliage gives the tree a fern-like appearance).

NATIVE AND ADAPTIVE RANGE: Isolated wild populations of coffee tree can be found in the vicinity of Lake St. Clair in southern Ontario, where it is listed by the Canadian Government as a threatened species. From there, it ranges westward to the upper Mississippi River Valley in southern Minnesota and the Missouri River Valley in southeastern South Dakota, through northern Oklahoma and down the Ohio and lower Mississippi rivers to central Arkansas. It can be found around the Finger Lakes of New York and in Pennsylvania, West Virginia and Tennessee, and it has spread elsewhere from cultivation. It can be grown in USDA zone 3, and there are healthy planted trees in Ottawa, Ontario.

CULTURE: Kentucky coffee tree can be tricky to transplant and establishes slowly. The root system is deep and sometimes seems as coarse as the branches. Wild saplings frequently originate as root suckers and are more difficult than seed-grown trees to dig. Scarified seed will start easily, and trees of known sex can be propagated from suckers or root cuttings. It likes full sun and is more tolerant of alkaline soils, though less so of acidic ones, than many other tree species. Its light, filtered shade encourages healthy turf under its canopy.

With their coarse branching patterns, coffee trees are rarely damaged by winter storms.

Young trees are almost devoid of branches until they reach nearly the diameter of a baseball bat, and it takes a little faith to believe that such an ungainly sapling will ever amount to much. But with sufficient sunlight, ample moisture and deep, rich alluvial soil, such faith will be rewarded with a vigorous, well-formed young tree.

PROBLEMS: Once established, coffee tree will be bothered little by heat, cold, road salt, insects, diseases or drought. The tree is rather slow-growing but not strong-wooded. But because its branching is so coarse that ice has little to cling to, it is rarely damaged by winter storms. Occasional root suckers should be pulled. In manicured lawns, the leaflets, rachises and pods, all of which fall at different times, need to be raked up repeatedly.

CULTIVARS: Selections should be made for trees with superior growth rate, form, fall color and known gender. None are widely available yet, but Chicagoland Grows, a cultivar-development cooperative, is evaluating at least one potential male cultivar. A variegated selection can be found growing at Kew Gardens in England.

RELATED SPECIES: One other *Gymnocladus* grows in China. The genus is related to other legumes like locusts (*Gleditsia* and *Robinia*).

COMMENTS: A magnificent old coffee tree still grows in Chancellorsville, Virginia, where it shades the grave of General Thomas "Stonewall" Jackson's amputated arm, buried there after a battle in 1863.

The satin-smooth seeds of this species make wonderful lucky charms or worry-stones to carry in a pocket; they are smaller and much more durable than the "lucky buckeyes" (*Aesculus* spp.) that traditionally assume such a role (but they are equally toxic if eaten). They have served generations as superior slingshot ammunition and can be drilled and strung as beads.

One wonders about the scattered populations of this species. It has jumped entire states in search of preferred habitat. The seeds do not seem to be sought by birds, nor can they be carried by the wind. So how has it spread in such a checkerboard pattern?

We could speculate that gomphotheres, giant mammals that became extinct at the end of the last ice age, fed upon the pods, swallowing them whole and later depositing the hard seeds during their migrations. Or perhaps Native Americans carried the durable seeds to new locations as prehistoric "Johnny Coffeeseeds." Many seemingly natural groves of this tree in the northeastern part of its range are actually growing on the sites of ancient villages.

If coffee tree owes its spread to the wanderings of prehistoric people and extinct animals, its wild range will always be patchy. However, such localized populations may encourage the evolution of regionally adapted forms or subspecies, further enriching its diversity and usefulness for horticultural purposes.

SILVERBELL

Halesia carolina (H. tetraptera)

DESCRIPTION: Silverbell is not a common tree, but where it usually grows it can be found in abundance. It exists in several forms, varieties or species, depending upon the taxonomic authority consulted, ranging from large shrubs to slim trees that reach well into the forest canopy.

It makes its best growth in the cove forests and moist slopes of the southern Appalachians. The biggest of many large specimens in the Great Smoky Mountains in Tennessee is 86 feet (23 m) tall and more than 4 feet (1.3 m) in diameter. Even trees of this size retain the attractive bark pattern—whitened furrows between gray-brown plates—characteristic of the genus.

LEAVES: Silverbell leaves may grow as much as 6 inches (15 cm) in length and about half as wide. They are usually free from insect damage and maintain a bright green color until late summer, when they fade to yellow or, in drought years, drop without noticeably changing color.

FLOWERS AND FRUIT: The flowers, which are at their peak around Arbor Day, when we all should be thinking about trees anyway, are sensational. They are snow-white, sometimes with a touch of pink, and up to 1 inch (2.5 cm) long. They hang like bells in clusters from the twigs. In a careful landscape design, this tree should be placed where its flowers can be viewed from below. Flowers of all species and forms are similar.

The fruits are slender, winged drupes up to 2 inches (5 cm) long. Those of the common species and its forms have four wings, while those of the related *Halesia diptera* have only two. The tan fruits make an interesting fall display. They are not particularly attractive to wildlife, although some rodents will eat them.

Top: The hanging flowers of silverbell are best seen from below. Above: The winged fruits of silverbells ripen to a light brown color anddevelop a hard central seed.

SEASONS:

1. Spring (the flowers are the primary aesthetic feature of this tree);
2. Winter (for the striped bark and, in early winter, the clinging fruit).

NATIVE AND ADAPTIVE RANGE: The typical form, known as Carolina silverbell, has a spotty range centered in the southern Appalachians. They can also be found in the Ozark Plateau of Missouri, Arkansas and Oklahoma, the Shawnee Hills of southern Illinois and scattered locations north, east and south of the primary range, from the Ohio River Valley to northern Florida.

The two-winged silverbell is confined to the Gulf coastal plain, and the impressive mountain form, sometimes distinguished as *Halesia monticola*, is generally restricted to the higher mountains of Tennessee and North Carolina. All of them are adaptable under cultivation far beyond their natural range, and *Halesia carolina* and *Halesia monticola* are fully hardy in USDA zone 5.

CULTURE: Silverbells are tolerant of most moderate conditions and of sun or shade, but they can be sensitive to drought, salt and alkaline soil. They grow moderately fast and do best in a moist organic loam, with their roots in the cool shade and their leaves exposed to partial or full sun. They are not subject to serious insect or disease problems, but some of the outlying natural populations show the effects of environmental stress, and as a result, their natural range may be shrinking.

Silverbells are easy to transplant and can be grown readily from seed as long as you don't mind stratifying it or waiting two years for it to sprout. Seedlings frequently grow as volunteers in mulched planting beds under favorable growing conditions, and collecting them can give the propagator a head start. Young trees can also be started from sprouts that shoot up from stumps. The sprouts can be layered, or bent over, and the tips covered with soil until they send out roots. The shoots can then be cut away from the stump and will be independent plants.

PROBLEMS: The wood is somewhat brittle, but we have not noticed many trees with major storm damage. Insects and diseases seem to avoid silverbells.

CULTIVARS: A dwarf form, 'Meehanii', reported to be even more striking in bloom than the species, is available from a few nurseries. There are several pink-flowering selections, which are collectively listed as variety *rosea* or cultivar 'Rosea'.

This national champion two-winged silverbell grows in Spring Grove Cemetery Arboretum in Cincinnati, Ohio.

RELATED SPECIES: We are very impressed with the mountain silverbell (*Halesia monticola*), which is considered by many authorities to be a variety. It is larger, more erect and more dramatic in all aspects than any of the other species or varieties. We have grown *Halesia monticola* variety *vestita* from seed collected at the Washington Park Arboretum in Seattle and are delighted with the vigor, erect stature and large flowers of this selection. Occasional pink-flowered forms of this species are also seen.

Two-winged silverbell (*Halesia diptera*) is a smaller species with fruits that have two broad wings instead of four narrow ones. It has a reputation for sparse blooming, although its award-winning variety *magniflora* is vigorous, heavily flowering and more tolerant of dry sites than other silverbells. The United States national champion two-winged silverbell, in Spring Grove Cemetery Arboretum in Cincinnati, Ohio, is a fine tree 42 feet (13 m) tall with a triple stem. Another small species, *Halesia parviflora*, is confined to the Gulf coastal plain. An additional species is found in China.

Snowbells (*Styrax* spp.) are shrubby relatives of the silverbells. The most common native species is *Styrax americana*, a large shrub of rich woods and swamps. Several exotic snowbell species are frequently seen as garden shrubs.

COMMENTS: Blooming silverbell groves, which overhang winding mountain roads, provide quite a spring spectacle. We have felt compelled to stop at every overlook along the Blue Ridge Parkway during the silverbell bloom to enjoy the drifts of white flowers that, in places, cover the wooded slopes like snow. Few trees can match the beauty of the silverbells. Nurseries are distributing them widely now as ornamentals, but to thrive and maintain good foliage color in dry weather, they need to be mulched and given adequate soil moisture.

Silverbell was a favorite of the famous naturalist-landscape architect Jens Jensen, who established a grove in the Abraham Lincoln Memorial Garden in Lincoln's hometown of Springfield, Illinois, during the 1930s. This large lakeside garden is Jensen's most famous design. We think he would be delighted to hike through the garden now and see that his original silverbell plants have reproduced prolifically, even though the soil and climate would not be considered ideal for the species.

CULTURE: Witch hazels naturally select shady sites but will become full, symmetrical specimens in sun as long as they are protected from severe drought and heat. They can be slow to recover from transplanting when moved in large sizes and are best handled as small field-grown or container-grown plants. Selected types can be layered or rooted from cuttings, although success requires some practice. Plants can also be propagated from seed sown outdoors in the fall, but expect to wait two years for some of them to sprout. Ozark witch hazel is reported to be more tolerant of alkaline soil and easier to root from cuttings than other types. It frequently grows on the banks of raging Ozark streams, where its pliable wood springs back easily after being bent by flash floods.

The autumn flowers of witch hazel are most conspicuous after the foliage drops.

PROBLEMS: In areas prone to infestations of gypsy moth (*Lymantria dispar*), witch hazels are among the first plants to be defoliated. Elsewhere, as long as they are planted where they can avoid severe drought, heat reflection and sunscald, they have few serious problems.

CULTIVARS: Flowering qualities such as size, color, density and phenology (seasonal timing) are quite variable. Nearly every horticulturist who has studied autumn witch hazel recommends that superior selections be propagated and marketed, but nobody seems willing to start. One red-flowering cultivar, 'Rubescens', is listed, and some geographical varieties or races are separated by some taxonomists. The most ornamental specimens hold their blooms long after the leaves have fallen. Such special trees can be found occasionally in horticultural collections, including our own at Starhill Forest in central Illinois.

There are at least a dozen named selections of Ozark witch hazel, many of which have very abundant flowers of varying shades of yellow and orange. Because this species blooms in late winter after the leaves are gone, phenology is not such a concern in making selections.

RELATED SPECIES: A related southern plant, *Hamamelis macrophylla*, is generally considered to be a variety of *Hamamelis virginiana*. Reportedly, there is a white-flowering species or form from northern Mexico that blooms in the summer, but it has not been tested in our area. Some of the southern forms tend to be marcescent, so the clinging but withered leaves hide the fall flowers.

Ozark witch hazel is a more shrubby species in the wild than autumn witch hazel, but it can still reach tree size in cultivation. It has darker, slightly larger foliage than autumn witch hazel but without the bright outline or the red tint on new leaves. Ozark witch hazel, and most other witch hazels, including two Asian species and a host of their hybrids and cultivars, bloom in the early spring instead of the fall.

COMMENTS: A forked stem of witch hazel, which grows erect with one branch pointed north and the other south, is one of the traditional tools for witching water wells. Few people admit to taking this procedure seriously, yet many can testify to the uncanny "luck" of a dowser who walked their property with a forked stick then advised sinking a well in a particular spot—with good results.

Those who live in cities, where water simply flows from the tap, instead of in the country, where it rises from your own ground, may never know the eerie, throbbing, irresistible pull of a good witching stick as it passes over hidden intersecting veins of groundwater.

Of course, we don't personally believe in such a phenomenon. Certainly not.

AMERICAN HOLLY

Ilex opaca

DESCRIPTION: Many people who admire sprigs of holly are not aware that these seemingly exotic holiday decorations come from a fine native tree species. American holly is a deep-woods understory tree in the southeastern United States and the state tree of Delaware. Seen often as a lawn specimen, holly is more at home in moist, open woodlands. Wild specimens typically respond to their shady environment by becoming loose and irregular in form. Cultivated trees in full sun are densely symmetrical. American holly is one of about 20 native hollies, and the largest, the national champion, in Chambers County, Alabama, is 74 feet (21 m) tall and has a smooth gray trunk more than 3 feet (1 m) thick.

We will also briefly discuss a few other of the hardiest holly species and hybrids. Chief among them is possum haw (*Ilex decidua*), a stiff little clumping tree with sharp spur branches and striking gray bark. One tree, in the Congaree Swamp of South Carolina, reaches 42 feet (13 m) in height with its largest stem 1 foot (30 cm) in diameter. Winterberry (*Ilex verticillata*) is a similar decidious species that can become a small tree, especially in the southern part of its range. Specimens up to 20 feet (6 m) tall can be found in Shenandoah National Park.

It can take 75 years for the slow-growing American holly to reach the size of this one at Jim and Jane Wilson's home in South Carolina.

LEAVES: The leaves of American holly, though not of all hollies, are fully evergreen. They reach about 3 inches (8 cm) in length and are thick and stiff with sharply pointed teeth along the margins. New growth finally pushes off the old leaves in the spring. Possum haw and winterberry can develop a bright yellow fall color that provides the perfect visual background for the fruits on the female plants.

FLOWERS AND FRUIT: Hollies are dioecious, requiring both male and female plants to produce fruit. The flowers develop in the leaf axils—those on staminate trees are clustered and those on pistillate trees are usually solitary, with neither formation being very conspicuous.

Holly fruits can be the visual focus of the landscape for extended periods in the fall and winter. The pea-sized drupes, or holly berries, are borne in great quantities and can be bright red, dark orange or, occasionally, yellow. Those of our deciduous hollies, possum haw and winterberry, are even showier than those of American holly because they are more highly visible among the yellow leaves in fall or massed on the bare gray branches in winter. After a hard frost, the berries become choice food for bluebirds, robins, mockingbirds, cedar waxwings and many other birds in their winter range.

SEASONS:

1. Fall and winter (when fruits are on female trees and for the smooth gray bark that is exposed on the deciduous species);
2. All year (for American holly, if the evergreen foliage is bright and healthy).

NATIVE AND ADAPTIVE RANGE: American holly can be seen in isolated populations around Long Island Sound, south to central Florida and southwest to eastern Texas. Possum haw covers the same general area but extends northwest along streams of the Ozark Plateau and up the Mississippi River and its tributaries to southern Indiana, Illinois and the southern tip of Iowa. Winterberry, the smallest but by far the hardiest of the tree hollies, ranges north to

Most often celebrated in the winter season, American holly retains its glossy, pointed leaves year-round, even in the North.

Upper Michigan, the Ottawa River in Ontario and northeast to Newfoundland.

Hardy selections of American holly will survive north to USDA zone 5, possum haw to USDA zone 4 and winterberry to USDA zone 3. Different cultivars, though, will show considerable variation in hardiness, and locally adapted individuals should be selected when possible. The larger-growing selections of winterberry generally have been chosen from the southern part of its range, but they are still hardier than other hollies.

CULTURE: Most hollies like moist soil, and American holly needs some winter protection for its foliage when planted north of its natural range. Possum haw and winterberry are quite comfortable in swamp forests and tolerate poorly drained or flooded sites as easily as they do good garden soil.

Hollies can be grown from seed, but they take two or more years to germinate and grow frustratingly slowly. To gain a head start, try transplanting the volunteer seedlings that can usually be found in the mulch under fruiting American holly females. We have rooted American holly from cuttings without difficulty. This is the only sure way to guarantee the desired mix of male and female trees.

PROBLEMS: American holly is frequently planted in areas beyond its adaptive range, where it experiences periodic winter damage. Foliar diseases and the holly leaf miner (*Phytomyza ilicicola*) can disfigure the leaves of ornamental specimens. Scale insects may damage it as well. The deciduous hollies are usually trouble-free, although winterberry foliage can be affected by mildew. American holly is very slow-growing, but the deciduous species grow at a moderate rate.

If you are growing hollies for their fruit display, plant the proper mix of compatible male and female plants to ensure fruit set. Plant seedlings in large quantities or obtain cuttings of known sex and similar blooming time to produce abundant fruit. The plants don't need to be too close to one another—bees adore holly flowers and will bring pollen from a considerable distance. An old American holly growing at the Wilsons' Savory Farm in South Carolina is very fruitful without a staminate tree in sight.

CULTIVARS: Various sources list from 100 to more than 1,000 cultivars of American holly and dozens more deciduous hollies. Many are nearly identical, and it would be impractical to describe them all here, but a few examples are worth mentioning.

From American holly, the selections 'Amy', 'Cardinal', 'Dauber', 'MacDonald', 'Merry Christmas' and 'Old Heavyberry' (we've always liked that name) are vigorous females with red fruit that are reported to be more hardy in the north than most. 'Croonenberg' is slightly monoecious and therefore self-fruitful—a good choice for those who don't have room for a separate male tree. 'Fruitland Nursery', 'Canary' and 'Goldie' are selections from the yellow-fruited form *xanthocarpa*. For pollination, some attractive male selections include 'Isaiah' and 'Jersey Knight'. One popular, narrow-leaved new selection for southern areas, 'Savannah', is actually a hybrid with another native holly, *Ilex cassine*.

Possum haw has several good cultivars, mostly selected for ornamental fruit. They include 'Reed', 'Sundance', 'Warren Red' and the yellow-fruited 'Byers Golden'. Winterberry selections include 'Afterglow', 'Cacapon', 'Fairfax', 'Late Red', 'Red Sprite', 'Shaver', 'Sunset', 'Winter Red' and 'Winter Gold'. Of these, the last three are most likely to develop into trees. 'Winter Red' is a 1995 Pennsylvania Horticultural Society Gold Medal recipient.

RELATED SPECIES: Mountain holly (*Ilex montana*) is an upland Appalachian species nearly identical to winterberry. It is less ornamental but grows about twice as large, approaching possum haw in size. Dahoon (*Ilex cassine*) and yaupon (*Ilex vomitoria*) are small coastal evergreen trees of the southeastern United States. They have tiny, fine-textured leaves and are adaptable species, but, like most other smaller native holly species, they are not hardy in the north.

One very hardy holly is inkberry (*Ilex glabra*), but it remains a shrub. Several European and Asian hollies are popular as ornamental plants.

COMMENTS: We've become so accustomed to thinking about the leaves and fruit of holly that we sometimes forget about its bark. An old American holly, free of the lower limbs that frequently skirt its base, exhibits a smooth, convoluted, lichen-adorned stem and abrupt root flare that resemble the foot and toes of a giant elephant. This engaging character does not develop overnight but takes many decades to grow. A big holly is one of the few trees that, usually, is even older than it looks.

Top: Many people fail to notice the attractive, diminutive flowers of possum haw.
Above: Winterberry fruits mature in late summer, and persist through much of the winter.

The slow-growing American holly, like some of our finest oaks, is an investment in the future. George Washington certainly thought so, for his records show that his failed attempts to transplant wild trees led him to germinate seedlings, which gave rise to the holly grove in the South Semicircle at Mount Vernon.

BLACK WALNUT

Juglans nigra

DESCRIPTION: Our most valuable native hardwood lumber comes from one of our most interesting and resilient trees. Black walnut is a tall, strong forest tree of well-drained bottomlands, but it is seen just as often as a picturesque, weathered survivor in overgrazed pastures or on sterile, eroded old fields. Everywhere it grows, humans and squirrels compete for its valuable nut crop. Mature trees in the "back forty" must be guarded with vigilance against log poachers eager to turn the dense, dark timber into cash.

It is rare now to see massive old-growth walnuts with straight trunks clear of limbs for their first 80 feet (22 m), although some still stand along Sugar Creek in Turkey Run State Park in Indiana. Most of the old giants once found in national forests or on private land have been harvested for their valuable lumber and for gunstocks. In fact, the largest known black walnut is a planted tree on Sauvie Island, Oregon, more than 1,000 miles from its ancestral home. It was measured in 1991 at 130 feet (40 m) in height. It is a sprawling, low-limbed tree with a trunk 7 feet 4 inches (2.25 m) in diameter.

Black walnuts provide our most valuable native hardwood lumber.

Butternut (*Juglans cinerea*), our other relatively common walnut species, is a smaller tree. Its champion specimen also grows in Oregon, in Eugene. It is an exceptional example, standing 88 feet (27 m) tall with a double trunk about 6 feet (1.8 m) in diameter, that dwarfs a nearby house.

LEAVES: The highly aromatic, pinnately compound leaves of all of our native walnut species look similar, emerge very late in the spring and drop early in the fall. Those of black walnut are up to 2 feet (60 cm) long, with paired leaflets and no terminal leaflet. They can turn a good clear yellow in early fall, which contrasts nicely with the dark bark, but on many trees, the foliage is stripped by insects or leaf blights before it colors. Butternut leaves usually have a terminal leaflet.

FLOWERS AND FRUIT: Walnuts are close relatives of hickories, and their flower structures are nearly identical. Staminate catkins are produced in hanging clusters, like green tinsel. Pistillate flowers occur singly or in small groups at the ends of the twigs.

The fruits ripen in late summer, but many don't fall until after the first frost. They are among the largest of our native nut-tree fruits; before husking, they occasionally exceed the size of tangerines. The nuts are predictably variable from tree to tree in size, shape and quality. Lester Cox of Carlinville, Illinois, has gathered walnuts on his property for years. He can examine a nut and tell you which tree it came from and accurately predict its quality and oil content.

Butternut crops can be sporadic because of the sensitivity of the pistillate flowers to frost even when the staminate catkins develop normally. Black walnut and butternut nutmeats are used commercially for oil and flavoring and, on the farm, for walnut bread and other delights. Birds will pick through the debris left when humans shell out walnuts, but they are unable to crack the nuts without help. Squirrels are among the few creatures with strong enough teeth and the determination to gnaw through the extremely hard shells.

SEASONS:

1. Fall (for the nut harvest and the good yellow fall color on disease-resistant specimens);
2. Summer (for the open shade and aromatic, fern-like foliage).

NATIVE AND ADAPTIVE RANGE: Black walnut grows in scattered groves along the St. Lawrence River, southwest through southern Ontario, west to eastern South Dakota, then south throughout most of the eastern United States except for southern coastal areas. The smaller butternut is more northerly, but nowhere common. Its range extends north to Quebec City and southern New Brunswick.

Black walnut performance is closely tied to provenance, so the more local the seed the better. In any case, the seed should not come from trees growing more than 200 miles (320 km) to the south. Seeds from more southern sources, when moved north, grow more each year than those from local stock, but the trees are less hardy and more likely to die back in severe winters. With this in mind, locally adapted black walnut is hardy through most of USDA zone 4 and butternut well into USDA zone 3.

CULTURE: Black walnut is a tough tree that can survive abuse but that thrives with proper care. Such care includes full sun and a good, fertile, moist, well-drained soil (limed if too acidic). Black walnut and butternut can grow surprisingly quickly under such conditions. Butternut is more particular in this regard than black walnut. It will not succeed on a poor or dry site, but it tolerates rocky soil. Both can be readily propagated from fall-planted seed, which should be protected from squirrels for its entire first year. Selected trees can be grafted or budded.

Care should be taken to minimize pruning wounds to keep disease from entering the tree. Black walnut is resistant to damage from storms, drought, alkaline soil and atmospheric ozone. Its deep roots, the long, leafless dormancy period from early fall to late spring and the light shade cast even in summer allow grass to prosper under its canopy. All native walnuts develop long taproots and can be a challenge to transplant unless they have been undercut in the nursery.

PROBLEMS: Walnut foliage can be heavily attacked by the walnut caterpillar (*Datana integerrima*) and the related yellow-necked caterpillar (*Datana ministra*). A target canker, *Nectria galligena*, is destructive to damaged or weakened trees. The most noticeable, although not the most destructive, disease

Black walnut tolerates a variety of soils and makes a strong shade tree.

on some black walnuts is anthracnose, caused by *Gnomonia leptostyla*. Trees vary in resistance to this leafspot fungus, which harmlessly but conspicuously defoliates the most susceptible ones in late summer.

Butternut has a much more serious problem. Butternut blight is a fatal disease caused by the fungus *Sirococcus clavigignenti-juglandacearum*, which forms cankers that are later invaded by another fungus, *Melanconis juglandis*. These organisms are as difficult to cure as they are to pronounce, and they eventually

With full sun and fertile soil, the black walnut grows quickly.

kill the tree. This disease is spreading throughout the natural range of butternut, even into Ontario, and the tree may be on the road to extinction unless a cure is found.

All walnut species manufacture an allelopathic substance called juglone. When the roots of juglone-sensitive plants (including walnut seedlings) hit walnut roots, they can be stunted or killed. Turf grasses, most ferns and many ornamental plants are not harmed, but it is detrimental to some garden vegetables and apples (*Malus* spp.), birches (*Betula* spp.), azaleas (*Rhododendron* spp.) and pines (*Pinus* spp.).

The falling nuts of walnut and butternut can cause injuries or dent cars, and the husks can leave indelible stains on patios. Along with the leaflets and stiff leaf rachises, which begin to drop in late summer, the nuts also create a litter problem and complicate lawn mowing.

CULTIVARS: For many years, we have admired the lacy, ornamental, slow-growing selection called 'Laciniata' at the Morton Arboretum near Chicago. Most other walnut selections have been directed toward timber or fruit production, and many exist.

The Northern Nut Growers Association has worked for decades to identify superior trees throughout the range of the species. Some of the best are 'Cochrane' from Wisconsin, 'Edras' and 'Grundy' from Iowa, 'Hare' from Illinois, 'Schreiber' from Indiana, 'Bowser' from Ohio, 'Harney' and 'Victoria' from Kentucky, 'Norris' from Tennessee and 'Monterey', 'Pinecrest', 'Thomas' and 'Vandersloot' from Pennsylvania. Although the large-fruited 'Thomas' is most frequently offered by nurseries, 'Pinecrest' and 'Vandersloot' reportedly bear even larger nuts.

RELATED SPECIES: Besides butternut, four other walnuts are native to North America. Two of them, *Juglans major* from Arizona and western Mexico and *Juglans microcarpa* from Oklahoma, Texas and eastern Mexico, can be grown in the warmer portions of our area. The others are confined to California. About 14 additional species are found in other parts of the world, including some commercially productive nut-orchard species.

COMMENTS: Black walnut is a preferred host of the beautiful luna moth and the immense regal moth, which can be 6 inches (15 cm) across and is parent to the awe-inspiring larva of the hickory horned devil. Once seen, neither can be forgotten. It also hosts the larva of the walnut sphinx moth, a moth unusual because of the squeaking sound it makes.

Some creative uses have been devised for walnut. Dried walnut leaves can be mixed with straw as a flea repellent in animal bedding. Ground walnut shells have been used as specialty abrasives in sandblasting to polish metals. Some commercial orchardists who grow Persian walnuts graft them high on black walnut understocks. When their production declines, the trees are cut and sold as high-quality veneer logs.

Butternuts are so tasty that Native Americans are known to have planted them for food. The United States Forest Service (North Central Experiment Station, 1992 Folwell Ave., St. Paul, MN 55108) is leading an interagency effort to solve the butternut-blight problem through research and identification of resistant trees. If you know of mature, healthy butternut trees in an area with butternut blight, please tell the forest service or your state or provincial natural resource agency, which might use them in resistance-selection programs.

RED CEDAR

Juniperus virginiana

DESCRIPTION: Red cedar is actually a juniper, not a true cedar. It is one of our most adaptable conifers, and it occupies a larger and more diverse natural range than any other coniferous tree in eastern North America. Red cedar commonly grows on rocky ridges, in hill prairies and in open, dry woods, and it seeds prolifically into abandoned pastures and along fence lines.

Stunted, gnarly specimens more than 300 years old can be found clinging to rocky cliffs of the Ozark Mountains. Here, under the scorching summer sun, they grow less than 1 inch (2.5 cm) a year and look much like the ancient bristlecone pines (*Pinus longaeva*) of Nevada. Yet on very favorable sites, the same species grows moderately fast into a conical tree 100 feet (30 m) high. The largest known red cedar is not nearly so tall—only 55 feet (17 m)—but it has a trunk 5 feet 7 inches (1.7 m) in diameter and a broadly spreading crown that shades a large portion of the Lone Hill Cemetery in Coffee County, Georgia. There are many geographic forms of red cedar, each with a localized advantage. The branches of northern forms, for example, can shed snow without breaking.

A century-old red cedar shades a rural cemetery in Illinois.

LEAVES: The aromatic, evergreen needles of vigorous young red cedars are prickly, which provides some defense against browsing animals. As the trees grow above the reach of browsers, the needles change into a more efficient, water-conserving scale form, which is smooth like the foliage of arborvitae (*Thuja* spp.). Some trees remain green through the winter, while others develop a bronze or purple cast. The foliage patterns of some trees are erect, while others are clumpy, and still others droop at the tips.

FLOWERS AND FRUITS: Like many other junipers, red cedar is dioecious. When the trees bloom in late spring, the females show a reddish tint and males stay yellow-green. The flowers are not conspicuous in the landscape.

Female trees bear small, modified blue cones called juniper berries in late summer and hold them through most of the winter or until they are eaten by birds. Unlike some junipers, red cedar matures its seed in one year. The fruits are metallic blue and can reach ¼ inch (0.6 cm) in diameter. The trees don't bear heavily every year, but a red cedar with a bumper crop appears to be covered with bright blue frost.

SEASONS:

1. Winter (most conifers are trees of the winter, and fruiting female red cedars are particularly colorful in an otherwise bland landscape);
2. Late spring (actually for the telial spore horns of rust galls, which are as bright as orange Christmas lights and, although a health menace to some other trees, are relatively harmless to red cedar);
3. All year (for picturesque old trees or selections with dramatic form).

NATIVE AND ADAPTIVE RANGE: Various races and provenances of red cedar can be found from the Ottawa River and the Georgian Bay area of Lake Huron, down through southern Ontario, east to Maine, west to the Dakotas and south to the coastal plains of the southeastern United States. It is hardy in cultivation from USDA zone 3 south.

CULTURE: Extremes of heat, drought, wind, cold and soil are not significant to this tree. It cannot tolerate shade or swampy sites and avoids very alkaline conditions in the wild. Beautiful old specimens with fluted trunks and tufted foliage, reminiscent of miniature sequoias, can be seen in cemeteries, pastures, river bluffs and parks on almost every soil type imaginable, wherever faster growing but less stalwart tree species have been kept in check.

Powder-blue fruits are borne on female red cedars.

Seed germinates slowly, sometimes not until the second year after planting, unless elaborate stratification and scarification practices are followed. Selected forms are rooted from cuttings. Where red cedar has invaded old fields or fence lines, it is usually so abundant that wild collection can be desirable to thin the stand. Such volunteers are best relocated when fairly small, before the root system has grown large and deep.

PROBLEMS: Wild red cedar trees in prairies and pastures are extremely sensitive to fire. Red cedar is also an alternate host to some rust diseases, including cedar-hawthorn rust (*Gymnosporangium globosum*), cedar-apple rust (*Gymnosporangium juniperi-virginianae*) and cedar-quince rust (*Gymnosporangium clavipes*), which infect fruit orchards and certain ornamental trees in the rose family. Rust-resistant varieties of these species should be used near groves of red cedar for their own sake, because the rusts do not seriously damage the red cedar.

It can be difficult to grow other plants beneath red cedars because of their competitive roots and the deep duff of decay-resistant needles. Red cedars, like most junipers, should not be pampered with irrigation because shallow root development may lead to toppling in a windy, wet spring.

CULTIVARS: Red cedar has given rise to many selections of both tree and shrub form. Some of the most popular and useful tree forms are 'Burkii' (a pyramidal male with a blue foliage tint), 'Canaertii' (a picturesque, tufted female form), 'Emerald Sentinel' (a narrow, pyramidal form), 'Hillii' (a compact, columnar selection with purple winter color), 'Pendula' (with drooping foliage) and 'Skyrocket' (a narrow, spire-shaped silvery blue accent plant that might be a hybrid with Rocky Mountain juniper, *Juniperus scopulorum*).

The USDA Soil Conservation Service began testing 307 selections of red cedar in 1986 and should release the winners for commercial use in 2005. An impressive collection of red cedar selections may be viewed at the North Carolina State University Arboretum at Raleigh.

RELATED SPECIES: The shrubby common juniper (*Juniperus communis*), which grows throughout much of our region and most of the northern hemisphere, is closely related to red cedar and may hybridize with it. Ashe juniper (*Juniperus ashei*) is a related western species that enters eastern North America only on the Ozark Plateau. Southern red cedar (*Juniperus silicicola*) is a southern coastal swamp tree, and the closely related Rocky Mountain juniper (*Juniperus scopulorum*) is planted frequently in the East. Approximately 10 additional species can be found in western North America and 50 more worldwide, some of which are common in cultivation.

COMMENTS: The first aroma many of us can recall from childhood is the wonderful pungency of the cedar chest or cedar-lined closet where our blankets were kept moth-free. The wood is equally resistant to decay organisms, so many young red cedar trees are harvested for fence posts.

Red cedar is one of our most valuable wildlife trees. Cedar waxwings earned their name from their preference for its fruits, which are a staple for more than 40 other wildlife species. Some of our fence-sitting birds have deposited red cedar seeds along nearly every fence within its range. The birds might also be transmitting rust diseases to fruit trees, because red cedar seedlings frequently pop up in orchards where they feed. The dense foliage furnishes cover and nesting sites for many birds and hosts the iridescent olive hairstreak butterfly. On a less noble note, red cedar fruits provide the raw material for gin.

TAMARACK

Larix laricina

DESCRIPTION: Tamarack is one of three larch species native to North America and the only one found east of the Rocky Mountains. The larches are conifers closely related to pines (*Pinus* spp.), firs (*Abies* spp.) and spruces (*Picea* spp.), but they are unique in that they are deciduous, like bald cypress (*Taxodium distichum*). Tamarack is perhaps the most cold-hardy of any native tree, and, among conifers, it has some of the strongest wood.

It grows in extremes of cold and wet, but seldom attains great size under such conditions. On good sites, it becomes a tall and picturesque specimen. One venerable tree near the northern tip of Maine is 92 feet (28 m) tall with a trunk almost 4 feet (1.2 m) in diameter. Larger individuals probably grow in remote areas across the breadth of Canada, especially in the prime tamarack habitat around Lake Winnipeg in Manitoba.

In the background, a large tamarack displays the irregular appearance characteristic of age.

LEAVES: Unlike most conifers, tamarack provides colorful seasonal variation. In the spring, the needles emerge a bright lime-green and contrast nicely with the dark foliage of pine and spruce. The needles grow in circular tufts on spur branches along the previous season's growth. On new twigs, they develop individually. The needles slowly mature to a length of about 1 inch (2.5 cm).

In late fall, tamaracks become golden searchlights over the muskegs and bogs of the North. Few other conifers provide any fall color, and those that do generally turn more somber tones of russet. The larches are without parallel among them.

FLOWERS AND FRUIT: Tamarack bears separate staminate and pistillate flowers on the same tree. The flowers are small, inconspicuous and visually overwhelmed by the emerging foliage. Male flowers are yellow-green and female flowers are a soft red.

Tamarack cones are among the smallest of any member of the genus, or of any other conifers, and rarely grow much more than ½ inch (1.3 cm) long. Young cones emerge from a basal whorl of short needles. They are pleasantly waxy and look (but do not taste) like some kind of tropical vegetable. They mature to a warm brown color and gradually fade to gray-brown as they continue to cling to their short spur branches for two or three years.

SEASONS:

1. Fall (the yellow needles, even during those years when their color is straw-tinted by cold or drought, add sparkle to any evergreen forest);
2. Spring (the fresh green of new needles, which emerge early from a bare coniferous tree, is the essence of a woodland awakening).

NATIVE AND ADAPTIVE RANGE: Tamarack forms our northernmost line of tree growth, from northern Newfoundland and Ungava Bay in Quebec, across James Bay and the central Canadian provinces to the southern end of Great Bear Lake and on to the Arctic Circle in central Alaska. From there, it follows suitable habitat south around the Great Lakes and southeastward to Pennsylvania and New Jersey.

This is one of the few trees whose hardiness in cultivation is expressed more appropriately in terms of its southern (not northern) limit, which depends on soil moisture and summer heat. Wild tamaracks are known to survive temperatures at least as low as –79 degrees F (–62 degrees C) without harm, thus cold is of no concern. They also experience short periods of summer temperatures exceeding 100 degrees F (40 degrees C). So, under ideal moisture conditions, tamarack can be grown south through much of USDA zone 6, especially if summer heat is moderated by a cool breeze from a nearby lake or evaporation from a sphagnum bog.

CULTURE: This tree requires moisture and cool temperatures. It also needs acidic soil and full sun. Long, cool summer days at high latitudes are ideal. Tamarack often grows slowly in the wild because of its stressful environment, but it can shoot up nicely with cultivation. It has a shallow, compact root system, so nursery-grown specimens can be easily transplanted when dormant, or it can be grown from seed sown in the fall. Tamarack will do well in any moist acidic soil, from sand to clay, but prefers a mulched organic loam. It casts a very light shade and may be underplanted successfully with acidic-soil wildflowers and shrubs.

PROBLEMS: Native stands of tamarack can be damaged severely by porcupines. The trees are shallow-rooted, especially on wet sites, and can be toppled by high winds. Shade and drought are probably the primary constraints on growing larch in a managed landscape.

The larch casebearer (*Coleophora laricella*) is a serious pest introduced from Europe. It is a tiny, fascinating insect that lives inside a hollowed-out needle, which it carries on its back while it feeds on other needles. Larch sawfly (*Pristiphora erichsonii*) can also be a troublesome defoliator, as can the gypsy moth (*Lymantria dispar*). Importation of unprocessed larch timber from Europe or Russia should be monitored closely because exotic borers and other serious pests exist there and might be introduced into North America.

CULTIVARS: Tamarack seems to be a very homogenous species, considering the extent of its natural range and the variability of habitat conditions in

Tamarack cones emerge from a whorl of waxy needles. They are among the smallest cones of any conifer.

Young tamaracks in cultivation exhibit an erect and symmetrical form.

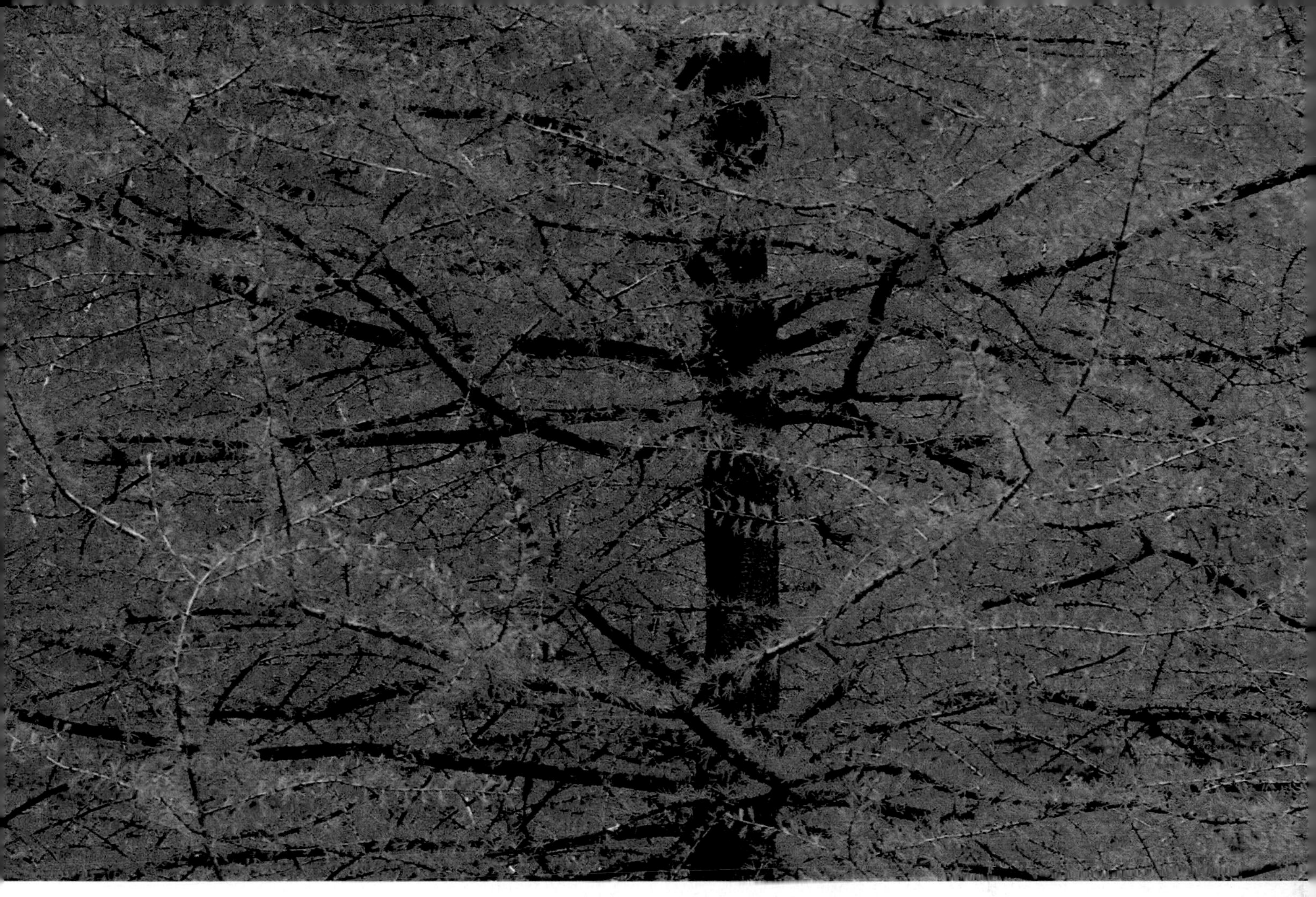

The tufted foliage, which emerges bright green in spring, is characteristic of tamarack.

which it thrives. A few obscure selections for blue or yellow leaf color have been made, but none are common in cultivation.

RELATED SPECIES: Two other beautiful larch species, *Larix occidentalis* and *Larix lyallii*, are found in the mountains of western North America, but they are not commonly found in cultivation in the East. European larch (*Larix decidua*) and Japanese larch (*Larix kaempferi*) are commonly grown in our area. Several other Asian species are cultivated in parts of North America, and the related golden larch (*Pseudolarix amabilis*) from China may also be seen occasionally.

COMMENTS: The irregular horizontal layers of branches and rough, excurrent form can make the deciduous tamarack look like a bare, dead evergreen in winter. It more than compensates, however, during the rest of the year with its colorful foliage and seasonal variation. Under the midnight sun in the North Country, this deciduous conifer photosynthesizes almost around the clock in summer to compensate for its lack of needles in winter. Its deciduousness makes it nearly immune to winter road salt, which severely damages many other conifers.

The seeds of tamarack are a favorite of crossbills, and the buds are eaten by spruce grouse. Many other birds value this species as a nesting site.

Many of us know that northern indigenous tribes used birch bark for their canoes, but few realize that these watercraft were sewn together with strips of tough, pliable tamarack root.

The famous nineteenth-century American horticulturist Andrew Jackson Downing recognized as early as 1849 that the flexible tamarack had an "expression of boldness and picturesqueness peculiar to itself." It is indeed an expressive tree, and we agree with him that it should be used with greater frequency to, in Downing's words, "give spirit to a group of other trees, to strengthen the already picturesque character of a scene, or to give life and variety to one naturally tame and uninteresting."

Very well said, Mr. Downing, and still true.

CORKWOOD

Leitneria floridana

DESCRIPTION: One of the pleasures of writing a reference book about plants lies in the occasional opportunity to include and promote the unusual. Corkwood provides such a pleasure.

Corkwood is aptly named. It has the lightest wood of any tree in North America, weighing less than half as much as cottonwood and less than a third as much as oak. The tree forms thickets in a few scattered, sandy or peaty wet areas in the southern United States and has not been found to grow anywhere else in the wild. Although not yet classified as a federally endangered species, this tree is rare enough that nature preserves have been established specifically to safeguard its regional existence.

Corkwood's summer foliage is glossy and lush.

Corkwood forms clonal colonies in the wild and also under cultivation. Although corkwood trees 25 feet (7.5 m) tall have been found, none that size are known to be alive now. Several of the largest specimens in Missouri, which has some of the best and most northern stands, are dying from competition with other species. Yet this unusual tree, with such a tenuous hold in the wild, has much to recommend it for the landscape.

LEAVES: Corkwood leaves emerge leathery and woolly in the spring, with wrinkled, rugose surfaces, and eventually reach almost 6 inches (15 cm) in length by less than half as wide. They are the primary aesthetic attraction of this species and look as if they belong on some tropical evergreen. But corkwood is quite at home in our temperate climate and is fully, if tardily, deciduous in the autumn. Some leaves turn a pleasant yellow before dropping, while others on the same tree might remain green until a hard freeze.

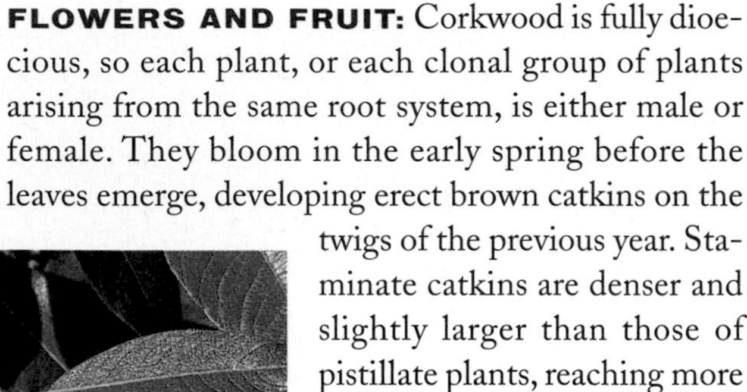

FLOWERS AND FRUIT: Corkwood is fully dioecious, so each plant, or each clonal group of plants arising from the same root system, is either male or female. They bloom in the early spring before the leaves emerge, developing erect brown catkins on the twigs of the previous year. Staminate catkins are denser and slightly larger than those of pistillate plants, reaching more than 1 inch (4 cm) in length.

Fruits are produced on female plants, but only on those that have been pollinated and usually only on wild trees that grow in an ideal habitat. They reach about 1 inch (2.5 cm) long, are conspicuously laced with surface veins and form small brown clusters in late spring. The fruits are timed to fall with the floodwaters of late spring, which carry them along to new homes where they promptly germinate on bare wet sand or muck.

SEASONS:

1. Summer (for the lush foliage) and late fall (for the green and yellow color effect);
2. Winter (for the huge flower buds, which look like small pine cones, and for the interesting architecture of the plant) into early spring (when the buds expand into a textural spectacle).

NATIVE AND ADAPTIVE RANGE: Corkwood is so limited in distribution that you could almost duplicate the backwoods familiarity of Davy Crockett and "know every tree." They grow in small, isolated groves in southern Missouri, eastern Arkansas, eastern Texas, northern Florida and southern Georgia. Most landscape reference books don't even acknowledge corkwood's existence, and the few that do generally rate it hardy north to USDA zone 6, probably based upon its natural range rather than first-hand experience with cultivation. We have grown it easily in USDA zone 5, and it does well in northern Illinois, nearly to zone 4.

CULTURE: Corkwood requires full sun and reasonable moisture but little else. It is not bothered by insects, diseases or gross inattention.

Under cultivation, it is amenable to almost any soil and does not seem to need the swampy conditions of its native habitat. Perhaps, like many other wetland trees, corkwood uses soggy soil to keep competitors at bay or to facilitate the establishment of its seedlings because almost all such species thrive in ordinary garden soil.

PROBLEMS: This species forms thickets and can become frustrating if your landscape design calls for a single-stemmed tree. It reaches its best ornamental potential, though, when left to its own devices and allowed to clump, as this eliminates the only maintenance (pulling sprouts) required for growing corkwood. It will be interesting to see its winter hardiness fully tested.

Above: Corkwood trees always grow in clumps as clones.
Below left: The catkins of staminate corkwood trees expand in very early spring, while most of nature is still asleep.

CULTIVARS: There are no named selections of corkwood. In fact, the species itself is barely known in cultivation. Selecting for male and female plants is simple, because corkwoods are so easy to propagate asexually from root cuttings or sprouts. Once you find a garden-club friend or local botanic garden with a corkwood, all you have to do is ask for a start.

RELATED SPECIES: Corkwood is the only species in the genus *Leitneria*, and *Leitneria* is the only genus in the family *Leitneriaceae*. One would expect the tree to have a few tropical or Oriental relatives, but in fact it is one of the true loners of the plant kingdom. It has only a distant relationship with willows (*Salix* spp.) and bayberries (*Myrica* spp.).

COMMENTS: It would be fun to grow corkwood, if only for a supply of balsa-like wood from its surplus stems. The wood is soft and easy to carve and also makes great fishing bobbers. The tree is an interesting ornamental, too, and is so easy to grow that there seems no good reason not to, if you can find some plants to start with.

It is interesting to note that species such as corkwood, bald cypress (*Taxodium distichum*) and water tupelo (*Nyssa aquatica*) exhibit much greater winter hardiness and accept drier soils under cultivation than their natural ranges and habitats would seem to indicate. This suggests that they are confined in nature to southern wetlands only by the winter ice of more northerly habitats and by the competition of other less flood-tolerant species on higher ground, or that their seedlings are unable to establish except under a southern swamp environment. Many such tree species thrive if planted and tended where they would be unable to establish naturally from seed. Corkwood is a great and very useful example.

SWEET GUM

Liquidambar styraciflua

DESCRIPTION: A young sweet gum, bare of foliage in winter, looks like a conifer and develops a distinctive conical form, with its trunk extending straight to the pointed tip. As it matures, the tree loses this characteristic architecture and begins to blend in with the oaks (*Quercus* spp.) and other deciduous trees in the vicinity. With age, sweet gum begins to fork at about half its ultimate height, resulting in one of the most sudden and dramatic architectural transformations from juvenile to adult form anywhere in our native forests. Many people have seen only the juvenile trees in urban landscapes and might be amazed to see an old-growth sweet gum swamp.

Bottomland woods are home to this tree, but it is almost as comfortable in old upland fields and grows at elevations up to 3,000 feet (900 m) in the lower Appalachian Mountains. It also extends south into Mexico and Central America, where it truly becomes a mountain tree. The most massive sweet gums are found in deep, well-drained bottomland soils of the southeastern United States. The largest known specimen stands 136 feet (42 m) high in Craven County, North Carolina, on a base more than 7 feet (2.1 m) in diameter above the root buttress. It is a magnificent tree, but many old sweet gums come close to such dimensions.

A young sweet gum develops a distinctive conical form, with its trunk extending straight to the pointed top.

LEAVES: Sweet gum leaves are like maple leaves (*Acer* spp.) in two respects: they are palmately lobed, or star-shaped, and they color magnificently in the fall, turning various shades of gold, red, pink and purple, often on the same tree. Unlike the maples, sweet gum bears its lustrous leaves alternately along the twigs. Leaves can grow up to 7 inches (18 cm) wide on vigorous shoots and are pleasantly fragrant when crushed. Fall color will develop even without cold temperatures, so sweet gum is a favorite tree for color in warm-climate areas.

FLOWERS AND FRUIT: The inconspicuous flowers are small and greenish and emerge just prior to the foliage, which tends to conceal them. Pistillate flowers develop in spherical clusters, while the more prominent staminate flowers occur in upright clusters.

The fruits, conversely, are among the most conspicuous and notorious of any of our native trees. These woody seed capsules ("gumballs") grow to a little more than 1 inch (3 cm) in diameter. They hang by the thousands from the dormant branches through much of the winter and gradually fall after releasing their small seeds. The fruits do not readily decompose, and when they land on a lawn, their horn-like projections cling like velcro, jamming reel mowers and causing a hazard and a maintenance headache. While attached to the tree, however, swinging from their flexible stalks, they enhance sweet gum's ornamental value. Many are collected and painted as holiday decorations.

SEASONS:

1. Fall (midseason for the colorful foliage and later for the attractive fruit capsules);
2. Summer (for the glossy, leathery leaves) and winter (for the gray bark, corky winged twigs, gumballs and symmetrical outline, most striking during the dormant season).

NATIVE AND ADAPTIVE RANGE: Sweet gum can

be found, often in pure stands on good sites, from southern Illinois, east to Long Island and south throughout the southeastern United States to eastern Texas and central Florida, except in the higher mountains. It reappears in the Sierra Madres of Mexico and at high elevations in Central America. Fossils of sweet gum have been found in Siberia, Greenland and Switzerland, which suggests not only an extensive earlier range but dramatic climatological change. Although geographic races are not recognized, this species is a good example of the effects of provenance. Trees from comparable hardiness zones should be selected for optimum vigor and hardiness in local conditions. With this caution, sweet gum can be considered hardy north through USDA zone 5.

CULTURE: This tree is quite adaptable but prefers deep, moist, acidic soil and full sun. It grows rapidly in such conditions but more slowly on dry sites or in less ideal soil. It is tricky to transplant because of its coarse root system, but root-pruned or container-grown trees establish quickly. The tiny seeds germinate readily if stratified and surface-sown in the spring. Collect seeds in early fall, before the gumballs open and release them to the wind.

PROBLEMS: Trees in natural stands are very susceptible to fire, and many planted specimens suffer from animal browsing. Sweet gums of southern origin are damaged by late-spring freezes and winter cold in the North. The species is generally sensitive to ozone pollution. Although it is a favorite target of gypsy moth (*Lymantria dispar*), most other insects and diseases seldom attack this tree.

Sweet gum can become chlorotic on insufficiently acidic soil or drought-stressed on shallow, very sandy or gravelly soil. Its gumballs can be a major litter problem. The extensive root system, which invariably projects above ground, needs room and protection from lawn mowers. Making a mulch bed around the tree rather than trying to grow grass might be the least frustrating way to accommodate both the surface roots and the accumulating gumballs.

CULTIVARS: For northern areas, 'Gold Dust', a variegated form, and 'Moraine' are hardy selections with good fall color. Southern gardeners who want brilliant fall color might consider 'Burgundy', 'Festival' or 'Palo Alto'. 'Obtusiloba' and 'Rotundiloba', which look similar and may have originated from the same plant, are the first of several selections developed for reduced fruiting. Several nurseries are testing selections for corky bark, and we expect to see some of these on the market eventually. 'Gumball' is a novelty form that is propagated for its dwarf, globose, shrubby growth pattern. Other cultivars exist, but many people prefer to select seedling trees of known local provenance. Though not as predictable as the cultivars, they are seldom disappointing. Choose one in the fall, when it reveals its colors.

RELATED SPECIES: One or two exotic species might be cultivated in the South, but none are as hardy as or aesthetically superior to our native species. Sweet gum is more closely related to witch hazels (*Hamamelis* spp.) than to any of our other trees.

COMMENTS: Sweet gum was one of the first trees in the western hemisphere to be historically documented. The Aztecs called it *xochiocotzoquahuitl*, and Aztec Emperor Montezuma smoked a medicinal sweet gum concoction with the explorer Hernando Cortés in 1519, one year before the Aztec Empire was destroyed in a bloody conquest by the Spanish. The species was given its modern common name, which is certainly easier to pronounce, from the gummy resin that coats fire scars and other wounds.

The vast quantities of tiny seeds produced by sweet gum are a favorite snack for finches and many other birds. They are carried far by the wind, which enables the tree to succeed as a pioneer species on abandoned fields and floodplains. The foliage serves as a preferred host for larvae of the beautiful luna moth, and the much despised gumballs have potential benefit in the flower garden; as a mulch, they reportedly repel cats seeking an outdoor litter box.

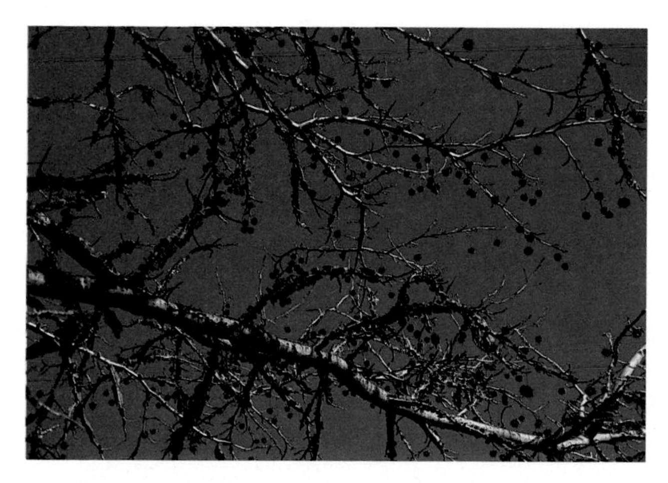

The corky bark that develops on some sweet gum twigs gives them texture and winter appeal.

TULIP TREE

Liriodendron tulipifera

DESCRIPTION: A special ambience comes with the tulip tree, or "yellow poplar" as it is known over much of its range. In the old-growth cathedral forests encountered by early settlers, tulip trees were like columns. Massive and straight, supporting a crown of foliage often lost to sight high above the canopy of its lesser neighbors, a great tulip tree might be 200 feet (60 m) tall. No other broadleaf trees in eastern North America grew so tall, and only the most exceptional white pines (*Pinus strobus*) were their equals.

The tulip-sized flowers of tulip tree are carried above the leaves and best viewed from a hilltop or upper-story window.

Some of these patriarchs still exist, but there are so few that it might be possible to become acquainted with each one. The current king stands in Bedford, Virginia. It is only 146 feet (45 m) tall, but its forked crown is supported by a base 10 feet (3 m) thick. The most impressive tulip tree grove surely must be the one above Little Santeetlah Creek in Joyce Kilmer Memorial Forest, which boasts dozens of massive trees much taller than the national champion. This remnant of our natural heritage provides an inspiring link to the once-vast old-growth forests of North America. It is part of the Nantahala National Forest in western North Carolina.

LEAVES: Many people who have not seen its flowers believe this species is named for the tulip-shaped silhouette of its leaves. Each leaf develops a truncated outline with four or occasionally six lobes and reaches about 5 inches (13 cm) in width and length; the leaf quivers at the end of an equally long petiole. The leaves, which are waxy and smooth, emerge folded and are fascinating to watch unfold in the spring. They seem impervious to insect damage and retain their clean appearance through the summer. Fall color is a dependable bright gold.

FLOWERS AND FRUIT: The flowers are, indeed, the size and shape of tulips, with two-toned orange and yellow petals around pale orange anthers, all surrounding a central cone-cluster of pistils. They bloom in May, after the first leaves have expanded, and must be seen from above to be fully appreciated. People who don't have second-story windows or balconies adjacent to their tulip trees sometimes miss one of the best floral displays of late spring. Tulip tree flowers are attractive to bees and produce nectar for gourmet honey.

The central cone, green and lemon-scented when young, matures into a tan woody cluster of winged seeds. The seeds gradually break away in the winter wind, leaving behind only the woody core by spring. While they remain intact, the fruits provide visual interest in early winter.

SEASONS:

1. Fall (the gold color of this tree, combined with its large size, makes it a prominent feature of the landscape);
2. Spring (if the spectacular flowers were not partially concealed from below by the foliage, spring might rate as the best season of all);
3. Summer (for the bright, clean foliage) and winter (for the persistent fruit).

NATIVE AND ADAPTIVE RANGE: Tulip tree covers a broad area from Grand Rapids, Michigan, Hamilton, Ontario, and Burlington, Vermont, south to the Gulf of Mexico. Within this range, it selects growing areas that meet its need for moderate, mesic conditions. As with some other such broadly adapted trees, provenance plays an important part in its success. Relatively local seed sources are best for areas near the northern or southern limits of its natural range. With this in mind, tulip tree is hardy north through USDA zone 5.

CULTURE: Tulip tree needs many things to succeed, but when it has all its requirements, it does extremely well. It is a mesic species and likes deep, rich, well-drained soil with uniform rainfall (or irrigation) throughout the growing season. Although late-season droughts affect its growth less than dry springs, hot, dry summer weather causes physiological problems, such as sunscald and early leaf abscission. However, with good moisture, good drainage, sun on the leaves and shade on the roots, tulip tree becomes one of our fastest growing and most magnificent trees.

When transplanting this species, select a large, open area with good deep soil. Transplanting can be a little tricky because of the tree's fragile, fleshy roots and juvenile taproot, so move it with a deep and generous soil ball in early spring. Seed germinates readily if sown in the fall, but do not expect more than 10 percent of the seed to be viable.

PROBLEMS: Tulip tree is remarkably free from insect and disease pests. Where gypsy moths (*Lymantria dispar*) have denuded forests for miles in every direction, the tall islands of green that remain are invariably tulip trees. This species is quite susceptible, however, to *Verticillium* wilt (*Verticillium dahliae* and *Verticillium albo-atrum*) and to environmental problems including air pollution, ice storms, drought, spring frosts, soil compaction, sapsucker pecks, animal browsing and (while still young) sunscald and fire. We have seen many unhappy tulip trees in urban settings. Because of its immense mature size, it also becomes an exposed target for wind and lightning.

CULTIVARS: This tree is not known for its cultivars, but a few exist. Several variegated forms are known, and botanical gardens sometimes grow the globe-shaped selection 'Compactum' or the narrow 'Fastigiatum'. A few forms with abnormal foliage shape are listed in horticultural literature. In general, these selections offer little advantage over the species type, but they are interesting curiosities.

Tulip tree's fall color is vibrant and dependable.

Massive and straight, a great tulip tree might be 200 feet (60 m) tall.

RELATED SPECIES: One other tulip tree exists in China. It is a smaller tree with deeply lobed leaves that is not nearly as hardy as our native species (although the Sternbergs are testing it, with early success, at Starhill Forest in Illinois). The genus is closely allied with the magnolias (*Magnolia* spp.).

COMMENTS: Tulip tree is the state tree of Indiana and Tennessee. It is a favorite nesting tree for many birds, and the flowers are a choice nectar source for hummingbirds. The tiger swallowtail butterfly uses this species. Bears sometimes spend the winter in large hollows that can develop in old trees.

Its great size and rich history have given the tulip tree a broad and deserved reputation. Daniel Boone reportedly built a 60-foot pirogue, or dugout boat, from a single tulip tree to carry his family down the Ohio river from Kentucky to the western frontier. George Washington and Thomas Jefferson planted what have grown to become some of the largest tulip trees in the East. The largest one at Mount Vernon, started by Washington in 1785, has been designated Mount Vernon's official Bicentennial Tree.

OSAGE ORANGE

Maclura pomifera

DESCRIPTION: Osage orange is a wind-resistant, drought-resistant, disease-resistant, pollution-resistant—seemingly everything-resistant—survivor with considerable aesthetic potential. Some individuals are picturesque ornamental plants, while others make impenetrable hedgerows. The species displays wide genetic variation, although generally individuals will become medium-sized trees that are stout in girth and artistic in form. In the Midwest, gnarly Osage oranges, or hedge-apples, are frequently found in pastures and along the edges of fields. Throughout much of the South they are called *bois d'arc* (pronounced BO-dock) from the words of French explorers who learned that Native Americans preferred the tough wood for bows.

Trimmed hedgerows planted more than a century ago from seed collected in the species' natural range protected cropland from wandering livestock. Later, in the Dust Bowl Era, the trees, which had grown taller, stood up to the wind and kept it from stealing tons of topsoil from the fields.

In the United States, the champion Osage orange is found at Red Hill, the home of Patrick Henry, in Charlotte County, Virginia. It stands 64 feet (20 m) tall with a branch spread of almost 100 feet (30 m) and has a short trunk 8 feet (2.4 m) in diameter. It is much larger than any of the trees remaining in the species' difficult natural habitat and shows how energetically the tree responds to a favorable site and horticultural attention. Local lore says that Mr. Henry often sat under this great tree, and it certainly looks old enough. But the legend is inconsistent with the fact that the species was not cultivated until a few years after the old patriot had died.

Top: Male Osage orange, here gracing the Sternbergs' home in Illinois, makes an attractive, clean shade tree. Above: In a productive year, a female Osage orange may be covered with large, heavy fruits.

LEAVES: Osage orange leaves appear citrus-like and are long-pointed, smooth and glossy. They reach about 5 inches (12 cm) in length by half as broad. They emerge very late, so they avoid frosts and allow the early-spring sun to warm the ground below them (or house behind them). The fall color is a rich, clear gold.

FLOWERS AND FRUIT: This species is fully dioecious. The inconspicuous flowers emerge with the leaves and are important only for gender identification. Distinguishing sexes can be important because female trees produce pebbly, grapefruit-sized yellow "hedge-apples" that can put a dent in your car if they fall on it. Any resemblance to citrus is merely superficial; the fruits are filled with sticky white sap. While they can be a hazard or at least a nuisance in managed landscapes, in the right place, the fruits can be ornamental and a curiosity for those unfamiliar with Osage orange.

Folklore holds that the fruits repel roaches, but we

suspect they are effective only if they happen to fall directly on one. Female trees should be relegated to agricultural landscapes or to large, mulched borders, where the fruit display may be appreciated from a distance, then harvested for a roach-repelling test or left for the squirrels, which will tear the fallen fruit apart to retrieve every seed. Finches, grosbeaks and crossbills also eat the seeds.

SEASONS:
1. Fall (the gold foliage color can hardly be surpassed; after the leaves drop, the fruit on the female trees is displayed to best advantage);
2. Winter (for the rugged dark orange and gray bark, especially on trees that have developed an artistic form);
3. Summer (for the glossy foliage).

NATIVE AND ADAPTIVE RANGE: Before the Lewis and Clark expedition introduced it to the North and East, Osage orange was found only in a small area of Texas and adjacent Oklahoma, where it had been forced by ancient glaciers. This range limitation is meaningless today. Hedgerow plantings of the past century have reintroduced the tree to much of its prehistoric range in the central and eastern United States. Its climatological limits are still being tested as it spreads into the agrarian landscape of the Corn Belt. But under suitable conditions, it can be grown in the north at least through USDA zone 5.

Beautiful bark and a convoluted trunk are typical of a mature Osage orange.

CULTURE: This species may experience dieback if it is transplanted carelessly. Move it with a soil ball in the spring, just as the buds begin to show signs of life. It will thrive in most soils, including tight clay, compacted urban subsoil and floodplain sand, and it is not fussy about soil pH. Seeds grow readily. To sow them, chop the ripe fruit into pieces and plant each piece in the fall (using the same technique as for planting seed potatoes). You can also let the fruit freeze. When it thaws, you can pick the seeds from the sticky pulp. Selected trees can be reproduced asexually from root or softwood cuttings.

Osage orange is like a spirited horse. It becomes valuable only with some training. Thinning the tangle of hard wood (and thorns on many wild trees) and removing all of its dead branches can test your resolve. But without attention, it will become completely unruly. As with a high-spirited horse, it may be easiest to guide it in the direction it already wants to go, with a saw cut here and a light pruning there, rather than trying to wrestle it into a formal shape. Vertical sprouts and root suckers should be removed, but you do not need to prune attentively and train for structural integrity. The wood doesn't break and it doesn't rot, so don't worry about narrow crotch angles.

Keeping a few mature trees on a lot and incorporating a landscape design around them may show Osage orange at its best. Magnificent old specimens shade the Sternberg residence at Starhill Forest in Illinois. Fortunately, many older trees are relatively thornless, and their gender can be determined from the flowers once they are old enough to bloom. During the winter, you can make an educated guess as to the tree's sex by looking for fruit remnants and by observing the crown structure with a practiced eye: male trees are often more upright. These tough trees are nearly immune to the ravages of ice and wind. Also, they are more tolerant of construction disturbances than most other trees. Of course, it pays to give them good care.

PROBLEMS: This species does have its drawbacks, and they can be serious. Most juvenile trees and sprouts are armed with vicious thorns, strong and sharp enough to puncture a tire. Some trees, though, particularly older ones, are nearly or completely thornless. Females bear the attractive but messy fruits, which can weigh up to 3 pounds (1.4 kg). On a calm, sunny, late-fall morning following a hard freeze, we once watched a single female tree drop several hundred fruit in less than one hour, pulverizing everything beneath it.

CULTIVARS: John Pair of Kansas State University is in the forefront of cultivar selection with this species. He is introducing several excellent forms chosen for their lack of thorns or fruit. Among these are 'Altamont' (an upright male selection from Illinois), 'Park' (from a superior tree found in Ottawa, Kansas), 'Pawhuska' (another release from Kansas stock, named for an Osage Indian) and 'Wichita' (from a tree found south of Wichita, Kansas. The current favorite is 'Whiteshield', from Oklahoma.

Osage orange can be spreading and picturesque, as shown by this century-old specimen in Illinois.

We are evaluating our own selections as well. The most intriguing have the temporary experimental names "Beta" (a majestic, thornless male tree shaped like an American elm, *Ulmus americana*), "Delta" (a spreading female with picturesque horizontal branching and cantaloupe-sized fruit, for ornamental and wildlife applications where massive fruits are desired) and "Hamel" (a dwarf, dense, thorny form, promising as a hedge plant for historic restorations).

RELATED SPECIES: *Maclura* is a monotypic genus, but it is closely related to the very similar Chinese *Cudrania tricuspidata*, with which it can be crossed to produce an unusual bigeneric hybrid. It is in the same family as the mulberries (*Morus* spp.).

COMMENTS: Osage orange is home to the hagen sphinx, a large, host-specific moth. The tree also offers valuable wildlife habitat. It is an ecological setback each time an old hedgerow is bulldozed in the Midwest to make room for an extra few rows of corn. Its bright yellow wood is the heaviest of any of our native woods and the most decay-resistant because of a natural fungicide, 2,3,4,5-tetrahydroxystilbene, which is concentrated in the wood. We have fence posts made from untreated Osage orange that have remained solid for more than 60 years; they have outlasted ones made later from treated pine (*Pinus* spp.). The wood burns with almost as much heat value as coal, but it generates an endless shower of sparks.

Most of the remaining old trees are no longer trimmed or hedged unless they are part of a historic restoration. But one famous old male tree near Bondville, Illinois, has been trimmed several times every year since 1900 by Neimiah Jacobs and his descendants. This trimming cycle was not begun for hedge purposes but to save the tree from removal when the first overhead utility lines were being installed. Its dense crown still can be seen (under the wires) along Illinois Route 10, west of Champaign.

The fossil record of Osage orange makes for fascinating speculation. Native as far north as Minnesota and Toronto during the Sangamon interglacial period of 100,000 years ago, Osage orange was driven south by the last Pleistocene glaciers. The large, heavy fruits of this species probably fed the great North American mammals like mastodons, which could consume them whole or in large pieces and drop the seeds intact along their migration routes.

Those magnificent animals were hunted to extinction at the close of the last ice age. Osage orange thus lost the only carriers by which it could move its seed and reclaim its former territory when the ice retreated. It had to wait 10,000 years for humans (the very species that had eliminated those carriers) to find it valuable and to transport the seed. This we have done, with great success, during the past 150 years.

CUCUMBER TREE

Magnolia acuminata

DESCRIPTION: People think of magnolias as Oriental flowering shrubs, but several magnolia tree species are native to North America. The largest and hardiest is the cucumber tree. It becomes a canopy tree in mesic forests, where it looks more like a large timber tree than a cousin of the dainty, pastel-flowered hybrid magnolias. It prefers evenly moist conditions similar to those enjoyed by its other cousin, the tulip tree (*Liriodendron tulipifera*), but tolerates more shade.

Cucumber tree is the only native magnolia of Canada, and unfortunately it is endangered there—it is found only in a few stream valleys and on protected slopes near Lake Erie. At this northern limit of its natural range, it grows only about half as large as it does in the cove forests of the southern Appalachians. The largest specimen of all, though, is a planted tree in Waukon, Iowa. It is a respectable 75 feet (21 m) tall, which is not particularly large, but it is nearly 8 feet (2.4 m) in diameter. This tree has attained such a distinguished girth because it is free from the competition of a forested habitat. Only an open-grown specimen can develop the massive lower limbs that build such a stout trunk.

A giant old cucumber tree at the peak of its fall color.

LEAVES: Cucumber tree leaves look much like those of pawpaw (*Asimina triloba*). They reach approximately 8 inches (20 cm) in length and develop acuminate points at their tips, which give the tree its species name. Fall color can be pale yellow or a warm, bright tan. Sometimes the leaves are hit by frost before any color develops.

FLOWERS AND FRUIT: The magnolias are known for their flowers, but those of this species are relatively modest. They are greenish yellow (some trees show more yellow than others) and grow to about 3 inches (8 cm) wide. They would be much more conspicuous if they emerged before the foliage. Several ornamental hybrid cultivars have incorporated the hardiness and yellow flower color of this species with the flower size and timing of some of the Asian species.

The aromatic fruit follicles that develop from the flower core resemble small cucumbers when green. Later, they turn deep red, and the compartments split open to expose the bright orange-coated seeds. Many fruits fall to the ground with their seeds still enclosed and become forage for towhees and other ground-feeding birds, as well as small mammals.

SEASONS:

1. Fall (for the red fruits and occasionally nice leaf color);
2. Summer (an attractive shade tree with clean foliage);
3. Spring (the flowers are attractive if seen close up).

NATIVE AND ADAPTIVE RANGE: Cucumber tree can be found from southern Ontario and western New York, southwest through the mountains of the eastern United States, with outlying populations in suitable habitats to the south and west as far as the Gulf coastal plain and eastern Oklahoma. Under cultivation, it is hardy north into USDA zone 4.

CULTURE: Most of our native deciduous magnolias require deep, moist, well-drained soil and protection from extreme wind and heat. They will accept partial shade and any moderate pH, but they will not tolerate wet soil or drought. As with the commonly cultivated Asian species, cucumber tree should be transplanted in the spring. The coarse, fleshy roots should be dug with a large soil ball and set in a shallow hole. The seed will germinate readily if removed from the fruit, cleaned of its colorful soft coating and planted in the fall. This magnolia grows rapidly once established in a suitable site.

PROBLEMS: All magnolias are brittle and reluctant to heal wounds or pruning cuts. Cucumber tree is less prone to storm damage than some, but it should be trained while young into a strong branching pattern. Try to remove unwanted limbs while they are still small. Native deciduous magnolias are more sensitive to drought and ground fires than are most associated species. They are also frequently damaged by the heavy pecking of sapsuckers.

CULTIVARS: Only two cultivars are widely known. 'Variegata' has white-speckled leaves and 'Golden Glow' has yellow flowers. Cucumber tree and its close relative, yellow cucumber tree (*Magnolia cordata*), have been very useful in breeding programs using Asian species. 'Elizabeth', 'Evamaria' and 'Yellow Bird' are some of the most promising offspring.

RELATED SPECIES: Half a dozen additional deciduous magnolia species are native to the southeastern United States. The one most closely allied to the cucumber tree, and the one seen most often in hybridization programs, is the yellow cucumber tree, which has been treated by some authorities as a subspecies or variety of cucumber tree. It is a smaller tree with larger, showier flowers.

Umbrella magnolia (*Magnolia tripetala*) is also seen occasionally in cultivation. It resembles a small

Bigleaf magnolia has beautiful flowers and the largest simple leaves of any tree in North America.

The large, velvety buds of cucumber tree are attractive all winter.

The rusty-red fruits of umbrella magnolia provide a colorful, long-lasting display.

version of the cucumber tree with immense 15-inch (38 cm) leaves, large creamy flowers and fruits up to 8 inches (20 cm) long. It is nearly as hardy as cucumber tree if given a protected location where its leaves will not be torn apart by wind. Fraser magnolia (*Magnolia fraseri*) is a small, fragrant, basal-branching tree of the southern Appalachians. Sometimes called earleaf magnolia, it has narrow, earlobed leaves and white flowers. A variety (often considered a distinct species), *pyramidata*, extends southward into the Gulf coastal plain.

Another species with earlobed leaves is the bigleaf magnolia (*Magnolia macrophylla*). Its leaves are even larger than those of the umbrella magnolia, sometimes reaching nearly 3 feet (90 cm) in length. A young specimen with a single stem capped with a ring of long, drooping foliage looks a bit like a banana plant. It is an attractive tree with huge 8-inch (20 cm) fragrant white flowers, but it needs a totally protected site and careful design placement because of its fragile leaves. Bigleaf magnolia is very rare and widely scattered in the wild; few people have seen it except in cultivation. The southern variety *ashei* has slightly smaller flowers and leaves and is listed by some as a distinct species. It grows into a compact, shrubby tree.

All of the above trees are fully deciduous and surprisingly hardy north of their native haunts. The Sternbergs grow every one in USDA zone 5, and some can be seen even farther north. Two other native magnolias are evergreen or semievergreen and are discussed separately.

COMMENTS: Cleaning magnolia seed for planting can be messy, but working in the fragrant, citrus-like aroma from the brightly colored seed coats makes the job more pleasant. The real reward, however, comes the following June, when—after you become convinced that the seed will never sprout—you see the little magnolia trees bursting out of the soil.

Old cucumber trees are occasionally seen around homes in the North, where they were not intentionally placed. This species has been popular as a grafting understock for some of the tender hybrid magnolias. When the grafted scion is killed by a hard winter, the hardier cucumber tree root sends up a sprout of its own to claim the spot. Years later, an inattentive gardener might never know why his delicate grafted magnolia became such a magnificent tree but never had those pink flowers he expected.

SOUTHERN MAGNOLIA

Magnolia grandiflora

DESCRIPTION: One of the most envied landscape trees at the Wilson house at Savory Farm in South Carolina is the perfect evergreen southern magnolia in the side garden. Nearly every southern town has at least one such stunning specimen that captures the attention of the community and conveys upon its owner the distinction of having what is locally described as "the house with the beautiful magnolia tree." But southern magnolia also grows in the forest, where it becomes not a leafy specimen with branches to the ground but a canopy tree with a tall, straight trunk, clear of limbs for half its height. Of all the magnolias, this is the species most often harvested for timber.

In South Carolina, the Wilsons' southern magnolia is loaded with fruit in late October.

Southern magnolia is the state tree of Mississippi, and the largest individual known grows in the south-central part of the state, in Smith County. It stands 122 feet (38 m) tall and has a trunk over 6 feet (2 m) in diameter. Southern magnolia is usually found growing with beech (*Fagus grandifolia*), sweet gum (*Liquidambar styraciflua*), oak (*Quercus* spp.) and other forest trees in sandy, fertile, well-drained soil on the fringe of wet areas. While it is very adaptable under cultivation, it is curious to note that nearly the entire natural range of this tree lies in lowlands, within 200 feet (60 m) of sea level.

LEAVES: The leaves are thick, shiny, stiff and creased along the midrib. They grow up to 10 inches (25 cm) long. They are the darkest of greens, with woolly undersides that vary from pale green to rusty red. Old fallen leaves are almost woody and look like miniature brown canoes skimming the forest floor. This species is fully evergreen, and the leaves remain for two years under most conditions. At the northern limits of cultivation, they will bronze, blotch and burn in severe winters, but most of them still cling, at least until they are replaced by new foliage in the spring.

FLOWERS AND FRUIT: This is one of the most showy of the magnolias for both its flowers and fruit. The white, waxy flowers can be up to 1 foot (30 cm) across and are powerfully fragrant. They are borne on the ends of nearly every twig on mature trees in late spring, and a few continue to open through the summer. The cone-like fruits that follow are heavy and symmetrical and have a crimson-velvet surface. The individual seed compartments split open to reveal bright flame-red seeds in each seam.

SEASONS:

1. Spring (for the striking appearance and powerful fragrance during the primary blooming period);
2. Fall (for the ripening fruit);
3. All year (for the evergreen foliage).

NATIVE AND ADAPTIVE RANGE: Southern magnolia is found in mixed stands along the coastal plains from North Carolina to eastern Texas. Its seedlings are extremely sensitive to frost, which is the primary reason its natural range is so limited. Some selections (mostly of the type with reddish-backed leaves called "brown-backs") are being tested as far north as USDA zone 5. An experimental plant from Mike Stansberry, a plantsman in Knoxville, Tennessee, has been the only selection we have tested that has endured more than two winters as far north as central Illinois. Most selections are reliably hardy in the North only through USDA zone 7 or barely into USDA zone 6. The species should probably not be planted beyond that range for general landscaping purposes, unless it is to be grown experimentally or as a shrub and cut back to the ground after every hard winter.

CULTURE: Except in the Deep South, this tree must be container-grown or transplanted with a soil ball, preferably in early spring. Young transplanted trees must be watered during dry spells until they are well established.

Southern magnolia likes deep, rich, acidic, gritty soil with good drainage. Partial shade is acceptable, and winter shade is preferred in northern areas where the ground freezes and immobilizes the extra soil moisture needed by sunlit leaves. The most dense form and flowering occurs in full sun. Southern magnolia seeds germinate more quickly than those of some of the deciduous species. Clean seed can be sprouted without a winter cold period.

PROBLEMS: Southern magnolia drops old leaves almost continuously and casts a dark shade, so you cannot grow lush turf beneath its canopy. It is best grown in a mulched border, with its lower branches left to blanket the ground. The fallen leaves should be chopped with a rotary mower and blown back under the branches to recycle the minerals in the leaf litter.

Specimens grown under severe winter conditions, especially in full sun, develop sunscald and foliage damage that, if not fatal, will at least destroy their ornamental value. This tree seems immune to insect and disease problems, and its waxy leaves make it resistant to salt spray and air pollution, unlike most other magnolias. Once established, it is the most drought-resistant of the magnolias, which isn't saying much.

CULTIVARS: More than 100 selections of this species have been made for superior flowers, foliage, growth rate or other merits. 'Little Gem' is a reblooming dwarf form from Warren Steed's Nursery in North Carolina. 'Majestic Beauty' is another popular selection from Monrovia Nursery in California.

The brilliant flowers of southern magnolia contrast strikingly with the dark, glossy evergreen leaves.

Persistent red fruit follicles and glossy evergreen foliage combine to give southern magnolia multiseason appeal.

Top: The undersides of the leaves are tawny on a hardy "brown-back" strain of southern magnolia. Above: The northerly, deciduous form of sweet bay is a graceful small tree.

Both are very ornamental but tender and suitable only in the South.

The current trend is to select for increased winter hardiness for gardeners in the northern part of the South. 'Edith Bogue' is an award-winning tree suitable for such areas that has been the winner of laboratory testing for hardiness. 'Bracken's Brown Beauty' and 'Russet' are selections that have shown hardiness in early testing. 'Victoria' is another hardy type—one of the few hardy "green-back" forms, which do not have rusty-colored leaf undersides.

Many other new selections, such as the one we are testing from Knoxville and another found by Matt Vehr at Spring Grove Cemetery in Cincinnati, show promise. But keep in mind that the term "native" for this species usually means south of USDA zone 6.

RELATED SPECIES: Northern gardeners who covet a semievergreen magnolia and southern gardeners who seek a refined, graceful small evergreen tree without some of the gaudy qualities of the southern magnolia should look at the sweet bay (*Magnolia virginiana*). It is more diminutive in all respects. Unlike southern magnolia, its leaves have silvery undersides that flash in the wind, and it has the ability to shed its foliage during severe winters, before physiological drought causes damage to the woody tissue. Northern-provenance sweet bays are at least a full zone hardier than the hardiest southern magnolia cultivars. This is also our most flood-tolerant magnolia, but it will do fine in average garden soil. The evergreen southern variety (*australis*) is more upright-growing than the deciduous form. Watch for superior new selections like 'Silver Sword' from Touliatos nursery in Tennessee.

COMMENTS: Southern magnolia might rank second only to some of the oaks in the number of events and legends with which it has become associated. It is a handsome, long-lived, commanding tree, worthy of commemorating history. The Jones Magnolia is a venerable southern magnolia growing in Washington State Park, Arkansas. Two men named Jones, who would become, respectively, governor and senator of Arkansas, were born near the tree in 1839, the year it was planted. The tree was placed just east of the inn where Sam Houston, William Travis and others met in 1835 to plan the independence of Texas, and a short distance south of the blacksmith shop where James Black and Jim Bowie made the first Bowie Knife. Bowie and Travis died with Davy Crockett at the Alamo in 1836, but Houston went on to become the first president of the independent Republic of Texas and lived to see the Jones Magnolia reach its twenty-fourth year. The historic tree is now an impressive 14 feet (4.3 m) in circumference.

PRAIRIE CRAB

Malus ioensis (Pyrus ioensis)

DESCRIPTION: In the savannas and borders of the prairie that once dominated so much of the heart of North America, one of the most beautiful and useful small trees was the prairie crab. It is a miniature apple tree in most respects, and its fruit is sought by wildlife, just as it was by early settlers in the days before Johnny Appleseed brought domesticated apples to the frontier.

The pale pink flowers of prairie crab cover the tree in spring.

We actually have three nearly identical species of native apple in eastern North America. Prairie crab is generally a little smaller than the others, and its prairie-fire heritage has encouraged it to evolve into a cloning species that sprouts from the roots—a means of survival if its top is burned. As a single specimen, it grows much larger than it does when allowed to clump. The United States national champion prairie crab, located in Oakland County, Michigan, is nearly 50 feet (14 m) tall and has a trunk diameter of 1 foot (30 cm).

The other two species are sweet crab (*Malus coronaria*) and southern crab (*Malus angustifolia*). The largest sweet crab grows in Hampstead, Virginia, and stands 37 feet (12 m) tall; the champion southern crab (on page 154) grows in Swannanoa, North Carolina, and is about the same size. Both have trunks twice as large as that of the champion prairie crab.

LEAVES: The leaves of our native crabapples look much like those of cultivated apples. Those of the prairie crab are the largest, up to 4 inches (10 cm) long, and are frequently shallow-lobed. Southern crab is also known as narrow-leaved crab, and its leaves are only about half as large and are seldom lobed. The leaves are red when they emerge in early spring and are quite attractive as they highlight the intricate tracery of twigs against the colorful scaly bark. Vigorous trees that escape premature defoliation from fungus diseases can develop a glowing orange-red color in fall.

FLOWERS AND FRUIT: Crabapples, whether native or exotic, are spectacular in bloom. Our native species have fragrant, light pink flowers that resemble single roses but grow in clusters that cover the trees in spring. Again, those of the prairie crab are the largest, sometimes up to 2 inches (5 cm) across. They bloom later than most of the exotic cultivated ornamental crabapples. The attractive flower buds are deep pink to red before they open, and the flowers on some trees fade to nearly white as they expand.

The fruits are not ornamental by crabapple standards, but they do add landscape interest in the fall after the leaves drop. They grow almost as big as golf balls and remain pale green until they fall and are eaten by wildlife or are gathered by humans.

SEASONS:

1. Spring (the flowers rival those of many of the most admired exotic species and hybrids);
2. Fall (for the fruit and the leaf color, but only if the tree has not been disfigured by leaf-fungus diseases);
3. Winter (for the silvery reddish bark and the intricate twig patterns, which cast fascinating shadow designs on the snow).

NATIVE AND ADAPTIVE RANGE: Our three native crabapple species are nearly allopatric, overlapping very little in their ranges, but together they cover a large territory. Prairie crab is the western species, which grows from Minnesota and Wisconsin south through Illinois and Missouri to scattered locations in Louisiana and Texas. Sweet crab dominates the northeastern part of the crab territory, from Michigan, southern Ontario and New York, south through Indiana and Ohio to areas in the southern Appalachians.

Southern crab begins to dominate where sweet crab fades out, extending its range to the Gulf Coast. Under cultivation, prairie crab and sweet crab are perfectly hardy north into USDA zone 4, while southern crab can perform well as far north as portions of USDA zone 5. Each species occurs in small areas within the range of the others. But generally, each is best when planted in its own home territory.

CULTURE: Native crabapples thrive anywhere that their exotic relatives do, and they also have similar limitations. They will not tolerate poor drainage and become scraggly in shade. They are very susceptible to the various disfiguring leaf diseases that plague so many members of the genus, but each spring they leaf out again without any perceptible loss of vigor.

PROBLEMS: Apple scab (*Venturia inaequalis*) is the most serious of the many leaf diseases that affect the native crabapple, and it frequently defoliates the trees by late summer. Several leaf rusts (*Gymnosporangium* spp.) are also common defoliators. These trees tend to form clonal thickets, so if you want a single stem you have to occasionally pull the suckers. The large fruits of native crabapples can be a nuisance if they fall on pavement or manicured lawns, and the sharp spur branches can be hazardous near sidewalks or other high-traffic areas.

Unhealthy trees are prone to attack from borers, such as the round-headed apple borer (*Saperda candida*), which occasionally inflicts so much damage to the base that the tree is eventually toppled by the wind. Rabbits cut or girdle many young crabapples in winter. While not a problem in wildlife plantings or natural thickets because the roots send up new stems, girdling can damage or kill a specimen tree.

The national champion southern crab graces a youth center in North Carolina.

The spherical, swelling buds of prairie crab open into attractive pink flowers.

CULTIVARS: Native crabapples are usually naturalized or maintained as wild trees. Selecting and breeding disease-resistant hybrids of exotic crabapples for the domestic landscape has been carried on almost to the exclusion of work with our native species. However, several prairie crab cultivars have been propagated for their superior ornamental qualities. 'Plena' includes a group that encompasses the old form 'Bechtel' and the improved selections 'Nova', 'Fiore's Improved Bechtel', 'Klehm's Improved Bechtel', 'Fimbriata' and 'Brandywine'. All are cultivars with double flowers. 'Nevis' and 'Boone Park' are more like the wild form, with single flowers.

'Big O' is a seed-propagated ecotype of sweet crab from Georgia that is resistant to rust diseases. 'Charlottae', 'Elk River' and 'Nieuwlandiana' are other sweet crab selections that have semidouble flowers. 'Callaway' is a southern crab selection from Callaway Gardens in Pine Mountain, Georgia. 'Prince Georges' is a form with large double flowers that is reported to be a hybrid of prairie crab and southern crab. Other hybrid selections resulting from crosses of our native species with some of the exotic crabapples are available from some nurseries.

RELATED SPECIES: One additional native crab, *Malus diversifolia*, is found in western North America. Some taxonomists separate a few varieties and probable hybrids into additional species in the southeastern United States. The differences, even among our three primary species, are so obscure that further splitting of the genus would accomplish little from a horticultural standpoint.

There are more than 500 crabapple cultivars on the market, which were derived from about 35 species, and hundreds of selections of edible apple species and hybrids exist. Technically, the difference between an apple and a crabapple is a matter of fruit size—a crabapple has fruit that does not exceed about 2 inches (5 cm) in diameter. There is no real taxonomic distinction between the two. It is interesting to note that the historic name of the genus (*Pyrus*) now applies only to the true pears but once included such trees as apples and mountain ash (*Sorbus* spp.).

COMMENTS: Crabapple thickets provide some of our most valuable wildlife habitat—they protect nests from predators and offer shelter to many species. Wild crabapples are sought by many mammals and large birds, especially ground-feeders that find the fruit under the snow when other food is scarce. Wild crabs also host the chocolate moth, a gentle and benign relative of the blood-sucking "vampire moth" of the Malay Peninsula.

RED MULBERRY

Morus rubra

DESCRIPTION: Unlike its weedy exotic cousins, which neither receive nor deserve much respect in horticultural circles, our native mulberry is a handsome, mild-mannered forest tree. And, much unlike the exotic species, which seem to favor sidewalk cracks, red mulberry inhabits rich, fertile, mesic forest soils. In the open, it becomes a vase-shaped, spreading shade tree, not unlike a small American elm (*Ulmus americana*).

Seldom merging into the top of the forest canopy in the wild, it is content to remain in the midstory under the shade of its tallest neighbors, where its large, round leaves capture the occasional sunlight that sneaks through. One at Tower Hill in Illinois has a trunk nearly 7 feet (2 m) in diameter.

LEAVES: This species has larger, hairier leaves than do most exotic mulberries. In the deep shade of its native forest habitats, the leaves can grow more than 8 inches (20 cm) long by almost as broad, making this species easy to identify from a distance. Red mulberry leaves are occasionally lobed like those of the Asian white mulberry (*Morus alba*), especially on vigorous sprouts, but they more often resemble the unlobed leaves of linden (*Tilia* spp.). The strong golden fall color of red mulberry ranks with that of hickories (*Carya* spp.).

Red mulberry has large leaves, often without lobes, and long edible fruits.

FLOWERS AND FRUIT: Mulberry is usually, but not always, dioecious. Sometimes, individual branches on the same tree will be either male or female, like those of honey locust (*Gleditsia triacanthos*). A few trees reportedly change their gender from year to year. The green staminate flowers grow in clusters up to 2 inches (5 cm) long, while the pistillate flower clusters are about half as large.

The flowers appear with the leaves in spring and are not very conspicuous, but the dark red fruits that follow on female trees are attractive and blandly sweet. The fruits, which grow in cylindrical clusters of individual drupes similar to long, narrow blackberries, are longer and narrower than those of white mulberry and generally ripen slightly later. Individual fruits mature at different times over several weeks, which benefits the more than 30 species of nesting songbirds and mammals that relish them.

SEASONS:

1. Fall (the huge, golden leaves of a deep-forest red mulberry, backlit along a dark, wooded streambank, can be visually striking);
2. Summer (for the foliage texture and, where they don't create a litter problem, the tasty fruit).

NATIVE AND ADAPTIVE RANGE: Red mulberry is never a dominant species, but it can be an indicator of good soils over an extensive range. It occurs as a rare species (listed as threatened by the Canadian Government) in southern Ontario and from there extends without a break southward throughout the eastern United States to Bermuda and southern Florida. Its western natural limit runs from southern Minnesota to the Pecos River Valley of western Texas (where its range overlaps that of the smaller Texas mulberry, *Morus microphylla*). It extends northeast through southern Pennsylvania to the Hudson River in New York and sporadically beyond. While provenance is certain to play a role in the local adaptability of such a wide-ranging tree, it definitely can be grown throughout eastern North America up into USDA zone 4.

CULTURE: Red mulberry can tolerate full sun un-

Above : This huge red mulberry grows near a school in central Illinois. Below right: Red mulberry's leaves cling to the tree in late fall.

der mesic conditions, yet it will grow in the dense shade of taller trees. While not as immune to drought and poor soil as some exotic mulberries, it will persist under some very trying conditions. If given ample moisture throughout the summer, red mulberry will grow quickly; if dry, it may languish. This tree responds well to fertile soil and is very resistant to air pollution and decay.

All mulberry trees are easy to transplant. They can also be grown from seed sown in the fall. To remove the seeds for storage, let the fruits ferment for a few days and squeeze them through a strainer. Intact fruits can be sown outside without cleaning. Cuttings of selected male or female trees can be rooted in late summer.

PROBLEMS: The main problem with mulberries in landscapes is the mess birds make when they eat the fruit and then roost above a patio or car. This is the cost of a tree that attracts so many songbirds, and it is too high a price for some people to pay. In other less fastidious settings, the birds and fruit can be a harmonious amenity.

Some minor leaf mildews (notably *Mycosphaerella mori* and *Phyllactinia guttata*) afflict red mulberry, but they do no serious damage. The tree is little troubled by the notorious twig blight, *Fusarium lateritium*, which causes brooming on white mulberry, and it is seldom attacked by defoliating insects such as gypsy moth (*Lymantria dispar*). Trees in the South can be damaged by the mulberry borer (*Dorcaschema wildii*). But, in general, this tree has fewer problems than its exotic relatives if given a decent site.

CULTIVARS: All mulberry cultivars at nurseries can be traced back to white mulberry. Red mulberry is seldom available, even as seedling stock. You have to really look for it or start it at home from seed or cuttings.

RELATED SPECIES: Of perhaps 10 or 12 mulberry species, only two are native to North America. Besides red mulberry, we can find the smaller but similar Texas mulberry growing in Texas, Arizona and Mexico. Mulberries are also closely related to Osage orange (*Maclura pomifera*) and several tropical food-producing trees such as breadfruit (*Arctocarpus communis*).

COMMENTS: Most people either love or hate mulberries because of the fruit. The early American tree expert D. J. Browne, in his 1846 book on the trees of North America, reported that red mulberry had already been cultivated in Europe for well over a century as a fruit tree and potentially for silkworm food. And in 1839, John Clarke, superintendent of the Morodendron Silk Company of Philadelphia, recorded that red mulberry from Missouri yielded a silk "stronger and finer than that of France," although the silkworms seemed to prefer the smoother leaves of white mulberry. Eventually, the silk industry abandoned the tough red mulberry because of the picky taste preferences of the worms.

The tree had other equally important values to earlier Americans. Its fibrous bast, or inner bark, was woven into blankets by the Choctaw and into ropes to refit the ships of DeSoto in 1540. This makes sense because mulberries are in the same plant family as hemp (*Cannabis sativa*), the preferred natural fiber worldwide for making rope. Mulberries are also closely related to *Broussonetia*, the trees that furnish bast for Polynesian *tapa* cloth, which Samoan people decorate with dyes made from their volcanic soil.

BLACK GUM

Nyssa sylvatica

DESCRIPTION: Architecturally, young black gum has one of the most refined silhouettes of any tree, resembling a fine-textured pin oak (*Quercus palustris*). Its twigs and small limbs beautifully catch the sunlight because of their perfectly horizontal growth and their reflective, pewter-colored bark. They can make the tree glisten, as if it is covered with ice on a sunny winter day.

A young black gum in fall shows its typical pyramidal form.

This species has several close relatives. Each is known respectively within its home range as "tupelo" (pronounced TWO-pillow), a name derived from a Creek Indian word meaning "swamp tree." The species we call black gum, or sour gum (to distinguish it from the unrelated sweet gum, *Liquidambar styraciflua*), is an adaptable tree of both upland and bottomland forests, while the other species and varieties of this genus are limited to wetland habitats.

Black gum can become a large specimen after many years, although storm damage and dying branches can reduce the stature of old trees. The United States national champion black gum is located near Barrackville, West Virginia. When measured in 1991, it stood 132 feet (40 m) tall, and its trunk was nearly 5 feet (1.4 m) in diameter.

LEAVES: The leaves are so smooth, waxy and glossy that they seem to plead "Touch me!" Except on vigorous sprouts, most leaves reach only about 4 inches (10 cm) in length by less than half as wide. They are very dark (as is the alligator-skin bark on old trees), hence the tree's common name. Foliage is arranged in horizontal layers, which reinforces the layered appearance of the branches.

Black gum is famous for the intensity of its crimson fall color, but this varies somewhat from tree to tree and sometimes does not develop fully in warm-climate areas. If you intend to purchase a black gum specifically for its foliage, visit your nursery in the fall and pick out the most brilliant of the bunch.

FLOWERS AND FRUIT: Although we grow black gums and see them every day, we never notice the flowers until honeybees attract our attention to them. If you search, you can find them in tiny axillary clusters as the leaves are expanding to full size. Black gum is most often dioecious, so staminate and pistillate flowers are usually borne on separate trees. The fruits that appear on female trees grow to about the size of navy beans, turn dark blue in the fall and hang in small clusters or pairs. They are a favorite food of many birds, so they don't last long.

SEASONS:

1. Fall (few trees can match the lustrous red color);
2. Summer (for the shiny foliage, which seems immune to the ravages of summer that tatter and tarnish the leaves of many other trees);
3. Winter (for the strong framework, fine texture and silvery bark of young trees).

NATIVE AND ADAPTIVE RANGE: Black gum is similar to red maple (*Acer rubrum*) in that it grows in very wet areas and sometimes on dry, rocky uplands. It ranges from Sarnia and Hamilton in Ontario, across to southern Maine, down through the eastern United States into Florida, west to Texas and sporadically farther south into central and southern Mexico. This immense range, coupled with its fondness for upland as well as lowland sites, makes it one of our most adaptable native trees.

Old black gums outgrow their symmetrical juvenile form and become ruggedly picturesque.

Specimens of local provenance should be used when planting this species. Trees that originate from tropical Mexico are not likely to thrive in the climate and photoperiod of Canada or vice versa. By using locally adapted sources, black gum can be grown in every USDA zone from the northern edges of zone 11 to the warmest parts of zone 3.

CULTURE: Black gum is a slow-grower that does best on moist, acidic soil, but it is adaptable to many different soil types and climate extremes. Once well established, it is resistant to drought and flooding, and the tough wood of healthy young trees remains firm against the forces of wind and ice. The glossy, waxy leaves are resistant to salt spray. This species can usually be propagated from seed sown in the fall. But in the most southern areas where soil temperatures might not become cold enough, the seed should be stratified over winter to break dormancy, then sown the following spring.

Black gum is very difficult to transplant from the

wild or as a field-grown tree. Mechanical transplanting machines that dig a deep, pointed rootball should be used for moving any landscape-sized nursery specimen that has not been undercut or grown in a root-control bag.

Small trees should be grown in containers designed for self-pruning of the root system in order to minimize taproot development and subsequent root girdling. Move black gum in early spring to expedite healing of its sensitive roots.

Top: The glossy summer foliage of a black gum nearly hides the inconspicuous developing fruits. Above: Symmetrical black gum trees tower over hollies and red cedars in a southern fencerow.

PROBLEMS: This tree often does not age gracefully. Some black gums in parts of the Appalachians have recently begun to develop cankers and leaf spotting similar to that found on flowering dogwood (*Cornus florida*) caused by anthracnose (*Discula destructiva*). Sometimes just branches are killed; sometimes it is the entire tree. This decline is evident where dogwood anthracnose damage is most concentrated. There may be a biological connection between the diseases. Black gum and dogwood are so closely related that they formerly were classified in the same plant family.

Our trees are occasionally attacked by leaf-eating caterpillars, such as the forest tent caterpillar (*Malacosoma disstria*). The tupelo leaf miner (*Antispila nyssaefoliella*), a shield-bearing insect, can cut disfiguring holes in the leaves.

The primary problem with this otherwise carefree tree, however, is how difficult it is to transplant. But this can be solved by using the same techniques employed for moving other taprooted species. The job may be challenging, but black gum is worth the effort.

CULTIVARS: There are no cultivars readily available for this species nor for any other members of the genus. 'Sheffield Park' was selected from a tree planted in England and might become available here. Provenance is very important and should be considered before purchasing a black gum tree.

RELATED SPECIES: Swamp tupelo, a narrow-leaved form restricted to swampy areas in the South, is listed as *Nyssa biflora* by some authorities but considered a variety of black gum by most. Another shrubby, suckering relative, Ogeechee tupelo (*Nyssa ogeche*), is confined to swamps in the coastal plains of Georgia and adjacent South Carolina and Florida. The biggest one known, in Columbia County, Florida, is more than 5 feet (1.6 m) in diameter, but its tapering trunk ascends only a few feet before dividing into many small limbs. This species' chief value is its larger, edible fruit, used locally as a substitute for limes. It develops a more uniform, round-headed appearance under cultivation than it does in the wild, looking much like an orchard tree, and some specimens have good red fall color.

The other major North American member of the genus is the water tupelo or cotton gum (*Nyssa aquatica*). This species ranks with bald cypress (*Taxodium distichum*) as the most flood-tolerant large tree in

Water tupelo, shown at sunrise, is an aquatic relative of black gum.

temperate North America. It moves air to its flooded roots through numerous pores that make the wood so light that it is used by fishermen for floats. Once established (often from a seedling on a mud flat or floating log), it can grow with its base continuously submerged, but it will also do fine on a moist upland site if planted. Its fruits will drift on the water until they hit a log or mud flat where the seed can then germinate.

Water tupelo is a coarse tree with larger leaves and fruit than black gum, and it develops a more irregular form. It is even less tolerant of shade and turns yellow in the fall instead of red. This species becomes huge. The record tree in Southampton County, Virginia, is 105 feet (32 m) tall with a trunk 9 feet (2.8 m) in diameter above the basal buttress. It is hardy on well-drained sites (where winter ice cannot girdle it as it could in a frozen swamp) north to USDA zone 5. Two other species of *Nyssa* also occur in Asia, and the dogwoods (*Cornus* spp.) are distant relatives.

COMMENTS: The tupelo genus collectively contains some of our best trees for honey nectar. Tupelo honey is sold by apiarists throughout the South. Fire-damaged water tupelo typically decays from the inside out. Hollow tupelo logs were used for drainage culverts during logging operations years ago.

The common names of the various tupelo species are used interchangeably in their home regions, so it pays to know the botanical name of the tree you wish to buy from your local nursery. Make sure that the nursery knows the difference too.

Black gum is the food plant of the Hebrew moth, a handsome black and white moth of the noctuid family. This interesting family of moths has developed the special ability to detect the sonar of predatory bats and then take evasive action.

IRONWOOD

Ostrya virginiana

DESCRIPTION: In many respects, ironwood is the upland analog of hornbeam (*Carpinus caroliniana*). It is often called hop-hornbeam, just as the true hornbeam is frequently labeled ironwood. Both trees have some of the hardest wood in the specialty lumber business. In fact, they have so much in common that it is easier to review their few differences than their similarities.

Ironwood is a small understory tree of well-drained deciduous forests. It loves hilly ground but cannot survive flooding and is typically found up the slope from the valley floors occupied by hornbeam. Its reddish bark will shred from large stems and limbs, most unlike the smooth gray bark of hornbeam, but young trees about broom handle-size have smooth bark and, in all seasons, look remarkably like sweet birch (*Betula lenta*) saplings. It also grows a little more erect than hornbeam, with a strong central leader (although old open-grown trees spread broadly), and it usually becomes slightly larger. The United States national champion, near Grand Traverse, Michigan, is 74 feet (22 m) tall and has a trunk 3 feet (1m) in diameter.

The hop-like fruits of ironwood are hidden among its leaves.

LEAVES: Ironwood leaves are oval-pointed, paper-thin, and feel like felt to the touch. They are not uniform in size: those on the ends of shaded lower branches can reach 6 inches (15 cm) in length, while those farther back on the twigs or higher in the crown remain much smaller. Like those of the hornbeam, they sometimes emerge with an ephemeral red tint. The mild yellow fall color of this species is enhanced by its contrast to the dark bark.

FLOWERS AND FRUIT: The flowers are not conspicuous in the spring when the leaves are unfolding, but the unopened catkins are visible in the winter and add even more interest to this fine-textured tree. The fruit strobiles that develop in summer are visually effective into fall—they reach about 2 inches (6 cm) long and resemble those of hops (*Humulus* spp.). They are pale green tightly bunched clusters of inflated papery capsules, each of which encloses a small nut. Ground-dwelling forest birds, such as grouse and turkey, feed on the nuts as they fall.

SEASONS:

1. Fall (for the fruits and dependable yellow color);
2. All year (for its fine-textured appearance).

NATIVE AND ADAPTIVE RANGE: The immense natural range of ironwood is nearly identical to that of hornbeam. It extends even farther to the northeast (Chaluer Bay in New Brunswick) and northwest (Winnipeg, Manitoba) and is absent only from the southern Atlantic coastal plain in the eastern United States. Like hornbeam, it grows in Mexico and Central America. Trees of locally adapted provenance can be grown north through USDA zone 3.

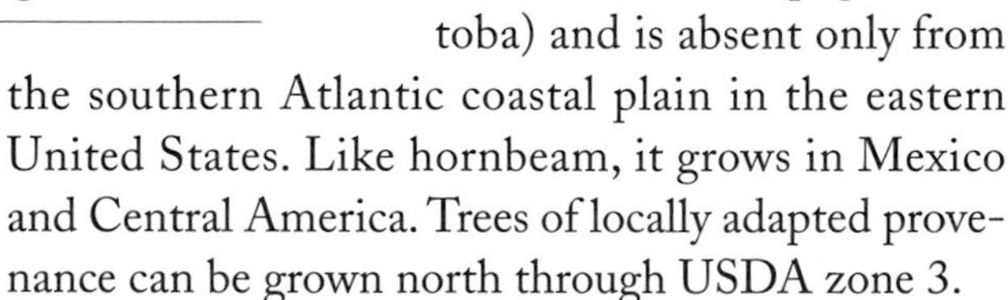

CULTURE: This is one species that really does thrive on neglect. It is not sensitive to drought (but will not tolerate flooding), and it seems impervious to most of the tree-testing forces of nature: soil and temperature variations, insects, diseases, wind and ice. It does well in full sun, where it becomes broader than it is tall, or in shade, where it retains its juvenile pyramidal form. It can be tricky to transplant, but we have moved young ironwood trees up to 10 feet (3 m) tall in the spring, even bare-root (not recommended), with success. The seeds have a physiological dormancy that delays germination. They are best planted outdoors in early fall or treated with a moist warm-then-cold stratification sequence.

PROBLEMS: Ironwood's primary limitations are slow growth and difficulty to transplant. Both can be largely overcome with the appropriate horticultural techniques. The tree responds well to a combination of mulch, moderate irrigation, fertilizer and increased sunlight, and it will grow reasonably fast under ideal conditions once it is well established. Its deep taproot can be undercut in the nursery to produce a root structure more amenable to future relocation, or it can be grown in containers or root-control bags.

This species is notoriously sensitive to salt, whether from ocean spray or from salted roads in winter. It is one of the first trees in any woods to be defoliated by the gypsy moth (*Lymantria dispar*), but it is not insect-prone in general. If you are extracting the seeds from the fruit by hand, consider wearing rubber gloves. The fruit clusters look harmless, but they can cause itchy fingers.

Above: In full sun, ironwood becomes more broad than tall. Below left: With age, the bark of ironwood shreds from large stems and limbs.

CULTIVARS: No ironwood selections have been marketed. Presumably, the tree's overall quality but absence of spectacular ornamental features have left superior individuals largely unnoticed. The challenges of transplanting and propagation might discourage researchers from tinkering with it and nurseries from growing it.

RELATED SPECIES: There are several *Ostrya* species native to various parts of the Americas, Europe and Asia, and their differences are subtle at best. *Ostrya knowltonii*, the Knowlton ironwood, is a smaller species with a very restricted natural range in canyons of the southwestern United States, and *Ostrya chisosensis* is a rare shrubby tree known only from the botanically rich Chisos Mountains of western Texas. Ironwood is a member of the birch family and closely related to hornbeam.

COMMENTS: While this tree can be frustrating to grow from seed, difficult to transplant and unavailable from many nurseries, we frequently find it growing wild in the understory of undeveloped wooded lots. Instead of bulldozing every small tree (a process that is likely to kill some of the large ones as well), landowners should consider understory species like ironwood a gift from nature and appreciate them wherever possible.

One of the great temptations in landscape design is to overuse ornate focus-species that, planted in imprudent combination, can create a discordant disaster. A purple-leaved something here, a yellow-leaved something there, a weeping or contorted something in the corner and a gaudy yard ornament in the middle—suddenly we have a visually cluttered landscape. Every work of art needs a focus and a harmonious setting. The trouble-free ironwood provides such a graceful background.

SOURWOOD

Oxydendrum arboreum

DESCRIPTION: This is a medium-sized tree of outstanding ornamental value in every season. It can be found in the forest understory or along roadsides and in clearings, and within its natural range, it adapts to a wide variety of habitat types. We most often see sourwood as a neighbor of oaks (*Quercus* spp.) on some of the better soils just uphill from wet bottomlands. It does not compete as well on the poor, disturbed soils inhabited by opportunistic successional trees, such as persimmon (*Diospyros virginiana*) and sumac (*Rhus* spp.), where grazing and cropping have depleted the land.

Open-grown sourwood trees are pyramidal and frequently branched to the ground, while those in forests can become surprisingly tall and develop straight, limbless trunks. They thrive along road cuts that are protected from the hot afternoon sun, where they defy slash-and-burn road maintenance crews and sprout vigorously from the cut stumps. Some of these sprout-formed trees are the most colorful of all in the fall.

Sourwood, shown in summer bloom, is an outstanding ornamental in every season.

We have seen sourwoods along the Roanoke River in Virginia that formed part of the forest canopy and were as tall as the adjacent oaks. The largest known specimen in North America is located in Robbinsville, North Carolina. Obviously a forest-grown tree, it is 118 feet (36 m) tall and has a trunk 2 feet (60 cm) in diameter. We once saw a planted specimen near the city center of Hamilton, New Zealand, that was even larger. Halfway around the world from its native range, this great, spreading tree resembled an oak; only close inspection revealed its identity.

LEAVES: The silky-smooth deciduous leaves resemble the leaves of black cherry (*Prunus serotina*) and attain an average length of 5 inches (12 cm). Thirsty hikers in the Appalachians seek the twigs and leaves of this tree for a chew or to make brew, just as those in the Midwest seek sassafras (*Sassafras albidum*). Sourwood twigs in sunny areas are reddish, but on shaded branches, they so closely match the rich green color of the summer leaves that they appear to be part of a compound leaf structure. They are not, however. In early fall, the brilliant crimson or purple-red leaves stand apart from everything else in the woods.

No other tree colors up earlier in the forests of the South. Tourists along the Blue Ridge Parkway in early October fall in love with this species, and many try (unsuccessfully) to take starts of it back home to the North and Midwest. This tree makes a great fall color combination when planted next to black gum (*Nyssa sylvatica*).

FLOWERS AND FRUIT: Turn a lily-of-the-valley plant upside down, hang it with hundreds more blossoms from the end of every twig in early summer and you will have the look of a sourwood tree in full bloom. The drooping panicles of white bells of this tree seen against the pea-green foliage is one of nature's finest floral displays. The flowers are very attractive to honeybees, and sourwood honey is considered a delicacy.

The clusters of upturned pale yellow fruit capsules that follow, highlighted against the spectacular color of the foliage, are nearly as impressive. They darken and cling through the winter, long after the tenacious red leaves have fallen.

SEASONS:

1. Late spring to early summer (for the blooming pe-

Waxy white flowers drape from the ends of sourwood twigs in summer.

riod, which reaches its peak after most spring-flowering trees have faded);

2. Fall (for the long-lasting color display);

3. Winter (the persistent fruits emphasize the picturesque winter outline of the branches).

NATIVE AND ADAPTIVE RANGE: Sourwood is primarily a tree of the hill country, ranging from southern Pennsylvania and Ohio south to the Gulf Coast, west to the Mississippi Valley and east to the Atlantic Coast along streams and bluffs. Scattered populations can be found in southern Indiana and west to eastern Texas. Some authorities list it hardy north to USDA zone 4, but we have found it to be marginal even in zone 5.

CULTURE: Sourwood is in the heath family. Like some of its relatives, which include rhododendrons (*Rhododendron* spp.) and mountain laurel (*Kalmia latifolia*), this plant needs good drainage, acidic soil and protection from climatic extremes. Either full sun or partial shade will do, and fairly dry soils are no problem. It is a difficult tree to transplant, so move it as a small container plant in the spring. The minute seeds are also tough to manage. They should be sown under mist on the surface of a finely sifted seedbed.

PROBLEMS: Sourwood is slow-growing and sensitive to air pollution, poor drainage, root disturbance and soil compaction. It often does poorly on exposed sites beyond its natural range, and it needs a gritty, woodsy soil and a gardener's skillful attention. It is generally free from insects and diseases if its site requirements are met.

CULTIVARS: Surprisingly, no cultivars of this outstandingly ornamental tree are available, possibly because of difficulties in its propagation and culture. These same difficulties have kept it out of many landscapes in the South, where it is best adapted. Container-grown sourwood trees and small field-dug plants are available from some nurseries that specialize in native trees, but there never seem to be enough to meet the demand. Researchers are refining laboratory methods for micropropagation from shoot tips, so we expect to see some sourwood cultivars in the future.

RELATED SPECIES: *Oxydendrum* is a monotypic genus. However, this tree does have many ericaceous, or heath family, cousins, including blueberries (*Vaccinium* spp.) and rhododendrons.

COMMENTS: Few trees, native or not, can match the sourwood's combination of early and intense fall color, extravagant blossoms that are followed by equally showy bracts and seedpods and shiny, deep green summer foliage. This is one of our premier landscape plants where it is native and well adapted, and it deserves all the praise it receives from those who know it well.

The foliage of sourwood turns brilliant red in fall.

Many of our native trees are species endemic to North America and occur nowhere else in the world except where planted as specimens. Generally, however, they have close relatives in Asia or Europe. The sourwood joins *Maclura* and *Robinia* as one of our few endemic genera of native trees. There is only one species of sourwood, and it can be found growing wild only in the eastern United States.

WHITE SPRUCE

Picea glauca

DESCRIPTION: Three closely related and similar species of spruce are native to eastern North America, all with colorful names: red spruce (*Picea rubens*), black spruce (*Picea mariana*) and white spruce (*Picea glauca*). They are among our most cold-hardy trees and are extremely valuable as nesting sites for birds. Under favorable conditions, they develop symmetrical, pointed crowns and are dense and full to the ground, like the more commonly cultivated exotic species. Spruces basically are Canadian trees: white spruce is the official arboreal emblem of Manitoba, red spruce is that of Nova Scotia and black spruce is that of Newfoundland.

The typical eastern form of white spruce is the fastest growing of the lot, though it is not as fast as some less hardy exotic species. It is the dominant forest-canopy tree over much of its natural range, which extends to the north of the most populous regions of Canada. Even under such extreme climatic conditions, white spruce frequently exceeds 100 feet (30 m) in height. The largest known specimen in the United States is near the Canadian border, in Koochiching County, Minnesota. It stands 128 feet (39 m) tall and has a long, straight trunk over 3 feet (1 m) in diameter.

Symmetrical and stately, white spruce is the arboreal emblem of Manitoba.

Black spruce is typically a long-lived tree of infertile, acidic northern bogs, where it grows extremely slowly to about half the size of white spruce. Under cultivation on better soils, its growth rate approaches that of some of the slower, western forms of white spruce. It develops a narrow, irregular crown with a dense top.

Red spruce is a more broadly pyramidal tree of the eastern mountains that reaches its most impressive dimensions near the southern end of its natural range, in the Great Smoky Mountains. It is very long-lived, but it grows nearly as slowly as black spruce. The largest, in Great Smoky Mountains National Park, is about the same height as the record white spruce but half again as large in diameter.

LEAVES: Our spruces all have pointed, evergreen needles that are square in cross section and less than 1 inch (2.5 cm) long. The malodorous needles of white spruce have a waxy coating, which gives the tree a frosted appearance. Black spruce needles are shorter, darker colored and tightly packed on the dense, dark twigs of old trees. This makes a mature grove of black spruce look almost black when seen against winter snow. Red spruce needles are more yellow-green, and the twigs and buds are reddish.

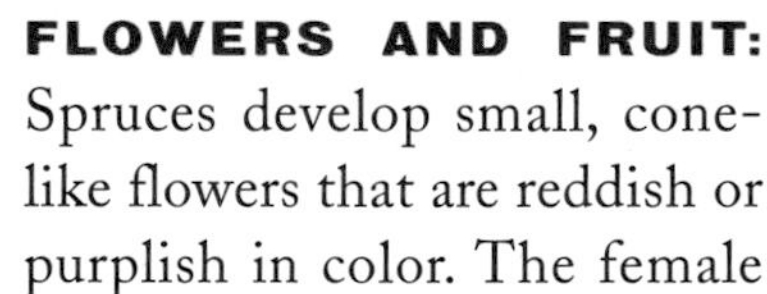

FLOWERS AND FRUIT: Spruces develop small, cone-like flowers that are reddish or purplish in color. The female flowers grow into papery, woody cone fruits that range from less than 1 inch (2 cm) long on black spruce to 2 inches (5 cm) long on white spruce, with those of red spruce in between. Neither the flowers nor the cones are particularly noticeable.

SEASONS:

1. Winter (for the fine-textured evergreen foliage and conical form);
2. Fall (the dark needles contrast beautifully with the colored foliage of deciduous trees);
3. Spring and summer (as a dark, pyramidal visual accent).

NATIVE AND ADAPTIVE RANGE: White spruce and black spruce share nearly identical territories, which extend to the northern limits of tree

White spruce needles are square in cross section and have a waxy coating, which gives the tree a frosted appearance.

growth in Canada and Alaska. They descend southward into the contiguous United States only in the Great Lakes region and northern New England and (for white spruce varieties) to a limited extent in the northern Rocky Mountains in Montana and the Black Hills of South Dakota and Wyoming. Red spruce is the predominant spruce of Nova Scotia, New Brunswick, southern Quebec and New England. It follows the mountainous subalpine zones southward into North Carolina and Tennessee.

All three species can be cultivated from the northern limits of tree growth in USDA zone 2 south into USDA zone 6. Summer heat and drought, rather than deep cold, are their limiting climatic factors.

CULTURE: White spruce, unlike the others, is somewhat drought-resistant and can be grown on almost any reasonable planting site. All three species tolerate wind, cold, sun and shade. White spruce is one of the toughest conifers—most unusual for a spruce—and it does well even in windbreak plantings on the Great Plains. There are several geographic races or varieties, and the western ones are better adapted to western and southern climates than the typical form of the Northeast. All varieties tolerate a wide variety of soil types.

Black spruce will perform satisfactorily under mesic conditions, but it is not genetically equipped to handle heat and drought. Red spruce does not do well beyond its natural mountain habitats unless its requirements can be closely replicated. Of the three species, white spruce is by far the most amenable to landscape use over most of our area.

Our native spruces are resistant to damage from snow loads and other winter hazards. They are all easy to transplant with a soil ball in fall or spring, and the seeds germinate so readily that they are often used in sampler packets to encourage young children to plant trees.

PROBLEMS: Spruces are frequently damaged or killed by salt spray, root rots, air pollution, insects and fire, and their wood decays rapidly after an injury. Watch for several major insect and mite pests, especially the spruce budworm (*Choristoneura fumiferana*), the European spruce sawfly (*Diprion hercyniae*), various gall adelgids (*Adelges lariciatus*, *Adelges abietis* and *Adelges laricis*), spider mites (*Oligonychus ununguis*) and bagworms (*Thyridopteryx ephemeraeformis*). Also, birds like to perch on the growing tips of spruces and break off the succulent new leaders. This can deform a tree, giving it a flat-topped shape.

CULTIVARS: There are several varieties and many cultivars of white spruce. The Black Hills spruce (*Picea glauca* var. *densata*) is a tough, drought-resistant, slow-growing tree that survives on difficult sites and develops a very dense crown. It has been designated the state tree of South Dakota and is a popular landscape selection.

Red spruce follows the high country of the Appalachians far to the south of our other spruces.

We have observed picturesque natural bonsai specimens of the western variety, Alberta spruce (*Picea glauca* var. *albertiana*), growing extremely slowly at the edge of the harsh tundra in Alaska. It has a dwarf form, 'Conica', which is often seen in rock gardens and dwarf conifer collections and has given rise through mutations to several other dwarf selections. 'Sander's Blue' has slate-blue needles. A few weeping and variegated selections are also known.

Sunlight dapples the open understory in the shade of a red spruce forest in Maine.

Most cultivars of black spruce are dwarf forms that emphasize, to an extreme, the naturally slow and compact growth of this species. Black spruce also has some variegated, weeping and prostrate selections. They are available only at nurseries that specialize in unusual conifers. Red spruce has a dwarf form, 'Nana', and a misshapen, unbranched mutant, 'Virgata', which are found only at botanic gardens.

RELATED SPECIES: Several spruces are major components of the forests of western North America. They include the ubiquitous Engelmann spruce (*Picea engelmannii*) of the Rocky Mountains, which is sometimes cultivated in the East, the less common but more frequently cultivated Colorado spruce (*Picea pungens*) and the giant Sitka spruce (*Picea sitchensis*) of the Pacific Coast. About 50 other spruce species grow in various regions throughout the northern hemisphere.

Our native spruces are known to hybridize with one another and with other exotic spruce species. The variety Alberta spruce, at least in part, might be a stabilized cross of white spruce with Engelmann spruce. There is no sharp distinction between the two species, and they blend completely where their ranges overlap. Engelmann spruce, in turn, crosses with Colorado spruce in the Rocky Mountains. Red spruce and black spruce hybrids can be found in the wild as well, where they grow together in eastern Canada.

COMMENTS: Although white spruce is a resilient tree, high-elevation forests of red spruce are following the ominous pattern of *Waldsterben* (forest death), which has caused so much concern in Europe. Red spruce is dying over much of its subalpine southern range, probably because of a tragic combination of human-generated acidic precipitation, human-caused climatic warming and human-introduced exotic insects. Along with the associated Fraser fir (*Abies fraseri*), it is becoming the arboricultural poster-child for conservation groups concerned with reversing the environmental degradation of our planet.

A century ago, red spruce was more endangered by logging than pollution and was the subject of a study conducted by a bright young forester in the undeveloped wilds of the western Adirondacks, at Nehasne Lake. The forester sampled the biology of a 40,000-acre (16,000 hectares) private timber holding and made recommendations for the sustained yield of the red spruce. He published the results of his work in an unassuming little book, *The Adirondack Spruce*, in 1898.

Today, the book is an obscure volume of interest largely to collectors. The bright young forester is remembered more for other accomplishments: as the founder of modern forestry in North America and as the first chief of the United States Forest Service, created by President Theodore Roosevelt. The forester's name was Gifford Pinchot.

PINCKNEYA

Pinckneya bracteata (P. pubens)

DESCRIPTION: When in full color, a pinckneya tree can cause traffic jams. No gardener can see one without burning to know its name. A few years ago, we planted two small container-grown pinckneyas at the Wilsons' Savory Farm in South Carolina, and throughout the month of June, they reward us with pink flower clusters about 5 inches (12 cm) across. They provide an astonishing color display, even while very young. Pinckneyas are stiff little trees that look like overgrown house plants—sparsely clothed with rather large, coarse leaves concentrated at the ends of the branches. Often the tree occurs as a cluster of upright stems that sprout from the base.

A pinckneya tree in peak bloom.

The largest pinckneyas we have seen were planted at Callaway Gardens in Pine Mountain, Georgia, more than 20 years ago. The trees quickly reached at least 20 feet (6 m) in height. Knowing their need for moist soil, Fred Galle (then Director of Horticulture) planted the trees near the bases of the earthen dams that retain Callaway's artificial lakes. An even taller specimen is reported in Orange Springs, Florida. It stands 32 feet (10 m) tall but has a slender trunk only 3 inches (8 cm) in diameter.

LEAVES: Pinckneya leaves are wide, thick, soft, pointed at both ends and about 5 inches (12 cm) long. They have wrinkled surfaces and are rough to the touch. The foliage may turn yellow for a few days before dropping in the autumn, but the tree usually shows little or no fall color.

FLOWERS AND FRUIT: The greenish white flower petals are small and inconspicuous but are surrounded by prominent, irregular sepals, which appear rather tousled. These sepals are the most noticeable part of the calyx and vary from creamy white through pink and rose to red, which creates a poinsettia-like effect. They are borne in late spring on new growth at the tips of the plump, furry twigs. The clustered, round pale yellow fruit capsules that appear later are about 1 inch (2-3 cm) across and seamed at the center. They turn reddish brown as they split in half to release the flat seeds.

SEASONS:

1. Late spring (or early summer north of its natural range) when the large flower clusters appear.

NATIVE AND ADAPTIVE RANGE: Pinckneya is a tree of the coastal plains of Georgia, northern Florida and extreme southern South Carolina, and it is limited to sunny wetland areas. Under cultivation in protected sites, it can be grown well into USDA zone 7.

CULTURE: In the wild, this species grows in the light shade of scattered pine trees in wet acidic soil along the margins of sloughs, bays, swamps and streams, where it forms thickets by sprouting from lateral roots. Under cultivation, it responds well to rich, loose, moist, fertile soil. Like many other wetland trees, it grows in wet areas not because it requires such conditions but because wet soil minimizes competition from upland trees.

Under cultivation, well-drained soils will minimize the tendency of this tree to sucker and will slow its growth rate. Without adequate irrigation, though, the leaves will respond to drought by bleaching or dropping. A consistently moist soil can be maintained by mulching heavily and watering every week during dry spells. Drip irrigation is ideal for watering wetland trees such as pinckneya. A little afternoon shade is beneficial, and winter protection is vital in areas north of pinckneya's natural range.

Propagation by seed is simple. Gather the capsules after the leaves have fallen, allow them to dry until they begin to split open, and plant the seed in rich soil in the fall. Seedlings will emerge with warm weather the following spring. Softwood cuttings (taken after flowering from twigs that grow from leaf axils below the inflorescence) will root easily. Propagate this tree frequently, and keep a few replacement plants coming along. It is quick to develop into a beautiful specimen but is frequently short-lived under cultivation, and once you have grown accustomed to pinckneya, you won't want to go through a single summer without its color.

PROBLEMS: On old cotton land, pinckneya trees may succumb to root diseases. If your tree dies, plant the next one in a different spot and modify heavy soil with peat moss and pulverized pine bark. Pinckneya may become stressed under drought conditions, and it is intolerant of both deep shade and dry sunny exposures. This is a short-lived tree for warm climates only, and it is not adaptable (except as a greenhouse plant) to northeastern North America, where winters are cold.

Few nurseries, except those that specialize in southern native species, carry pinckneya, probably because it doesn't become showy until several years after propagation and because its color develops in early summer—the off-season for nursery sales in the hot climates where pinckneya grows best.

CULTIVARS: Some nurseries are selecting informally for plants with red sepals, but pink forms seem at least as attractive and useful in the landscape. We are unaware of any named selections, but with the growing interest in pinckneyas, the variable flower color and the ease of propagation of selected forms from cuttings, improved cultivars should be expected in the future.

RELATED SPECIES: Pinckneya is the only species in its genus. Most of its woody relatives are tropical plants, with the unique exception of buttonbush (*Cephalanthus occidentalis*), which is hardy north into central Canada.

COMMENTS: Pinckneya received its other common name, Georgia fever-bark, from the use of its bark to treat malaria. It is a close relative of the cinchona tree (*Cinchona ledgeriana*) of South America, the original source of quinine. In colonial times, malaria affected many people in the southern coastal plains where pinckneya grew, particularly where rice was cultivated in impounded water.

The flowers of pinckneya provide an astonishing color display.

JACK PINE

Pinus banksiana

DESCRIPTION: Several small- to medium-sized, short-needled pine species thrive on difficult growing sites. All these species are similar, and most are very closely related. In eastern North America, jack pine and its southern highland counterpart Virginia pine (*Pinus virginiana*) are the most common. They are in the "hard pine" subgenus (*Pinus*, also known as *Diploxylon*), which includes most of our eastern pines.

Jack pine forms a ragged crown of long, uneven branches. It is a short-lived but tough little tree that colonizes dry, sandy areas after forest fires. It seeds by the thousands and often grows in dense, pure stands. The branches of most other pines grow in whorls at annual nodes. However, jack pine develops internodal branches because of a phenomenon called "lammas growth," which means that some of the next year's growth buds open and develop during the current season. The age of a young jack pine tree is thus difficult to estimate by counting whorls of limbs.

Jack pine develops an irregular crown even while still young; it lacks the whorled appearance of most other pines.

On good sites, and with protection from competition and from the frequent fires common in jack-pine habitat, this species can grow reasonably large. Bigger specimens surely exist in Canada, but the record tree in the United States, in the Upper Peninsula of Michigan, is 84 feet (26 m) tall and has a trunk 29 inches (75 cm) in diameter. This species is not only one of our fastest growing pines but also one of the fastest growing of all conifers in its sapling stage.

LEAVES: The curled, flat, dark yellow-green needles of jack pine grow in pairs from the rough, scaly twigs. They mature at less than 2 inches (4 cm) in length and are pointed but not prickly. The foliage is evergreen and persists for three to four years.

FLOWERS AND FRUIT: Staminate and pistillate strobiles, or flower clusters, occur separately on the same tree. Bumping into a jack pine (or any pine) at the peak of pollen release will leave you coated with pollen and will set more drifting off in a dense cloud. Pines are wind-pollinated species, so copious amounts are needed to ensure that some grains land in the right place.

The crooked pinecones do not have long-lasting, sharp spines like those of many of the hard pines. However, each scale, like those on all hard pinecones, has a dorsal umbo, which for a time tightly seals the surface like a series of interlocking armor plates. The scales give the cones a pineapple-like appearance instead of the shingle overlap seen on soft pines or spruce (*Picea* spp.). The cones grow to about 2 inches (5 cm) in length and persist indefinitely, sometimes becoming ingrown and enclosed by wood as the branch thickens.

This species has what are called serotinous cones that often remain closed (but viable) for decades unless loosened by the heat of a forest fire. Then they may release many years' worth of seeds to be scattered by the wind across the ash-covered forest floor. Trees from the southern part of the natural range usually open at least some cones each year, with or without the stimulation of fire.

SEASONS:

1. Winter (any evergreen tree with a little dusting of snow is most appreciated during bright days; jack pine also makes a great windbreak);

The attractive staminate strobiles of jack pine are loaded with bright yellow pollen.

Jack pine cones are smooth, crooked, and serotinous; they can take many years to open unless stimulated by fire.

2. Spring and summer (its critical importance is as nesting habitat for many birds, including, in the Pine Barrens of Michigan, the globally endangered ground-nesting Kirtland's warbler, *Dendroica kirtlandii*).

NATIVE AND ADAPTIVE RANGE: Jack pine is our northernmost pine species. Its range reaches nearly to the Arctic Circle in northwestern Canada and extends eastward across the continent only as far south as the Gulf of St. Lawrence, except for spotty distribution in New Brunswick and New England. It also follows the western Great Lakes to the southwest and occurs across the northern portions of the Great Lake states.

Winter hardiness is obviously not of concern for jack pine because it grows naturally as far north as USDA zone 1. Surprisingly, however, it seems to do nicely when planted at least as far south as USDA zone 6. This overlaps the northernmost growing region of the very similar Virginia pine and extends the combined ranges of these species to the highlands of central Alabama. From there, other short-needled hard pines, all closely related and very similar, continue south into Florida and west to the Pacific Coast.

CULTURE: Jack pine and its relatives will grow well on many different soils and in many climate zones. It must be given good drainage, full sun and, preferably, acidic soil. It is simple to transplant with a soil ball in either spring or fall. Ripe cones may be soaked in hot water overnight then left on a sunny windowsill to open. The seeds can then be shaken out. They require no stratification and may begin to germinate within a week of sowing.

PROBLEMS: Three physiological stresses cause more problems for cultivated jack pines than any insect or disease: shade, heat and wet feet. In natural stands, fire is responsible for the death of many trees, but it creates the conditions that ensure reproduction and survival of the species.

CULTIVARS: A few prostrate and weeping forms are grown in botanic gardens. For gardeners in most of the eastern part of North America, trees of southern provenance (such as the Great Lake states) should perform best.

RELATED SPECIES: Virginia pine is the southeastern mountain and Piedmont look-alike of jack pine. It has spiny cones, can grow a little larger than jack pine and has slightly longer, twisted needles. It shares jack pine's enthusiasm for eroded, burned, inhospitable terrain. Virginia pines from the northern edge of their natural range (Pennsylvania and southern Indiana) perform as well as jack pines at Starhill Forest in USDA zone 5 in Illinois. Virginia pines also thrive in a large wild patch at the Wilsons' Savory Farm in western South Carolina. The famous Hennepin Virginia Pines outline a block in the town of Hennepin, in northern Illinois, surrounding the site of the town's first schoolhouse. Planted in 1857, these trees remain in good condition, despite the fact that they are growing far northwest of their native habitat.

Table mountain pine (*Pinus pungens*) is a stiff cousin of Virginia pine that grows in scattered locations in the Blue Ridge Mountains and has done well at our Illinois arboretum. It has sharp needles, attractive purple staminate strobiles and large cones covered with fierce claws. This is a picturesque evergreen when seen along the borders of steep mountain roads in winter.

In the low country of the South, Virginia pine and table mountain pine give way to spruce pine (*Pinus glabra*). We have seen beautiful old specimens of this short-needled pine growing at the north end of its natural range in the Francis Biedler Wildlife Sanctuary in South Carolina. It grows somewhat larger than Virginia pine and tolerates light shade and wet soil better than most pines. Farther south, sand pine (*Pinus clausa*) is the equivalent of jack pine in the sandy barrens of Florida.

Westward, jack pine merges into lodgepole pine (*Pinus contorta*), which itself is divided into several varieties or subspecies. Lodgepole pine has prickly cones like Virginia pine, but it is otherwise barely distinguishable from jack pine. The Rocky Mountain type (*Pinus contorta* var. *latifolia*) is a tall, slender tree with a life-from-death cycle, like jack pine, which means it frequently falls victim to forest fire and then freely germinates after the blaze. It was used by western Native Americans for poles to support their lodges. It can be grown in the East, but we have found that it grows more slowly in Illinois than jack pine or Virginia pine.

Additional pine species, more distinct from jack pine, are treated separately.

COMMENTS: Jack pine is viewed with disdain by many self-proclaimed tree-lovers as a scrubby runt that occupies space where more stately species ought to grow. Over much of its territory, however, the jack pine exists simply because other trees cannot survive the winter cold, sterile sand and relentless wind that seek to convert the forest, such as it is, to tundra. Its tenacity is so appreciated that jack pine has been designated the official territorial tree of the Northwest Territories of Canada; likewise, its cousin the lodgepole pine is the provincial tree of Alberta.

A thoughtfully tended jack pine, planted in a friendlier environment, can rise to an aesthetic standard that might surprise some folks who have seen it only as a weather-beaten survivor of some of the most inhospitable conditions in North America.

Jack pine sheds snow and resists wind damage.
It can grow farther north than any other pine.

SHORTLEAF PINE

Pinus echinata

DESCRIPTION: The several members of a group of large, valuable timber trees of the southeastern United States are known collectively as southern pine to many people. These trees, perhaps more than any others, are the ubiquitous symbols of the South. Pollen research indicates that they have been a dominant forest type there for at least 5,000 years. Of the group, the hardiest and most adaptable species is shortleaf pine. It is the most widespread pine in the eastern United States and has been designated the state tree of North Carolina and Arkansas.

Shortleaf pine is typically an upland tree, but it grows just as well in sandy, well-drained stream valleys. It flourishes on farmed-out fields and acidic, infertile ridgetops where competition from other, faster-growing pines and from hardwood trees is minimal. While sometimes not as large as other southern pines on more productive sites, it definitely is a forest-canopy species. The largest shortleaf pine is located in a rural yard in Myrtle, Mississippi. It is 138 feet (42 m) tall and has a trunk 3½ feet (1.1 m) in diameter. Even larger specimens grew in the Ozarks until about a century ago, when voracious logging operations decimated the virgin pines in less than three decades.

The classic form of shortleaf pine stands out in a grove mixed with sweet gum.

LEAVES: The common name of this tree is misleading, for the leaves are short only in comparison to other southern pines. The evergreen needles are borne in fascicles, or bundles. On the same tree, indeed on the same branch, some fascicles may have two needles and others three. They are dark yellow-green and flexible, reach 5 inches (12 cm) in length and persist for several years in mild-winter areas.

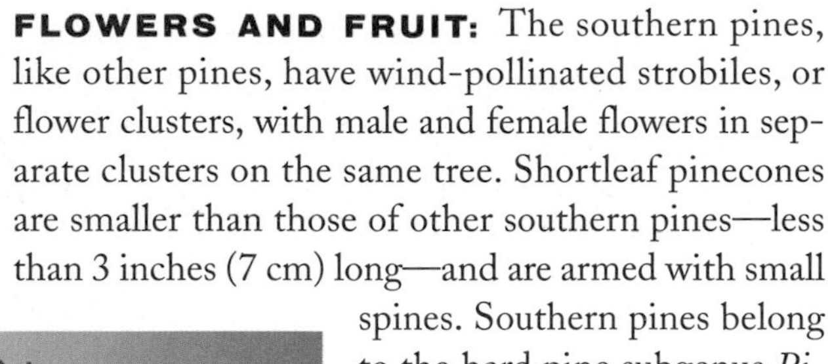

FLOWERS AND FRUIT: The southern pines, like other pines, have wind-pollinated strobiles, or flower clusters, with male and female flowers in separate clusters on the same tree. Shortleaf pinecones are smaller than those of other southern pines—less than 3 inches (7 cm) long—and are armed with small spines. Southern pines belong to the hard pine subgenus *Pinus* (called *Diploxylon* in some references), so their cone scales each have a dorsal umbo (like those of jack pine, *Pinus banksiana*) rather than the shingled scales of white pine (*Pinus strobus*).

SEASONS:

1. Fall (when interspersed with xeric hardwoods on rocky hillsides and bluffs, the green of this tree accents the colors of other species);
2. Winter (the hardiest southern pine, it is planted in areas where the others cannot grow; it occasionally suffers foliage discoloration in severe winters but survives nonetheless).

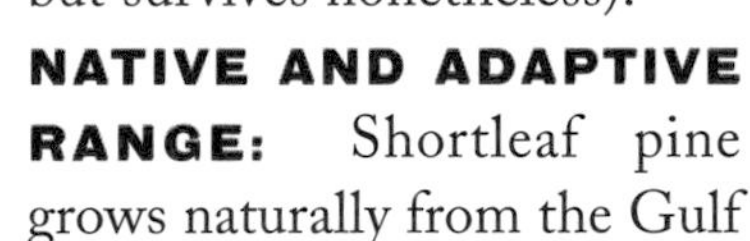

NATIVE AND ADAPTIVE RANGE: Shortleaf pine grows naturally from the Gulf coastal plain northwest through the Ozark Plateau into southern Illinois, northeast along the Cumberland Plateau to southern Ohio and east to the Pine Barrens of New Jersey and to Long Island Sound. Although it is generally not as prevalent or vigorous as other southern pines in mild-climate areas of the Southeast, it is the predominant pine of the Ozark Plateau and Ouachita Highlands west of the Mississippi River, where it grows best. It can be easily cultivated north into USDA zone 5, although cold, dry conditions will occasionally burn its needles.

CULTURE: This tree will grow in sandy or rocky soils or on well-drained silty clays. Like most southern pines, it must have full sun. Along with pitch pine (*Pinus rigida*), shortleaf pine has adapted to its fire-prone natural habitat by sprouting from dormant buds if the top is killed.

Shortleaf pine is hard to transplant unless its taproot has been severed in the nursery at an early age, but it grows easily from seed. It has a reputation as a slow-grower, mostly because of the marginal sites where it is found in the wild. A specimen growing in the irrigated herb fields at the Wilsons' Savory Farm in South Carolina has developed nicely into a dense, picturesque, spreading tree, demonstrating the species' response to favorable conditions. The Missouri Department of Conservation recognizes this potential and is promoting the restoration of shortleaf pine to its former habitat there.

PROBLEMS: All of the southern pines are attacked by boring beetles, especially the southern pine beetle (*Dendroctonus frontalis*). The needles are eaten by the redheaded pine sawfly (*Neodiprion lecontei*). Shortleaf pine is resistant to the *Sphaeropsis sapinea* leaf blight that attacks some of the other pines but is subject to damage from the twig-boring Nantucket pine tip moth (*Rhyacionia frustrana*). It is also susceptible to various root-rot organisms.

The cones of shortleaf pine are spiny like those of Virginia pine.

This round-headed, long-needled hybrid of pitch pine and loblolly pine makes an attractive yard tree and generates mulch as its old needles fall.

Most of the hard pines show little resistance to the pinewood nematode (*Bursaphelenchus xylophilus*), which is so deadly to several European hard pine species. All pines and their products are subject to regional quarantine in the United States because of the European pine shoot beetle (*Tomicus piniperda*). This pest was recently brought from Europe, where it is the most serious bark beetle in pines. Southern pines are also very vulnerable to ice storms, because they tend to collect so much freezing rain on their long needles.

CULTIVARS: No horticultural cultivars have been selected for shortleaf pine. All of the southern pines, however, have been examined for genetic variation that might affect their performance as timber trees.

Southern pines of selected provenance are recommended for timber plantations.

RELATED SPECIES: The only other pine in most of our area with the ability to sprout from old wood is pitch pine (*Pinus rigida*)—a small, irregular, picturesque species that grows on barren highlands and sands in the Appalachian Mountains and New England. Pitch pine is one of the few hard pines reported to be resistant to pinewood nematode. In plant-breeding programs, it has been paired with the closely related loblolly pine (*Pinus taeda*) to produce a hybrid, *Pinus* x *rigitaeda*. The intent was to combine the hardiness and adaptability of pitch pine with the larger size, straightness and fast growth of loblolly pine. Both pitch pine and the hybrid are hardy and fast-growing in the Sternbergs' test plantings in central Illinois, but neither has a tall trunk.

Loblolly pine is one of our largest, most productive pines and the most common tree in southern forest plantations.

Loblolly pine, popular throughout the Deep South, cannot survive the occasional severe winters of central Illinois (USDA zone 5) and is very susceptible to fusiform rust disease (*Cronartium quercuum*). It is the most common tree in southern forest plantations and in wet areas, where most other pines cannot live, and is one of our largest and most productive pines. The United States national champion, in King William County, Virginia, is 135 feet (41 m) tall with a trunk nearly 7 feet (2 m) in diameter. Genetically improved loblolly is grown in the timber plantation at the Wilsons' Savory Farm in South Carolina.

Another southern pine, the longleaf pine (*Pinus palustris*), grows for us in USDA zone 5 but only as a struggling botanical curiosity. In the sandy pine savannas of the South, this species becomes a magnificent tree. Its needles grow in bundles of three, up to 18 inches (46 cm) in length, and droop gracefully from the coarse, stubby branches. The cones, too, are decorative, growing up to 10 inches (25 cm) long. Young saplings are sparsely branched and often look like giant bottlebrushes. Seedlings don't put forth much stem growth for several years, and they initially resemble clumps of ornamental grass. This beautiful pine is the state tree of Alabama.

Slash pine (*Pinus elliottii*) has needles nearly as long as those of longleaf pine. It is a fast-growing timber tree, but it is not hardy in the north. Pond pine (*Pinus serotina*) resembles a small loblolly pine. It shares the ability of shortleaf and pitch pines to sprout from the stump on small trees and grows in swamps and pocosins on the coastal plains.

COMMENTS: The southern pines are so ubiquitous where they do well that many people fail to appreciate them as a wonderful evergreen. Recently, new-home construction has probably invaded piney woods more than any other forest type in the southeast. Many fashionable subdivisions around cities such as Atlanta are being carved from pine forests. The trees seem able to cope surprisingly well and share their landscape with human tenants in quiet dignity. However, they occasionally take revenge for root damage inflicted during construction and drop huge dying limbs or topple onto the roofs of encroaching houses.

RED PINE

Pinus resinosa

DESCRIPTION: Red pine is the northern counterpart of the southern timber pines. It belongs to the hard pine (*Pinus*, or *Diploxylon*) subgenus and shares many characteristics with the other hard pines previously described. The coarse twigs and flaky bark have a reddish cast, unlike that of other native pines of the North. Red pine is a tree of sandy soil. It prefers more moisture and organic matter than the scrubby little jack pine (*Pinus banksiana*) with which it grows, but it will thrive on poorer sites than white pine (*Pinus strobus*).

Red pine becomes a large tree. The United States champion in Watersmeet, Michigan, is 154 feet (47 m) tall and has a long trunk more than 3 feet (1 m) in diameter. It is the state tree of Minnesota, and we have seen some of the best-looking red pines growing along lakeshores there and in northern Wisconsin and Ontario, where their roots can probe into sandy soil with good drainage but have access to a high water table.

Red pine develops a broad, stately crown in open settings and favors sandy lakeshores.

LEAVES: Red pine's slender yellow-green needles are bundled in pairs within each fascicle and generally last for two full years before falling. They are long for a northern pine, up to 6 inches (15 cm), and very flexible, but they will snap cleanly when bent too far. The needles usually don't persist as long as those of other hard pines. The branching pattern is very coarse on young trees (because of limited early formation of lateral buds), so unsheared saplings have a very open, fluffy look reminiscent of longleaf pine (*Pinus palustris*) in the South.

FLOWERS AND FRUIT: The staminate strobiles of red pine are a striking violet color and develop conspicuously at the ends of the branches. The cones, which grow from pistillate flowers usually high in the tree, are not as large as those of most of the southern pines, barely reaching 2 inches (5 cm) in length. The unopened cones are smooth and without prickles, like those of jack pine. Each cone scale has a dorsal umbo, making the surface of a tightly closed cone appear as smooth as a ceramic-tiled floor.

SEASONS:
1. Winter (the fluffy foliage looks appealing when frosted with snow);
2. All year (the evergreen needles and red bark make a striking combination).

NATIVE AND ADAPTIVE RANGE: Red pine is a prominent forest tree in the Great Lake states and eastern Canada. It extends northwest to Lake Winnipeg in Manitoba and eastward to Lake St. John and the Gaspé Peninsula of Quebec, with isolated stands as far east as Newfoundland. To the south, it can be found through northern New England and the northern portions of the Great Lake states, with outlying natural groves as far away as Illinois and West Virginia. The cold tolerance of this tree is well established; it grows naturally in USDA zone 2. Summer heat might be more of a problem, but healthy specimens can be found as far south as USDA zone 6.

CULTURE: Red pine must have sun and very good drainage, although it does well in tight soils on slopes where water cannot puddle. It is the most difficult of the northern pines to transplant because of its long, deep root system. Small trees can be dug by hand with a deep soil ball. Mechanical tree movers, with deep, conical blades, work well for larger sizes. The seed has no dormancy requirement and will germinate within a week or two of planting.

The staminate strobiles of red pine help give the entire tree a reddish tint in spring.

Because of the limited early formation of lateral buds, young red pines have an open, fluffy look.

PROBLEMS: Red pine is a favorite target of the European pine sawfly (*Neodiprion sertifer*) and is sensitive to ozone pollution. It is also among the most sensitive of the pines to the allelopathic effects of walnut roots and should not be planted in the same backyard as black walnut (*Juglans nigra*). In areas south of its natural range, where blizzards often turn into ice storms, red pine can be heavily damaged as the ice builds up on its long needles. Its primary limitations, though, are poor drainage and shade.

Young saplings sometimes put out double leaders if they do not have a symmetrical ring of lateral buds. Red pine trees develop only one or two lateral buds each year, until they are five or more years old. Double leaders are readily apparent and simple to correct by removing the less dominant one while the tree is still small. Christmas tree growers shear the new twig growth, or candles, on young red pines to induce more bud development and to limit the lengths of internodes, thus producing denser trees.

CULTIVARS: Red pine is notably devoid of genetic variation, and the only cultivars likely to become available will probably develop from witches'-brooms or mutations. We know of none at present.

RELATED SPECIES: Along with the southern pines and the short-needled hard pines, red pine is related to the hard pines of western North America, Europe and Asia. Notable among these are ponderosa pine (*Pinus ponderosa*) and its varieties, some of which grow well when planted in the eastern part of our continent. Several exotic hard pines are commonly seen in cultivation, including Scots pine (*Pinus sylvestris*), Austrian pine (*Pinus nigra*) and the shrubby mugo pine (*Pinus mugo*). All three are quite variable, with numerous ecotypes, varieties or subspecies.

COMMENTS: A red pine fireplace mantle graces the Sternberg home, wrought from the hand-hewn beams of a pegged barn built generations ago by family ancestors. Red pine—strong, light and workable—was the logical choice for a barn-raising on the prairie before cranes, gasoline engines and stamped-steel gusset plates made easier work of lifting and connecting the bones of such a structure.

We used to grow red pine for Christmas trees on our Illinois tree farm. It taught us much about how willfully some trees resist all human attempts to mold their loose, airy forms into tight cones of foliage.

Although we know it served well as barn beams and grudgingly as Christmas trees, we have come to appreciate red pine most as a majestic large conifer that should be left alone, free to grow better with age.

WHITE PINE

Pinus strobus

DESCRIPTION: White pine is the tallest tree native to eastern North America. It is the state tree of Maine and Michigan and the provincial tree of Ontario. The long, straight, strong stems of this tree were coveted for masts during the days of sailing ships. None of its associates can match its mature stature, rarely seen these days because virtually all of the giant pines of the primeval forest have been harvested for timber.

Massive white pine logs were cut during the past century—one tree 12 feet (3.6 m) in diameter was logged in 1899—but isolated stands such as the one at Hearts Content in the Allegheny National Forest remain to offer a hint of this tree's former greatness. The largest known white pine today is 200 feet (60 m) tall and 5 feet (1.5 m) in diameter. It grows in Marquette, Michigan.

The soft, friendly needles of white pine grow in fascicles of five.

LEAVES: White pine is the only soft pine (subgenus *Strobus* or, by some authorities, *Haploxylon*) in eastern North America. It bears aromatic blue-green needles in fascicles, or bundles, of five. The evergreen needles are flexible and friendly to the touch, unlike the prickly needles of many other conifers, and they have lines of white stomata (pores) along the lower surface. They reach about 5 inches (12 cm) long and droop from the twigs, which gives the tree a graceful weeping aspect and an unmistakable wind-song. Played by the breeze, it accompanies the call of the loon to provide haunting nighttime harmonies familiar to those who have visited areas such as the Quetico wilderness of Ontario.

White pine needles develop only toward the ends of the twigs, instead of along their full length, and they fall after their second year. This gives vigorous young specimens a "see-through" structure, which is filled in as the tree ages and branches (or, on Christmas trees, by shearing).

FLOWERS AND FRUIT: The staminate and pistillate strobile flowers of white pine are borne in separate clusters. The cones are longer and proportionately more slender than those of most of our other pines, reaching up to 8 inches (20 cm) long and maturing in two years. The scales each have a terminal umbo, which makes them overlap loosely like shingles. They are smooth but gummy to the touch. Unripe cones look like green hot dogs hanging from the upper limbs of mature trees.

SEASONS:
1. Winter (our most massive evergreen tree and one that holds its color well; its picturesque silhouette is visible for miles when adjacent deciduous trees shed their foliage);
2. All year (especially for the fragrance and for the haunting sound of the wind rustling its crown).

NATIVE AND ADAPTIVE RANGE: This is one of our most adaptable pines. It thrives from southeastern Manitoba across the Lake Country of western Ontario to the south shore of Lake Nipigon and from the northeast shore of Lake Superior, across to the Gulf of St. Lawrence and Newfoundland, then south throughout the Great Lake states and New England and in the Appalachians to northern Georgia. During earlier postglacial times, it grew farther to the southwest, and isolated populations remain in Indiana, western Kentucky and, as variety *chiapensis*, even as far as southern Mexico.

Many provenance studies have shown that white pine exhibits clinal (genetic) variation in response to climatic extremes, so locally adapted stock performs

White pine is the tallest tree native to eastern North America. In the open, old specimens retain their lower limbs.

best. In general, white pine from appropriate sources will grow as far north as USDA zone 2 and as far south as USDA zone 8 with adequate soil moisture.

CULTURE: As pines go, white pine is a mesic tree. It grows in many soil types, from fairly wet to quite dry and from silty clay to dune sand, but it does best on good soil. It loves full sun but can tolerate a little more shade than the hard pines. It is very easy to transplant with a soil ball, either in fall or spring. Seed should be sown outside in the fall for best results. It takes several years before the seedlings begin rapid growth. Once they take off, they will outgrow most other pines on good sites, sometimes adding annual "candles" of growth more than 4 feet (1.2 m) long.

PROBLEMS: White pine is extremely sensitive to salt and air pollution, so it should not be planted close to highways. The smooth, thin bark of young trees is damaged easily by fire or by careless use of string trimmers. The twig-boring white pine weevil (*Pissodes strobi*) and white pine blister rust disease (*Cronartium ribicola*) can be problems in portions of the tree's natural habitat. Other insects such as pales weevil (*Hylobius pales*), pine bark aphid (*Pineus strobi*) and white pine aphid (*Cinara strobi*) also cause problems locally. Mound-building ants (*Formica integra*) at the Sternbergs' tree farm inexplicably kill sapling white pines within about 20 feet (6 m) of their nests by girdling their bases.

White pine is one of the most resistant of our pines to the deadly pinewood nematode (*Bursaphelenchus xylophilus*) and is less prone to attack by the defoliating European pine sawfly (*Diprion similis*) than the hard pines. Leaf diseases such as tip blight (*Sphaeropsis sapinea*) occasionally spread from the more susceptible hard pines to the more resistant white pine. White pine is subject to more different minor diseases than any other North American species, but it is still one of our most trouble-free pines in terms of serious problems.

CULTIVARS: Many dwarf selections have been

propagated from the frequently seen witches'-brooms of white pine. Of the selections that become real trees, though, we particularly like 'Fastigiata' because its broadly ascending form is more elegant than the exclamation-point forms of most fastigiate plants. 'Pendula' and 'Inversa' are weeping forms, and 'Contorta' has twisted branches. Several selections have been propagated for their leaf color, including 'Alba', 'Gracilis Viridis', 'Variegata' and the impressive blue form 'Glauca'.

RELATED SPECIES: There are many soft pines in western North America and Asia, several of which are found in cultivation in parts of our area. Limber pine (*Pinus flexilis*), southwestern white pine (*Pinus strobiformis*) and western white pine (*Pinus monticola*) all grow well in our tests in central Illinois. Another western relative, bristlecone pine (*Pinus aristata* and, by some authorities, *P. longaeva* in its westernmost form), is the longest-lived tree species in the world. It can be planted in the East, but it should not be expected to live for 5,000 years like it does in the West. Himalayan pine (*Pinus walichiana*) and Chinese white pine (*Pinus armandii*) are occasionally cultivated in the eastern United States.

A dwarf species, *Pinus culminicola*, is found in alpine conditions, at 13,000 feet (3,500 m), on the mountain Cerro Potosi in Mexico. It might be useful in the Southeast as a possible substitute for the European mugo pine (*Pinus mugo*). It is one of the piñons, a group of small southwestern soft pines with large, edible nuts.

COMMENTS: The crown of white pine is made up of long, fluffy limbs that give mature trees a layered appearance when viewed from a distance. These same plume-like limbs, when seen from above, make this species among the easiest of all conifers to identify from an airplane. An illustrated training manual for aerial timber surveying, published by the Canada Department of Forestry, shows the characteristic star-shaped crowns of white pines emerging above the surrounding forest canopy like starfish on an ocean floor.

A tradition of early American settlers moving west was to plant "coffin pines" at their new homes. The native forests of the frontier were composed of hardwoods that could not be fashioned quickly into a coffin, so white pine from the East was used. A matched pair of pine trees was often planted for husband and wife. Many of the trees never served their intended purpose and still survive.

Although conifers and broadleaf trees are not closely related, members of each group have evolved in a parallel fashion to fill analogous positions in natural communities. In many ways, the various pines (*Pinus*), which are our largest and most important conifer genus, parallel the oaks (*Quercus*), our largest and most important genus of broadleaf trees.

Pines and oaks both invade habitats that have been opened (or kept open) by fire, logging or poor soil. Both are resistant to drought but have low to intermediate tolerance for shade. Without periodic disturbance or dry, sterile soil to keep other species under control, pines and oaks may eventually be replaced by more shade-tolerant species. However, the disturbances that set the stage for their reproduction need only occur once every few centuries to keep the species in place because many individual oak and pine trees survive to become old and huge, dominating their corner of the woods.

Southwestern white pine is a tough tree well suited to dry, exposed sites.

SYCAMORE

Platanus occidentalis

DESCRIPTION: Sycamore is a tree of the winter valley. For the four to six months of winter dormancy each year, the huge, white-speckled boles and limbs of this great tree make it the most conspicuous living organism along every river within its range. It commonly grows with cottonwoods (*Populus deltoides*), walnuts (*Juglans nigra*), bottomland oaks (*Quercus* spp.) and other trees that have rough, dark bark. Every white-barked sycamore is visible among these trees like a fire in the night.

Sycamores never seem to slow down in growth, and those that manage to outgrow storm damage, stream undercutting and heart rot can become the most massive trees in eastern North America. We have seen some that exceed 150 feet (46 m) in height and 6 feet (2 m) in trunk thickness. The largest one known is only 129 feet (40 m) tall, but it is 15 feet (4.6 m) in diameter, with its multiple trunks rippling with bulges and burls. This patriarch is unquestionably the largest broadleaf tree in North America, and it is three-fourths as large in overall size as the national champion California redwood (*Sequoia sempervirens*). It lives in Jeromesville, Ohio.

The bark at the base of a sycamore frequently becomes dark and scaly; many specimens with multiple stems develop from stump-sprouts.

This species follows soil disturbances caused by floods and channel-braiding along rivers and by people on some upland sites. It bears great quantities of seed, which are scattered by the wind and, with sufficient light and moisture, take root on any open ground and outgrow most competitors.

LEAVES: The size of sycamore leaves can vary on the same branch. Those that develop in midseason on vigorous stems can reach as much as 10 inches (25 cm) in width by nearly as long. They have three or five very shallow lobes and a hollow petiole that encloses the bud. The creamy early-spring color of woolly new sycamore leaves adds to the spectacle of the white bark, but fall color is only a dull tan.

FLOWERS AND FRUIT: Spherical reddish flower clusters emerge with the leaves in spring. The pistillate flower clusters develop into seed heads about 1 inch (2.5 cm) in diameter and hang from the tree on long, flexible stalks through most of the winter. They gradually break apart in spring storms, just in time to cast seed across the sandbars and mud flats exposed by receding floods.

SEASONS:

1. Winter (a large sycamore stands out among its associates for the bright hues of its mottled, peeling bark);
2. Spring (the colorful young foliage and flowers are impressive but only when they are unmarred by disease).

NATIVE AND ADAPTIVE RANGE: Sycamore, in its varieties and forms, grows from Iowa south into Mexico, east across Ontario (south of Georgian Bay) to southern Maine and southeast throughout most of the eastern United States, except for the Gulf Coast and peninsular Florida. It does best in the central part of this range, but it can be cultivated north into USDA zone 4.

CULTURE: This is one of the simplest of our trees to grow or transplant. We once moved several 27-foot (8 m) trees successfully with a 44-inch (112 cm) transplanting machine. Sycamores may be grown from cuttings or from seed, or wild seedlings can be transplanted from areas they overpopulate. Cutting-grown trees might be used to select for the whitest

Sycamore is fast-growing and will often be the largest and most distinctive tree in the bottomland woods.

The reddish, spherical flower heads of sycamore will ripen into golf-ball-sized fruits.

bark, a variable trait from tree to tree. If grown from seed, the seeds should be fresh and sown thickly on the surface of a wet seedbed. They require only sunlight and ample moisture for optimum growth. Seedlings in our seedbeds have grown as much as 4 feet (1.2 m) in their first year.

This rapid growth can be expected to continue almost indefinitely under ideal conditions. Undamaged seedlings usually develop a strong central leader and require no corrective pruning, but double leaders occasionally emerge. Trees that develop wide multiple forks become very picturesque as they age, but those with narrow forks should be pruned to a single leader while small in order to preserve structural soundness.

PROBLEMS: The most important, and least known, problem with this tree is that the fuzz on its leaves, fruits and young twigs can cause allergic reactions, including temporary blindness, if the branches are handled roughly during pruning. This hazard is magnified greatly if you are using a brush chipper. When in doubt, wear protective goggles and a dust mask when working with a sycamore.

Conversely, a less serious but widely known problem is the spring anthracnose disease, *Apiognomonia veneta (Gnomonia platani)*, which annually kills young leaves and sometimes even twigs on susceptible trees. The symptoms look like the results of a late frost, browning the first new leaves. As secondary shoots develop, the weather generally warms and dries to the point where the fungus disease shuts down for the year, and little harm is done. In very wet years and on especially susceptible trees, this anthracnose disease causes significant twig dieback and noticeable delays in leaf development. Still, much of the damage is cosmetic and will eventually be overcome by new growth.

We have observed native sycamores growing wild along Rock Creek in central Illinois for many years and have found that they consistently show much less damage from anthracnose than dozens of trees of unknown provenance planted a few miles away in Springfield. We have also noticed that a few of the trees in Springfield are consistent from year to year in being more severely affected than others, showing the knobby growth that results from repeated twig dieback. It would be interesting to learn how much of this apparently variable resistance is genetic and how much is environmental.

Sycamore hosts a variety of canker diseases and wood-rotting organisms. Most of them gain entry through pruning wounds or other damaged areas, so proper tree care will generally prevent them. Many streamside sycamores have been hollowed out by decay that entered through wounds from winter ice flows. Some of them live on for centuries, providing wildlife habitat and children's playhouses, but their structural integrity is always in doubt and they shouldn't be trusted within falling distance of a house. The shedding bark, large leaves and blight-killed twigs cause significant littering throughout the year. The fallen leaves are allelopathic and can be toxic to turf, and the roots can be invasive, so there are additional reasons to keep this tree away from carefully tended lawns, pavement and buildings.

CULTIVARS: Available cultivars seem to be selections of a hybrid with an Asian species, *Platanus orientalis*. The hybrid, *Platanus* x *acerifolia*, is known as London plane because it has been grown for centuries in England. It is more resistant to pollution, drought and anthracnose than the native species, but it has duller bark and is frequently plagued by serious canker problems. Many of the London planes grown in North America seem to be backcrossed to our native species, but there are some that have retained their intermediate appearance.

Selections should certainly be made from native sycamores for bark color and anthracnose resistance because these traits show great variability and account for the best and the worst aesthetic qualities of this species. Sycamores from the southwestern part of North America, and especially from Texas and Mexico, have smaller, tougher leaves and might be useful for cultivar selection on that basis if they were more winter-hardy. Several of them are now classified as separate species.

RELATED SPECIES: A similar tree with more deeply lobed leaves, *Platanus racemosa*, grows along streams in California, and another with even more pronounced lobing, *Platanus wrightii*, can be found in the canyons of the Southwest. Several additional species are recognized in Mexico, Europe and Asia. The sycamore genus is the only member of its plant family and has survived for 100 million years, since the late Cretaceous Period, making it one of the true elders of the tree tribe.

Our species is considered to be the most evolutionarily advanced, and it is certainly first in at least one respect: a sycamore now growing across from Independence Hall in Philadelphia was germinated from seed carried to the moon in 1971 by Apollo Astronaut Stuart Roosa. Several of its sister seedlings can be found in other locations, all germinated by the USDA Forest Service upon Roosa's return to Earth.

COMMENTS: Noted ornithologist Robert Ridgeway wrote in 1889 that the cerulean warbler was "the most abundant of the summer-resident members of the family in Illinois." Today, this migratory bird has become a threatened species because of habitat destruction. Cerulean warblers seem to set up their mating territories around venerable old sycamores, which they prefer above all other trees for singing perches.

We have an old photograph, a treasured gift from a good friend. It shows Ridgeway in 1882 along the Wabash River in southern Indiana. He and his brother, Charles, are posed by a sycamore with two trunks, the larger one 15.5 feet (4.8 m) in diameter and 168 feet (50 m) tall. It was the largest tree of any species ever measured in North America east of California. The tree might still be there to admire but for the short-sightedness of its owner who reportedly had it cut down soon after the picture was taken so he wouldn't be inconvenienced by more tree-gazers.

Stewardship connotes responsibility to the future. We often ponder the wisdom of giving individual humans "ownership" rights over such wonders of nature.

The upper bark on some sycamores is snowy white.

COTTONWOOD

Populus deltoides

DESCRIPTION: "Cottonwood" is a name that means different things to different people. Cottonwoods of various species and varieties are found almost throughout North America, and all look and behave very much alike. They are rugged, water-seeking trees that grow faster and larger than nearly all of their associates in any region of the continent. But they are also weak and very prone to damage and decay, and female trees release a summer snow of cottony seeds that become entangled in window screens from the Atlantic to the Pacific.

Cottonwoods are most appreciated in the Great Plains, where other trees are rare and more difficult to grow. Here, they make vast riparian forests that shade the rivers and furnish the structural bones upon which wildlife habitat is built. Kansas, Wyoming and Nebraska have each designated a cottonwood as their state tree, but there is some confusion whether the honored tree is the eastern cottonwood (*Populus deltoides*) or the closely related plains cottonwood (*Populus sargentii*). Some authorities consider them to be varieties of the same species; their ranges do overlap in Kansas and Nebraska.

Weather-beaten old cottonwoods are striking visual features of the Great Plains.

We have known old, hollow cottonwoods that had enough room inside for a poker game. The current national champion, in a pasture near Minadoka Dam in Idaho, has the spreading form characteristic of plains cottonwood; it is only 85 feet (26 m) tall but has a trunk 11.5 feet (3.5 m) in diameter. A comparable specimen 96 feet (30 m) tall with a trunk 11 feet (3.2 m) in diameter grows in Gosper County, Nebraska. For many years, the recognized national champion was an eastern cottonwood growing along the Illinois and Michigan Canal in Illinois. Before it fell in 1991, entire grade-school classes could convene within the massive tree's hollow base (although the entrance was too small to admit most teachers).

LEAVES: Toothed and triangular, the leaves average about 4 inches (10 cm) long and broad. Those on the shoots of western species and varieties are generally smaller and more leathery, but the leaves on vigorous shoots of any species grow much larger. We have found that trees from different geographic regions planted together at Starhill Forest in Illinois retain the foliage characteristics of their home habitat.

The leaves hang from flexible petioles and clack together even when the breeze is too subtle to be felt on the ground. Their music is especially pleasant in late summer, when the leaves begin to dry and their sounding boards resonate. Cottonwood foliage becomes a warm yellow if the tree has had an insect-free summer and a gradual transition to fall.

The autumnal display is made more dramatic by the typical, fungus-induced early abscission of the oldest leaves, which, in falling, highlight the bare structural form of the branches.

FLOWERS AND FRUIT: All cottonwoods are dioecious, so only female trees bear the cottony seeds for which they are notorious. The fruit capsules begin as strings of green pearls in early spring, and the ripe capsules split open synchronously to fill the late-spring air with a beautiful but messy display of cottony snow.

SEASONS:

1. Fall (there is something unforgettable about a

grizzly old cottonwood on a lonesome ranch, its foliage reduced to a smattering of golden leaves rattling in the breeze, the scene lit by a ray of sunshine breaking through the dark clouds of a lowering sky); 2. Late spring (the cotton is truly the best and the worst of this tree; it is festive in wild areas where it may be enjoyed without inconvenience).

NATIVE AND ADAPTIVE RANGE: The combination of eastern cottonwood and plains cottonwood blankets low ground and riparian habitats across the eastern and midwestern United States. Plains cottonwood extends into Alberta and Saskatchewan, north at least to Saskatoon. Other species, which are similar in most details, range north throughout much of Canada, west to the Pacific Ocean and southwest into Mexico, where the cottonwoods are known as *los alamos.* Our eastern native species is adapted from the Gulf Coast north into USDA zone 3, but local races exist. So if you are doing some planting, look for trees of local provenance.

Cottonwoods are resilient trees that grow well in exposed locations.

CULTURE: Cottonwood is probably our fastest growing large tree. It is fairly easy to transplant when small, but it grows so readily from unrooted cuttings that transplanting an established tree seems pointless. Seed is perishable and difficult to handle. Tiny seedlings volunteer everywhere, however, and they may be moved about with abandon as they germinate.

The trick with propagating cottonwood is to start in late winter with a hardwood cutting of known gender. Plant it in open, weed-free soil, give it excessive amounts of water and get out of the way. We have seen groves of cottonwoods that grew more than 100 feet (30 m) tall in less than 20 years. Soil type is not critical, but the trees must have water, full sun and little competition to flourish.

PROBLEMS: Whole books have been written about the insects and diseases of cottonwood. Two cankers, *Cytospora chrysosperma* and *Dothichiza populea*, are especially troublesome on trees that have been injured by pruning or extreme weather. The trees are notoriously prone to damage from lightning, beavers, ice, wind, insects, decay and nearly every other force known to nature. Yet they are so resilient that some live to take their place among the largest of our deciduous trees. A few of the venerable cottonwoods that shaded Lewis and Clark on their Journey of Discovery in 1804 are still growing along the Missouri River.

Cottonwoods' worst problems are amplified by their sheer size. This translates into massive, brittle limbs and extensive, invasive roots. Then, if your trees are females, there is the cotton. Some communities have actually passed ordinances prohibiting the planting of female cottonwoods. The cottonwood is a picturesque, fast-growing giant at its best where its negative traits are of no consequence.

CULTIVARS: Because cottonwood has immense value for paper pulp, many superior production clones with elaborate pedigrees are grown in forestry plantations. Cottonwood has been used in a vast forestry hybridization program with European, Asian and western North American poplar species. Several nurseries offer "cottonless" ornamental cultivars, which are nothing more than staminate trees grown from cuttings. Anyone interested in growing one need only look around during the blooming period for a male tree, then return in late winter to harvest a dormant cutting.

RELATED SPECIES: Eastern cottonwood and plains cottonwood are the primary species in the eastern and midwestern United States. People in the northern part of our area will find balsam poplar (*Populus balsamifera*) an aromatic species that ranges

The golden foliage of the cottonwood reigns over the landscape in early fall.

north as far as the Arctic Circle. It has narrower leaves than cottonwood, and it seldom grows as large.

Swampy areas in the eastern United States sometimes support swamp cottonwood (*Populus heterophylla*). It has beautiful emerging foliage in early spring and becomes a large, tall tree, like eastern cottonwood. The national champion (named "the Little Big Tree" from associations with Native American lore) grows along the Black River in Spencer, Ohio, and stands 140 feet (43 m) tall with a straight trunk nearly 9 feet (2.75 m) in diameter.

There are other cottonwood-like poplars in western North America. They include black cottonwood (*Populus trichocarpa*), a giant tree of the Pacific Northwest; narrowleaf cottonwood (*Populus angustifolia*) of the Rocky Mountains; and several varieties of Fremont cottonwood (*Populus fremontii*) in the Southwest. The aspens are poplars, too, although they have more in common with some European and Asian species than with other North American poplars. They are covered separately.

COMMENTS: Enter a cottonwood grove on a hot summer day and you will receive a standing ovation from the clapping leaves and the comfort of the dappled shade. In the nearly treeless landscape of the Great Plains, this can be a memorable and welcome experience. If contemporary life were not so dependent on window screens, air conditioners, swimming pool filters and all manner of sensitive gadgets that clog and choke, we might also appreciate the drifting summer snow of cottonwood seeds, just as it must have been admired by the early Native Americans who revered this great tree.

The Arapaho believed that great cottonwoods cast the stars into the sky, and many tribes found mythic and pragmatic value in virtually every part of the tree. The famous photographic portfolios of Edward Sheriff Curtis, compiled at the beginning of this century as the sun was setting on the ancient ways of Native American life, help document the importance of cottonwoods to his subjects. Two of his more dramatic images depict a Navaho weaver's loom set beneath the exposed root of a huge cottonwood and a ceremonial hat made from cottonwood leaves for the Sun Dance of the Cheyenne.

QUAKING ASPEN

Populus tremuloides

DESCRIPTION: Aspen is a tree born of fires, landslides and other disasters. It colonizes disturbed areas and masses at the sunny edges of forests and meadows, where its white bark and gentle grace make it a favorite subject for nature photography. Aspens grow as clones—colonies of stems with a common root system. Fires and other disturbances periodically clear away the older stems, allowing ever more vigorous new sprouts to grow.

Quaking aspens are slender and graceful trees. Their white bark and delicate branching pattern might contribute to the illusion of small size, but aspens can become quite large on favorable terrain. The biggest single quaking aspen tree known was found in Ontonagon County, at the western end of Upper Michigan. It is 109 feet (33 m) tall and over 3 feet (1 m) in diameter. The closely related bigtooth aspen (*Populus grandidentata*) can grow even larger. One specimen in Marquette, Michigan, is 132 feet (40 m) tall, and a venerable specimen in Caroline County, Maryland, has a trunk 4 feet 7 inches (1.4 m) in diameter.

Quaking aspens grow as clones; all of the aspens in this coppice originated from the roots of a single tree.

LEAVES: Quaking aspen derives both its common and scientific names from its foliage. The round leaves hang from flexible, flattened petioles and tremble with the slightest breeze. The scientific name actually means "like *tremula*," a reference to the nearly identical European aspen (*Populus tremula*), which is known for its similar shivering movement. The leaves are very finely toothed along their margins.

We have an experimental provenance plot of aspen at Starhill Forest in Illinois; the trees have been propagated vegetatively from more than 30 locations across the entire natural range. The leaves vary in size, shape, fall color and phenology (seasonal timing), depending on where the parent tree grows. Most turn bright gold in the fall, and some clones from the Rocky Mountains include a little orange. Those from the East generally have the largest leaves, up to 3 inches (8 cm) in diameter; those from central Alaska and the southern Rocky Mountains seem to have the smallest.

The foliage of bigtooth aspen is similar, but it has coarse, irregular teeth along the margins. The two species are easy to tell apart in early spring because bigtooth aspen leafs out later, and its new foliage is covered with a white wool, as though cotton balls decorated the crown of the tree. The two species are more difficult to distinguish from a distance during other seasons.

FLOWERS AND FRUIT: Aspens, like all poplars, are dioecious, and each clone is either staminate or pistillate. In the high mountains, staminate clones seem to survive better than pistillate ones, but the genders are evenly mixed in most areas. The flowers are small catkins similar to those of willows (*Salix* spp.), and they are not particularly conspicuous. Those of bigtooth aspen open later than those of quaking aspen.

Female trees release great quantities of seed in early summer every few years, but the tiny seeds are so perishable that few remain viable long enough to

The bark of quaking aspen usually remains smooth throughout the life of the tree.

Top: Occasionally, a quaking aspen will develop red or orange fall color. Above: Less widely appreciated, bigtooth aspen also displays good fall color.

sprout. This does not pose a challenge to the tree's survival because almost endless generations of clones may grow from the few seeds that do take root.

SEASONS:

1. Fall (the golden foliage, backlit and shivering on white stems among stands of dark evergreens, is perhaps the most popular of all nature photographs for calendars);
2. Early spring (as the misty, lime-green new leaves of quaking aspen and the white leaves of bigtooth aspen expand);
3. Summer (when the foliage dances in the wind).

NATIVE AND ADAPTIVE RANGE: If you live anywhere in the cooler portions of North America, quaking aspen trees are probably near. Aspen ranges from northern Alaska to the mountains of central Mexico, eastward across every portion of Canada that has a growing season long enough to support tree growth, south through the moist, cool highlands of Virginia and Missouri and throughout the mountains of the West. Our testing indicates that trees of western mountain origin are not as vigorous in the Midwest as those from local or more eastern sources. Root cuttings or small sprouts should be gathered locally when you are planting near the limits of the species' natural range. Locally adapted provenances of quaking aspen are hardy north into USDA zone 1.

Bigtooth aspen shares much of the same range in the East, with the exception of Newfoundland, and does not extend west very far beyond the Mississippi River Valley. It can be grown a little farther south, in the hot, humid Southeast, than quaking aspen and north through USDA zone 3.

CULTURE: Aspens are best established from root cuttings set directly into their permanent planting location. However, trees can be started from small sprouts lifted in the dormant season from disturbed areas at the edge of a clonal clump. They should be set in their new hole with the roots at their previous depth and the tops pruned back to soil level. Aspen is difficult to direct-seed because the seed is so small and perishable. Moving established trees is also problematic. It seems that any injury leaves the transplant prone to cankers, insect attack, bark blemishes and, ultimately, premature death. Cutting back the top, after the tree is moved and allowing it to resprout offers the best chance for a successful transplant.

Aspen tolerates many soil extremes, from sandy fields and cinder ballasts to rocky taluses and peaty bogs. Bigtooth aspen does better in dry, sandy or clayey soils than quaking aspen. It can be a tenacious tree. A bushy specimen has been growing on the tile roof of the Decatur County Courthouse in Greensburg, Indiana, since 1870, with its roots sustained only by the windblown dust that has accumulated in the cracks between the tiles. Both species do best in full sun and on moist, well-drained soils of limestone origin. In any soil, weeding around the tree can boost its growth surprisingly.

The white spring foliage of bigtooth aspen makes it easy to distinguish from quaking aspen.

Either species of aspen can be attractively grown in a clump if you periodically remove the older, damaged stems and allow new sprouts to fill in. Better still, preserve the area around a natural aspen coppice and allow it to develop on its own, interfering only to cut shade-tolerant trees that try to invade.

PROBLEMS: Aspens are very sensitive to environmental degradation and are host to more than 500 species of parasites, herbivores, diseases and other dependent organisms. Thus, while these trees contribute to ecological diversity, the chances are poor that any one aspen will be healthy and long-lived in a home landscape.

Bark injuries, even superficial scratches from climbing squirrels, become permanent scars. The above-ground parts of the trees are also extremely susceptible to fire, wind and ice. Some say a loud "Boo!" will scare an aspen to death. New stems always emerge to replace the old, damaged ones, unless roots become waterlogged or poisoned with herbicides. Resprouting perpetuates the clone but frustrates anyone trying to grow aspen as a single-stem shade tree.

CULTIVARS: Our native aspens will hybridize with each other and can be crossed with European aspens. There are many such hybrids, which are developed mostly for pulpwood, but ornamental cultivars of either of our native species are uncommon. If aspens were better suited as lawn trees and easier to propagate from cuttings, many beautiful cultivars of both species could be developed from their variations in bark color, branching structure, foliage, growth rate and regional adaptability.

RELATED SPECIES: Our native aspens are closely related to the European *Populus tremula* and *Populus alba* and to the Asian *Populus tomentosa* and *Populus sieboldii*. All of these poplars, in turn, are more distantly related to our other poplars, such as cottonwood (*Populus deltoides*). The entire genus is in the same family as *Salix*, the willows.

COMMENTS: Known across the North as popples, aspens host an amazing array of birds, mammals and butterflies. If the damage these animals cause can be tolerated, aspen will serve as one of the premier wildlife trees in your landscape. They require attention, particularly culling old, damaged stems, but the work becomes pleasurable when you consider the cheerful fires you can start with this wonderful kindling.

Quaking aspen is a tree for the record books. It occupies a larger range than any other North American tree, spreading over 110 degrees of longitude (nine time zones), over 47 degrees of latitude (northern Alaska to central Mexico) and from sea level to the timberline. Some individual aspen clones are among the largest living organisms known anywhere. A single clone in Utah has 47,000 stems and is estimated to weigh at least three times more than the world's single largest tree. Another clone, in Minnesota, has been estimated to be 8,000 years old, placing it among the oldest living organisms on Earth.

Bigtooth aspen develops thick, rough patches on its otherwise smooth bark.

WILD PLUM

Prunus americana

DESCRIPTION: The genus *Prunus* includes two of our most ornamental groups of native trees: cherries and plums. Most of the plums are quite similar, and none is more attractive in bloom nor more widespread in the landscape than the common wild plum. A thicket-forming small tree in the wild, similar to the wild crabapples (*Malus* spp.), wild plum can be domesticated into a splendid flowering specimen for the ornamental garden.

When the internal competition of its own suckers is eliminated, a wild plum will develop into a fruit tree of substantial proportions. The United States champion in Oakland County, Michigan, is 35 feet (11 m) tall with a branch spread of the same dimension, and it has a trunk 1 foot (30 cm) in diameter. Several closely related species become at least as large, although all of them grow naturally as dense thickets of small stems.

The flowers of wild plum rival those of any exotic flowering tree.

LEAVES: Wild plum leaves closely resemble those of their domesticated cousins. They are usually recurved and keeled down the midrib and reach up to 5 inches (12 cm) long. They have toothed margins and rough, rugose surfaces with deeply set veins. Leaves of this species emerge after the flowers, while those of most other plum species develop concurrently with the flowers. If the leaves survive early defoliation or disfigurement by fungus diseases, many take on a nice yellow-orange fall color, often while some on the tree are still green.

FLOWERS AND FRUIT: Plum flowers, especially on this species, rival those of any of our popular exotic flowering trees. Wild plum flowers are pure white and emerge from a showy red calyx that sets them off sharply. They bloom early, at the same time as the exotic ornamental pears (*Pyrus calleryana*), and are every bit as attractive.

The plum flowers appear in clusters and reach their peak as redbuds (*Cercis canadensis*) begin to bloom, making a rich combination along roadsides and fencerows. Many people praise the floral beauty of redbud and dogwood (*Cornus florida*) in late spring, but the earlier combination of plum and redbud is just as spectacular. Plum bark is curly and dark, often nearly black on some species. The contrast of snowy flower clusters against an ebony bark makes the trees seem to glow.

The tangy fruits that develop later in the summer are a colorful plum-red with yellow flesh and reach about 1 inch (2.5 cm) in diameter. One would expect plum fruits to be an avian treat. Woodpeckers, jays and robins will take a few, and quail feed on them when they fall, but they are sought mostly by foxes and other mammals, including humans.

SEASONS:

1. Spring (wild plum is one of our finest flowering trees);
2. Fall (for those trees that develop color);
3. Late summer (for the fruit harvest).

NATIVE AND ADAPTIVE RANGE: This is one of our most adaptable plums. It grows naturally from southeastern Saskatchewan, east to New England and south to northern Florida. This species and several of its close relatives can be grown throughout most of USDA zone 3.

CULTURE: Plums like sunny sites and good soil drainage. They benefit from the same spray program as a home orchard, especially if you want insect-free and disease-free fruits and attractive foliage. They are easy to raise from seed if the seeds are gathered as soon as the fruits are completely ripe, then cleaned and planted in the early fall. Be sure to protect the seedbed from mice. Because they are shallow-rooted, plums are easy to transplant or to divide from suckering clumps in early spring.

PROBLEMS: Wild plum and its relatives are subject to many leaf-spot fungi, to black knot disease (*Dibotryon morbosum*) of the stem and to the common brown rot fungi (*Monilinia* spp.), which destroys many stone fruits in the home orchard. They can also be attacked by some of the same borers and other insects that bother stone fruits in commercial plantings.

Because of the sharp spur branches and the falling fruit, plums can be a hazard, or at least a nuisance, if planted near walks, patios and driveways. Unless you want a thicket, it is important to cull suckers as soon as they emerge by mowing or, preferably, by pulling them.

CULTIVARS: There are several hundred selections of wild plum chosen for fruit production and wildlife habitat. The species is also used in hybridization programs and as a rootstock for domestic plums. We have not seen any cultivars selected for ornamental use.

RELATED SPECIES: Chickasaw plum (*Prunus angustifolia*) is similar but shrubby and a more southern species. Canada plum (*Prunus nigra*) is limited to the states and provinces along the international border, from Manitoba eastward. It can become a fairly large tree and, like wild plum, it blooms before the leaves emerge. This species is used widely for food.

The wildgoose plums (*Prunus hortulana* and *Prunus munsoniana*) are restricted to the Midwest and bloom later, when the leaves are beginning to expand. There are several other regional plums in eastern North America, and they can be difficult to distinguish from one another. Plums are in the same genus as other stone fruits, a genus that includes more than 200 species worldwide.

COMMENTS: Ethnobotanists have documented the value of wild plums to Native Americans and have recorded examples of their cultivation of plum crops. Spanish explorers discovered the flavorful fruit early in their travels, as noted in a May 30, 1539, journal entry of the Hernando de Soto expedition. Europeans had first written of the wild plum 15 years earlier, when Giovanni da Verrazano found what was probably the shrubby looking beach plum (*Prunus maritima*) during his explorations along the East Coast. More than 450 years later, the beach plum is popularly cultivated and its wild cousins are still high on people's lists of tasty uncultivated fruits.

Somewhat surprisingly, plums are not a choice food for wildlife, but they join hawthorns (*Crataegus* spp.) in providing valuable nesting cover throughout their extensive range. They are useful for erosion control, too, because of their tendency to form thickets and their tolerance of poor, dry soil. They host many butterflies, including several colorful hairstreaks and the giant cecropia moth, with its 6-inch (15 cm) wingspan.

The wildgoose plum (*Prunus munsoniana*) is more valuable for its fruit than its flowers. It has some of the tastiest plums of all and has furnished several pomological selections. Guy discovered the largest *Prunus munsoniana* ever found, at New Salem, the Illinois village where Abraham Lincoln lived in the early 1800s. It was 18 inches (45 cm) in diameter and grew east of the first store that Lincoln operated as a young man in the 1830s. A tornado later damaged the tree, but we are working with the manager of the historic site to protect and restore it.

Wild plums are tangy and tasty and about 1 inch (2.5 cm) in diameter.

WILD CHERRY

Prunus serotina

DESCRIPTION: Of all the cherries and plums, this species is by far the preeminent forest tree. It is a classic dominant species of the Allegheny Mountains, where it becomes a tall, straight canopy tree and a superior source of fine hardwood lumber. Smaller trees shoot up in almost every fencerow from the Atlantic seaboard to the prairies of the Midwest. But the biggest cherry of all grows in Washtenaw County, Michigan; it measures 138 feet (42 m) in height and nearly 5 feet (1.5 m) in diameter.

Wild cherry is a tree that follows disturbances. Its seeds are spread by birds to forest openings created by tornadoes, fire, logging or other calamities. Seedlings also attempt to establish under the forest canopy, but they fail or stagnate within a few years unless a storm topples some of the taller trees and opens the area to sunlight. Those that survive grow tall and slender if crowded by their neighbors, but in the open, they become spreading, heavy-limbed trees with arching branches.

Free from competition, wild cherries become broad, spreading trees with arching branches.

LEAVES: Wild cherry leaves resemble those of cultivated cherries, but they have smooth, glossy upper surfaces, finely toothed margins and long, acuminate points. They contain cyanic acid and can be toxic to browsing animals, especially if the acid is concentrated by wilting on broken or pruned branches. Cherry leaves are very uniform in size and shape and grow to about 5 inches (12 cm) long. They turn a deep yellow or orange in autumn, but they are not always as impressive as some of their forest neighbors.

FLOWERS AND FRUITS: The flowers are white and hang in racemes that grow to 5 inches (13 cm) long in early summer after the leaves have developed. Trees sometimes seem covered by these flower clusters, but the foliage detracts somewhat from their beauty. The clusters of tiny, pungent cherries that appear after the flowers are at first green, then red and finally a dark purplish black. The fruits of some trees are tolerably edible but only when absolutely ripe. They ripen sequentially within each cluster, so it is not practical to strip entire clusters at one time. Generally, they would be acceptable for the human palate if only the birds had left them just one more day.

SEASONS:

1. Late spring (for the white flowers);
2. Summer (for the colorful fruit clusters, where they do not create a litter problem, and for the shiny foliage).

NATIVE AND ADAPTIVE RANGE: There are several geographic races of wild cherry, and they combine to cover a lot of ground. The species, in its various forms, grows from Nova Scotia, west to central Minnesota, south to central Florida and the Edwards Plateau of Texas, then southwest through Mexico to Guatemala. Locally adapted selections are hardy throughout eastern North America north into USDA zone 3.

CULTURE: Wild cherry prefers full sun and moderate soil conditions. Good drainage is probably the factor most critical to its success, as is true with many plants of this genus. Seeds germinate readily under a variety of conditions. We have seen wild cherry seedlings emerge from beneath deep layers of mulch, from the middle of a gravel driveway and from piles of old leaves, as well as thousands that volunteer into

The white flowers of wild cherry hang in racemes that grow to 5 inches (13 cm) long in early summer.

The small fruits ripen sequentially within each cluster and sometimes become sweet enough to eat.

cultivated perennial beds. Growing them intentionally, however, requires stratification or fall planting, with foolproof protection from mice. A few mice gathering winter stores can clean out an entire seedbed.

This tree does not seem to appreciate being transplanted, and it should be moved only in the early spring with a good-sized soil ball. Be sure not to plant it too deep or it will wither almost as soon as it tries to leaf out. If your seedling struggles into a nondescript leaning form for a year or two after transplanting, cut it to the ground in the dormant season and it will respond with a vigorous, straight shoot.

PROBLEMS: Wild cherry is a member of one of our most disease- and insect-prone families of trees, but it is more trouble-free than most of its relatives. Its most conspicuous pest, surely, is the eastern tent caterpillar (*Malacosoma americanum*), which totally defoliates entire fencerows of cherry, leaving the branches covered with webs. Trees weakened by these insects, or by any of several other defoliators or fungus diseases, are prone to attack by borers, which inflict wounds on the trunk and limbs and cause them to ooze a gummy sap.

In the forest, wild cherries frequently fall victim to fires, deer, porcupines and other natural hazards. Those in exposed settings in the South are often stunted and disfigured by burls (which are coveted by woodworkers). In cultivation, these trees can be allelopathic to garden plants. They are sensitive to soil disturbance, bark injury and the chain saws of impatient homeowners who tire of the messy fruits and ceaseless twig litter.

CULTIVARS: Geographic races are known to exist over the broad natural range of this tree, but horticultural selections are almost unknown. Upright, weeping and cut-leaf forms are listed in the literature but are not commercially available.

RELATED SPECIES: Pin cherry (*Prunus pensylvanica*) is a slender look-alike that becomes a vigorous early pioneer on disturbed sites. It is more colorful than wild cherry and faster growing, but it is not very long-lived. This is a cold-climate species that ranges across most of Canada and southward into the Great Lake states, New England and the Appalachians. We have seen brilliant, fiery orange fall color on specimens along the north shore of Lake Superior and in the Adirondacks. Old specimens can reach 80 feet (24 m) in height, with thin, straight trunks. A similar species, *Prunus emarginata*, grows in the western mountains of North America.

Chokecherry (*Prunus virginiana*) is a shrubby, suckering species that, in its several varieties, covers an immense natural range that includes 40 states and almost every Canadian province. Chokecherry is an understory tree with remarkable shade tolerance for a cherry. It tends to form clumps of upright stems and has impressive resilience under variable growing conditions.

Unfortunately, the only cultivar of chokecherry commonly sold is a selection variously called 'Canada Red' or 'Shubert', a purple-leaved form totally incongruous with the natural settings that suit this species best. Luckily, wild plants can be propagated easily from seed or by dividing the clumping stems. The Canadian Prairie Farm Rehabilitation Administration's Shelterbelt Centre in Saskatchewan is testing selections of chokecherry for the northern Great Plains, so selected releases for conservation planting may become more readily available.

Wild cherry and its native kin are closely related to the cultivated cherries that originated in Europe and Asia and less closely related to plums, apricots, peaches and almonds, all in the genus *Prunus*.

COMMENTS: Approximately 30 species of *Prunus* are native to North America; together, they constitute some of our most valuable wildlife plants. The half of this group that includes the native cherries is especially important. Cherries are a major food source for more than 100 species of wildlife, and wild cherry is a primary host for over 200 species of butterflies and moths.

Wild cherries in midwestern farm fencerows are often among the first, and the easiest, trees climbed by young farm children. The limb structures of a few of those trees (right foot here, left foot there, handhold above-left) still remain sharply engraved on our memories, many decades later, as do the spacious rural panoramas that became visible from high in those trees and the feelings of freedom and exhilaration that increased with each step upward. Our climbing days are behind us, but some of our old climbing trees remain, ready to thrill new generations of children awakening to the miracles of their natural environment.

Peeling bark is characteristic of wild cherry.

Wild cherry turns yellow or orange in the fall.

WHITE OAK

Quercus alba

DESCRIPTION: Oaks suffer from people's shortsighted demand for trendy but short-lived exotics. As we tree planters gain wisdom and patience and begin to focus more upon the longevity of our work, we turn to our native oaks.

Oaks occur naturally in vast numbers in every one of the 48 contiguous states except for Idaho, and cultivated oaks grow there. Nearly 100 oak species are native to the United States and Canada, and many more can be found in Mexico. Just as the maple (*Acer* spp.) is the official tree of Canada, the oak is the emblematic tree of the United States. And the flagship species of the oak genus is probably white oak, the state tree of Connecticut, Maryland, Iowa and Illinois.

White oaks can live for centuries, becoming ever more massive and picturesque.

White oak is a dominant tree in many landscapes. It lives for centuries under favorable conditions, becoming more massive and picturesque with every passing human generation. Like most oaks, it establishes from acorns sown by wildlife into openings caused by fire, logging, wind or other disturbances, and it grows slowly but relentlessly to become, after the first century or so, the lord of its locality.

While every portion of its natural range can boast notable and noble white oaks, nothing else can quite match the Wye Oak, which grows in its own park (Wye Mills State Park) next to a little brick building in Maryland. This famous national champion is 79 feet (24 m) tall with a canopy that spreads more than 100 feet (31 m). It is supported by a trunk 10 feet (3 m) in diameter. Its enormous spreading limbs have been braced and cabled to discourage injury from windstorms and lightning. So it lives on, as it has since before the birth of this nation, to awe every visitor who knows enough about trees to comprehend its antiquity. The photogenic qualities of such specimens, as they surpass their second or third century, are without parallel in a misty purple sunrise or a moody winter fog.

LEAVES: White oak leaves show the classic rounded-lobed outline used by graphic artists everywhere to symbolize the genus. The logo of The Nature Conservancy, one of our finest natural heritage preservation groups, consists simply of the silhouette of a white oak leaf. The leaves emerge white or pink in the spring and turn medium green as they expand to about 7 inches (18 cm) long. In the fall, they are among the most colorful of all oak leaves, turning various shades of crimson.

FLOWERS AND FRUIT: Oak flowers develop as the leaves expand in spring. Pistillate flowers are minute and barely noticeable, but staminate catkins, seen *en masse* from a distance, give the entire tree a veil of pastel green smoke.

Oaks are wind-pollinated, so tremendous numbers of these catkins are produced to ensure that some of the pollen gets to the right place. To minimize self-pollination, many trees are protogynous, with male and female flowers opening at different times.

The fruits are acorns whose caps and pointed ends are familiar to anyone who has ever walked an oak woods in the early fall. White oak is in the taxonomic subdivision of oaks traditionally known as subgenus *Lepidobalanus* (more recently reclassified as section *Quercus*; see the discussion under Shumard oak, *Quercus shumardii*). This group ripens their acorns in one year. The acorns will sprout without a dormancy period and begin to germinate as soon as they fall from the tree. They are among the very best sources of

White oak leaves display the classic "oak leaf" outline.

food for wildlife and are gathered and hoarded by birds and rodents.

SEASONS:

1. Fall (for the rich color and the acorn crop, which draws a fascinating array of wildlife);
2. Spring (when the tiny new leaves and staminate catkins combine to cast a pastel tint on the artistic superstructure of limbs);
3. Winter (for the character of the tree's architecture and bark);
4. Summer (as a superior shade tree).

NATIVE AND ADAPTIVE RANGE: The natural range of this species is a nearly perfect square whose corners are defined by Minneapolis, Minnesota; Augusta, Maine; Brunswick, Georgia; and Houston, Texas. This range extends across southern Ontario and the edge of Quebec, and trees from northern sources can be planted safely in USDA zone 3.

CULTURE: Plant young white oak in a neutral to acidic soil. Water and fertilize to promote quick growth or "double-flushing" (developing two years' worth of shoots in one year), control competition from weeds and turf, and wait. Planting a white oak shows faith in the future: to nestle an acorn in the earth and start it on its path is to leave a legacy for others to sit beneath or look up at and admire.

Propagation is simple. Healthy acorns (those not infested with insect larvae) should be planted on their sides in the fall, as soon as they mature, and protected from squirrels and mice for the entire first growing season. If you intend to transplant the seedlings, prepare the acorns by putting them in a sealed bag in the refrigerator until the hypocotyls (primary roots) emerge. Pinch back the tips of those roots before planting. This will encourage a branched root system, without which oaks can be difficult to transplant.

Acorns grown in pots tend to develop long, circling roots that, years later, can girdle a young tree. Some nurseries address this problem by using deep, ribbed pots. We prefer root-control pots coated inside with copper (which curtails root growth) or bottomless pots (on raised benches or pallets) because the taproots will stop growing as soon as they emerge from the soil into the air. But the best solution is to plant the acorn where you want the tree to grow for the next 500 years.

PROBLEMS: White oaks will not survive long in shade and are intolerant of poor drainage and alkaline soil, which will cause chlorosis. Old trees are extremely sensitive to construction disturbance within their root zones and to planting turf around a tree on what had been a forest duff ground cover. The acorns can be a litter problem, but birds and squirrels usually clean them up before winter. Anthracnose

These odd bark patterns on white oaks are the work of a harmless fungus.

(*Gnomonia quercina*) disfigures many oaks during wet years and can be particularly severe on white oak, but it generally does not cause permanent damage. New foliage that develops in the summer as a second growth flush can be particularly susceptible to mildew from *Microsphaera* species and related fungi.

As the preeminent genus of hardwood trees in North America (*i.e.* the most species, the most individual trees, the widest distribution), oaks, in general, are subject to many other nuisance diseases and insects, which usually are not serious. They are famous for the beauty and variety of the galls (mostly harmless growths) they support. A benign bark condition, *Corticium* patch, causes interesting smooth, patchy patterns on the bark of this and some other white oak species.

All oaks are cake and ice cream to the notorious gypsy moth (*Lymantria dispar*), which was introduced in the 1860s from Europe. This insect defoliates more than 6,000 square miles (15,000 square km) of oak forest each year, killing some trees and stressing others. Oaks are our most important hardwood timber genus, so many forestry scientists are working furiously to bring this epidemic under control. Specimen trees may be sprayed by an arborist, if necessary, to minimize gypsy moth damage.

A better long-term solution would be to enlist the aid of biological controls, such as the fungus *Entomophaga maimaiga*, which is showing great success in controlling this pest in experimental evaluations. Other promising tools for control include the braconid endoparasite *Rogas lymantriae* (an ichneumon fly), *Cotesia melanoscela* (a small parasitic wasp), a nucleopolyhedrosis virus called Gypchek and several parasitic *microsporidia* organisms.

Oaks hold great promise for landscaping, but they have not been promoted for this use because of several other perceived problems. Until recently, they have been difficult to propagate from cuttings or even by grafting, so exceptional selections could not be replicated easily. Many oak species are difficult to transplant, but root-training techniques used in modern nurseries overcome this. Old oaks on upland sites are often troubled by sudden competition from and excess irrigation of newly planted lawns. For these trees to remain healthy, we must understand this and respect their root zones.

CULTIVARS: A few variant forms of white oak are described in the literature, but no selections are commercially available yet. White oak can be hybridized with other oaks in its subgenus, and some of the hybrids are magnificent. Starhill-Heritage Trees, a horticultural research association owned by Guy Sternberg and Earl Cully, is at the forefront of hybrid oak cultivar research in North America. Guy and Earl have studied hybrid oaks for more than two decades and have recently selected several superior white oak hybrids for release to the nursery trade. More are under evaluation now.

Old white oaks are dignified trees that lend serenity to cemeteries and other pastoral landscapes.

Above: White oak develops richer fall color than most other members of its section. Below left: Oaks hybridize freely; this hybrid of white oak and chestnut oak is one of several superior new cultivars being developed for the landscape industry.

RELATED SPECIES: Post oak (*Quercus stellata*) is an even slower growing version of white oak. It is the ultimate drought-resistant tree. We have seen stunted 400-year-old post oaks growing on xeric south-facing rock ledges with their roots in hot, thin, sterile soils. It also tolerates flatwoods soils, which are soggy in the spring and brick-hard in summer. Post oak makes a fine, firm tree on a good site, but it usually does not attain the size of other white oaks, although the record tree in Surry County, Virginia, is 85 feet (26 m) tall and more than 6 feet (1.9 m) in diameter. It really excels, though, as an ancient, gnarled "hangman's tree" in a xeric setting too severe for a lesser tree. It should be preserved wherever it occurs.

The related sand post oak (*Quercus margaretta*) is thought by some to be a stabilized natural hybrid of post oak with the Rocky Mountain oak (*Quercus gambelii*), a small species from west of our area sometimes seen in cultivation and useful in experimental hybridization. If this is true, the establishment of such a hybrid swarm would have to date back to a prehistoric time when the range of the two parent species overlapped. The largest sand post oak, a symmetrical spreading tree in a cemetery in Augusta, Georgia, is 67 feet (20 m) tall but almost 100 feet (30 m) across the canopy, with a trunk 3 feet 5 inches (1 m) thick.

There are many other members of the white oak taxonomic section (*Quercus*) in North and Central America, Europe, Asia and Africa and many additional oaks in the western hemisphere in sections *Lobatae* (red oaks) and *Protobalanus* (golden oaks). Worldwide, there are several hundred species and countless hybrids within the genus and many more in the closely allied genus *Lithocarpus*, the tan oaks. Oaks are in the same family as chestnuts (*Castanea*) and beeches (*Fagus*). Some of our other native oak species are discussed in the following pages.

COMMENTS: Ancient white oaks probably appear on more inventories of historic trees, over a broader area, than any other species. Because of their predominance within their range, many historic events took place near them; and because of their longevity, many of them survive as witnesses to those events. One of the most impressive is the Richards white oak in Cecil County, Maryland, which served as a landmark on a map made for William Penn in 1681. It provided a camp shelter for General Lafayette in 1781 and for a cavalry unit during the Civil War. By 1965, it shaded an area 115 feet (35 m) across.

Among the Sternbergs' collection of tree memorabilia is a small piece of white oak wood from the frontier fort of Jacob Zumwalt, built in the 1790s northwest of St. Louis. This structure hosted Daniel Boone and Chief Blackhawk, was passed by the Lewis and Clark Expedition on May 22, 1804, and was the site of the first Missouri battle of the War of 1812. Zumwalt's Fort sheltered its builder and his successors for about a century; it was then abandoned to the elements for another century. Yet the scrap of wood remains rock-hard today. It holds a special meaning for Edie Sternberg, who is Jacob Zumwalt's great-great-great-great-great-great-granddaughter.

BUR OAK

Quercus macrocarpa

DESCRIPTION: Anyone who grew up on the prairies of the Midwest knows the classic North American savanna tree species, bur oak. It belongs to the white oak group, or taxonomic section *Quercus* (formerly called subgenus *Lepidobalanus*), which is the most widespread subdivision of oaks. Although bur oak as a species is widespread as well, it is most appreciated on the Great Plains, where it stands resolute against the elements that devour all lesser trees.

The classic open form of the bur oak is well represented by this state champion in Missouri.

Just as white oak (*Quercus alba*) is the lord of the eastern deciduous forest, bur oak is the preeminent tree of Midwest savannas, although each extends considerably into the habitat of the other. It is a majestic, rugged tree—extremely variable even for an oak—that tolerates a very wide range of habitats. In the extreme northwest sector of its range, it survives as a shrub. Under more favorable conditions, it ranks among the most impressive of all trees. The champion bur oak, which grows by a rail fence in Paris, Kentucky, is 95 feet (29 m) tall and more than 8 feet (2.6 m) in diameter.

LEAVES: If bur oak had better fall color, instead of its dull tan hue, it might be rated the king of the oaks. Its summer foliage is beautiful, with dark upper surfaces accented in the wind by shimmering light undersides. The mature leaves reach about 7 inches (18 cm) long, although the size varies from region to region. The leaves have deep indentations, or sinuses, that separate the base of the leaf from the distal end.

FLOWERS AND FRUIT: Bur oak flowers are similar to those of the other white oaks. The fruits can be among the largest of acorns, sometimes exceeding 2 inches (5 cm) in diameter, and they come equipped with a cap-fringe beard that makes them appear even larger. These acorns are among our most valuable wildlife foods, especially on the prairies where other mast is scarce.

SEASONS:

1. Winter (perhaps no other tree can match the rugged venerability of an old bur oak with frost or snow accenting its rough bark);
2. Summer (a most-appreciated shade tree on the hot prairie).

NATIVE AND ADAPTIVE RANGE: Bur oak, one of the hardiest of all oaks, grows from well north of Winnipeg, Manitoba, down to the Gulf Coast of Texas and northeast across southern Ontario to isolated populations in New Brunswick. It will grow under cultivation from USDA zone 2 south.

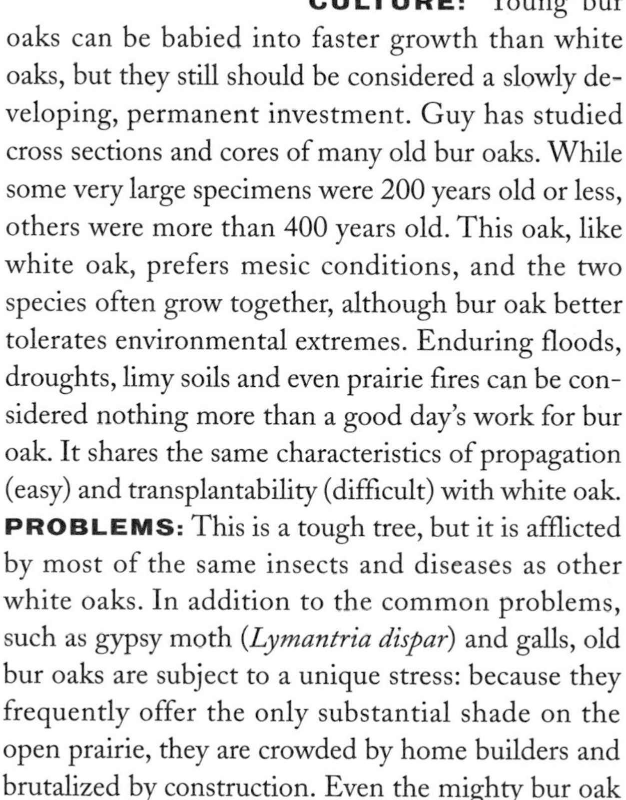

CULTURE: Young bur oaks can be babied into faster growth than white oaks, but they still should be considered a slowly developing, permanent investment. Guy has studied cross sections and cores of many old bur oaks. While some very large specimens were 200 years old or less, others were more than 400 years old. This oak, like white oak, prefers mesic conditions, and the two species often grow together, although bur oak better tolerates environmental extremes. Enduring floods, droughts, limy soils and even prairie fires can be considered nothing more than a good day's work for bur oak. It shares the same characteristics of propagation (easy) and transplantability (difficult) with white oak.

PROBLEMS: This is a tough tree, but it is afflicted by most of the same insects and diseases as other white oaks. In addition to the common problems, such as gypsy moth (*Lymantria dispar*) and galls, old bur oaks are subject to a unique stress: because they frequently offer the only substantial shade on the open prairie, they are crowded by home builders and brutalized by construction. Even the mighty bur oak has its limits, and the ravages of development often bring it to an untimely end.

CULTIVARS: The USDA Soil Conservation Service has released two vigorous seed-propagated selections of bur oak from Oklahoma called 'Boomer' (from Boomer Creek) and 'Lippert' (from Payne County) for windbreaks on the Great Plains. Other bur oaks collected from the entire western range of the species in the United States and Canada are being tested by the USDA Agricultural Research Service Laboratory in Mandan, North Dakota. Some of these same selections are under evaluation at Starhill Forest in Illinois, together with specimens from farther east. The Prairie Farm Rehabilitation Administration of Canada is conducting similar tests in Saskatchewan.

Another seedling strain, 'Sweet Idaho', was selected for its palatable acorns by Bear Creek Nursery. The parent is of unknown provenance (it grows in northern Idaho, where no oaks are native). Some seedlings exhibit red fall color, so we suspect it to be of hybrid origin. Oikos Nursery offers, among its extensive oak listings, seedlings of 'Ashworth' (a precocious, hardy northern selection) and several bur oak hybrids from Texas oak breeder Miguel Marquez. Starhill-Heritage Trees also has several bur oak hybrids under study for possible introduction as cultivars.

RELATED SPECIES: Swamp white oak (*Quercus bicolor*) is a close mimic of bur oak and shares its adaptability to various site conditions. As its name implies, it is one of the oaks most tolerant of poor drainage, but it does well when planted on upland sites. Swamp white oak has very sweet acorns, and those from some trees can be eaten fresh, without leaching or roasting. This species is one of the easiest of the white oaks to transplant, so it has become popular with nurseries. It is a northern species, growing from the Great Lakes region south to the Ohio River Valley. Wayne County, Michigan, boasts the largest known specimen, a tall, straight tree that towers 144 feet (44 m) on a 6-foot-thick (1.9 m) trunk.

Bur oak struggles to display a little fall color; its foliage is more impressive, though, during the growing season.

In the South, swamp white oak is replaced by its southern counterpart, overcup oak (*Quercus lyrata*). Probably the most flood-tolerant white oak of all, it thrives in swamps that sometimes remain underwater for the entire growing season. The overcup oak acorn is almost fully enclosed by the involucre, or cup, and falls from the tree with the cup intact. The cups float, which helps the floodwaters disperse the seeds. The largest overcup oak is 156 feet (48 m) tall and nearly 7 feet (2.1 m) in diameter. Other white oaks, worldwide, are closely related.

COMMENTS: Bur oak is one of our most variable oak species, and it is very prone to hybridize with other white oaks. Many intermediate forms show genetic influences from white oak, swamp white oak and other neighboring species. It has been crossed successfully with many North American, European and Asian oak species.

Because of its preferred open-country habitat, bur oak often develops into a spreading shade tree—the form most familiar to its admirers. In the deep woods of northern Indiana, however, and the terrace forests of the Wabash River valley in southeastern Illinois, we know old monarch bur oaks with tall, straight trunks, bare of limbs for more than half their height.

This species is among the toughest of a hardy family, about which the noted horticulturist John Evelyn remarked, "Oaks prosper exceedingly even in gravel and moist clays, which most other trees abhor; yea, even the coldest clay-grounds that will hardly graze . . . there grow oaks . . . out of the very walls of Silcester in Hantshire, which seem to strike root in the very stones." Evelyn made these observations on October 15, 1662, during a presentation before one of the first meetings of the respected British Royal Society. The evidence of ensuing centuries affirms their accuracy.

CHINKAPIN OAK

Quercus muhlenbergii (Q. muehlenbergii)

DESCRIPTION: Within the white oak taxonomic section (*Quercus*; also known as subgenus *Lepidobalanus*) are several species that have handsome leaves with serrate margins, like those of chestnuts (*Castanea* spp.). They are called chestnut oaks, and we separate them from the other white oaks here merely on the basis of their foliage. All white oak types are closely related.

The most adaptable and widespread of the chestnut oaks is chinkapin oak (*Quercus muhlenbergii*), which is also called chinquapin or yellow chestnut oak. It is unusual among our native oaks in that it is very well adapted to alkaline soil. We have found this species growing on xeric limestone bluffs, in floodplains and in mesic forests and savannas without apparent preference. It seldom dominates any ecological community, but it plays a minor part in many different settings over a broad range.

Chinkapin oak seldom dominates any ecological community but plays a minor role in many different settings.

Chinkapin oak is at its best in the Midwest, where many outstanding specimens can be seen. The current United States national champion grows on the Union County Waterfowl Refuge in Illinois. It is 120 feet (37 m) tall with a trunk more than 6 feet (1.9 m) in diameter. Guy has found one with an even larger trunk growing nearby at Horseshoe Lake in southern Illinois, one of the premier locations in the Midwest for big-tree hunters.

LEAVES: The leaves of this species are unlobed but consistently serrate along the margins, with acute, incurved teeth. They grow up to 8 inches (20 cm) long on vigorous young trees but usually stop at about 6 inches (15 cm) on mature specimens. They can be more than half as wide as they are long, but they are often very narrow. Their light-colored underside contrasts attractively with the lustrous yellow-green upper surface. Chinkapin oak usually develops a pleasant yellow or light orange fall color and stands out among associated oaks, which turn red or tan. The fall color is accented by the bright gray bark and the convoluted branch structure on picturesque old specimens.

FLOWERS AND FRUIT: The chestnut oaks as a group have flowering characteristics as described under white oak (*Quercus alba*). Chinkapin oak has the smallest acorns of any of the chestnut oaks and some of the most precocious. They mature in one year and in humid climates often begin to germinate before falling from the tree.

SEASONS:
1. Summer (for the attractive foliage, making it one of our most beautiful shade trees);
2. Fall (not the best of the oaks for color, but not bad);
3. Spring (for the pastel smoke of the catkins);
4. Winter (for the bright bark and picturesque branching).

NATIVE AND ADAPTIVE RANGE: Chinkapin oak grows in a diagonal band from scattered areas in New England and southern Ontario southwest through the central states to isolated populations in Mexico and New Mexico. It is hardy north into USDA zone 4, with attention to provenance.

The other chestnut oaks are not as widespread, but they are often more common where they occur. Rock chestnut oak (*Quercus montana*), which was formerly called *Quercus prinus*, is a mountain tree that grows along the Appalachians. Swamp chestnut oak (*Quercus michauxii*), which is also called *Quercus prinus* (by different authorities), grows in well-drained bottomlands of the Southeast. Both are large, magnificent trees. Dwarf chinkapin oak (*Quercus prinoides*) is a shrubby species that forms thickets in dry, rocky areas in the central states. All three are hardy north into USDA zone 5.

An ancient chinkapin oak shows the characteristic branch spread of most trees of this species.

CULTURE: Chinkapin oak is not easy to transplant because of its deep taproot. Like most oaks, it can be successfully moved by mechanical transplanting machines, which excavate a deep, cone-shaped soil ball.Oaks are best moved in the early spring. This species, though, is very easy to start from seed. The acorns should be sown in the fall as soon as they can be picked easily from the cups without tearing at the point of attachment. They absolutely must be protected from rodents for the entire first growing season. We have lost seedlings in late summer to chipmunks digging them up to eat the remaining food in the cotyledons of the attached acorns.

Unlike the other chestnut oaks, and the genus as a whole, chinkapin oak loves alkaline soil. It will grow very rapidly (for an oak) under attentive cultivation if given water, fertilizer and mulch, as needed.

PROBLEMS: The chestnut oaks are susceptible in varying degrees to the problems that affect other white oaks, with the exception that chinkapin oak will not suffer from chlorosis on alkaline sites. Refer to white oak (*Quercus alba*) for additional information.

CULTIVARS: We are not aware of any selections currently available in the nursery trade. Chinkapin oak is a variable tree and deserves some attention in this regard. Starhill-Heritage Trees is working with several superior hybrids involving chinkapin oak and rock chestnut oak. Some of them may become available in the near future.

RELATED SPECIES: Rock chestnut oak is a handsome and durable tree with rich fall color that varies from old gold to deep maroon. It is one of the few white oaks available from many nurseries. Like chinkapin oak, it is very resistant to drought once established. Its bark is dark and deeply furrowed, an unusual trait for a native white oak. The biggest rock chestnut oak was found in Northport, New York, with a height of 95 feet (29 m) and a trunk 7 feet (2.1 m) in diameter.

Of any oak, swamp chestnut oak may have the most striking combination of scarlet fall foliage and whitened bark. It prefers deep, rich soils, where it grows straight and tall to immense proportions. The largest one known stands in a forest opening in

Fayette County, Alabama. It is the tallest of all national champion oaks, rising 200 feet (61 m) on a clear trunk more than 5 feet (1.6 m) thick. Rock chestnut oak and swamp chestnut oak have large, sweet acorns relished by wildlife and livestock.

Dwarf chinkapin oak is a shrubby species that is otherwise very similar to chinkapin oak. Because it was described first, it takes priority taxonomically for those who argue that one is a variety of the other. Some authorities, therefore, list chinkapin oak as a variety (*acuminata*) of dwarf chinkapin oak.

Like other oaks, chestnut oaks commonly hybridize with other species in their taxonomic section. Guy nominated the current national champion Deam oak (*Quercus alba* x *Q. muhlenbergii*), which he found in Sangamon County, Illinois. It is a stately specimen 77 feet (24 m) tall with a branch spread of more than 100 feet (31 m) and has a trunk nearly 5 feet (1.4 m) in diameter. Refer to white oak (*Quercus alba*) for additional information on related species.

COMMENTS: On a trip into the isolated cloud forests of Mexico, one may encounter strange oaks of every shape and size. Many are evergreen and tropical in appearance. Some are dwarf and reminiscent of the chaparral oak species of the western United States. Among the hundreds of these unfamiliar species can be found one old friend—the chinkapin oak. It is the only oak from the eastern United States and Canada that is adaptable enough to grow side by side with the unusual oaks in the Mexican mountains.

Top: Chinkapin oak develops a dependable yellow fall color. Above: The typical autumn color of chestnut oak is a rich crimson.

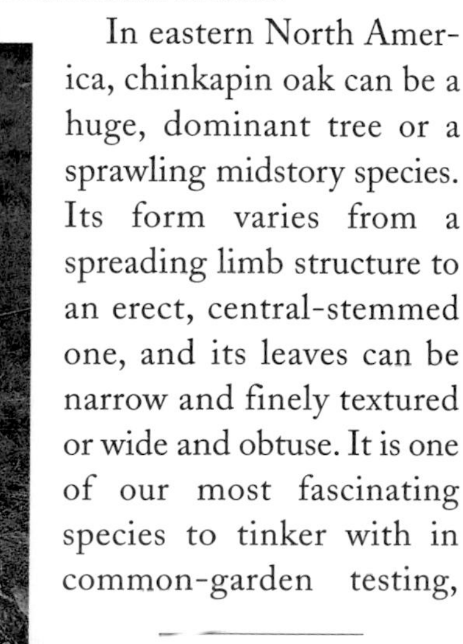

In eastern North America, chinkapin oak can be a huge, dominant tree or a sprawling midstory species. Its form varies from a spreading limb structure to an erect, central-stemmed one, and its leaves can be narrow and finely textured or wide and obtuse. It is one of our most fascinating species to tinker with in common-garden testing, where specimens originating in different areas, from Mexico to Canada, are planted together under identical conditions so that genetic variations can be directly compared. Chinkapin oak is also quite useful for hybridization experiments. Traits such as its alkaline soil tolerance, narrow serrate foliage and unique growth forms might be combined with the red fall colors, large leaves or persistent foliage of some other white oaks to derive offspring with exceptional ornamental value and adaptability. Depending on hybrid vigor, some of these crosses will be faster growing than either parent species—a very valuable trait when working with the oaks.

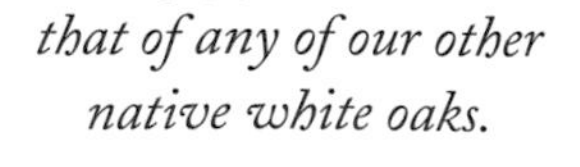

Chestnut oak bark is rough and deeply fissured, unlike that of any of our other native white oaks.

WILLOW OAK

Quercus phellos

DESCRIPTION: A surprising number of native oaks have narrow leaves that look anything but oak-like. Most belong to the red oak section *Lobatae* (formerly known as subgenus *Erythrobalanus*), a group limited to the western hemisphere. The narrow-leaved species in this group grow mostly in the South, and the most widely known example is probably the willow oak.

Willow oak is an upright, fast-growing red oak species native to alluvial soils in warm, humid climates. It is one of the most frequently planted landscape oaks in the Southeast because of its fine-textured foliage, rapid growth and ability to be easily transplanted. It is not generally among the largest oak species, but huge specimens can be found on moist, well-drained sites. The record tree is located in Oxford, Maryland. It is 112 feet (34 m) in height with a branch spread of the same dimension and a trunk more than 7 feet (2.2 m) in diameter.

Willow oak, like this one at the White House, is a popular shade tree throughout the South.

LEAVES: Willow oak leaves are among the narrowest of any of our oaks; they reach about 4 inches (10 cm) long but are less than 1 inch (2 cm) wide. They are without lobes or teeth on the margins. Like those of many of the narrow-leaved oaks, they stay green late into the fall, and in mild climates, some persist into winter. Occasionally willow oaks will develop a dark yellow fall color.

FLOWERS AND FRUIT: The flowering characteristics of willow oak and the other oaks in this section are identical to those previously described under white oak (*Quercus alba*), with one major exception: willow oaks and all of our other eastern native oaks in section *Lobatae* require two years to mature their acorns. They are more bitter than those of white oaks but have a higher fat content and become valuable to wildlife later in the winter. Acorns of most of our narrow-leaved oaks, and particularly willow oak, are very small and do not cause a significant litter problem. Their size is particularly appreciated by many wildlife species that cannot handle the large acorns of some other oaks.

SEASONS:

1. Summer (the fine texture of the foliage is the primary aesthetic attribute);
2. Spring (during the blooming period).

NATIVE AND ADAPTIVE RANGE: Willow oak is native on moist sites throughout the Southeast and north to southern Illinois and New Jersey. It is one of the hardiest of the narrow-leaved oaks and can be planted north into USDA zone 5. The similar shingle oak, (*Quercus imbricaria*) is primarily an upland species that grows naturally as far north as the southern edge of the Great Lakes and can be planted into USDA zone 4. The other species are best used in USDA zone 6 or southward.

CULTURE: Willow oak is a popular street tree in the South and seems capable of adapting to a variety of growing conditions. It likes moisture and full sun and does best in acidic soil. Fairly large trees can be transplanted successfully with care. Seeds (acorns) may be sown—and protected from rodents—in the fall as soon as ripe or, because they have a dormancy period, stratified until early spring. Most of the narrow-leaved oaks tend to develop weak crotches, so saplings should be trained and pruned to a strong form.

PROBLEMS: Red oak types, such as willow oak, are

The fine-textured foliage of willow oak is one of its primary aesthetic attributes.

much more susceptible to oak wilt (*Ceratocystis fagacearum*) than most of the white oaks (section *Quercus*) because of their wood structure. Red oaks have open pores that allow the wilt to invade their vascular system quickly, with fatal consequences. The disease can best be discouraged by promptly removing dead trees, by cutting root grafts to adjacent trees and by not pruning in early summer in areas where the wilt is prevalent. Also, the wood of these narrow-leaved oaks is more brittle and subject to decay than that of white oaks. They should be planted away from houses so any falling limbs will not cause damage.

The red oaks in general are subject to severe defoliation from gypsy moth (*Lymantria dispar*) and suffer most of the other problems described in the white oak section. However, the primary leaf ailment in this group is not anthracnose, as in the white oaks, but pine-oak rusts (*Cronartium* spp.) and leaf blister (*Taphrina caerulescens*).

CULTIVARS: Species in the red oak section have been difficult to propagate asexually. Consequently, very few cultivars of willow oak and its relatives have entered the nursery trade. Researchers are finding ways to graft the red oaks now and propagate them from cuttings and tissue culture, so we expect to see a surge in cultivars soon.

RELATED SPECIES: Shingle oak is the closest mimic of willow oak in the Midwest and is certainly the hardiest. Its leaves are about twice as large as those of willow oak, and it is not restricted to bottomland sites. Shingle oak grows in disturbed areas across a variety of habitats. Its leaves sometimes turn dark red or yellowish in the fall, but they may remain green until browned by a hard freeze and then cling to the tree until spring. The largest shingle oak is in Cincinnati, Ohio; it is 104 feet (32 m) tall with a trunk more than 5 feet (1.6 m) in diameter.

Like willow oak, water oak (*Quercus nigra*) is planted along streets in the South. It is another wetland species with slightly wider, spatula-shaped leaves. Water oak can be grown north through USDA zone 6, but careful early pruning is needed to keep

Top: Shingle oak leaves unroll as they expand in the spring. Above: The small acorns of shingle oak grow in clusters and require two years to mature.

this beautiful but brittle species from developing a weak structure and breaking in ice storms. Kept intact, a water oak can grow quite large in a relatively short time. The national champion is 128 feet (39 m) tall and 7 feet (2.1 m) in diameter. It grows in Calhoun County in northwest Florida, where ice is not much of a problem.

Two other large oaks resemble willow oak; both are called laurel oak. Swamp laurel oak (*Quercus laurifolia*) is a bottomland species with leaves intermediate between those of willow oak and water oak. The similar upland laurel oak (*Quercus hemisphaerica*) has thicker, leathery leaves with sharper points and retains its green leaves for most of the year. Some authorities don't distinguish between the two species, but upland laurel oak is typically a larger tree of upland, sandy soils. The largest reported swamp laurel oak grows in Marengo County, Alabama. It stands 93 feet (29 m) tall and is over 7 feet (2.1 m) in diameter. The champion upland laurel oak, also known as the Darlington Oak, is found in Wrens, Georgia. It stands 96 feet (29 m) tall with a trunk more than 6 feet (1.9 m) in diameter.

Bluejack oak, *Quercus incana* (*Q. cinerea*), is a small understory tree of sandy pine forests. It has attractive blue-green foliage that becomes wine-colored in the fall in northern areas. It has been root-hardy in USDA zone 5 in Illinois under our limited testing. Bluejack oak forms thickets in the wild, but individual trees can reach into the forest canopy. A dwarf, related oak of sandy soils in the Atlantic coastal plain is the thicket-forming runner oak (*Quercus pumila*). It lives as an understory shrub in piney woods, where it forms clonal colonies by sprouting from the roots. Refer to white oak (*Quercus alba*) and to the other oak sections for more information on related species.

COMMENTS: Fort Massac State Park was dedicated in 1908 as the first state park in Illinois, and for good reason. The site has a commanding, strategic view of the lower Ohio River, it has been occupied for military purposes by Spanish explorers and French traders and it has been the site of two French forts, a British fort, an American fort (Fort Massac, 1794-1814) and a Civil War training camp. Three willow oaks grow within throwing distance of the restored American fort. A few historians had suggested that all of the scenic old trees should be removed to recreate the freshly cleared landscape that would have existed around a fort. Luckily, their views did not prevail. Much care was taken decades ago, during the initial reconstruction, to protect the significant trees, including the willow oaks, two of which are very large. (Guy was the state's landscape architect on the project.) These efforts proved worthwhile. The willow oaks and surrounding trees offer a picturesque backdrop for views and photographs of the fort and help screen out the intrusive new Interstate 24 bridge across the Ohio River.

Since the passage of the Endangered Species Act, willow oak has been recognized as a protected species in Illinois, where it reaches the extreme northwestern limit of its natural range. Seedlings from the unique, hardy provenance at Fort Massac can be planted far north of their natural range with great success, providing northerners with willow oaks they might not otherwise be able to enjoy.

RED OAK

Quercus rubra (Q. borealis)

DESCRIPTION: Like willow oak (*Quercus phellos*) and the other narrow-leaved oaks, the lobed-leaved red oaks belong to the taxonomic section *Lobatae* (also called subgenus *Erythrobalanus*). Some species are northern, others are distinctly southern. The recognized king of the northern species is "northern red oak," or simply "red oak." It is the state tree of New Jersey and the provincial tree of Prince Edward Island. This is the familiar oak seen in nearly every mesic deciduous forest, with a huge, columnar trunk that rises half its height to the first massive limb and its dark bark striped with long, smooth plates separated by deep furrows. This smooth, striped bark is a primary ornamental feature. We have noticed beautiful red oaks planted in the Pacific Northwest that have not yet begun to develop bark furrows, though they exceed 2 feet (60 cm) in diameter.

Northern red oak becomes one of the largest oaks in North America.

Red oak is a tree of coves, northern exposures and moist but well-drained soils. It grows rapidly for an oak and becomes one of the largest trees in the deciduous forests of eastern North America. We have seen many red oaks more than 120 feet (36 m) tall. The United States champion is shorter, at 66 feet (20 m), but its trunk is nearly 10 feet (3 m) in diameter.

LEAVES: Red oak leaves are smooth and lustrous but thin compared with those of similar species. They have pointed, shallow lobes, each ending in several aristae (small, flexible bristles). They grow up to 9 inches (23 cm) in length by half as wide and are broadest at the middle. Most species in this taxonomic section have nice fall color, and red oak can turn crimson, golden orange or russet.

FLOWERS AND FRUIT: The flowers are like those of willow oak (*Quercus phellos*) and develop into mature acorns after two years. Red oak acorns are some of the largest of any of the red oak subgenus; they often exceed 1 inch (2.5 cm) in length and have a shallow, plate-like cup that covers only the end of the fruit.

SEASONS:

1. Fall (many of these trees develop outstanding color);
2. Winter (the clean, open branching pattern and the smooth, striped bark are attractive and best seen in the dormant season);
3. Spring (during the blooming period);
4. Summer (a clean, attractive shade tree).

NATIVE AND ADAPTIVE RANGE: Together with bur oak (*Quercus macrocarpa*), red oak is our hardiest species for northern climates, and it is the most widely distributed oak in Canada. Although it has a smaller stature in the far northern end of its range, it can be found from northern Minnesota around the northwest shore of Lake Superior and eastward north of Lake Huron and Lake St. John to Chaleur Bay in Quebec. From there, it is distributed south throughout the eastern United States to the Atlantic coastal plain and southwest to eastern Oklahoma. Red oak can be grown in USDA zone 3.

CULTURE: Red oak prefers everything in moderation: moist but well-drained soil and lots of light, but not necessarily full sun. This is one of the more shade-tolerant of our large red oaks, and it can develop well under a broken canopy of older trees. It is relatively easy to transplant for an oak and should be moved with a deep soil ball in early spring.

The smooth green leaves of northern red oak have colorful petioles.

The fall color of northern red oak varies from amber to crimson.

Acorns may be sown in the fall or stratified for spring sowing. Either way, protect them from rodents for the first growing season. Ohio State University has experimented with cultural techniques for growing red oak and has perfected the "Ohio Production System" for producing 7-foot (2.1 m) seedlings in containers, from acorns, in six months.

PROBLEMS: All of the northern red oak species are very susceptible to oak wilt (*Ceratocystis fagacearum*). This disease is becoming an epidemic in the northwest part of the range of red oak. Infected trees should be removed immediately, and root grafts with adjacent susceptible trees should be cut to prevent vascular infection. Because the primary insects that carry this wilt are attracted to pruning wounds, it is inviting trouble to prune any red oak species in wilt-infested areas during the growing season. Arborists can offer trees some protection by injecting them with fungicides. However, the cost makes the treatment impractical on a large scale.

The "king" of the northern oak species, red oak is the provincial tree of Prince Edward Island.

Some fascinating insects dine almost exclusively on red oaks, including common walkingstick (*Diapheromera femorata*) and giant walkingstick (*Megaphasma dentricus*), neither of which really damage the tree. Other problems are listed under white oak (*Quercus alba*) and willow oak (*Quercus phellos*). Northern red oak is less subject to weather damage than most of the other red oaks.

CULTIVARS: This tree is so predictably variable from region to region that natural geographic varieties were once separated on the basis of acorn size, but taxonomists now seem reluctant to maintain such distinct classifications. Foresters have invested much research into the effects of provenance and of genetically induced improvements in form and growth rate, so many superior strains and geographically adapted types have been identified and propagated for timber.

Such variability should lead to cultivars with exceptional horticultural or ornamental merit as well, but this has not happened yet. However, with the problems of vegetative propagation now being solved, we expect to see some red oak selections in the nursery trade in the future.

RELATED SPECIES: Black oak (*Quercus velutina*) is a comparable tree that covers much the same southern and central range, but its range stops around Kingston, Ontario, in the North. It occupies poor, dry sites, is intolerant of shade and is more prone to structural damage and decay than red oak, but some trees escape such injury to reach massive proportions. The largest one grows in East Granby, Connecticut. It is a stout specimen that is 84 feet (26 m) tall and more than 8 feet (2.5 m) in diameter.

Black oak leaves are thick, glossy and stiff, and they often turn deep orange or red in the fall. Their early-spring color is just as attractive: a bright, velvety red. The inner bark of this tree was a primary source of yellow dye for early Americans and was harvested for export as quercitron. Black oak is extremely difficult to transplant and is best grown from seed or preserved in place.

Northern pin oak (*Quercus ellipsoidalis*) shares much of the northwestern range of red oak. It appears similar to black oak, with comparable susceptibility to damage and decay, but in youth, it maintains a classic pyramidal form and its red fall color is outstanding. It is a smaller species than northern red oak, usually found on poor soils. The largest is 85 feet (26 m) tall and 4 feet 5 inches (1.3 m) in diameter.Some authorities believe northern pin oak is simply a northern race of scarlet oak (*Quercus coccinea*) or a stabilized hybrid of some combination of scarlet oak, red oak, black oak and possibly pin oak (*Quercus palustris*).

Pin oak looks much like northern pin oak, but it usually has smaller leaves and prefers wet, acidic soils. It can be found from the southern edge of the Great Lakes south through Tennessee and under cultivation throughout most of the United States. We have found old references to "pine oak" in the literature, probably because of its excurrent, conifer-shaped juvenile form. This might have been shortened to the present name, but the tree also has numerous small twigs, which makes it look like a pin cushion. Our old friend Floyd Swink at the Morton Arboretum wryly claims wood from this tree was used to make the wooden puppet Pinocchio (pin-oak-io). The national champion pin oak is a beautiful, symmetrical tree that grows in a pasture in Henderson County, Tennessee. It is 110 feet (34 m) tall and more than 6 feet (1.9 m) in diameter.

Pin oak becomes very chlorotic on neutral or alkaline soil, but it grows so rapidly, displays such nice red fall color and develops such a symmetrical form as a young sapling in the nursery that it sells well and has been our most popular oak in cultivation. We expect to see the sales of pin oak decline as other, more adaptable oak species and hybrids become more widely known and grown.

Of all the native oaks, the pin oak, such as this one on the grounds of the Illinois State Capitol, is the most commonly planted landscape tree.

COMMENTS: Many old red oaks are associated with historical events. The Salt Fork Oak growing in Champaign County, Illinois, was Abraham Lincoln's landmark for finding the ford he used to cross the Salt Fork of the Vermilion River on his trips as an attorney to the circuit court in Danville.

Red oak is becoming steadily more popular in the nursery trade and might soon take the best-seller position ahead of pin oak. It is also the most intensively managed of all our oak species for timber production because of its growth rate, good form and wood quality. Red oak is the most popular of our native oaks for planting as an exotic species in Europe; it grows there with great vigor.

SHUMARD OAK

Quercus shumardii

DESCRIPTION: The northern red oaks (*Quercus rubra* et al.) have several counterparts in the southern United States. We have selected Shumard oak, one of the largest and most popular, as the example to describe in detail here. Shumard oak is a giant bottomland tree. Its columnar trunk, striped smooth bark, branching pattern, foliage, large acorns and great proportions all remind one of northern red oak. The current recordholder, in Lake Providence, Louisiana, is 97 feet (30 m) tall. Its branch spread exceeds its height, and its trunk is nearly 7 feet (2.1 m) in diameter.

Shumard oak forms a strong, tapered buttress of roots in the seasonally wet bottomlands where it grows best.

LEAVES: Every botany student knows the Shumard oak leaf. It appears on the cover of *Gray's Manual of Botany*. The leaves are the size of northern red oak leaves but are proportionately wider and more deeply and intricately lobed. Most Shumard oak trees develop beautiful red foliage in the fall, and they are among the first of our oaks each year to change color.

FLOWERS AND FRUIT: These characteristics are similar to northern red oak (*Quercus rubra*).

SEASONS:

1. Fall (this oak and its close relatives are some of our most spectacular trees for color);
2. Summer (an excellent shade tree with glossy, deeply lobed leaves);
3. Spring (during the blooming period).

NATIVE AND ADAPTIVE RANGE: This is a dominant tree of the lower Mississippi River Valley, but it can be found over a considerable natural range from Pennsylvania, Indiana and Missouri southward. It even grows in southern Ontario, where it is rare enough to be listed as a vulnerable species. The range is not precisely defined because this species grades, or blends, into other similar species on upland habitats and toward its western limit. Shumard oak is a popular tree in cultivation, and it has performed well in the north at least through most of USDA zone 5.

CULTURE: Certain geographic races of this species have proven to be quite tolerant of alkaline soil, an unusual quality in oaks. Shumard oak also tolerates short-term flooding but not shade. It grows very quickly for an oak and very large. It is relatively easy to transplant and to grow from seed. Refer to the previously described oaks for more general information.

PROBLEMS: Shumard oak is subject to the same problems that affect red oaks in general. Refer to red oak.

CULTIVARS: This species is becoming popular as a landscape tree, but cultivars are not yet available. As far as we know, nobody is even studying the species in an attempt to identify superior ornamental selections. This may be due, in part, to an enzyme-incompatibility problem that causes frequent graft-union failures on all oaks in this taxonomic section, thus complicating the asexual propagation necessary for cultivar development. Horticultural techniques to overcome this problem are being perfected, so we might eventually see some selections on the market.

RELATED SPECIES: Oak nomenclature has been confused for many years, partly because these trees are so variable and cross-fertile and are difficult to fit precisely into somewhat subjective botanical categories. There is a smaller, upland tree that was considered a variety or form of Shumard oak until 1993. Then, our friend Bill Hess, the herbarium curator for the Morton Arboretum, studied this tree in great detail and affirmed that it should be classified as a separate species, *Quercus acerifolia*. It is found growing wild only on Magazine Mountain, the highest point in Arkansas, and in a few mountainous localities nearby, but it does fine in cultivation north through USDA zone 5 and makes a beautiful medium-sized tree.

The western upland variety, Texas Shumard oak, has been separated into a distinct species as well and was until recently called *Quercus texana*. It was renamed *Quercus buckleyi* based on naming precedence and current interpretations of the international rules of plant nomenclature. Texas Shumard oak, like *Quercus acerifolia*, does not grow as large or as quickly as the eastern lowland Shumard oak, but it is tolerant of drought and alkaline soils. We are currently evaluating a promising selection at Starhill Forest that was propagated from a fine-textured tree with exceptionally small leaves and acorns found near Dallas. Some of the seedlings are showing dependable winter hardiness, fine diminutive foliage and brilliant fall color.

One reason Texas Shumard oak can no longer be called *Quercus texana* is that this name is now assigned to Nuttall oak (formerly *Quercus nuttallii*) because of historical precedent. Nuttall oak is a southern look-alike of pin oak that was classified as a separate species in 1927. In the wild, it is largely confined to wet ground in the lower Mississippi River Valley and adjacent lowlands, but it grows very well when planted on higher ground.

Guy was the first to discover Nuttall oaks in Illinois, and they constitute the northernmost natural population of this tree. Their unique genetic qualities are being preserved by cuttings, using an emerging technology. Their offspring are proving to be winter-hardy far north of the natural range of the species.

Shumard oak and its kin are very closely related to scarlet oak (*Quercus coccinea*), the official tree of the District of Columbia. A beautiful specimen planted by President Benjamin Harrison grows next to Pennsylvania Avenue at the White House. This is a very common tree of sandy upland sites in the South, but it also grows naturally in scattered locations as far north as southern Michigan and coastal Maine. The forest at Jim and Jane Wilson's farm in South Carolina has some scarlet oaks that brighten the woods each year with their brilliant fall color. Some taxonomists believe that the northern stands of scarlet oak are actually northern pin oak (*Quercus ellipsoidalis*) because the only reliable distinction between them is a minor difference in the acorn cup scales.

Scarlet oak is more easily distinguished from Shumard oak and Nuttall oak by its upland habitat than by any conspicuous differences in general appearance. The surest way to identify all of these species is to look at the acorns with an identification key and magnifying glass and study the leaves under a microscope. Like Shumard oak, scarlet oak is popular in the nursery trade. It has the breathtaking fall color that is the source of its name, but it is difficult to transplant unless it has been grown in the nursery using root-training techniques. The national champion of this species is a vase-shaped roadside tree in rural Hillsdale County, Michigan; it reaches 117 feet (36 m) high with an even larger branch spread and has a short trunk 6 feet 5 inches (2 m) in diameter.

All of these trees are red oaks (section *Lobatae*) and are basically southern in distribution, but another species is given the actual title of southern red oak. This tree, *Quercus falcata*, can subsist on some of the most abused, degraded red soils found anywhere in the South. Old southern red oaks frequently appear weather-beaten and unkempt because of their hard life, but this species (also known as Spanish oak) can make a magnificent tree in a favorable location and can grow rapidly in good soil.

The Texas Shumard oak is a medium-sized tree that thrives on upland sites with alkaline soil.

The national champion southern red oak has lost

a few lower limbs, but it maintains a cathedral-like arching form. It grows in Harwood, Maryland, and is 104 feet (32 m) tall with a branch spread of 135 feet (42 m) and a trunk nearly 9 feet (2.6 m) in diameter.

Southern red oak has such variable foliage that botanists have argued for years about the existence and number of taxonomic varieties and forms. We have observed that seedlings propagated from trees with different leaf forms are not readily matched to their parents by leaf shape. Some have three lobes, some have more. Some have long, tail-like central lobes, while others are barely lobed at all. Some have rich crimson fall color, others are drab. But we have seen some southern red oaks with foliage in spring, summer and fall that ranked them among the most beautiful of trees.

A closely allied species, often listed as a variety of southern red oak, is cherrybark oak, *Quercus pagoda* (formerly *Quercus pagodaefolia* or *Quercus falcata* var. *pagodaefolia*). This tall, massive tree is a fast-growing canopy species of rich, wet, fertile bottomlands. It may be the most valuable oak for timber production in the South, and it makes an attractive landscape tree. The straight, columnar trunks of forest-grown cherrybark oaks really do resemble those of wild cherry (*Prunus serotina*) with their dark, curly, cherry-like bark. Like Shumard oak, this is one of our tallest and most vigorous oaks. The largest of all grows in Sussex County, Virginia; it stands 124 feet (38 m) tall on a trunk almost 9 feet (2.6 m) thick.

Shumard oaks are among the first of the oaks to turn color in the fall, becoming a glossy red.

These southern red oaks all resemble pin oak (*Quercus palustris*), northern pin oak (*Quercus ellipsoidalis*) and the other trees we have called northern red oaks. Refer to the other oak descriptions for additional information.

COMMENTS: There might be no better path to humility as an amateur botanist than to wade headlong into the oaks. The genus *Quercus* consists of hundreds of species throughout the northern hemisphere, some in areas so remote that their acorns or other characteristics have yet to be observed.

There are the red oaks of section *Lobatae* (former subgenus *Erythrobalanus*), with acorns that mature in two years (barring a few exceptions); the white oaks of section *Quercus* (former subgenus *Lepidobalanus*, also known as *Leucobalanus*), with acorns that mature in one year (again, with some exceptions); and some intermediate, or golden, oaks (section, or subgenus, *Protobalanus*), with characteristics akin to both red oaks and white oaks. In Asia, there are oaks classified in a completely different subgenus, *Cyclobalanopsis*, with ringed acorn cups and leaves that resemble anything but those of an oak.

Parallel centers of speciation and diversity for the genus exist in North America and Asia. There are evergreen oaks and deciduous oaks, and many in between; giant tree oaks and sprawling scrub oaks; desert oaks and swamp oaks; tropical oaks and temperate oaks. Then there are tan oaks (*Lithocarpus* spp.), a related genus with nearly as many variables of its own.

While some oak species are distinct and consistent, many are similar and seem to melt imperceptibly into one another where their ranges overlap. Sometimes this is caused by hybridization among species. Most of the differences that do occur within species result from heterozygosity, or natural genetic variation, and from natural selection within particular habitat types in response to environmental pressures. As climatic change and the more local impacts of human activity create new ecological niches, oaks seem to diversify even further in a race to occupy them.

The oaks are evolving—even exploding—as a genus, right before our eyes. And one of the best places to begin looking at these changes is among the confusing, interrelated grex of magnificent trees we call southern red oaks: the Shumard oak and its many kin.

LIVE OAK

Quercus virginiana

DESCRIPTION: The state tree of Georgia is the emblematic tree of landscapes throughout the Deep South. In the forest, it becomes an erect tree up to 100 feet (30 m) tall, but it is best known as a spreading tree with sinuous limbs that rest their giant elbows on the ground. The squat, leaning, tapering trunks of such trees grow larger in diameter than those of any other oak. Many live oaks have been described as the biggest or the oldest, but their irregular growth forms make it difficult to discern between specimens of roughly equal bulk. The recognized United States national champion is located near Lewisburg, Louisiana. Although only 55 feet (17 m) tall, its sprawling canopy shades an area 132 feet (40 m) across, and its short, divided trunk is almost 12 feet (3.6 m) in diameter. The most massive overall, though, might be the famous Middleton Oak in South Carolina.

Avenues of live oaks are a signature of the South.

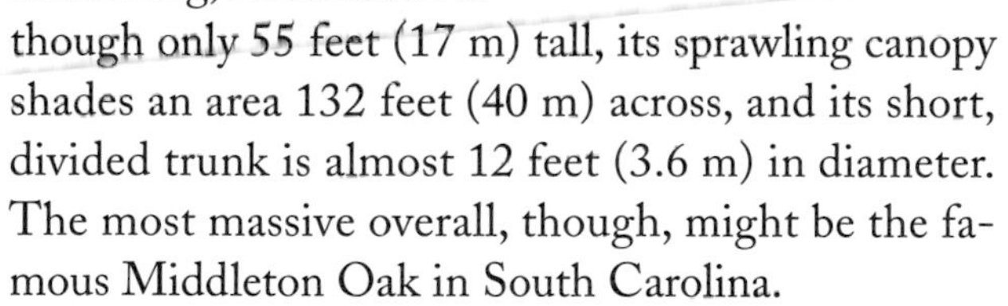

No one seems to have accurate data on the longevity of this species, but such venerable specimens are almost certainly among the oldest oaks in North America. Perhaps the most inspirational, although not quite as large, are the old planted trees that make up the cathedral-like alleys lining the approaches to places such as Boone Hall in Mount Pleasant, South Carolina; Oak Alley in Vacherie, Louisiana; and Rosedown in St. Francisville, Louisiana. Surely the most haunting is the Windsor Oak, near Port Gibson, Mississippi, when viewed at dusk through the remaining columns of the burned antebellum plantation house.

LEAVES: Unlike the leaves of most other oaks discussed in this volume, most of those on live oak are fully evergreen. They reach about 3 inches (7 cm) long by 1 inch (2.5 cm) wide and have smooth margins or, especially on vigorous shoots and second (summer) growth flushes, scattered teeth. The leaves are waxy and resistant to salt spray, which allows this tree to grow where others can't—on coastal dunes and barrier islands.

FLOWERS AND FRUIT: Live oak is a member of the white oak taxonomic section *Quercus* (former subgenus *Lepidobalanus*) and has acorns that mature in one season. The acorns are narrow and tapered, very dark when ripe and less than 1 inch (2.5 cm) long. They are the primary food for many wildlife species in coastal habitats.

SEASONS:

1. Winter (this is an evergreen tree and shows to best advantage when its neighbors are bare);
2. Summer (for the welcome shade it provides in the hot, humid climate of its home range).

NATIVE AND ADAPTIVE RANGE: Live oak grows throughout Florida and extends in narrow coastal bands north to Virginia and west into Texas. It is hardy into the warmer parts of USDA zone 7. Within the warm, humid environment of its natural range, it is among the strongest, largest and longest-lived of trees. It does not do well very far inland from the coastal plain and usually becomes semideciduous and slow-growing when planted in the Piedmont.

CULTURE: This oak, like most others, grows readily from seed, but live oak seeds should be planted as soon as they are ripe. Refer to white oak (*Quercus alba*) for hints on propagation. Once established, live oak is drought-resistant and so will thrive on sandy soils in coastal cities. It also tolerates more shade in summer than most other oaks because its evergreen leaves can function through most of the winter. Young trees grow quickly but need to be trained to an upright form for use in parkway planting strips and similar areas where their natural tendency to sprawl

Venerable live oaks, such as this champion in Louisiana, are certainly among the oldest oaks in North America.

would most likely be unwelcome.

PROBLEMS: Live oak is unusual among our native tree-sized oaks in its proclivity to send up vegetative sprouts from surface roots some distance from the base of the parent tree; this results in clonal thickets. Although this is great for erosion control on coastal dunes, it can be annoying in the garden.

Live oak is similar to the red oaks in its susceptibility to leaf blister from *Taphrina caerulescens*, and it is one of the only white oaks seriously bothered by oak wilt, *Ceratocystis fagacearum* (refer to both problems under willow oak, *Quercus phellos*). Oak wilt can be fatal, but valuable trees in wilt-infested areas can be protected with fungicide injections.

Live oak is also one of several oaks known to be somewhat susceptible to chestnut blight (*Cryphonectria parasitica*). This disease persists on "carrier" oaks to reinfect chestnuts (*Castanea americana*) planted within range. (For other problems, see white oak.) The Spanish moss, *Tillandsia usneoides*, that drapes many live oaks is a harmless epiphyte and is valuable to many birds for nesting material.

CULTIVARS: As popular and variable as this tree is, it might seem surprising that cultivars are not available. Still, almost any seedling live oak makes a great tree. Irregular, unpredictable form is considered characteristic and desirable, and fall color and flowering are not issues upon which to base cultivar selection with evergreen oaks.

RELATED SPECIES: There are several other evergreen oaks in our area, most of which once were (or still are) considered varieties or forms of live oak. Reference books list them in various ways. The current approach, which we follow here, is to separate several of them into distinct species. All belong to the white oak taxonomic section.

An upland form, *Quercus fusiformis* (*Q. virginiana* var. *fusiformis*), grows in interior parts of Texas. We have also collected this species from the temperate mountains of eastern Mexico. It is much hardier than *Quercus virginiana*. Planted specimens have survived to maturity through the winters of USDA zone 6 in the mountains of New Mexico and on the high plains of Oklahoma.

We are testing the hardiness of this species from an isolated northern provenance in Oklahoma. They tend to be partially deciduous in Illinois in USDA zone 5, and some of the seedlings even develop a bit of red fall color. They are not fully hardy there in severe winters, but their tolerance of winter cold has been surprising so far. This tree is nearly identical to the eastern coastal species except for its pointed acorns and its greater hardiness, so it would make a good substitute for use in the mid-South where the coastal species cannot survive.

Sand live oak, *Quercus geminata* (*Q. virginiana* var. *maritima*), was named for its habit of bearing acorns in pairs and for its sandy habitat. Its leaves are cupped and have deeply set veins, but there are few other differences between this tree and live oak. Another similar species, dwarf live oak (*Quercus minima*), remains a shrub and grows as an understory plant in sandy woods under southern pines (*Pinus* spp.).

Our eastern live oaks resemble the live oaks of California in many ways, but none of those species are classified in the same taxonomic section. *Quercus agrifolia*, the coast live oak, and *Quercus wislizenii*, the interior live oak, are red oaks (section *Lobatae*), while *Quercus chrysolepis*, the canyon live oak, and its relatives are intermediate (or golden) oaks (section *Protobalanus*). The Engelmann oak (*Quercus engelmannii*), a semideciduous species, is probably the closest counterpart of our eastern live oaks on the Pacific Coast. It even has fused cotyledons in its acorns, like live oak.

Live oak will hybridize with other white oaks. Oak breeders like Miguel Marquez of El Paso, Texas, are attempting to incorporate its evergreen foliage characteristics into hardy hybrids by crossing it and the related *Quercus fusiformis* with northern species such as bur oak (*Quercus macrocarpa*). The progeny of such crosses might be neither hardy nor evergreen, but they certainly will be interesting.

COMMENTS: In the Deep South, every town seems to have its own famous resident live oak tree. A registry is maintained by the National Live Oak Society of venerable trees that have obtained a certain size and age.

One of the notable members is the Jim Bowie Oak at the Bowie Museum in Opelousas, Louisiana, on land once owned by Bowie's father. The Lafitte Oaks, a pair of trees at Jefferson Island, Louisiana, supposedly conceal the lost buried treasure of the pirate Jean Lafitte. The Sunnybrook Oaks near Covington, Louisiana, sheltered Andrew Jackson on his way to the Battle of New Orleans. The Big Oak at Thomasville, Georgia, is listed in the National Register of Historic Places.

These living landmarks are not immortal, and one succumbs every now and then to a hurricane or a disease. But far worse is the magnetic appeal such ancient and inspirational trees seem to have for the vandals of our society. The Treaty Oak in Texas, the last living witness to many peace treaties and boundary agreements negotiated under its canopy among various Native American tribes, was to have been removed in 1937 by the owner of the land where it grew. The town leaders intervened and made the site a city park. This preserved the great oak for more than half a century, but the tree was eventually poisoned with herbicide by a vandal. Arborists from around the world flocked to the site and attempted to revive it, but their attempts were unsuccessful.

The ancient Inspiration Oak at Magnolia Springs, Alabama, has a similar story. During a property dispute in 1990, this giant tree was spitefully girdled with a chain saw. After three years of bridge-grafting, watering, misting, fertilizing, pruning and hoping, the arborists who had volunteered to try to reverse the damage finally gave up. One of them hopes to inject the tree with preservatives so at least its structure will remain intact as a reminder of the centuries of life that can be suddenly ended in a thoughtless act of anger.

Even after a hard winter, many of the leaves of live oak are still green when the tree blooms in the spring.

OTHER OAKS

Quercus species

Oaks in North America can generally be segregated by range into eastern, southwestern and western species. In the East and Midwest, we frequently encounter several eastern species in addition to those already covered, and occasionally one of the hardier Pacific or southwestern species will show up as a cultivated specimen.

Among the red oaks (refer to the taxonomic discussion under Shumard oak, *Quercus shumardii*), a few small- to medium-sized trees are found, mostly on xeric soils or in other rugged habitats. One of the most widespread and well-known is blackjack oak (*Quercus marilandica*). It occurs from New Jersey and southern Iowa south to the Gulf Coast and is restricted by competition to sandy soils, hardpans, bluff ledges and similar sterile habitats. In such inhospitable locations, it is seen as a ratty little fiddle-leaved tree, but it can grow into a pleasant surprise when cultivated in good soil and given room to develop. The national champion is a street tree in Greenville, South Carolina, with a perfect, symmetrical crown that reaches to 90 feet (28 m).

Blackjack oak is a small, tough tree that grows slowly but is able to survive on very poor soils.

Blackjack oak grows very slowly and is nearly impossible to transplant unless the roots are trained or pruned during its early growth. It develops a dense, twiggy crown and can make a good screen or windbreak. Burnt orange fall colors are common, and the dead leaves often cling throughout the winter. Arkansas oak (*Quercus arkansana*), also known as upland water oak, resembles blackjack oak. It inhabits sandy or rocky sites, and its distribution is very localized in southwestern Arkansas and scattered areas of Alabama, Georgia and the Florida panhandle.

Turkey oak (*Quercus laevis*) is a common shrub or small tree of sandy scrub woodlands of the Atlantic coastal plain. Isolated trees on fertile sites can become as large as blackjack oaks, but the species usually grows in dwarf thickets. Turkey oak leaves are deeply and narrowly lobed, and some resemble turkey footprints. They provide good red fall color.

Two other species that remain small are bear oak (*Quercus ilicifolia*) and Stone Mountain oak (*Quercus georgiana*). They look much alike and occupy similar, stark habitats. Bear oak grows from the mountains of Virginia northeast to Mt. Desert Island, Maine; Stone Mountain oak grows only on the rock surface of its namesake mountain near Atlanta, Georgia, and in a few similar, isolated areas nearby. Both color nicely in the fall to a bright crimson, and both are showing USDA zone 5 hardiness in our tests. Myrtle oak (*Quercus myrtifolia*) is a semievergreen shrub confined to warmer parts of the Atlantic coastal plain; *Quercus inopina* is similar but with convex leaves.

From the white oaks (section *Quercus*), we have Oglethorpe oak (*Quercus oglethorpensis*). It becomes a medium-sized tree with unlobed leaves and, like live oak (*Quercus virginiana*), we have seen it become infected with chestnut blight (*Cryphonectria parasitica*). Although it is a very rare species known only from a few isolated populations in South Carolina and Georgia, it is surprisingly hardy when planted in the north. Young seedlings are doing well in our central Illinois testing, and a specimen can be seen at the Morton Arboretum near Chicago, in USDA zone 5.

Bluff oak (*Quercus austrina*) and the closely related Durand oak (*Quercus sinuata*) are similar to Oglethorpe oak, but they have wavy-edged leaves.

Blue oaks are North American natives from the West Coast, adaptable in our area only if the climate and soil of their home habitat can be duplicated.

Some authorities classify the two as varieties of the same species. Neither is very common, growing only on limestone soils and bluffs scattered throughout the South. Like Oglethorpe oak, they seem more cold-hardy than would be expected from their limited distribution. Chapman oak (*Quercus chapmanii*) is a shrubby species that grows naturally on the sand hills and dunes of Coastal Georgia and south into Florida.

We sometimes find hardy selections of Rocky Mountain oak (*Quercus gambelii*) doing well in the East. We are testing the similar California species *Quercus oerstediana* (synonym *Quercus garryana* var. *semota*) as well and are also having success with *Quercus garryana*, the only oak of the Pacific Northwest. Valley oak (*Quercus lobata*) and its foothill associate, blue oak (*Quercus douglasii*), may survive in the Southeast on well-drained soils. High-elevation selections of other western oaks such as *Quercus kelloggii* (a red oak) can also be hardier than expected.

The foliage of Stone Mountain oak turns deep red in the fall.

It should be noted that winter cold is not the only climatic difference to be overcome when planting oaks from the West and Southwest in the East. They are, in effect, exotic species that evolved in very different climate cycles. Most of the western oaks are damaged by artificial irrigation because they are accustomed to dry summers similar to those in the Mediterranean region of southern Europe. In fact, several exotic oak species from Asia are better adapted to eastern North America than any of those from the western part of our own continent, since they evolved in analogous climates. Northern Europe has also supplied a few of the exotic oaks commonly seen here in cultivation, especially some of the cultivars of English oak (*Quercus robur*).

Those who would like to know more about this most fascinating family of trees would do well to join the International Oak Society (P.O. Box 310, Pen Argyl, PA 18072-0310).

STAGHORN SUMAC

Rhus typhina

DESCRIPTION: The sumacs are a genus of small trees and shrubs with some very special attributes. Their clumping habit, outstanding fall color, sparse branching, large pinnate leaves and persistent fruit clusters all help to identify most members of the genus from a distance.

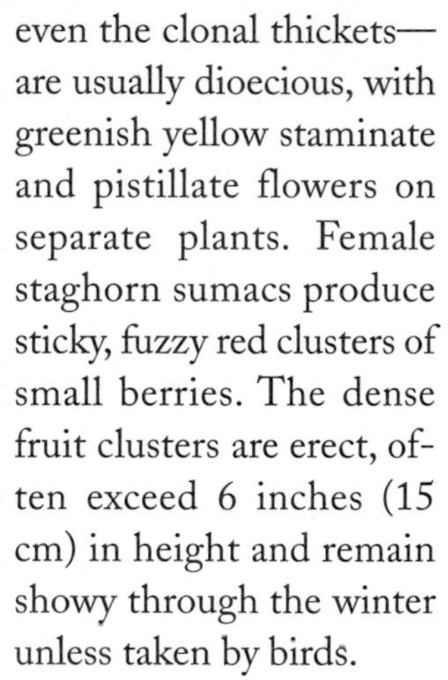

Wild staghorn sumac, shown with pistillate flowers, thrives at the forest edge.

The largest and hardiest of our native sumacs is staghorn sumac, which gets its common name from its hairy, velvet-antler twigs. Like most of the others, it sprouts readily from the roots to form clonal thickets as does aspen (*Populus tremuloides*). The individual stems in such thickets seldom attain the size of those that grow as individual trees, but original stems in old thickets can exceed 30 feet (9 m) in height. The largest known individual staghorn sumac tree (although not the largest clone) is 61 feet (19 m) tall with a trunk 15 inches (40 cm) in diameter. It was found growing in Tallapoosa County, Alabama.

Staghorn sumacs were once trees of the prairie-forest interface. Now they have found homes along fencerows and railroad lines and in abandoned pastures and roadside thickets. They aggressively colonize clearings that offer full sun and good drainage and have been quick to follow in the footsteps of "progress" across North America.

LEAVES: The leaves of most sumac species are pinnately compound and quite large. Staghorn sumac leaves are typically composed of up to 31 toothed leaflets, each about 4 inches (10 cm) long, supported by a rachis, or stalk, almost 2 feet (60 cm) in length. The fall color of this species is lighter than that of most sumacs: they turn a glowing flame-orange. Smooth sumac (*Rhus glabra*) turns scarlet, and winged sumac (*Rhus copallina*) turns a rich crimson. The most striking sumac color of all, however, might be the translucent ruby red of the untouchable poison sumac, *Rhus vernix* (classified under genus *Toxicodendron* with the poison ivies by some botanists).

FLOWERS AND FRUIT: All of our sumacs—even the clonal thickets—are usually dioecious, with greenish yellow staminate and pistillate flowers on separate plants. Female staghorn sumacs produce sticky, fuzzy red clusters of small berries. The dense fruit clusters are erect, often exceed 6 inches (15 cm) in height and remain showy through the winter unless taken by birds.

The seeds, although rich in vitamins and fat, are not a tasty first choice for most birds, so fruit clusters remain intact into the winter and are consumed when other foods are gone. Some authorities have observed that female clones might live longer than males, persisting in the landscape even as taller trees begin to overtop them.

SEASONS:

1. Fall (their early colors rank our sumac species among the elite trees of autumn);
2. Winter (for the trees' architecture and the clinging fruit clusters of females, especially on staghorn sumac and smooth sumac);
3. Early summer (for the flowers, most attractive on male plants of winged sumac).

NATIVE AND ADAPTIVE RANGE: Each of our eastern sumacs covers a lot of territory. Staghorn sumac is found from Cape Breton in Nova Scotia and Lake St. John in Quebec, south through the Blue Ridge and Cumberland Plateau of Tennessee and northwest out to eastern Minnesota. Smooth sumac ranges from the southern edge of Ontario and the vicinity of Lake Manitoba south throughout eastern North America to the Atlantic coastal plain. Winged sumac ranges from southern Indiana and Illinois down to the tip of Florida. Poison sumac has a polka-dot range, in response to its wetland habitat requirements, throughout the eastern United States and the southern end of Ontario. All of these species seem equally tolerant of winter cold and summer heat north to USDA zone 4. Staghorn and smooth sumacs push into zone 3.

CULTURE: Most sumacs need only a sunny location and well-drained soil. Staghorn sumac will respond to good soils and adequate moisture with more vigorous growth. Poison sumac is unique in its preference for swampy ground, which is just as well because its ability to cause contact dermatitis would create havoc if it grew in accessible upland areas.

Sumacs should be planted or preserved where they can be allowed to form thickets. This is their natural growth habit, and their blaze of fall color is splendid. Individual specimens, if trained and restrained from suckering, make artistic small trees with sinuous limbs and graceful, leaning trunks. If a sumac stem is wounded, it becomes prone to attack by various borers and cankers. Often it is best to cut it back to ground level and let a sucker take its place.

Sumacs are simple to transplant in the dormant season as small suckers or root cuttings from the edges of established clones. All of the stems in any one clone will be of the same sex, so for a mixed-gender planting, you will need material from more than one clone. They can also be grown from seed, but they may take two to three years to sprout without the right combination of acid scarification and stratification. Established seedlings or previously transplanted suckers that have developed branching root systems can be relocated without difficulty.

PROBLEMS: Like many other clonal trees, sumacs develop root sprouts as an adaptation to a fire-prone environment. With their sprouting capability, they have little need to invest their metabolic resources in thick, protective bark. Consequently, their thin skin makes them sensitive to fires, lawn mowers and string-trimmers. White gummy sap bleeds from injuries and dries to a persistent black varnish.

Serious wounding triggers the development of replacement shoots. Those who desire a thicket should cut back their sumacs every few years. Those who don't should be careful to avoid injuring the bark.

A significant problem centers around the toxicity, or perceived toxicity, of sumacs. They can be toxic to other plants, through allelopathic chemicals released by their roots, and some are toxic to humans as well. Because one native species (poison sumac) can cause severe skin inflammation, some folks fear all sumacs. On the other hand, because most of the familiar sumacs are benign, other people don't give the one toxic native species the respect it deserves. Unless you are immune to poison sumac, admire its rare beauty from a distance; but appreciate the other species at close range.

CULTIVARS: Two female cultivars of staghorn sumac are popular for their deeply lobed foliage. These selections, 'Dissecta' and 'Laciniata', tend to be more spreading and suckering than the species type; 'Laciniata' also develops fern-like bracts in its flower clusters. There is a 'Laciniata' form of smooth sumac as well. Three additional selections of smooth sumac are under final evaluation for conservation use by the USDA Soil Conservation Service.

Smooth sumac is frequently cultivated for its outstanding flaming red fall foliage.

Although no other cultivars have been named, we have noticed that staghorn, smooth and winged sumacs are variable in form, from tall and upright to low and spreading. Because sumacs can be propagated asexually from root cuttings, growth form could be a practical criterion for selection of a specimen or patio tree.

Above: Black locust develops a picturesque crown of lacy branches. Below right: Bristly locust is a small species with bright pink flowers that blooms at the same time as black locust.

Black locust can be grown from root cuttings or by dividing thickets of suckers in the dormant season, and young trees either of seedling or sucker origin transplant without difficulty. Seeds germinate quickly once the hard seed coat has been cracked or scarified to allow it to soak up water.

PROBLEMS: The classic pest that attacks black locust is the locust borer (*Megacyllene robiniae*). It can turn pole-sized trees into Swiss cheese, and many trees break in the wind where the borer tunnels are most concentrated. Vigorous locusts growing with other species of trees in a forest are seldom damaged. Stressed trees in monotypic stands invite attack. Some black locusts seem resistant, while others are vulnerable. Researchers are uncertain whether genetic or environmental factors are to blame.

Some of the tree's other problems stem from its untamed nature. Vigorous young twigs have sharp, strong thorns paired at each leaf axil, which makes leather gloves mandatory when pruning. Black locust roots are allelopathic to some other plants (although they encourage turf growth), and in turn they are suppressed by the allelopathy of goldenrod (*Solidago* spp.), the food plant of the adult locust borer. Suckers can spring up virtually overnight and grow head-high or more in one year if not removed promptly.

When the tree is on a mesic site with its roots undisturbed and growing in loamy, neutral soil, suckering is not an unmanageable problem. Understory shade also seems to inhibit suckering. But trees growing on strip-mine tailings, degraded pastures or sandy prairies and savannas seem almost desperate to claim territory and soon dominate their area with a maze of thorny, impenetrable suckers.

Black locust is also notable for the problems it resists. Gypsy moth (*Lymantria dispar*), the scourge of the eastern deciduous forest, won't touch it. Drought has no effect on established trees, nor does salt spray from road deicing. Sterile, infertile soils are perfectly satisfactory for it and are improved by its presence. The wood is as strong as that of any native tree, unless it has been damaged by locust borers, and it resists ice, wind and decay.

CULTIVARS: Europeans have been fascinated with this American tree for centuries and have developed most of its cultivars. 'Idaho' and 'Decaisneana' are hybrids with pink flowers. There are forms with no thorns ('Crispa' and 'Inermis'), with unique foliage ('Aurea', 'Dissecta', 'Frisia', 'Macrophylla' and 'Unifolia') and with unusual form ('Pendula', 'Pyramidalis', 'Tortuosa' and 'Umbraculifera').

The pea-like white flower clusters of black locust are a favorite of honeybees and hummingbirds.

The last is called parasol locust in the nursery trade. It is a fanciful lollipop tree consisting of a shrubby form grafted high on a standard trunk, and it is all too common in the gardens of North America.

The "Steiner Group" consists of 'Appalachia', 'Allegheny' and 'Algonquin'—vigorous USDA Soil Conservation Service selections reportedly resistant to locust borer. The group originated from trees in Virginia and West Virginia and excelled in tests for growth rate and straightness. 'Appalachia' was named in 1956, while the others were added to the group in 1987, following many years of evaluation.

RELATED SPECIES: A complex of species called bristly locust consists of *Robinia fertilis* (a diploid) and *Robinia hispida* (a triploid). Both are low, suckering plants with prominent pink flowers. 'Arnot' locust, promoted by the USDA for erosion control, is a selection of bristly locust. It tends to do its job too well, spreading and suckering with a vengeance. Clammy locust (*Robinia viscosa*) is a small, pink-blooming tree from the southern Appalachian Mountains. Other locust species grow in western North America and Mexico.

COMMENTS: Black locust sleeps at night. The leaves fold together like pages of a book and wait for daylight before opening again. This trait is shared by many tropical and herbaceous legumes, but it is unusual among temperate trees.

Black locust was one of the trees cultivated by Native Americans prior to the arrival of European colonists. They planted it near their dwellings along the Atlantic Coast and used the wood for bows. Later, pioneers found the decay-resistant wood ideal for the sills of their buildings, fence posts and (even today) firewood.

The genus is endemic to North America, but most true locust-lovers seem to live in Europe (where locust borer, a North American insect, is apparently not a problem). Botanist Jean Robin brought black locust seeds back to Paris as early as 1601, and his son transplanted one of those locusts in 1636. This specimen, the oldest on record, still grows in Paris in the garden of the Museum of Natural History. Its old limbs are propped up with bars, and its trunk is adorned with a crude sign that outlines its history and reveals its remarkable antiquity.

CABBAGE PALM

Sabal palmetto

DESCRIPTION: This species, the state tree of South Carolina and Florida, is unique among the trees in this book because it is a monocot. This makes it a closer kin to grasses and cereal grains than to the conifers and broadleaf dicots we commonly think of as "trees." The palms as a family are the most valuable trees for food, shelter and barter material in tropical regions throughout the world. Cabbage palm is the one we will discuss here because it is the most common and one of the few large palms in North America, and because it and some of its relatives are the hardiest of all palms.

A palm doesn't add growth rings to its diameter each year, like other trees. Its trunk rarely becomes much thicker than when the tree develops its terminal bud, regardless of how tall it grows. We have never seen a cabbage palm 2 feet (60 cm) in diameter, but some come close. The national champion is considerably leaner than that, but it stands 90 feet (28 m) tall. Cabbage palms grow slowly, so this one must surely be one of the senior citizens of Highlands Hammock State Park in central Florida.

The cabbage palm is one of the few palm species that can tolerate hard winter freezes.

LEAVES: Cabbage palms are evergreen, shedding older leaves (stalk and all) as new ones emerge from the growing tip. They maintain a constant array of 30 to 40 leaves. The feathery leaves are supported by hard, woody stalks and form the visual branches of the tree; they sometimes extend as much as 8 feet (2.2 m) from the trunk on all sides.

FLOWERS AND FRUIT: Huge clusters of tiny flowers hang several feet (1-2 m) from the crown of the tree among the new leaves. Originating from the growing point, they are greenish white and develop into dark, pea-sized, spherical, edible fruits. Each fruit contains a brown pit, or seed. Ground-foraging birds like turkeys eat the fruits as they fall, and gulls and jays pick them from the trees.

SEASONS:

1. Winter (for its evergreen foliage);
2. All year (a graceful accent plant in any season).

NATIVE AND ADAPTIVE RANGE: This is a tree of Florida and the Atlantic coastal plain that ranges up the coastline to Cape Fear in southern North Carolina. Its smaller relative, bush palmetto (*Sabal minor*), extends farther west along the Gulf Coast and grows as far north as Albemarle Sound in northern North Carolina. They both tolerate hard winter freezes and can be grown in cultivation north into the warmer parts of USDA zone 7, especially in the coastal habitats they prefer.

CULTURE: Cabbage palm is a carefree tree that likes full sun, but it will grow in partial shade. It inhabits sandy soil in the wild but seems willing to adjust to tighter soil in cultivation as long as it has good drainage. It seems immune to the salt spray of its coastal habitat, joining live oak (*Quercus virginiana*) on beachheads and barrier islands.

This tree grows slowly in the nursery, but large, old specimens can be transplanted easily with virtually no rootball because new adventitious roots regenerate from the base of the tree, not from cut root ends like those of other trees. Move it in the heat of early summer, when its roots will regenerate quickly, and keep its root zone well aerated and porous.

Some landscapers trim away most of the fronds when transplanting these trees in order to reduce transpiration and balance root loss. This practice can lead to a waistline indentation in the trunk as the tree grows, which forms a conspicuous weak spot. We have noticed good results when arborists simply remove the oldest fronds and tie the rest up temporarily to reduce transpiration until the tree is established.

Old leaves will turn brown and hang from the base of the crown unless they are trimmed away. They make great habitat for birds and bats and also for some of the undesirables of the rodent clan. The decision to trim or not to trim is a matter of aesthetic preference. The palm does fine either way, as long as the trimming is done correctly without damaging the trunk or bud. Tall specimens should be trimmed by a certified arborist who knows about proper palm maintenance. Some homeowners may also choose to have fruit clusters removed before they begin to shed, especially if the tree overhangs a driveway or walk.

PROBLEMS: This tree has one apical meristem, or growing point, located in the cabbage-like bud at its tip. If the bud is destroyed, the tree cannot grow new leaves and eventually dies. Because it has no cambium, it is unable to overgrow or "heal" trunk wounds, and this should be remembered if you are climbing or trimming the tree. Never use climbing spikes or other devices that pierce the trunk, and preserve the terminal bud or you will lose the tree.

A widespread decline is affecting some cabbage palm groves in Florida. Most noticeable in low areas, it has been attributed to the intrusion of salt water into the root zone. Scientists believe this is due to a subtle rise in sea level caused by global warming. Several palms, including this one, are also susceptible to a fatal fungus, *Ganoderma zonatum*, which was introduced from Malaysia.

CULTIVARS: Because cabbage palms cannot be grafted or grown from cuttings, cultivars have not been developed and propagated.

RELATED SPECIES: Besides the bush palmetto, there are a few other shrubby species of this genus and of the similar genus *Serenoa* in our area. They are known by names such as dwarf palmetto, saw palmetto and scrub palmetto, and they seldom develop erect, tree-like stems of any significant size. *Sabal minor* and *Serenoa repens* form understory thickets and are among the hardiest of all palms.

Sabal mexicana is a large species from southern Texas and subtropical Mexico, similar to cabbage palm. *Sabal louisiana* is similar to bush palmetto and occupies much of the same range, but it more often reaches tree size. There are perhaps 7,000 other palm species found in tropical areas around the world.

Cabbage palms are characteristic street trees of the South.

COMMENTS: The hardy palmetto palms can create the illusion of a tropical paradise in an artful landscape design, but their placement must be guided by a sense of harmony. Strong design elements like palms call attention to themselves and appear ridiculous in a poorly conceived plan. They always look great, though, in their natural setting and should be preserved wherever they occur in the wild.

On the seashore, cabbage palms serve a vital ecological function as the first line of defense against hurricanes and storms: they bend and recoil before winds that shatter other trees. We have watched a group of cabbage palms on the seaward side of Hunting Island, South Carolina, during a fierce Atlantic storm. With roots firmly anchored in the beach at the high tide mark, the palms rolled with every punch of the wind, like the flexible sea-oat grass that stood beside them, impervious to gusts, waves and salt spray. The next morning, they stood calmly in the warm Carolina sun with every leaf intact, just as their species has done for centuries through countless storms.

SHINING WILLOW

Salix lucida

DESCRIPTION: Willows are the ubiquitous trees and shrubs of moist soils throughout the temperate climates of the world. The genus comprises countless species and hybrids and, like the oaks (genus *Quercus*), seems to be evolving before our eyes. Many willows offer highly ornamental bark, flowers or foliage. In the foliage category, the finest of all must be the shining willow.

This species is always admired in landscape settings, perhaps in part because it is a mimic of bay willow (*Salix pentandra*), an Old World species that has been used in European ornamental horticulture for centuries. It forms a dense pyramidal shape when grown in the open, generally topping out as a bushy small tree in cultivation but often forming shrubby thickets in the wild. The largest recorded shining willow was measured in Traverse City, Michigan, in 1985: it stood 74 feet (22 m) tall and had a trunk more than 3 feet (1 m) in diameter.

Catkins emerge with the new leaves of shining willow.

LEAVES: Some willows are planted for their early catkins, others for their colorful winter bark. But if you are looking for a native willow that offers gorgeous, lustrous foliage for the entire growing season, plant shining willow. The leaves resemble those of wild cherry (*Prunus serotina*) in general outline and are similar in size, growing to about 5 inches (12 cm) in length. But the leaves are smooth and glossy, as if lacquered; they shimmer in the sun and turn yellow in the fall, like most other willows.

FLOWERS AND FRUIT: All willows are dioecious, and their pistillate flowers and fruits are miniature versions of those of poplars (*Populus* spp.), with which they share a common lineage. The flowers of many male (staminate) willows are the "pussy" catkins seen in the early spring wherever these plants grow. Those of male shining willows emerge late, with the leaves, and their rich yellow anthers highlight the gloss of the leaves.

SEASONS:
1. Summer (the shiny foliage adds life to any landscape);
2. All year (the first-year twigs are attractive and show to advantage even after the foliage has dropped. Many other willow species are at their best in winter or early spring).

NATIVE AND ADAPTIVE RANGE: Shining willow covers the Laurentian Shield of eastern Canada, dipping to encircle the Great Lakes, and extends eastward throughout New England and the Acadian Provinces. Many other willows also exhibit amazing cold tolerance. We have hiked on ground covers of alpine willows in central Alaska, and a few shrubby species grow on tundra and permafrost right up to the Arctic Ocean. Shining willow can

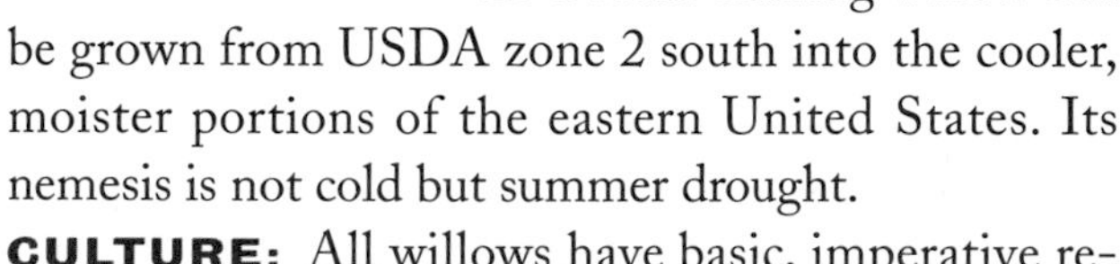

be grown from USDA zone 2 south into the cooler, moister portions of the eastern United States. Its nemesis is not cold but summer drought.

CULTURE: All willows have basic, imperative requirements: full sun, uninterrupted access to moisture during the growing season, loose, sandy or organic soil and occasional control of the myriad organisms that attack them. Given this, they are fascinating plants to work with.

The perishable seeds of willows are tricky to germinate, but most species, including shining willow, can be propagated from dormant hardwood cuttings by simply jamming a fresh stick into the ground (top end up) in late winter. The more scientific method is to clip a finger-sized section about 12 inches (30 cm) long from a vigorous stem of the desired gender in early spring. Immerse its bottom half in water at room temperature for a few days and keep it in total darkness; pot it up as soon as bumpy white primordia and adventitious roots begin to break through the bark.

For the more recalcitrant species, allow the cuttings to callus first, then pot them and add a little bottom heat. Willow cuttings contain salicylic acid—a rooting stimulant as well as a headache remedy—and are useful in promoting rooting of other cuttings immersed with them.

Willows grow very quickly, at least the tree forms do, and they can be transplanted with no difficulty. Seedlings sometimes spring up by the thousands in newly disturbed sites and may be moved with a trowel to preferred locations. The ornamental values of the willows (bark, male flowers, foliage) are enhanced by vigorous growth, which, in turn, is stimulated by adequate water and heavy but judicious pruning. Such pruning is also necessary to remove broken and diseased wood.

PROBLEMS: Willows are brittle and messy, with aggressive roots that exploit the moisture found in drains and sewers. They are short-lived, quick to decay and prone to damage from nearly every insect and canker that lives. We have had willows in our study collection in Illinois disfigured by antler-rubbing deer, cut by beavers, skinned by rabbits, peeled by squirrels, mutilated by fungus diseases and defoliated by countless types of insects. They are particularly tasty to the gypsy moth (*Lymantria dispar*). Some people have little good to say about willows, but others are willing to overlook their many faults and admire their seasonal beauty and vigor.

CULTIVARS: There are no cultivars of shining willow on the market. It is difficult enough to find the plant for sale, even as a species, and much simpler to propagate it by cuttings from a wild plant. Other willows, chiefly those that have been cultivated in Europe for millennia, are available as selected clones. Willows are promiscuous; they hybridize without shame, and some of the hardy weeping forms have developed from such crosses.

RELATED SPECIES: Willows of various sizes can be seen along every stream, pond and swamp throughout North America. Some of the largest become massive trees, but they are brittle and seldom grown in developed landscapes. Black willow (*Salix nigra*) is typical of these. It is a huge species, with clumping, leaning, often hollow stems. One was measured in Grand Traverse County, Michigan, that stood 114 feet (35 m) tall and had a trunk 10 feet (3 m) in diameter. We have many tall black willows along Rock Creek at Starhill Forest. This species and the similar peachleaf willow (*Salix amygdaloides*) may be the most common large native tree willows in the eastern United States.

The European species *Salix fragilis* (crack willow) and *Salix alba* (white willow) are widely naturalized here and grow just as large. Several selections

Shining willow maintains its lustrous foliage throughout the entire growing season.

Most native willows, including the black willow, above, are resistant to winter cold but break easily in ice storms.

and hybrids of white willow are seen in cultivation, displaying the traditional "weeping willow" form or their golden or red bark.

Pussy willow (*Salix discolor*) is a small native tree or shrub that is famous for its satiny male catkins. Actually, staminate plants of many willows have outstanding catkin displays in late winter or early spring, including native species like *Salix bebbiana* as well as some popular exotic species. Sandbar willows (*Salix interior* and *Salix exigua*) occasionally reach tree size, but they more often form stoloniferous thickets that stabilize soil and provide wildlife cover along streams and lakeshores. Some superior clones of sandbar willow are being tested now, and the best will be released by the USDA Soil Conservation Service for erosion control.

Willows are basically northern trees, but the South has the Carolina willow (*Salix caroliniana*), which grows in wetlands south to the Florida Everglades. In all, there may be close to 100 species of willows in North America, 200 more worldwide and innumerable hybrids.

COMMENTS: Many of our most beautiful butterflies are drawn to willows, including the distinctive mourning cloak, the red-spotted purple, the twin-spotted sphinx moth, the giant poplar sphinx moth, several underwing moths, the magnificent cecropia and the monarch-like viceroy, with its larvae that mimic bird droppings. Each causes a little damage, but they should be encouraged in moderation for their aesthetic contributions to the landscape. When the larvae become too concentrated, they may be relocated by hand to wild willows nearby or to acceptable alternate plants.

Willows require from their planters a certain tolerance, a commitment to routine maintenance and the realization that nothing is forever. However, they are simple to propagate and transplant, rapid to grow, graceful in form, attractive to wildlife and colorful. As they grow and decline, to be cut and grown again, willows remind us that the garden is a dynamic entity that is constantly in flux.

Some believe that fast-growing, short-lived trees like willows are best planted by elderly gardeners, who have no time to waste. We disagree. Older, experienced gardeners have acquired the patience and wisdom to know that a tree can become a memorial to its planter, so they often plant the most permanent species. It is the young gardener, the novice, to whom we should introduce the willow. Start with an unrooted cutting, and watch your fascination grow with the tree.

SOAPBERRY

Sapindus drummondii

DESCRIPTION: Our native soapberry is the hardiest member of a genus comprising perhaps 40 species, mostly tropical and ranging here and there from Hawaii to Florida, Mexico and Asia. Surprisingly, this distinctive little tree is not very well known in cultivation except within its natural range. We have admired soapberry at the Missouri Botanical Garden in St. Louis for many years, but it seems nearly impossible to find in the nursery trade.

This species is adaptable to many conditions, including some of the most severe, but it grows best on rich limestone soils. It often forms streamside thickets of small stems in the southern Great Plains, but isolated individuals can become much larger. The current national champion was found recently in Corpus Christi, Texas. It stands 62 feet (19 m) high and has a trunk 3 feet 4 inches (1 m) in diameter. Three trees previously shared the record, growing respectively in Texas, Oklahoma and Alabama. The former champions, and most specimens we have seen in cultivation, are more slender, but several approach the height of the record tree.

A graceful, small tree when cultivated, soapberry deserves a broader appreciation.

LEAVES: Soapberry leaves are pinnately compound, leathery and fine-textured. They reach about 1 foot (30 cm) in length and are like those of black walnut (*Juglans nigra*) in that the terminal leaflet is seldom present. They turn a rich gold in autumn.

FLOWERS AND FRUIT: Soapberry's flowers are dioecious and form showy white clusters in early summer. Pistillate (female) trees bear grape-like clumps of translucent yellow spherical fruits, each with a single black seed. They look almost like fat golden raisins, but they are not palatable. Reportedly, these attractive fruits are poisonous, at least to the fish that inhabit ponds where they fall. The toxic substance involved is called saponin. Most of the fruit clusters persist into or through the following winter, giving female trees a golden sparkle on bright winter days. The hard seeds polish to a beautiful ebony color and may be drilled and strung as beads.

SEASONS:

1. Winter (for the combination of fruits, bark and picturesque form, which bring life to the most dreary of landscapes);
2. Fall (for the golden foliage and lacy appearance, much like Kentucky coffee tree, *Gymnocladus dioicus*;
3. Summer (this is an attractive, tough small tree with heavy, strong wood; it has a deceptively delicate appearance and nice flower highlights).

NATIVE AND ADAPTIVE RANGE: Our native soapberry is often called western soapberry and is encountered most commonly in the southwestern United States and adjacent Mexico. But it also thrives from Texas north through Oklahoma and most of Kansas, eastward into Missouri and southeast to portions of the toe of Louisiana. Under cultivation, we find it hardy north into the warmer parts of USDA zone 5, making it one of the hardiest of our basically subtropical desert trees.

CULTURE: Full sun is needed, but soapberry will grow well (but slowly) in most soils and tolerates a higher pH than most eastern forest trees. It seems to thrive on the prairie soils of the lower Midwest. Small soapberry trees are easy to transplant if grown under

Translucent and raisin-sized, soapberries make an impressive lather in water but can be toxic if eaten.

cultivation in decent garden soil with ample water to encourage a shallow root system. Once established, they tolerate drought, heat, wind, poor soil, air pollution and most other hazards of the natural or urban environment.

The seeds should probably be scarified to ensure uniform germination and planted outdoors in the fall or early winter. Rubber gloves are advisable when handling the fruits to guard against skin irritation when removing the seeds from the gummy pulp. Seedlings are easy to germinate and frequently volunteer near older trees. They develop taproots, so they should be transplanted early, undercut or grown in a moist, friable planting bed to discourage deep-rooting until they reach their permanent home.

PROBLEMS: If eaten, the fruits can be toxic to small children or pets. On the positive side, they become leathery and dry during early winter, so they usually don't create the slimy litter problem one might expect from their fall appearance. We have found no records of diseases or insects bothering this species. Perhaps the most frustrating aspect of soapberry is its lack of commercial availability; it seems to be a well-kept secret.

CULTIVARS: No cultivars of this tree are commercially available. Individual specimens selected for form, vigor, hardiness or gender may be grown from cuttings taken in the spring, so we would not be too surprised to learn that someone might be looking into cultivar development in the future.

RELATED SPECIES: Other soapberries are all tropical or subtropical trees or shrubs. Their most popular hardy relative is the exotic goldenrain tree (*Koelreuteria paniculata*).

COMMENTS: Native Americans in the southern Great Plains knew that soap could be made from the berries of this tree, just as they were aware of uses for so many native plants. When the fruits are squeezed and rubbed under water, they produce a surprising amount of lather, which makes any tree grower's first experience cleaning soapberries and separating the seed a memorable one. The pulp erupts into such a soapy froth that you wonder if bubble bath has somehow spilled into the water.

The gray, sculpted bark of soapberry gives the tree distinction in the dormant season.

SASSAFRAS

Sassafras albidum

DESCRIPTION: The aromatic sassafras is one of our most colorful medium-sized trees. It is very fast-growing in good soil and common in many forest openings, fencerows and old fields. Sassafras frequently forms clonal thickets by suckering, which tends to limit the ultimate size and growth rate of all the ramets, or stems, due to competition. However, single-stemmed trees over 60 feet (18 m) tall and 3 feet (90 cm) in diameter are not uncommon under favorable conditions.

The largest sassafras, in Owensboro, Kentucky, is 76 feet (23 m) tall and 6 feet 8 inches (2 m) in diameter. A grove of venerable 60-foot-high (18 m) trees, planted at the Helm farm near Tuscola, Illinois, during the Civil War, is a traffic-stopper each autumn. And we have seen ancient wild trees in old-growth forests in Illinois that exceeded 100 feet (30 m) in height.

Majestic, old-growth sassafras trees reach 120 feet (36 m) in a remote virgin forest remnant.

The sympodial, candelabra-like branching structure forms graceful horizontal layers like some of the dogwoods (*Cornus* spp.) by developing lateral twigs from current buds that initially outgrow the terminal shoot. Sassafras wood is light and brittle, but the excellent architecture of the branching makes the tree more resistant to storm damage than might be expected.

LEAVES: The leaves are smooth, sweetly fragrant when crushed and 3 to 7 inches (7-18 cm) long. They are frequently unlobed on young seedlings and on the basal (early-season) portions of twigs but mitten-shaped, with one or two lobes, on the upper parts of saplings and on vigorous shoots and suckers. The leaves are bright yellow-green in spring, maturing to a blue-green in summer and turning brilliant shades of red, gold, orange or purple in the fall.

FLOWERS AND FRUIT: Small yellow flowers appear before the leaves in early spring, which makes the trees look like clouds of gold when viewed against a dark background. Most individual trees are either male or female (dioecious). The females bear lustrous dark blue fruits on bright scarlet stalks in late summer. The ripe fruits are sought by squirrels and many birds, which spread the seeds along fencerow perching areas. Among their greatest fans are bluebirds, catbirds, vireos and quail.

SEASONS:

1. Autumn (with the persistent scarlet fruit pedicels on female trees and the brilliant, dependable foliage color);
2. Early spring (for the yellow flowers and branching pattern);
3. Winter (green twigs with artistic, sympodial branching) and late summer (dark fruit with contrasting pedicels).

NATIVE AND ADAPTIVE RANGE: Sassafras is native and well adapted throughout most of the East, South and Midwest and north through USDA zone 5 into southern Ontario.

CULTURE: Sassafras requires full sun for best growth. It is difficult to transplant from the wild unless true seedlings, not sprouts from roots, are selected. Transplant small wild seedlings in late winter (in the South) or early spring. Current-year seedlings can frequently be found in mulch beds under the trees and are easy to dig and relocate. New trees may be started from seeds planted outdoors in the fall. Individual trees or clonal thickets display different growth forms and fall color patterns, which can be reproduced vegetatively by taking root cuttings.

Maintain the young tree as a single stem by removing the occasional suckers, or cut back the stem and encourage sprouts to form a thicket for a mass of fall color at eye level. Once established, sassafras adapts to most soils, from dune sands to silty clays with hardpans. Clumps of sassafras even can be seen spreading along the rock ballast of abandoned railroad tracks.

PROBLEMS: This tree is not readily available from most nurseries because of its reputation as being hard to transplant. However, we have moved many trees up to 5 inches (12 cm) in diameter with success. The key is to avoid those that have developed from root suckers and to dig the young tree with a large rootball in late winter. Better yet, buy (or grow) a small container-grown seedling, which can be transplanted with proper care in any season as long as the ground is not frozen.

Sassafras is intolerant of heavy shade and road salt and has brittle wood. A broken young tree can be cut back to the ground and it will sprout a straight, vigorous shoot (which should be protected from abuse) to replace the lost stem. Sassafras has no serious insect or disease problems and is resistant to decay.

Root-suckering is considered a problem when it creates unwanted additional trees. Sassafras is less likely to send up suckers if its roots and stem are not damaged or disturbed. Any unwanted suckers can be pulled before they become woody. Sassafras is allelopathic and can discourage the growth of certain other plants within its root zone.

CULTIVARS: No named cultivars are available, but the natural beauty and variability of this tree make it a good candidate for horticultural selections. Propagation and transplanting methods, if researched further, would encourage the development of cloned varieties with predictable form, fall color and gender.

RELATED SPECIES: No close relatives of sassafras are found in the United States or Canada, although a similar species occurs in central China. Other aromatic plants like spicebush (*Lindera* spp.), bay tree (*Laurus nobilis*), cinnamon tree (*Cinnamomum zeylanicum*) and camphor tree (*Cinnamomum camphora*) are in the same family.

COMMENTS: This is one of our most striking and aromatic trees. It is rich in the herbal traditions of Native Americans and valuable for many wildlife species. The roots, dug in early spring, were used to provide the root-beer flavor of sassafras tea, and the medicinal bark was among the first products exported by the American colonies, beginning in the early 1600s. We have enjoyed chewing sassafras twigs and drinking sassafras tea from our own trees over the years, but the active ingredient (safrole) was listed in 1976 as a mild carcinogen by the United States government, so sassafras tea can no longer be purchased in interstate commerce. Still, the famous *filé* powder of Creole cooking is made from sassafras leaves.

Sassafras also serves as a host plant for some of our most spectacular moths and butterflies, including the colorful palamedes and spicebush swallowtails, the giant promethea, imperial and io silk moths, the furry little crinkled flannel moth and the tiny sassafras leafroller.

Sassafras leaves come in several shapes and, in the fall, several bright colors; fall color is consistent within each clone and is helpful in distinguishing between neighboring clones.

MOUNTAIN ASH

Sorbus americana

DESCRIPTION: This decorative small tree is one of the most colorful inhabitants of boreal forests. Its European and Asian cousins are more well known in cultivation, but our native species is every bit their equal within its natural range. It loves granitic rock outcrops, streambanks and acidic soils. There, it mixes with scattered conifers, bog plants and birches (*Betula* spp.), all of which combine in the natural landscape to create spring and fall scenes of postcard beauty.

Partly by nature and partly because of its environmental circumstances, mountain ash remains a small tree or large shrub. The largest specimen in the United States, which grows in West Virginia, is 62 feet (19 m) tall and 2 feet (65 cm) in diameter. Within the vast Canadian range of this species, other large specimens can no doubt be found. Sometimes, though, bigger is not better. We have admired many mountain ash shrubs on mountain balds, with their colors displayed at eye level, and others when viewed from below, clinging to rocky crags in Canada where their fall colors were intensified by a dark rock background. Mountain ash trees are equally impressive when viewed from above, with their bright fruits and foliage held high and showing nicely against the smooth, dark bark and the shaded valley floor. And they always look great in the garden, if they are healthy and well maintained.

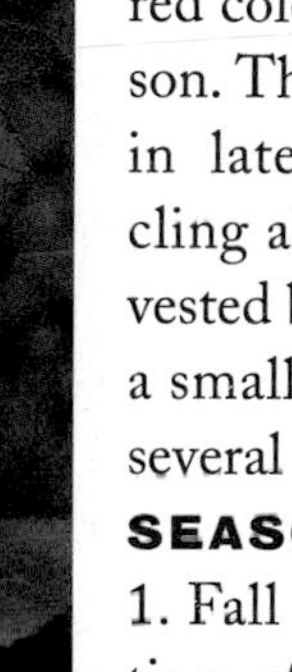

North of USDA zone 6, gardeners can grow mountain ash and enjoy its fall color.

LEAVES: Mountain ash leaves are pinnately compound. The 11 to 17 leaflets are sharply toothed and pointed, and each leaflet grows to about 3 inches (6-7 cm) in length. The leaflets turn golden-orange in the fall and cling to bright red rachises. This combines with the ripe fruit to create one of the most colorful displays of a very colorful season.

FLOWERS AND FRUITS: The fragrant flowers develop on new growth in late spring after the foliage and are positioned conspicuously at the ends of the twigs, not hidden among the leaves. They consist of broad white clusters, or corymbs, about 4 inches (10 cm) across and are very showy. The fruit clusters that follow are even showier, with their flame-red color and extended season. They ripen to full color in late summer and may cling all winter unless harvested by birds. Each fruit is a small pome that contains several small seeds.

SEASONS:
1. Fall (the color combination of leaflet, rachis and fruit ranks this tree with the finest of all autumn standouts);
2. Late spring (during the blooming period).

NATIVE AND ADAPTIVE RANGE: Most members of this genus do best at high latitudes or altitudes, and ours is no exception. It flourishes in eastern Canada north to Hudson Bay and penetrates southward into the United States, mostly around cool bogs and in mountainous areas down through the Appalachians. It prospers in USDA zones 2 and 3 and gradually declines southward, becoming very unhappy from USDA zone 6 southward.

CULTURE: Mountain ash is related to the cultivated fruit trees and was once classified in the same genus with the pome fruits. It benefits from the same insect- and disease-management programs that are used in the home orchard, because every borer and foliage disease that plagues fruit orchards also attacks mountain ash. Young trees can be transplanted easily, and seed can be germinated successfully if stratified over the winter or sown early in the fall. The fruits may be crushed or fermented to remove the seeds, but we have grown seedlings by squeezing the fruits and sowing them intact, then thinning any seedling clumps. Mountain ash is sought by rabbits, deer, moose and other browsing mammals for winter forage, so protection of the young stems and the thin bark may be needed. This tree requires a cool, mulched root zone and acidic soil. It is unusual within its family for its tolerance of wet soil, but it does best with good drainage. It will grow in full sun or, especially near its southern limit, in light shade.

The fruits of mountain ash add vibrant color to the northern landscape in late summer.

PROBLEMS: Refer to serviceberry (*Amelanchier*) for its similar problems with insects and diseases, and add sunscald, anthracnose (*Glomerella cingulata*) and the European mountain ash sawfly (*Pristiphora geniculata*) to the list. In warm climates, the round-headed apple borer (*Saperda candida*), a striped beetle with larvae that tunnel into the base of the tree, can be devastating. The thin bark is sensitive to sapsucker pecks and mechanical damage and must be protected from misguided mowers and string-trimmers. This tree is weak-wooded and develops multiple leaders, making it prone to ice breakage in portions of the Midwest and upper South, where freezing rain often replaces snow.

Although many people in the Midwest and South try to grow mountain ash, their efforts are rarely successful, and the trees often meet an untimely end. Like paper birch (*Betula papyrifera*), this tree should be left to the gardeners of the North and the coolest mountain areas.

CULTIVARS: Most cultivars of mountain ash are derived from exotic species. 'Belmonte' was selected from our native tree, but the selection was made from plantations in an arboretum in Holland. Given the propensity of this genus toward rampant hybridization, the selection might well be a cross with a member of another species.

RELATED SPECIES: Showy mountain ash (*Sorbus decora*) differs only in subtle ways. Its leaflets are a little wider and toothed only about half way to the base. Its fruits shade toward vermilion, and its individual florets are a little larger than mountain ash. Other species, all shrubby, grow in the Northwest, and perhaps 70 more can be found in Europe and Asia. Several of these are popular landscape trees, and at least one, *Sorbus aucuparia*, is widely naturalized across the boreal forests of North America. The true ashes (*Fraxinus* spp.) are not related to mountain ash.

COMMENTS: The mountain ash genus is a prime example of what botanists grudgingly call a plastic taxon. It refuses to stay between taxonomic lines: its many species interbreed not only with one another but even with *Aronia*, *Amelanchier* and other members of the great rose family. In areas where one mountain ash species overlaps in range with others, they can blend at the edges through a genetic mixing process called introgression to the point that the individual species cannot be distinguished. Tidy botanists don't like this because it is a violation of the "species" concept. A species is a taxonomic unit that does not interbreed with other species, and a genus is a collection of related species, so natural intergeneric crossing should be impossible. But mountain ash is a taxonomic rebel of the first order.

BALD CYPRESS

Taxodium distichum

DESCRIPTION: This state tree of Louisiana is the universal symbol of the southern swamp. It sometimes grows slowly in its watery habitat, but it can do so for a thousand years or more. Bald cypress is the largest and oldest tree in Illinois and no doubt in many states to the south. In fact, old-growth bald cypress stands, from southern Florida to southern Illinois, contain the oldest trees of any species in North America, except for two or three of the great conifers of the West.

The trees grow in excess of 100 feet (30 m) during their first century or two, but with time, some of the upper branches often die, and the trees become "stag-headed" because of drainage alterations in their habitat or the cumulative effects of fire, wind and lightning. The national champion on Cat Island, Louisiana, is only 83 feet (26 m) tall. Its trunk, however, is 17 feet (5.2 m) in diameter, making it one of the most impressive trees in North America or anywhere else. We have measured other bald cypress trees, some entering their second millennium, with diameters only about half that size. Most were damaged or hollow and thus useless for timber. Many more would still be growing if their durable wood had not been so valuable to loggers.

Cypress knees rise among Atamasco lilies and azaleas in a wetland landscape.

LEAVES: This is one of our few deciduous conifers—it loses its foliage each fall after turning a coppery bronze tone. The unique feathery foliage is composed of small individual leaves arranged alternately in tight, flat sprays along small twiglets, which themselves are deciduous.

FLOWERS AND FRUIT: The conspicuous staminate catkins of this tree are one of the first signs of life in the new year; they expand in late winter when the deciduous swamp forest is bare of foliage. The small, round pistillate flowers develop into spherical brown cones nearly the size of golf balls.

SEASONS:

1. Fall (to see this conifer turn a glowing copper color in a good year is reason enough to canoe through a southern swamp);
2. Late winter (the catkins are the only hint of life outdoors in this dormant season and combine nicely with the reddish bark and artistic form of the tree);
3. Spring (for the pale green color of the new growth);
4. Summer (for the airy shade it provides in a sweltering climate and its fine, graceful texture).

NATIVE AND ADAPTIVE RANGE: This is a low-elevation tree that grows wild in the Atlantic coastal plain and in the broad, flat valleys of the Lower Mississippi River and its tributaries and bayous. It ranges north to southern Illinois and Indiana in the interior and up to the Delmarva Peninsula and Delaware Bay along the Atlantic Coast. These northern limitations are not due to intolerance of the cold but to specific reproductive requirements.

Seeds must have constant moisture to germinate. Young seedlings must have constant access to surface water until they sink their roots below the water table. And saplings must have seasonal flooding to kill the hardwood competitors that would outgrow them. Such flooded areas are subject to freezing in the North, and the annual formation of heavy ice would kill the seedlings before they grew large enough to withstand it, so this tree does not usually grow naturally north of USDA zone 6. When saplings are planted and tended, making such flooding unnecessary, bald cypress can be grown on upland sites north into USDA zone 4 in Minnesota and Ontario.

CULTURE: Bald cypress prefers a heavy soil or one rich in organic matter. Seed will germinate in the spring following a winter of wet stratification and should be sown on sphagnum moss or some similar substrate that can be kept constantly moist. Small trees can be transplanted, but larger specimens become very deep-rooted on upland sites and can be a job to move. In swamps, however, the trees are more shallow-rooted. We have heard of large wild trees that were plucked from swamps by giant helicopters and replanted.

New trees should be watered regularly until their roots reach constant moisture in the lower soil horizons. Once they are well established, they tolerate any amount of water. They can grow fairly quickly in cultivation. Many trees less than 20 years old are 30 feet (9 m) tall or more. Specimens planted in about 1850 at Spring Grove Cemetery in Cincinnati, Ohio, look like forest giants. If they are planted in well-drained locations, bald cypress trees will probably not develop the porous knees (root growths that look like stalagmites) for which cypress swamps are famous. But if they do, the knees may be pruned off at ground level in areas where they constitute a hazard. In a mulched planting bed, out of the way of mowers and foot traffic, they become living sculptures. We have observed that the knees on our cultivated specimens at pondside in Illinois grow about 1 inch (2.5 cm) in four years, but we have seen magnificent knees 10 feet (3 m) tall in virgin bald cypress swamps.

Bald cypress is one of our few deciduous conifers, with new leaves opening feathery and green each spring.

PROBLEMS: Once this tree is established, it is one of our most carefree species. As a deciduous conifer, it resists damage from the ice storms that can tear apart evergreen trees whose needles collect freezing rain. Its strong wood is not very vulnerable to insects, cankers or wind and is even more resistant to decay once it ages for a century or two. The tiny leaves do not cause a litter problem, and the airy canopy allows other plants to be grown below. Alkaline soil can cause chlorosis, and some trees are susceptible to superficial damage from gall-forming mites and midges such as the cypress twig gall midge (*Taxodiomyia cupressiananassa*).

CULTIVARS: Earl Cully of Jacksonville, Illinois, is the acknowledged leader in cultivar development for bald cypress. His most popular selections include 'Monarch of Illinois', a massive, broadly pyramidal tree with a strong branching structure, and 'Shawnee Brave', which has a narrowly upright form.

He also selected 'Prairie Sentinel' from the related species *Taxodium ascendens*, or pond cypress, which many authorities argue is merely a smaller, southern variety (*imbricarium*) of bald cypress. It has thicker bark and linear foliage sprays that look like thick strands of green yarn. The tree resembles a young (and very small) version of Sierra redwood (*Sequoiadendron giganteum*). Several arboretums and nurseries are testing pond cypress selections such as 'Nutans' for hardiness in their search for marketable cultivars with superior cold tolerance.

Another selection of bald cypress has been around for over a century. It is called 'Pendens' and has a conical form with pendulous twigs. Earl is testing additional cultivars of bald cypress and pond cypress, and other desirable selections are certainly possible. Grafted trees, which look alike, give a uniform appearance in a stand. Otherwise, a bald cypress planting—like the one at Spring Grove Cemetery in Cincinnati—will be quite variable.

RELATED SPECIES: Other than the bald cypress/pond cypress grex, one other species of *Taxodium* can be found. It is called Montezuma cypress (*Taxodium mucronatum*), and it grows along rivers in southern Texas, Mexico and Guatemala. Some taxonomists classify this tree as *Taxodium distichum* variety *mexicanum*. We once saw a beautiful grove along the river Purificación in Mexico and a giant, 200-year-old tree at an old hacienda nearby in Tamaulipas. It becomes a great, spreading, weeping, nearly evergreen tree in its native habitat.

The Giant Tule Cypress, a Montezuma cypress in Santa Maria de Tule village, just south of Mexico City, reportedly has the largest-diameter trunk of any tree on Earth. Michael Melendrez of Los Lunas, New Mexico, is propagating an exceptionally hardy strain of Montezuma cypress that might be useful in the Southeast.

Bald cypress stand as a commanding centerpiece of this refined wetland design.

The closest living relative and mimic of the bald cypress and its clan is dawn redwood (*Metasequoia glyptostroboides*). This is the "fossil tree" that was thought to be extinct until it was discovered alive in China in 1945. The oldest specimens in North America, including the beautiful grove at Missouri Botanic Garden in St. Louis, date back only to 1947. Many other members of this family now exist only as fossils.

COMMENTS: Bald cypress is invariably the largest and tallest tree in old swamp forests of the South. In such settings, it attracts everything that likes high places over water, including eagles, ospreys, anhingas, cormorants, herons and lightning.

During a canoe trip from the Suwannee Canal west into the heart of Okefenokee National Wildlife Refuge in Georgia years ago, the birds, alligators and carnivorous plants were marvelous. But the most lasting impression is of a black night spent in total solitude, camping among islands of beautiful bald cypress trees that were draped with ghost-like moss and alive with tree frogs. Some of the trees had their roots anchored in nothing more than drifting batteries of peat that had floated up from the bottom of the swamp.

There are more convenient places to admire ancient bald cypress trees—beautiful places like Corkscrew Swamp in Florida, Heron Pond in Illinois, Reelfoot Lake in Tennessee and Francis Beidler Refuge in South Carolina, where boardwalks serve as dry sidewalks, elevated above the real world of water and snakes. But a solitary trip across the wilds of the Okefenokee is a chance to encounter the haunting beauty of ancient bald cypress trees, free from the intrusions of the modern world.

ARBORVITAE

Thuja occidentalis

DESCRIPTION: Often known as northern white cedar, a name that can lead to confusion with many other trees also called cedars, the arborvitae is a fragrant evergreen of the boreal forest. It grows slowly and lives to a venerable age on cliff faces and in swamp forests of the North.

Arborvitae seedlings germinate on rotting logs, organic peats and moist, calcareous mineral soils laid bare by fire. They can persist under the shade of taller trees for decades until they slowly claim their place in the sun. Those that grow on rocky upland sites assume bonsai forms with twisted, forked and gnarly crowns and look totally unlike the slender, erect trees found in dense stands in swamps. This is solely a function of environmental influence and is not due to genetic variation between the two types.

Arborvitae means "tree of life." Its foliage is fragrant, its bark tight and stringy.

Arborvitae is a compact tree that seldom attains the stature of its neighboring conifers, but very old individuals on productive upland sites can surprise gardeners who buy arborvitae as foundation shrubs. The United States champion in Leelanau County, Michigan, is 113 feet (35 m) tall and 5 feet 8 inches (1.7 m) in diameter. Arborvitae is primarily a Canadian tree, so one can expect to find comparable specimens in the North.

LEAVES: The foliage of arborvitae is soft and pleasant to the touch, and it is very fragrant. The flat, filigree sprays of tiny, scaly leaves are popular as background foliage for cut-flower arrangements and wonderful to scratch and sniff on walks through the woods. Some trees remain bright green all winter, while others turn a bronze tone and green up again in spring. Some leaves remain attached even after they have turned brown and been replaced by younger ones, and they eventually pop off as the twig expands in girth.

FLOWERS AND FRUIT: Tiny male and female flowers are borne on separate twigs of the same tree. The female (pistillate) flowers grow into oval, pea-sized cones with a few overlapping scales that ripen to a warm brown in late summer.

SEASONS:
1. Winter (evergreens become dominant in any landscape during the dormant season);
2. All year (a pleasant, fresh green foliage plant in youth and a picturesque tree as it matures).

NATIVE AND ADAPTIVE RANGE: This hardy tree grows from the northern end of Lake Winnipeg in Manitoba, across eastern Canada to the Gulf of St. Lawrence, around the Great Lakes and in isolated areas of suitable habitat south into Illinois, Ohio and the Appalachians. It can be grown in cultivation north into USDA zone 2, but it becomes stressed by heat and drought south of USDA zone 6 unless carefully sited and tended.

CULTURE: Arborvitae thrives in moist soil, loves limestone areas and can take full sun or light shade. It grows slowly, but it is easy to transplant. Seeds should be sown in the fall and not allowed to dry out. Wild plants often propagate by layering, when their lower branches sweep the ground, become covered with a litter mulch and take root. Favorite selections are easy to propagate by cuttings taken in winter.

PROBLEMS: Many small arborvitae trees are destroyed each winter by rabbits, deer, moose, other browsing mammals and snowmobiles. They must be given protection from such abuse as well as from foliage browning caused by dogs and cats marking their territories. Bagworms (*Thyridopteryx ephemeraeformis*) seem to prefer this tree above all others, but they cannot survive in the cold climate that prevails over much of its natural range. The bags, or sacs, should be removed over the winter to reduce the number of eggs that will hatch in the spring. Heavy infestations can be controlled with a timely application of the biological pesticide *Bacillus thuringiensis* (Bt).

Summer drought is a serious problem in hot climates, and low humidity desiccates trees planted in the Southwest. Within its natural habitat, it is affected most by animal damage and fire. The species tolerates air pollution and heat as long as it is rooted in cool, moist soil. It is tough and flexible and more resistant to damage from ice and snow than many other conifers, but some ornamental cultivars with multiple leaders will split under heavy snow.

Above : Arborvitae bears clusters of small cones among its sprays of foliage. Below left: Arborvitae has given us many cultivars, including this popular pyramidal form.

CULTIVARS: Many horticulturists have been attracted to this plant and have found and propagated numerous selections for foliage color, growth form and dwarfism. A plant of 'Hetz Midget' at Starhill Forest that Guy propagated from a cutting in 1967 is robust and healthy but has yet to reach waist height. Some of the best tree-sized cultivars, including 'Nigra' and 'Techny Mission', have been grown for their winter color. A seed-propagated strain, 'Affinity', is a tall, pyramidal type released in 1993 by the USDA Soil Conservation Service. It was propagated from a vigorous cultivated specimen in Indiana for conservation use in the Midwest.

RELATED SPECIES: Western red cedar (*Thuja plicata*) is a giant conifer of the Pacific Northwest that shows surprising adaptability under cultivation in the climate of the eastern United States. A plant in our Illinois collection that was propagated from the interior part of its range (Idaho) seems denser and perhaps hardier than specimens propagated from populations near the Pacific Coast. Several arborvitae species also grow in Asia and are progenitors of some popular cultivars.

The Atlantic white cedar (*Chamaecyparis thyoides*) is the only eastern North American native representative of a similar genus. It is a lowland tree of the Atlantic coastal plain, from Maine to the Mississippi River, and it is slow-growing and long-lived. Two related species grow on the Pacific Coast, and numerous cultivars have been derived from several Asian species. Cypress (*Cupressus* spp.) are closely related as well, as are junipers (such as our red cedar, *Juniperus virginiana*) and incense cedar (*Calocedrus decurrens*). None of these plants is closely related to the true cedars (*Cedrus* spp.) of Africa and Asia.

COMMENTS: "Tree of life" is the literal translation of arborvitae, and this species was one of the most common trees planted in old cemeteries to commemorate the afterlife. It has been used for this and other horticultural purposes since 1536, and it was the first of our native conifers to be cultivated in Europe.

Even before that, Native Americans were leaving offerings at a natural shrine known as the Witch Tree, which was growing on the exposed rocks of Hat Point along the northwest shore of Lake Superior. This crooked old arborvitae served as a landmark for early French voyagers on their way to Grand Portage and was noted as a very old tree by explorer Sieur de La Vérendrye as he passed it in 1731. The Witch Tree lives on, and we observed several recent offerings left by modern Native Americans when we inspected it a few years ago. We touched the tree, imagined the stories it could tell and left in silence.

BASSWOOD

Tilia americana

DESCRIPTION: Basswood, or linden, is one of those tenacious trees that can survive in remarkably adverse conditions. But it becomes a stately shade or timber tree only where its roots can find deep, moist, silt-loam soils. It is a climax species of sheltered valleys, the lower portions of north-facing slopes and the cool forests of the Great Lakes region.

This tree frequently grows in clumps or as a single trunk with several basal sprouts. It excels in its ability to regenerate by sprouting vigorously from the root collar after fire or other damage. The sprouts often seem too impatient for the main stem to be killed before racing to take its place. This sprouting ability has enabled basswood, which is generally slow-growing from seed, to dominate areas where previous disturbances have killed competing species. It also produces clumps that have very artistic forms.

'Boulevard' is a pyramidal selection of basswood with a strong central leader.

Given enough time, basswood can become one of our largest trees. The United States champion, which grows in Montgomery County, Pennsylvania, is 94 feet (29 m) tall and has a trunk nearly 8 feet (2.2 m) in diameter. But such giants don't develop overnight. During a historical reconstruction project at the Lincoln Home National Historic Site in 1993, several basswoods that appeared to be about 50 years old were discovered to actually date back to the Civil War.

LEAVES: Heart-shaped and sharply toothed, basswood leaves emerge from red buds and grow to nearly 8 inches (20 cm) long. They closely resemble the unlobed leaves of red mulberry (*Morus rubra*). The foliage is arranged on the tree in a pattern designed to capture every ray of sunlight that falls within the spread of its canopy, leaving the ground below in darkness. Basswoods seldom color well in the fall, but they sometimes turn yellow.

FLOWERS AND FRUIT: Basswood blooms in early summer, after the leaves are grown. Fragrant yellowish flowers hang in clusters from narrow leaf-like bracts. Basswood is one of our most important sources of nectar for honey. Bees quickly find the flowers and can arrive in such numbers that the tree hums like a power line in a storm. Clusters of dry, crusty, pea-sized round fruits appear after the flowers, and they fall in early winter while still attached to the bracts.

SEASONS:

1. Summer (for the cool, dense shade under their canopy and the flowers);
2. Winter (for the arching form and red buds).

NATIVE AND ADAPTIVE RANGE: This tree can be found in mesic forests from Winnipeg, Manitoba, south to northeastern Oklahoma, east across southern Ontario and Quebec to the St. John River Valley in New Brunswick and southeast to the mountain coves of North Carolina. Under cultivation, it rates hardy from USDA zone 2 southward.

CULTURE: Basswood is very easy to transplant and will survive on a variety of sites, but it will not perform well as a landscape tree unless given deep, moist soil. It grows in sun or shade and is indifferent to soil pH. In native stands, it is one of the best soil builders, bringing nutrients up from the subsoil and depositing them on the surface in its leaf litter, where they become available to understory plants. You have to prune basswood if you want a single stem or a uniform clump, but when removing surplus basal shoots, be careful not to damage the smooth, thin bark of the main stem or stems.

Growing these trees from seed can be frustrating because the seed remains dormant for up to four years until its requirements have been met. So we suggest that you obtain much more seed than you think you will need, then divide it into several batches and treat it in different ways. Stratify some; remove the seed coat from others; soak some in warm water; scarify others with acid; pick some before it is fully ripe in late summer and plant them immediately. Try all of these techniques and, with patience, you may succeed.

PROBLEMS: Basswoods can be defoliated by larvae of the linden leafroller moth (*Pantographa limata*) and the gypsy moth (*Lymantria dispar*). Early growth is sometimes killed by late-spring frosts, and the soft wood and narrow crotches are susceptible to storm damage. The foliage is subject to scorch from drought and to blotching from anthracnose (*Gnomonia tiliae*), although neither condition usually causes long-term damage. Canker diseases and heartrot fungi affect many wild trees, and vascular wilt from *Verticillium albo-atrum* is found on some landscape trees.

Browsing animals love basswood, and deer seem to prefer its smooth bark and soft wood for shadowboxing in the fall, testing their new antlers by scraping the bark away. Because of its dense shade, which restricts the options for ground covers, basswood can be difficult to place in the landscape.

CULTIVARS: 'Boulevard' and 'Frontyard' are forms selected for their strong central leaders, a natural characteristic on forest-grown trees but not on open-grown basswoods, which often form multiple leaders that weaken them. 'Pyramidal' is another cultivar, selected for its narrow crown, while 'Douglas' and 'Legend' have broad crowns and strong central leaders. 'Dakota' is a hardy round-headed selection from a cultivated tree that grows in South Dakota, and 'Rosehill' has a rounded pyramidal form. A few se-

Basswoods can develop into giants over time, in some cases becoming more than 90 feet (28 m) tall.

The clustered fruits of basswood hang from leafy bracts.

The flowers of basswood are attractive to bees and make a premium honey.

lections with variant foliage can be seen in botanical gardens.

'Redmond' may be the most popular *Tilia* cultivar on the market. It is often listed as a selection of our native basswood, but it seems to have developed from a hybrid, and possibly a backcross, involving basswood and some European linden species. Other cultivars have derived from European and Asian lindens, which are also known as limes (but are not related to the edible limes of the genus *Citrus*).

RELATED SPECIES: Taxonomy in this genus is hopelessly confused by variability and hybridization, and some authorities recognize five times as many species as do others. Most agree that the distinctive white basswood (*Tilia heterophylla*) of the Southeast is our only other definitive native species of consequence. It is very ornamental, with the woolly white undersides of its leaves flashing in the breeze. The record tree, a full-crowned specimen in Henderson County, North Carolina, is 101 feet (30 m) tall. Its trunk reaches a diameter of nearly 4 feet (1.1 m) before dividing into three equal leaders.

Other varieties or species occur in limited areas of the Southeast and Mexico, and numerous species and hybrids are found in Europe and Asia. Many of the street trees planted in North America are selections from some of these exotic varieties, particularly the littleleaf linden (*Tilia cordata*).

COMMENTS: Most authorities assert that basswood was cultivated in North America at least by 1752 for both its honey and its carvable wood. But at least one record indicates that trees growing in London in 1730 were from seed collected by the famous plant explorer Mark Catesby in Carolina in 1726. We suspect it might have taken the four intervening years just to germinate the seed.

Knowing that basswood is a tree of the mesic forest, we were startled years ago, while visiting the Indiana Dunes of Lake Michigan, to see a straggly little basswood emerging from the lakeward (retreating) side of an active sand dune. Closer inspection revealed that this tree had developed adventitious roots nearly to its top as the dune advanced upon it. Some of those roots reached more than 20 feet (6 m) down into the receding sand, making the tree look like a tropical fig or banyan with stilt roots. This specimen would never have made an acceptable lawn tree or sawlog, but its tenacity was stunning.

HEMLOCK

Tsuga canadensis

DESCRIPTION: Landscape professionals often speak of "quality plants" that are long-lived, are refined in character and have no off-season. Hardwood trees such as sugar maple (*Acer saccharum*), beech (*Fagus grandifolia*) and white oak (*Quercus alba*) come to mind, along with conifers like white pine (*Pinus strobus*). We find hemlock sharing the spotlight with these elite trees as well as many of the habitats where they grow best. Hemlock, the state tree of Pennsylvania, is certainly a member of the quality-tree fraternity throughout its range.

Hemlocks can be recognized from a distance by their nodding leaders, like those of some exotic cedars (*Cedrus* spp.). No other native conifer in eastern North America typically has this growth form. Large hemlocks are found only in old-growth forests or in the oldest of cultivated landscapes, and they are impressive. The United States national champion in Aurora, West Virginia, is 123 feet (38 m) tall and has a rugged trunk 6 feet (1.8 m) in diameter. Many magnificent hemlocks several centuries old can be seen in the Joyce Kilmer Memorial Forest in North Carolina and in the Tionesta Scenic Area of the Allegheny National Forest in Pennsylvania. The Tionesta grove offers an interesting contrast between virgin stands and new growth that has sprung up in a swath cut by a tornado. Early-successional species have become established among the old hemlocks.

The soft, graceful appearance of hemlock makes it a premium landscape evergreen.

LEAVES: The evergreen needles of hemlock are a dark, military-issue olive green with whitened bands of stomates underneath, and they reach about ½ inch (15 cm) in length. They are borne in flattened, two-ranked horizontal sprays on slender twigs. Hemlocks are willowy and flexible, lacking the stiffness and sharpness of most conifers.

FLOWERS AND FRUIT: The brown staminate (male) strobiles are tiny and inconspicuous. Pistillate (female) strobiles mature in a single season into seed cones at the ends of lateral twigs, which are less than 1 inch (2 cm) long but slightly larger than those of tamarack (*Larix laricina*). Cones open to release their seeds in early fall, then some drop before the next spring, crunching like popcorn underfoot.

SEASONS:
1. Spring (for the two-toned pattern of new foliage seen against dark, older growth);
2. Winter (the dark evergreen needles contrast sharply with snow; the tree's lacy form is most evident amid the bare branches of the neighboring deciduous trees);
3. All year (hemlock casts a deep, cool shade in summer and looks dark and regal among the bright colors of other trees in autumn).

NATIVE AND ADAPTIVE RANGE: This is a tree of mesic sites in the Great Lake states, in the Appalachians south to Alabama and in New England. It extends north into Nova Scotia, New Brunswick and southern Quebec and to the vicinity of Algonquin Provincial Park in Ontario. Isolated populations, left from the last glacial period, can be seen in cool canyons, such as those in and around Turkey Run State Park in Indiana. There, they modify the microclimate to their advantage by shading the soil and reducing evaporation. Hemlocks can be cultivated from USDA zone 3 southward, but they will begin to die in the warmer parts of USDA zone 7 unless they can be kept cool and moist.

Top: Old cones still cling to a hemlock as the new ones develop. Above: Hemlock needles are olive green on top and whitish with stomates underneath.

CULTURE: Like many of our other most prestigious landscape trees, hemlock needs moderate conditions. Cool-climate areas with moist, acidic soil and good drainage are best. It survives in the shade and grows best there in the South, but becomes more dense in full sun. Windy locations, in either summer or winter, should be avoided. Hemlock responds to pruning and shearing by becoming more dense.

Transplanting should be done with a soil ball in either spring or fall. Take care not to set the new tree deeper than it originally grew. Mulch a wide area around its base, and water it regularly but not excessively. Organic matter incorporated into a mounded planting bed (not just in the planting hole) gives good results. Hemlock is sensitive to provenance, so local sources should be used if possible.

Seedlings may be grown from seed sown in the fall or stratified until spring. The cones should be picked just as they begin to open and left in paper sacks for a few days until the seed can be shaken free. The warm, dry air rising from behind a refrigerator is great for drying and opening cones. New seedlings are tiny and fragile and must be given protection from wind and strong sunlight. Spreading a layer of compost on bare soil beneath a mature hemlock and allowing natural seeding to produce a few seedlings (transplanted about two years later) might be the easiest way to obtain a few starts of this beautiful tree.

PROBLEMS: Hemlock is sensitive to environmental extremes. Heat, drought, wind, salt spray, air pollution and poor drainage must be avoided. It tolerates winter cold but can be damaged by unseasonable frosts. It will bend and recover from ice and snow but may be toppled by wind because of its shallow roots. It can live for nearly a thousand years but it grows slowly, and during its long life, it does not adapt well to changes in its habitat. Hemlock is one of the indicator species that environmental scientists are watching to gauge the effects of global warming.

Our native hemlock is not related to the herbaceous hemlock (*Conium maculatum*) that poisoned Socrates. In fact, it is all too palatable to deer and porcupines. Rabbits damage small specimens as well. But the most serious pest is the woolly adelgid (*Adelges tsugae*), which was accidentally introduced in 1924 from Asia. It can be fatal, but infestations can be controlled with horticultural oil sprays or with systemic pesticides. A parasitic mite, *Diapterobates humeralis*, from the adelgid's home range in Japan may be used in the future as a biological control.

Hemlock needles are arranged in flat, overlapping sprays that intercept virtually all sunlight falling on the tree's crown. Unlike the translucent foliage of neighboring broadleaf trees, hemlock needles are opaque. The shallow roots of hemlock are very efficient at absorbing moisture from upper soil layers, and hemlock grows well in acidic soils. All of this does not bode well for the successful establishment of turf under a hemlock canopy.

CULTIVARS: This species has produced more than 50 prominent horticultural selections. Most of them are weeping, procumbent or dwarf and would not fall within our definition of a tree as such, but they are among the most prized plants for rock gardens and dwarf conifer collections. A few selections have been made for specimens with variegated or unique foliage or compact, dense growth.

RELATED SPECIES: Carolina hemlock (*Tsuga caroliniana*) can be found in the southern Appalachians. It is a more compact tree and perhaps not quite as graceful as its larger cousin, but it is reported to be a little more tolerant of heat in shaded urban plantings. Two other hemlocks, *Tsuga heterophylla* and *Tsuga mertensiana*, are giant timber trees of the far West. They are strikingly beautiful in their natural habitat but have not proven very adaptable in our area. Several more hemlock species are found in Asia and seen in some North American gardens.

In the spring, hemlocks may have a two-toned appearance, as light, new foliage contrasts with darker, older growth.

COMMENTS: Hemlock is a patient tree. Although it will grow at a moderate rate under ideal conditions, suppressed specimens no taller than a person but more than 100 years old have been found in the wild. George Washington planted a hemlock at Mount Vernon in 1785, and it has not yet reached 30 inches (75 cm) in diameter. This species can afford to grow so slowly because it is extremely shade-tolerant. It can succeed, over time, even where faster growing neighbors initially overtop it. After two or three centuries, the persistent hemlock usually wins out, rising through the crowns of other trees to dominate in the climax forest.

Such a forest is called climax because, once it has become dominated by mature hemlocks, no further natural succession takes place under their dark shade. A fire or storm, like the one at the Tionesta grove, must open the dense hemlock canopy enough to allow fast-growing, sun-loving, early-successional species to regain a temporary foothold. Without droughts, natural disasters and human impacts, climax forests would eventually rule much of the natural world, and hemlocks would rule many of those forests in the North.

AMERICAN ELM

Ulmus americana

DESCRIPTION: The American elm once reigned as the most favored of all shade trees. It is massive, long-lived, tough, easy to grow, adaptable and blessed with an arching, wine-glass silhouette that made it the perfect street tree. It is also valuable as a builder and stabilizer of forest soils and for the nutrient-rich leaves it sheds each fall that feed beneficial soil organisms. American elm was selected as the state tree by Massachusetts, and a few years later by North Dakota, and it was a favorite of many other areas as well. Then, a few decades ago, an epidemic turned our urban monocultures of elm into firewood.

This malady, commonly known as Dutch elm disease, has killed millions of elms of several species across our continent and in Europe. Many elms live on, though, to remind us of the great potential of this tree. Some of the survivors escaped the infection only temporarily, and a few of them succumb each year. But others are resistant and give us hope. In fact, research has given us not only optimism but confidence that the stately elm will be back.

Most elms are notable exceptions to the rule that narrow crotches make weak limbs. The wood of our native elms is so tough and cross-grained that the trees can develop massive crowns full of resilient forks. The United States national champion American elm is the Louis Vieux elm—a huge, leaning, historic specimen that grows along the Oregon Trail near Louisville in northeastern Kansas. It measures 100 feet (31 m) in height with nearly an equal spread, and it has a trunk more than 8 feet (2.5 m) in diameter. This tree is the centerpiece of the only state forest in Kansas—a city-lot-sized piece of rural land set aside specifically for the tree.

The cultivar 'Independence' was selected for resistance to Dutch elm disease. Perhaps the beauty of its fall foliage will be perpetuated for generations.

Other elms, even larger, have reigned, until they contracted Dutch elm disease. Still more contenders, almost as large, await the uncertain fate of the Louis Vieux giant. It is isolated from other elms, though, and has not yet become infected. Some of these potential challengers grow in mesic forests, some along prairie streams, some in the bottomlands of great rivers and some in the parks and parkways of nearly every part of North America.

LEAVES: Elliptical and pointed with prominent veins and asymmetrical bases, the leaves of all of our native elms look substantially alike. Those of American elm are large but variable in size—up to 6 inches (15 cm) long—and doubly serrate along the margin but relatively smooth on the upper surface. They often turn a rich gold in the fall, as do the leaves of most of our other native elm species.

FLOWERS AND FRUIT: Drooping clusters of small flowers appear early, before the leaves, on American elm and most other native elms. These flowers make our elms among the earliest of trees to show signs of life in spring, and they add a soft red tint to the crowns of blooming trees. The flowers expand into small, circular, winged seeds, which scatter by the thousands, helicoptering on the spring wind.

SEASONS:

1. Fall (on trees that exhibit the best fall color);
2. Spring (the early flowers and young leaves accentuate the characteristic arching limb structure);
3. Summer (this is an ideal shade tree when healthy) and winter (for the silhouettes of picturesque old specimens).

NATIVE AND ADAPTIVE RANGE: American elm is one of our most resilient and tractable trees. It grows in habitats ranging from rocky bluffs to flood-

Colorful leaves rain from an American elm on a frosty fall morning.

plains and from mesic forests to prairie valleys. It is ubiquitous and possibly grows wild in almost every county in North America east of Wyoming south of a line from Prince Albert in central Saskatchewan to the Gaspé Peninsula of Quebec, except for southern Florida. Under cultivation, it does well anywhere south of USDA zone 2.

CULTURE: Elms are adaptable to almost any climate and soil, wet or dry, sun or partial shade, and they are very easy to transplant at any size. Seeds of most species sprout immediately upon ripening (with no dormancy), and spontaneous seedlings can be found in every flower bed and sidewalk crack within reach of the wind-blown seeds.

Once established in the right setting, our several native elm species have only one significant cultural requirement, and that is management for control of Dutch elm disease.

PROBLEMS: Elm roots are shallow, with flaring buttresses, and invasive; they may lift adjacent sidewalks unless root barriers are installed. Small seedlings sprout everywhere, so periodic weeding is necessary where they are unwanted. Elms are susceptible to several vascular diseases caused by various fungi and viruses. Rabbits girdle many small elms in winter, so young trees should be protected. Elm leaf beetle (*Pyrrhalta luteola*) and many other insects feed on our native elms but cause more serious damage on exotic elm species.

The European elm bark beetle (*Scolytus multistriatus*) and a native bark beetle (*Hylurgopinus rufipes*) are the major elm pests, partly because they burrow under the bark as larvae but mostly because they spread Dutch elm disease when feeding on the twigs as adults. This disease, *Ophiostoma ulmi* (formerly *Ceratocystis ulmi*), was introduced accidentally into Europe and North America from Asia in the 1930s. An especially aggressive strain now predominant in North America has been given separate taxonomic status as *Ophiostoma novo-ulmi* by some pathologists.

Asian elms are resistant to Dutch elm disease, but most European and North American elms are not. Because elms are so valuable in landscaping, a horticultural war is being waged on several fronts against the disease and its vectors. One successful technique has been to use Asian elms, either directly or in hybridization programs with native elms, to breed disease-resistant trees. George Ware, dendrologist at The Morton Arboretum in Illinois, has led this effort since 1972. He furnished the resistant *Ulmus davidiana* planted at the Lincoln Home National Historic Site, and we are testing some of his most promising selections in our own Illinois planting at Starhill Forest.

Other research is focused on protecting existing trees. One approach is to control the bark beetles that spread the disease. They are attracted to weakened trees, so keeping elms vigorous lessens the likelihood of infection. Insecticides can be used to protect historic or valuable trees from the beetles, but they should be narrow-spectrum types that minimize damage to nontarget organisms. Fungicide injections to kill or block the fungus (done every three years by qualified arborists) can give excellent results at a modest cost per tree. Some success has been achieved by inoculating trees against the disease. By inspecting elms regularly during the growing season, we have cured the disease on two of our trees by simply pruning out the "flags" of dying foliage in the small twigs where the beetles feed. Such pruning must be done immediately, and with sterilized tools, several feet below the lowest detectable sapwood stain caused by the fungus. The disease also can spread through natural root grafts, so dying elms should be removed and their root systems cut to isolate them from healthy trees.

Winged elm is a tough, drought-resistant species. In the dormant season, the wings along its twigs may be etched with frost.

Laboratory techniques can be used to expedite screening for resistance in native elms, and such resistance is being found. It may vary with the size of vascular openings in the wood. An elm will be more resistant if it is managed to encourage strong but moderate growth as a sapling, minimizing the open pores that occur in rampant growth, because the disease must move through the xylem against the sap flow to become systemic.

Resistance in individual trees increases with age and seasonally after the initial spring growth flush. Hot summer temperatures also control the spread of the fungus, so it is not as serious in the Deep South as it is in the North. However, natural selection has removed many of the most susceptible trees in the North, so the remaining elm population there has a higher proportion of resistant trees and is a better source of native breeding stock for research.

Professor Ray Guries and his predecessors and associates at the University of Wisconsin have tested thousands of American elms since 1957 and have found varying degrees of disease resistance. Several of their first selections have been propagated by the Elm Research Institute in Harrisville, New Hampshire, and are commercially available as the 'American Liberty' multiclone. Dr. Guries began work on an improved "second generation" of resistant elms in 1986, incorporating the best genes of his original trees plus some new ones. We look forward to seeing the results of his work planted across the continent.

CULTIVARS: Most of the older cultivars, selected for growth form and other ornamental characteristics, are susceptible to Dutch elm disease. One clone, 'Delaware', originated in the city of Delaware, Ohio, and is reported to be disease-resistant. 'Moline', an upright selection from Illinois, is susceptible but has some latent resistance and has been one of the more useful parent clones in the Wisconsin breeding programs for disease resistance. The 'American Liberty' multiclone consists of six different selections bred from resistant trees chosen from across northern North America. Most are known only by experimental numbers, but clone #W510 has been named 'Independence'.

RELATED SPECIES: Slippery elm, or red elm, *Ulmus rubra* (*U. fulva*), is a forest tree of the eastern United States and southern Canada, west to the Great Plains. It is more stiffly erect than American elm and has larger, rougher leaves and more conspicuous flowers. This species is just as susceptible to Dutch elm disease as American elm, but 'Lincoln' is a disease-resistant hybrid of slippery elm. The largest slippery elm grows in Sugar Grove, Ohio. Its spreading crown is 100 feet (31 m) tall and wider still, with a trunk 6 feet 4 inches (1.9 m) in diameter. The village dedicated a small public park around the tree.

Rock elm, *Ulmus thomasii* (*U. racemosa*), grows primarily in the Great Lake states and southern Ontario. It is an upright tree that has decorative, corky twigs and beautiful gold fall color. Although usually seen as a smaller tree, this species can grow as large as red elm. The current record-holder, which grows next to a country road near Cassopolis, Michigan, is 117 feet (36 m) tall, at least as broad and more than 5 feet (1.6 m) in diameter.

The few remaining large American elms in the North should be preserved for their beauty and their scientific value in the fight against Dutch elm disease.

Several smaller elms grow in the southeastern United States. Winged elm (*Ulmus alata*) is a tough, drought-resistant tree of old fields and rocky bluffs. It develops broad wings on its twigs; some specimens we have seen in western Kentucky are spectacular in this regard. On productive sites, this tree can grow fairly large, but usually it is seen as a subdued inhabitant of poor, dry soil.

Cedar elm (*Ulmus crassifolia*) is similar, but it prefers wet sites and blooms in late summer. In general, all of these species are susceptible to Dutch elm disease, but individual trees can be resistant. We grow them all at Starhill Forest in USDA zone 5.

September elm (*Ulmus serotina*) is another small southern species, which blooms in early fall. Several other elms from Europe and many from Asia will grow in cultivation in North America. Water elm (*Planera aquatica*) is a small member of the elm family that grows in southern swamps. Hackberries (*Celtis* spp.) are also related to elms.

COMMENTS: Many people decide to cut down the living elms on their properties because they think the trees are likely to die anyway. But any native elm that has survived this long in disease-infested localities might have some degree of natural resistance and should be preserved at least until its response to the disease can be evaluated. Some elms will survive on their own, but remember that it will cost much less to have fungicide injected into a healthy old elm this year than it will to have a dead tree removed next year.

If you need further reason to take proper care of your elm, seek some inspiration from one of the majestic, 200-year-old bicentennial elms that can still be found in many areas.

SPECIALTY TREES

SOMETIMES, WHEN TRAVELING THE BYWAYS of eastern North America, we see various native woody plants that would fit perfectly into a niche in certain naturalized landscapes. Many of them are limited in their general usefulness. Some are not winter-hardy, except in the Deep South. Others are not typically trees but grow as shrubs unless they reach an advanced age or have specific growing conditions. But each has merit—for attracting wildlife, protecting the soil or for ornamental value. Preserving or planting these natives in your landscape will contribute, on a local scale, to that critical concept: biodiversity. Given the narrow but valuable role of these specialty trees, we have covered them here concisely, as a group.

FALSE INDIGO

Amorpha fruticosa

This woody legume grows in stream valleys and exposed sites throughout the eastern United States, from Minnesota south and east, and is hardy north into USDA zone 4. It forms an open, tall shrub in the wild, occasionally reaching tree-like proportions. Its spicy-fragrant compound leaves and unusual spikes of purple and orange flowers are subtle from a distance but attractive up close. False indigo thrives in almost any soil, even in sterile quarries and strip-mined lands, but needs full sun and judicious pruning to develop into an attractive specimen. It grows easily from seed.

ARALIA

Aralia spinosa

Usually seen in thickets along field borders from USDA zone 5 south, the prickly aralia can reach more than 30 feet (10 m) in height. Large, old aralias (often one of the similar Asian species) can be seen as landscape relics around some Victorian houses. Great masses of summer flowers and purple fruit clusters perched atop erect trunks combine with enormous, doubly pinnate compound leaves to make this species among the most unusual of all trees. It is most easily propagated by transplanting suckers and can be made more landscape-friendly by rubbing away the prickles that form on the bark.

WOOLLY BUMELIA

Bumelia lanuginosa

Woolly bumelia and its close southern relatives, buckthorn bumelia (*Bumelia lycioides*) and tough bumelia (*Bumelia tenax*), epitomize the concept of "tough native tree." Woolly bumelia is the hardiest of the group, growing north into USDA zone 5. This picturesque small tree thrives in wet soil or on barren rocky bluffs, in sun or partial shade, and will tolerate road salt, heat and drought with impunity. The black, olive-like fruits can be eaten by humans and wildlife. Seed should be scarified and planted in the fall.

BUTTONBUSH

Cephalanthus occidentalis

This wetland species, with golf-ball-like white flower buttons, ranks among our most flood-tolerant woody plants but it also thrives when cultivated in upland landscapes. It is found from Montreal southward and can become a multiple-stemmed tree reaching 20 feet (6 m) in height in the southern part of its extensive natural range. Buttonbush blooms in the summer, when few other woody plants display noticeable color. Seed clusters can be collected by canoeing into flooded wild stands in early fall. The seeds will germinate promptly without any special treatment if kept sufficiently wet.

SWAMP CYRILLA

Cyrilla racemiflora

One of the hardiest of southern semievergreen trees, this wetland species can be grown as far north as USDA zone 6. It actually may reach its ornamental peak north of its natural range. There, it not only bears fragrant white spring flowers, but its foliage turns a brilliant scarlet-orange in late fall then drops to reveal the plant's colorful stringy bark. Left alone, cyrilla (also known as "ti-ti") forms clonal thickets, but it can be grown as an erect small tree in moist areas in the garden. It can be propagated from seed or by transplanting suckers.

LEATHERWOOD

Dirca palustris

Leatherwood never really attains tree size but always grows in tree form. Where garden scale is restricted, it gives the aesthetic equivalent of a tree in a small space. It makes an intriguing landscape plant because of its rubbery twigs, which can be tied in knots without breaking. This species inhabits cool ravines and wet areas north into USDA zone 4. Leatherwood blooms in early spring and can be grown from seed sown in the fall.

YELLOW ANISE

Illicium parviflorum

The licorice-scented yellow anise and its close relative, Florida anise (*Illicium floridanum*), are small evergreen trees hardy only in the Deep South. Florida anise, the hardier of the two, grows naturally north into USDA zone 7, but yellow anise is more common in cultivation. Both species like shady sites with wet, sandy soil and have hanging flowers that are best appreciated when seen from below. Planted near a walkway, they emit an anise fragrance when brushed. Seeds germinate readily, and small volunteer seedlings are easily transplanted.

MOUNTAIN LAUREL

Kalmia latifolia

One of the most prized of ornamental flowering shrubs, mountain laurel becomes a small tree up to 25 feet (8 m) tall on ideal sites in mesophytic cove forests, where elevation, soil and moisture combine to create a species-rich environment. Wild plants typically have white or light pink blooms, but many horticultural selections with variously colored flowers are available. Mountain laurel is one of our hardiest broadleaf evergreens and can be grown successfully north into USDA zone 5 on protected slopes. Propagation is difficult: sow the tiny seeds on the moist surface of a peat bed in full light, or purchase a nursery-grown plant.

SPICEBUSH

Lindera benzoin

This dioecious plant grows in shrub form with multiple stems but can reach more than 20 feet (6 m) in height. It has such appealing red fruit (on female plants), yellow flowers (best on male plants) and spicy-fragrant leaves with bright yellow fall color that it deserves recognition. Spicebush grows north to USDA zone 4. It requires a moist, rich site but will tolerate shade well. It germinates easily from seed sown in the fall, and volunteer seedlings occasionally are found in moist mulch around the base of the plant.

WAX MYRTLE

Myrica cerifera

Our largest bayberry, this aromatic species grows up to 40 feet (12 m) tall in the South. It is a fast-growing, symmetrical, fine-textured small tree from the Atlantic coastal plain, hardy north to USDA zone 7. The smaller northern bayberry, *Myrica pensylvanica*, occasionally reaches tree size as well, and can be grown north into USDA zone 3. Both are dioecious, bearing their scented waxy fruits only on female plants. Bayberries survive on sandy, sterile soils but thrive under more fertile conditions. Fall-planted seeds, cleaned of their waxy coatings, germinate well.

RED BAY

Persea borbonia

The hardiest member of the avocado genus, the red bay grows along the Atlantic coastal plain north to the Delmarva Peninsula (USDA zone 7). A handsome broadleaf evergreen tree of sandy soils that is usually restricted in the wild to wetlands, it does well in cultivation on a variety of soils, as long as the winter is not too harsh. It is essentially free from pests and can reach 50 feet (15 m) or more in height. The spicy leaves may be used as bay leaves for flavoring casseroles. Seeds should be extracted from the small blue drupes and planted in the fall.

HOPTREE

Ptelea trifoliata

This is an inconspicuous understory shrub or small tree, growing up to 20 feet (6 m) tall, with compound leaves. It can be found in scattered locations throughout the eastern half of the United States and occasionally in southern Canada. It is officially listed as "vulnerable" in Quebec and Ontario because it is near the edge of its range. In cultivation, hoptree is reliable north into USDA zone 4. It likes moist soil best and will grow equally well in full sun or dense shade. Its winged seeds resemble giant elm (*Ulmus*) seeds and germinate well if sown in fall.

NATIVE BUCKTHORN

Rhamnus caroliniana

We call this tree, also known as Carolina buckthorn, "native" buckthorn to distinguish it from several exotic buckthorn species that have become serious weeds in North America. This native, as well as its smaller native relative, *Rhamnus lanceolata*, is safe to plant without fear of it becoming another biological pest. Both are hardy in USDA zone 5. Carolina buckthorn is the more colorful and tree-like of the two, sometimes reaching 40 feet (12 m) tall. It has attractive fruits that resemble small, dark cherries, and we have grown it from seed without difficulty.

ROSE BAY

Rhododendron maximum

Rose bay is one of several tree-size rhododendrons from the Southeast. It forms dense stands along mountain streams and can reach more than 20 feet (6 m) in height. It can be grown with protection in USDA zone 5. *Rhododendron catawbiense* is slightly smaller and hardier, being native to higher elevations and reliable in USDA zone 5. These evergreens are among the most spectacular of all flowering plants, native or exotic, and are used as parents in hybrid cultivar development. They are difficult to raise from seed but can be purchased as container-grown stock.

BLADDERNUT

Staphylea trifolia

Striped bark, compound opposite leaves, and inflated, papery seed capsules give bladdernut a distinctive appearance when seen close up. At a distance, though, it becomes an inconspicuous understory tree or shrub of moist woods and streambanks. A large specimen growing in a rich woods may reach 30 feet (9 m) in height. Bladdernut grows in scattered locations across much of eastern North America, north into USDA zone 3 in Quebec and Ontario. The stone-like seeds rattle in their pods when ripe and should be planted in late summer for germination the following spring.

HORSE-SUGAR

Symplocos tinctoria

Also known as native sweetleaf, this is another understory tree of southern swamp borders, useful under cultivation north into USDA zone 7. It develops an open, irregular framework that becomes picturesque with increasing age. Fragrant yellow-orange flowers are produced in large clusters in spring, after the semievergreen leaves have dropped to expose the branches. Horse-sugar can grow to 50 feet (15 m) or more in good soil. Seeds should be extracted from the orange fruits when ripe and planted in late summer.

FARKLEBERRY

Vaccinium arboreum

This is the largest of our native blueberry species but grows from a shrub into a tree only after many decades, especially on the dry, rocky, acidic bluffs where it adapts better than most woody plants. Seldom reaching more than 20 feet (6 m) tall, it often has the grizzled appearance of a bonsai tree. Farkleberry is a southern tree that displays fine red color in the fall and has attractive, peeling bark. It is hardy north into USDA zone 5. Seed can be sown into a sandy-peaty bed in fall.

BLACK HAW

Viburnum prunifolium

Viburnums are familiar as shrubs, but several species become small trees up to 24 feet (7 m) tall in the wild. Along with black haw, other tree-sized viburnums include rusty black haw (*Viburnum rufidulum*) and nannyberry (*Viburnum lentago*). All three occupy successive hardiness belts running from nannyberry in the north (to USDA zone 2) through black haw (USDA zone 4) to rusty black haw (USDA zone 5). They have impressive spring flowers, lustrous foliage and attractive fruit in late summer and grow easily from seeds, layers or suckers.

PRICKLY ASH

Zanthoxylum americanum

This tree is easiest to spot in early spring, when its thorny twigs are covered with delicate yellow flowers. Female trees bear clusters of small, dark red fruits in late summer. Prickly ash is not a true ash but is closely related to hoptree (*Ptelea trifoliata*) and can be found in various habitats across the northern United States and southern Canada north to USDA zone 3. It often grows as a clonal shrub, but we have seen individual stems 20 feet (6 m) tall and 6 inches (15 cm) in diameter. Propagate from suckers or from seed sown as soon as ripe.

GLOSSARY

Abscission: The natural process by which trees internally wall off and shed unneeded parts, such as ripe fruit, old leaves and dead branches.
Acuminate: Long-pointed, as in a leaf blade.
Adventitious: Roots or buds that develop in abnormal positions from cambial meristem, often in response to saturated soil or the loss or damage of normal buds or roots.
Allelopathy: The production and dissemination of chemicals by a plant to suppress the growth of competitors.
Allopatric: Said of plants that have completely separate natural ranges; compare with sympatric.
Apical dominance: The release of hormones that suppress the growth of lateral buds near the tip of a branch, stem or root.
Apomixis: Reproduction without male pollen.
Arboriculture: The professional care of trees.
Auriculate: A leaf shape with ear-like lobes at the base of the leaf blade.
Autochthonous: Aboriginal; an organism with a distribution remaining in the area where it evolved.
Axillary: In the axil; said of a lateral bud or flower that develops at a node, or leaf axil.
Backcross: A second-generation hybrid crossing with one of its parent species or varieties.
Berry: A fleshy fruit with many seeds.
Bog: A wetland area formed by the gradual filling of a marsh, lake or pond with organic material.
Bole: The main stem, or clear trunk, of a tree.
Bottomland: A flat, low area that is subject to occasional flooding; floodplain.
Broadleaf evergreen: An angiosperm (not a conifer) with leaves that remain green through the dormant season.
Canopy: In a forest, the average level of the treetops; on an individual tree, the branch spread.
Catkin: A spike or tassel-like flower structure with scaly bracts; may be either staminate or pistillate.
Chlorosis: The abnormal loss of chlorophyll, or green pigment, in a leaf, sometimes caused by a chemical imbalance, such as a deficiency of iron.
Climax forest: The population of plants and animals that will, in the absence of disturbance, ultimately dominate a site. The tree species that typically achieve such dominance are called climax species.
Clone: An individual organism (ramet), formed by asexual propagation, that is genetically identical to the original organism (ortet) from which it was developed; the sum of all such ramets, frequently seen as a thicket of coppicing trees. A clone may be propagated, named and registered as a cultivar.
Co-dominance: Two or more competing growing tips, or leaders; co-dominant leaders trap bark between them, known as included bark, and form weak crotches.
Compound leaf: A leaf composed of leaflets, which in our native trees may be arranged radially (palmately), in a feather-like pattern (pinnately) or in a branched pinnate form (bipinnately).
Conifer: A cone-bearing tree; our most familiar tree-sized order of gymnosperms; often, but not always, evergreen.
Coppice: A small grove or thicket; a sprout cluster; also copse.
Cove: A protected lower mountain slope or valley, concave in profile, that accumulates moisture and nutrient runoff; provides an ideal site for tree growth; also, a protected coastal bay or inlet.
Cultivar: A plant variety known only in cultivation (*culti*vated *var*iety) and, in the strictest sense, not reproducible except by asexual processes; often a named clone. Like a variety name (which is written in lower case Latin), a cultivar name (usually in English and in single quotes) follows the species name. Some authorities extend the definition to include closely related seed-propagated groups and hybrid series. (In this book, we have used single quotes unofficially to designate horticultural selections in general.)
Deciduous: A tree that sheds its leaves when entering its dormant season (winter in our area).
Dentate: Tooth-like; a leaf with evenly pointed, but not forward pointing, teeth around its margins; compare with serrate.
Dioecious: Having functionally staminate (male) and functionally pistillate (female) flowers on separate trees; only pistillate dioecious trees bear fruit.
Diploid: Having a double set of chromosomes; the typical genetic form of an organism.
Dripline: The circle beneath a tree where rain drips from the outer edge of the canopy, and where much of the absorptive root system is concentrated.
Drupe: A fleshy fruit with a hard seed, or stone, such as a cherry or plum.
Ecotype: Individuals within a species that share characteristics such as size, form or hardiness as a result of their common evolution within a particular habitat or provenance.
Endangered species: An organism at risk of extirpation from portions of its range or of complete extinction.

Protected by law, it cannot be collected or disturbed. Lesser degrees of risk are recognized under some laws, such as threatened (at risk of becoming endangered), vulnerable (at risk of becoming threatened), candidate (nominated for listing) and watch-listed.

Endemic: Restricted to a specific region or habitat; compare with pandemic and exotic.

Entire: Smooth, toothless; said of the margin of a leaf.

Excurrent: A growth form, prevalent in many conifers and some juvenile hardwoods, in which a single central stem extends up through the crown of the tree to its tip; also said of an element projecting beyond the surface or tip, such as a leaf bristle.

Exotic: Not native to an area; cultivated or naturalized.

Ex situ: Off-site; said of a plant cultivated outside its natural habitat; compare with in situ.

Fascicle: A bundle, or cluster, as of pine needles originating from a common point on the twig.

Fastigiate: Narrowly upright in form because of the erect growth of lateral branches.

Friable: Crumbly; said of soil easily penetrated by roots.

Fruit: Botanically, a fertilized ovary containing the seed(s); may or may not be edible or fleshy.

Genus: A group of closely related species. The genus name is written in Latin and capitalized. Some major genera like the oaks (genus *Quercus*), the maples (genus *Acer*) and the pines (genus *Pinus*) are divided into distinct groups, called subgenera and sections. The trees in this book are arranged alphabetically by genus and by species within each genus.

Glabrous: Smooth; without hairs or tomentum.

Glaucous: Waxy; covered with a frost-like coating.

Grex: A group of closely related hybrids or very similar species (sometimes occurs where the ranges of two species overlap); also, a hybrid swarm.

Growth habit: The natural shape of a tree, e.g. spreading, excurrent, fastigiate, columnar, pyramidal, weeping.

Habitat: A specific environment within which a tree naturally grows; compare with range.

Hardiness zone: See USDA zone.

Included bark: Bark trapped in a fork as two limbs grow and expand; a structural weakness in trees.

In situ: On-site; said of a plant managed within its natural habitat; compare with ex situ.

Layering: The rooting of a lateral branch by covering it with soil, allowing roots to form and then pruning it from the stem to create an independent plant; a method of propagation; occasionally occurs naturally.

Leaflet: One element of a compound leaf, consisting of a blade and its petiolule.

Marcescent: Withering but remaining attached through most of the dormant season, as with certain deciduous foliage or fruit.

Marsh: An area supporting mostly herbaceous plants, coursed by flowing water that may fluctuate in speed and depth; compare with swamp and bog.

Mesic: Evenly moist, neither saturated nor arid.

Microclimate: Immediate, localized climate shaped by factors like wind protection, shade, heat reflection from a building or temperature moderation by a nearby body of water; can influence survival of sensitive species or those of marginal hardiness.

Micro-propagation: The laboratory culture of cells to replicate a plant; a high-tech form of asexual propagation; tissue culture.

Monoecious: Having staminate (male) and pistillate (female) flowers or flower parts on the same individual; compare with dioecious.

Mycoplasma: An infectious organism without cell walls similar to a virus; like bacteria or fungi in some respects; lives outside the cells of its host and causes diseases, such as yellows; an MLO is a mycoplasma-like organism.

Mycorrhiza: A fungus that grows symbiotically with the roots of certain trees and aids the roots in absorbing nutrients; also, the combination of fungus and tree.

Mulch: Loose material such as bark, leaf or twig litter placed beneath a tree; mulch conserves soil moisture, inhibits weeds and promotes mycorrhizal development.

Old growth: Approaching or synonymous with virgin forest; characterized by a predominance of ancient trees, the remains of even older trees and the web of life associated with them.

Ortet: The original ancestral organism from which a clone of ramets develops.

Palmate: A leaf pattern with the lobes radiating from a central point, like fingers.

Pandemic: Present nearly everywhere; compare with endemic and exotic.

Panicle: A compound-branched tuft of flowers or fruits, composed of several combined racemes.

Pedicel: The stalk of an individual flower (or fruit) in a cluster, or of a solitary flower; compare with peduncle.

Peduncle: The basal stalk of a cluster of fruits or flowers (or a solitary inflorescence); compare with pedicel.

Persistent: Continuing to adhere even when no longer functional or living; said of leaves and fruits that cling through the dormant season; marcescent.

Petiole: The stalk of a leaf connecting it to a twig.

Petiolule: The stalk of a leaflet of a compound leaf; compare with rachis.

Phenology: The timing of biological phenomena, such as flowering, leaf development and fruit ripening.

Phyllotaxy: The arrangement of leaves on a twig; an important characteristic for identification. Opposite leaves occur in pairs, whorled leaves develop in groups of three

or more and alternate leaves are borne singly in a zigzag or spiral pattern along the twig.
Pinnate: Feather-like; the arrangement of leaflets of a compound leaf along a central axis, or rachis.
Pistillate: Having a pistil; a female flower or a functionally female dioecious plant.
Pocosin: A shallow, upland bog that supports woody plant species.
Pod: A fruit with a seam that will split open; usually dry, woody or leathery.
Pome: A fleshy fruit with seeds in a multicelled core, such as an apple or pear.
Prairie: A natural community dominated by grassy, herbaceous plants.
Propagation: Generating additional organisms by seeds, cuttings, layers or other means.
Protogynous blooming: Timing differences between male and female flowers on the same tree.
Provenance: An ecological pedigree; a specific combination of soil and climate that may lead to the evolution of an ecotype; also, the ecotype itself. Provenance considerations are important in selecting individual trees or cultivars for habitats that are marginal or stressful.
Raceme: A branched tuft of flowers or fruits.
Rachis: The stalk of a pinnate compound leaf.
Radicle: The embryonic root that emerges from a seed during germination.
Ramet: An asexually propagated individual, genetically identical to the ortet from which it originated; one member of a clone.
Range: The geographic area within which a tree grows; compare with habitat.
Rhizome: An underground stem.
Riparian: Occurring along a streambank.
Rugose: Wrinkled; with indented veins.
Samara: A winged, papery, wind-dispersed seed.
Semievergreen: Intermediate between being fully evergreen (holding green foliage throughout the dormant season) and deciduous (dropping foliage at the start of the dormant season).
Serotinous: Blooming or opening late; fall-blooming; seedpods or cones that do not open immediately when ripe unless triggered by a stimulus, such as fire.
Serrate: Sharply saw-toothed, with the teeth pointing forward; said of the margin of a leaf; compare with dentate.
Simple: An unbranched leaf or solitary flower structure; not compound.
Speciation: The development or evolution of new species.
Species: A group of similar, freely interbreeding individual organisms that consistently produce similar offspring; the taxonomic level below genus (or subgenus, if there is one). The species name, or specific epithet, is written in lower-case Latin and always follows the genus name; abbreviated sp. (singular) or spp. (plural).
Stag-headed: The antlered appearance of a severely stressed tree, caused by dieback in the upper canopy.
Staminate: Bearing stamens; a male flower or a functionally male dioecious plant.
Stolon: A creeping stem that roots along its length.
Stratification: In plant propagation, placing seed in a cold, moist medium for several weeks or months to simulate wintering and break dormancy; originally, placing seed in strata, or layers, of planting medium.
Strobile: A cone-like flower structure with tough, persistent bracts.
Swamp: A low, wooded wetland without surface drainage.
Sympatric: Said of plants that have overlapping natural ranges; compare with allopatric.
Sympodial: Candelabra-like branching caused by the precocious growth of lateral buds on the current terminal shoot. Sympodial branching contributes to the attractive architecture of several tree species.
Taxon: Any unit in the scientific classification of organisms, such as a genus, species or variety. The study of such classification of taxa is called taxonomy; those who do so are taxonomists.
Terminal: Occurring at the tip or distal end, as of a twig, leaf or fruit.
Tetraploid: Having four sets of chromosomes; tetraploid plants often display hybrid vigor and may be more robust than their diploid relatives.
Tomentum: A woolly coating on a leaf or twig.
Twig: The end of a branch, representing the current or most recent season's growth.
Umbo: The point of a cone scale.
USDA zone: A broad geographic area with largely consistent winter temperature extremes; a guide for plant hardiness; zones are delineated on the Plant Hardiness Zone Map published by the United States Department of Agriculture (USDA).
Variety: A taxonomic subdivision of a species with minor but consistent differences from other such varieties and with the general capacity to transmit those differences to offspring by normal (sexual) reproduction.
Vegetative propagation: Nonsexual reproduction of plants, using cuttings, layers, grafting or any method other than planting seeds.
Volunteer: Natural or unaided establishment of a tree by seed, suckering or layering; a tree thus established.
Xeric: Dry or excessively well-drained habitat.
Xeriscaping: Landscaping for dry or drought-prone areas using native plants that survive with little irrigation.

SOURCES: NATIVE TREES AND SHRUBS

THE FOLLOWING LIST IS BASED PARTLY on information supplied by the National Wildflower Research Center in Austin, Texas, *The Canadian Plant Sourcebook*, by Anne and Peter Ashley, and *Gardening By Mail IV*, by Barbara Barton. The list includes only the states east of Colorado and the prairie and maritime provinces of Canada. We acknowledge that this is an incomplete list. Many other nurseries sell native trees and shrubs but are so local in their advertising that they are not appropriate for a list such as this.

A few nurseries are included that sell only wholesale. So if you want to buy some of their plants, ask your local garden center to order them on your behalf. Be advised that the cost of catalogs changes frequently, and you may be asked to pay more for a catalog than the price listed here. We did not include the major mail-order garden seed companies because they sell only a few species of trees and shrubs, and most of them are exotic cultivars.

We encourage you to patronize nurseries that produce plants from sources within 100 miles of your home to be sure of getting locally adapted ecotypes. Where provenance is critical to the winter or summer adaptability of a species, always ask the nursery to identify the original source.

ALABAMA

Byers Wholesale Nursery
P.O. Box 560
Meridianville, AL 35739
Wholesale only. Plants of trees and shrubs, native species and cultivars.

Tom Dodd Nurseries
4595 Hawthorn Pl.
Mobile, AL 36608
Wholesale only. Nursery-propagated trees, shrubs and ground covers. Mostly cultivars, some native species.

International Forest Seed Company
P.O. Box 490
Odenville, AL 35120
Wholesale only. Seeds of trees and shrubs of native species, hybrids and other cultivars.

Southern Plants
P.O. Box 232
Semmes, AL 36575
Retail/mail order. Unusual plants adapted to the Southeast. Some native trees and shrubs. Catalog $1.50.

ARKANSAS

Ridgecrest Nursery
Rte. 3, Box 241
Wynne, AR 72396
Retail/no mail order. Cultivars and native trees and shrubs, seeds and plants of wildflowers, some wild-collected.

FLORIDA

Apalachee Native Nursery
P.O. Box 204
Lloyd, FL 32337
Wholesale and retail. Trees and shrubs grown in containers.

Birdsong Nursery
511 Royal Oak Rd.
Webster, FL 33597
Retail/wholesale/mail order. Cultivars and native trees and shrubs, some wild-collected. Free price list.

Blake's Nursery
Rte. 2, Box 971
Madison, FL 32340
Retail/wholesale/mail order. Nursery-propagated trees and shrubs, mostly native species. Free price list.

Breezy Oaks Nursery
Rte. 4, Box 6-A
Hawthorne, FL 32640
Retail/wholesale/no mail order. Native and cultivated trees and shrubs, cacti and succulents, all nursery-propagated. Seeds and plants of wildflowers.

Bullbay Creek Farm
1033 Old Bumpy Rd.
Tallahassee, FL 32311-8689
Wholesale only. Nursery-propagated, mostly native trees, shrubs, cacti, succulents and wildflowers.

Central Florida Lands and Timber, Inc.
Rte. 1, Box 899
Mayo, FL 32066
Wholesale by mail order. Native trees and shrubs and herbaceous wildflowers, some wild-collected. Write for price list.

Central Florida Native Flora, Inc.
P.O. Box 1045
San Antonio, FL 33576-1045
Wholesale only. Exclusively native trees and shrubs, cacti, succulents and wildflowers, some wild-collected.

Dan's Native Nursery
2325 Lake Easy Rd.
Babson Park, FL 33827
Retail/wholesale/no mail order. Principally plants of native trees and shrubs.

Ecohorizons, Inc.
22601 S.S. 152 Ave.
Goulds, FL 33170
Retail/wholesale/no mail order. Exclusively native trees and shrubs, cacti, succulents. Seeds and plants of native grasses and wildflowers, some wild-collected.

Environmental Equities, Inc.
12515 Denton Ave.
Port Richey, FL 34667
Retail/wholesale/no mail order. Mostly native trees and shrubs, cacti, succulents and wildflowers, all nursery-propagated.

Farnsworth Farms Nursery
7080 Hypoluxo Farms Rd.
Lake Worth, FL 33463
Retail/wholesale/no mail order. Mostly native trees and shrubs, all nursery-propagated.

Florida Division of Forestry
Herren Nursery
Lake Placid, FL 33852
Wholesale/walk-in and mail order in bulk quantities. Exclusively native species, all nursery-propagated. Write for price list.

Florida Keys Native Nursery, Inc.
102 Mohawk
Tavernier, FL 33070
Retail/wholesale/mail order. Exclusively native trees and shrubs, cacti, succulents and wildflowers. Seeds of wildflowers, some wild-collected. Free price list.

Florida Scrub Growers
730 Myakka Rd.
Sarasota, FL 34240
Retail/wholesale/no mail order. Exclusively native trees, shrubs, cacti, succulents, wildflowers and grasses, some wild-collected. ("Scrub" describes the ecosystems of mostly dry, sandy and infertile land in northern Florida.)

Gann's Native Tropical Greenery
22140 S.W. 142 Ave.
Goulds, FL 33170
Retail/wholesale/no mail order. Exclusively native trees and shrubs, cacti, succulents and wildflowers.

Horticultural Systems, Inc.
P.O. Box 70
Parrish, FL 34219
Retail/wholesale/no mail order. Cultivars and a few native trees, shrubs and wildflowers, some wild-collected.

Mandarin Native Plants
13500 Mandarin Rd.
Jacksonville, FL 32223
Retail/wholesale/no mail order. Mostly native trees and shrubs, cacti, succulents and wildflowers, all nursery-propagated.

Mesozoic Landscape, Inc.
7667 Park Ln. West
Lake Worth, FL 33467
Retail/wholesale/no mail order. Nursery-propagated, mostly native trees and shrubs, cacti and succulents.

MWN Nursery
P.O. Box 1143
De Funiak Springs, FL 32433
Retail/mail order. Mostly native species, some exotics. Free catalog with large SASE.

Native Green Cay
Rte. 1, Box 331-B
Boynton Beach, FL 33437
Wholesale only. Native trees and shrubs, cacti and succulents, some cultivars, all nursery-propagated.

Native Nurseries
1661 Centerville Rd.
Tallahassee, FL 32308
Retail only/no mail order. Nursery-propagated, mostly native trees and shrubs, cacti, succulents and wildflowers. Seeds of native grasses and wildflowers.

Native Southeastern Trees, Inc.
P.O. Box 780
Osteen, FL 32764
Wholesale only. Nursery-propagated, mostly native trees and shrubs.

The Natives
2929 J.B. Carter Rd.
Davenport, FL 33837
Retail/wholesale/no mail order. Nursery-propagated, exclusively native trees and shrubs, cacti, succulents and wildflowers.

Okefenokee Growers
P.O. Box 4488
Jacksonville, FL 32201
Wholesale; container and bare-root trees.

Pine Breeze Nursery
P.O. Box 149
Bokeelia, FL 33922
Retail/wholesale/no mail order. Native trees and shrubs and cultivars, some wild-collected.

Salter Tree Farm
Rte. 2, Box 1332
Madison, FL 32340
Retail/mail order. Nursery-propagated, mostly native trees, shrubs and wildflowers. Free catalog with SASE.

Suncoast Native Plants
P.O. Box 248
Palmetto, FL 34220
Wholesale only. Exclusively native trees and shrubs, cacti, succulents and wildflowers, some wild-collected.

Superior Trees, Inc.
P.O. Box 9325
Lee, FL 33059
Wholesale only. Nursery-propagated trees and shrubs, mostly native.

The Tree Gallery
8855 116-Terrace S
Boynton Beach, FL 33437
Retail/wholesale/no mail order. Exclusively native trees and shrubs, all nursery-propagated.

Upland Native Growers of Martin County
P.O. Box 855
Palm City, FL 34990
Wholesale only. Nursery-propagated, exclusively native trees and shrubs, cacti and succulents. Seeds and plants of wildflowers.

The Wetlands Company, Inc.
7650 South Tamiami Trail, Suite 10
Sarasota, FL 34231
Retail/wholesale/mail order. Exclusively native trees, shrubs, cacti, succulents and wildflowers, some wild-collected. Free price list.

Wetlands Management, Inc.
P.O. Box 1122
Jensen Beach, FL 34958
Wholesale only. Exclusively native trees and shrubs, cacti, succulents and wildflowers, some wild-collected.

Wild Azalea Nursery
Rte. 1, Box 54-B
Brooker, FL 32622
Retail/no mail order. Mostly native trees and shrubs, cacti and succulents, all nursery-propagated. Seeds of native grasses and wildflowers, some wild-collected.

Winding Roads Nursery Corporation
P.O. Box 15905
West Palm Beach, FL 33406
Wholesale only. Nursery-propagated, mostly native trees and shrubs.

GEORGIA

Baycreek Gardens
P.O. Box 339
Grayson, GA 30221-0339
Retail/mail order. Mostly exotic species but some native trees and shrubs. Free price list with large SASE.

Cedar Lane Farms, Inc.
3790 Sandy Creek Rd.
Madison, GA 30650
Wholesale only. Nursery-propagated cultivars of trees, shrubs and wildflowers, some native species.

Eco-Gardens
P.O. Box 1227
Decatur, GA 30031
Retail by appointment/mail order. Mostly herbaceous plants but some native trees and shrubs. Catalog $2.

Goodness Grows, Inc.
P.O. Box 576
Crawford, GA 30630
Retail/wholesale/no mail order. Mostly choice cultivars of trees, shrubs, cacti, succulents, perennials and ground covers. Some native species, all nursery-propagated.

Picadilly Farm
1971 Whippoorwill Rd.
Bishop, GA 30621
Mail order/retail on set days. Mostly herbaceous perennials and wildflowers but some native trees. Free price list with large SASE.

Seed Production, Inc.
1280 Atlanta Hwy.
Madison, GA 30650
Wholesale only. Seeds of trees, shrubs, wildflowers and grasses, some native species.

Twisted Oaks Nursery
P.O. Box 10
Waynesboro, GA 30830
Retail/wholesale/no mail order. Nursery-propagated trees and shrubs, mostly cultivars, some native species.

Wilkerson Mill Gardens
9595 Wilkerson Mill Rd.
Palmetto, GA 30268
Retail only/no mail order. Small nursery with many native tree and shrub species, along with choice exotic cultivars.

ILLINOIS

Genesis Nursery
Rte. 1, Box 32
Walnut, IL 61376
Retail/mail order. Nursery-propagated native trees, shrubs, cacti, succulents and wildflowers. Seeds of wildflowers and native grasses, some wild-collected. Free price list.

Greenview Nurseries
2700 West Cedar Hills Dr.
Dunlap, IL 61525
Retail; several locations throughout Illinois. Native and exotic species.

Greenwood Propagation
8805 Kemmen Rd.
Hebron, IL 60034
Wholesale/minimum order required if retail. Native and exotic trees and shrubs.

H.E. Nursery
Rte. 2, Box 173
Litchfield, IL 62056
Wholesale/retail/no mail order. Many native and exotic trees, shrubs and herbaceous plants.

Kankakee Nursery
P.O. Box 288
Aroma Park, IL 60910
Wholesale/retail/no mail order. Many native and exotic trees, shrubs and herbaceous plants.

LaFayette Home Nursery, Inc.
1 Nursery Ln.
LaFayette, IL 61449
Retail/wholesale/mail order. Nursery-propagated native trees and shrubs, cacti, succulents and wildflowers. Seed of wildflowers and native grasses, some wild-collected from abundant stands. Catalog $1.

Lee's Trees
Box 1666, Richview Rd.
Mt. Vernon, IL 62864
Wholesale/some retail/no mail order. Many cultivars, native and exotic.

Midwest Groundcovers
P.O. Box 748
St. Charles, IL 60714
Retail/wholesale/no mail order. Nursery-propagated trees, shrubs, ground covers, cacti, succulents and wildflowers. Mostly cultivars, some native species.

Onarga Nursery Company
Onarga, IL 60955
Wholesale/retail, no mail order. Many species of native trees and shrubs and exotic cultivars.

Possibility Place
7548 West Monee Rd.
Monee, IL 60449
Mostly wholesale/large-quantity retail/no mail order. Many native trees and shrubs.

Spring Bluff Nursery
41W130 Norris Rd.
Sugar Grove, IL 60554
Retail only. Trees, shrubs, cacti, succulents and wildflowers. Mostly cultivars, some native species, some wild-collected.

Starhill Forest
RR 1, Box 272
Petersburg, IL 62675
Research facility. Seeds of mostly native trees and shrubs by mail order, retail or wholesale. Oaks a specialty. Visits by appointment only. Price list for $1 or SASE.

INDIANA

Indiana Propagation Nursery
3 Lyon Block
Salem, IN 47167
Wholesale/retail/mail order. Native trees from selected provenances, specializing in oaks.

IOWA

Cascade Forestry Nursery
22033 Filmore Rd.
Cascade, IA 52033
Retail/wholesale/mail order. Nursery-propagated trees and shrubs, mostly native, for windbreaks, woodlots and reforestation. Free price list.

Mount Arbor Nursery
P.O. Box 129
Shenandoah, IA 51601
Wholesale only; major supplier of cultivars and native trees and shrubs.

Smith Nursery Co.
P.O. Box 515
Charles City, IA 50616
Retail/wholesale/no mail order. Nursery-propagated trees and shrubs, mostly cultivars, some native species.

KANSAS

T.M. Sperry Herbarium
Department of Biology
Pittsburg, KS 66762
Mail order. Seeds of native trees, shrubs, cacti, succulents, wildflowers and grasses, some wild-collected. Free price list.

KENTUCKY

Nolin River Nut Tree Nursery
797 Port Wooden Rd.
Upton, KY 42784
Retail/mail order. Nursery-propagated nut tree cultivars and species. Free price list.

LOUISIANA

Louisiana Nursery
Rte. 7, Box 43
Opelousas, LA 70570
Retail/mail order. Wide choice of plants of trees, shrubs, cacti, succulents and wildflowers. Mostly cultivars, with some native species, some wild-collected. Catalog $5.

Natives Nurseries
P.O. Box 2355
Covington, LA 70434
Retail/no mail order/wholesale. Nursery-propagated, mostly native trees and shrubs.

Prairie Basse Nursery
Rte. 2, Box 491-F
Carencro, LA 70520
Retail, no mail order. Nursery-propagated, exclusively native trees, shrubs and wildflowers.

Sherwood's Greenhouses
P.O. Box 6
Sibley, LA 71073
Retail/mail order. Nursery-propagated, mostly native trees, shrubs, cacti, succulents and wildflowers. Catalog $3.

MARYLAND

Behnke Nurseries
P.O. Box 290
Beltsville, MD 20705
Retail only/no mail order. Nursery-propagated stock, some native trees, shrubs and wildflowers.

Environs Conservation Nursery
1927 York Rd.
Timonium, MD 21093
Mail order. Native trees, shrubs and herbaceous wildflowers for habitat restoration.

MASSACHUSETTS

Donaroma's Nursery
P.O. Box 189
Edgartown, MA 02539
Retail/mail order. Nursery-propagated trees, shrubs, cacti, succulents and wildflowers. Wildflower seed, some wild-collected. Free price list.

New England Wildflower Society
180 Hemenway Rd.
Framingham, MA 01701-2699
Retail/mail order. Nursery-propagated, exclusively native trees, shrubs, cacti, succulents, grasses and wildflowers. Seeds of individual species of wildflowers. Annual spring plant sale. Seed price list $2.

Rockscapes
Silver Birch Ln.
Lincoln, MA 01773
Retail/wholesale/no mail order. Nursery-propagated trees, shrubs, cacti, succulents and wildflowers. Cultivars and some native species.

F.W. Shumacher Co., Inc.
36 Spring Hill Rd.
Sandwich, MA 02563-1023
Retail/wholesale/mail order. Nursery-propagated trees and shrubs, some native species. Catalog $1.

Tripple Brook Farm
37 Middle Rd.
Southampton, MA 01073
Retail/wholesale/no mail order. Nursery-propagated, mostly native trees, shrubs, cacti, succulents and wildflowers.

Weston Nurseries, Inc.
E. Main St., Rte. 135
Hopkinton, MA 01748
Retail/wholesale/no mail order. Nursery-propagated trees, shrubs, grasses and wildflowers. Mostly cultivars, some native species.

MICHIGAN

Cold Stream Nursery
2030 Free Soil Rd.
Free Soil, MI 49411-9752
Retail/mail order. Specializes in bulk quantities of seedling trees for woodlands, wildlife cover and windbreaks. Many hybrids, some native species such as American chestnut. Free price list.

Hortech
P.O. Box 16
Spring Lake, MI 49456
Wholesale only. Nursery-propagated plants, principally cultivars, some native trees and shrubs, grown from wild-collected seeds.

New Life Nursery
3720 64th St.
Holland, MI 49423
Wholesale/retail in bulk quantities/mail order. Native and exotic conifer seedlings.

Oikos Tree Crops
P.O. Box 19425
Kalamazoo, MI 49019
Retail/wholesale/mail order. Nursery-propagated, mostly cultivars, some native trees and shrubs. Specializes in fruiting trees and oaks for wildlife. Price list $1.

Vans Pines Nursery
7550 144th Ave. W
West Olive, MI 49460
Wholesale/mail order. Nursery-propagated, principally cultivars, some native trees, shrubs and wildflowers.
Free price list.

Wavecrest Nursery
2509 Lakeshore Dr.
Fennville, MI 49408
Retail/wholesale/mail order. Also wholesale. Nursery-propagated, principally cultivars, some wild trees and shrubs. Catalog $1.

MINNESOTA

Bailey Nurseries, Inc.
1325 Bailey Rd.
St. Paul, MN 55119
Major wholesale nursery. Nursery-propagated, principally cultivars, some native trees, shrubs, cacti, succulents, grasses and wildflowers.

Orchid Gardens
2232 139th Ave. NW
Andover, MN 55304
Retail/mail order. Nursery-propagated, mostly native trees, shrubs and wildflowers, including native orchids. Price list 75 cents.

Prairie Hill Wildflowers
Rte. 1, Box 191-A
Ellendale, MN 56026
Retail/wholesale/no mail order. Nursery-propagated, exclusively native trees, shrubs, cacti, succulents, grasses and wildflowers. Seeds of prairie grasses and wildflowers.

Prairie Moon Nursery
Rte. 3, Box 163
Winona, MN 55987
Retail/mail order. Nursery-propagated, exclusively native trees, shrubs, cacti, succulents, grasses and wildflowers. Seeds of prairie grasses and wildflowers. Catalog $2.

Prairie Restorations, Inc.
P.O. Box 327
Princeton, MN 55371
Retail/wholesale/mail order. Nursery-propagated, exclusively native prairie trees and shrubs, cacti, succulents, grasses and wildflowers. Seeds of prairie grasses and wildflowers. Free price list.

MISSISSIPPI

Flowerplace Plant Farm
P.O. Box 4865
Meridian, MS 39304
Retail/mail order. Nursery-propagated, mostly wildflowers, some native trees and shrubs. Catalog $3.

MISSOURI

Arborvillage Farm Nursery
P.O. Box 227
Holt, MO 64048
Retail/mail order. Nursery-propagated trees and shrubs, mostly cultivars, some native species. Price list $1.

Forrest Keeling Nursery
P.O. Box 135
Elsberry, MO 63343
Wholesale only. Nursery-propagated trees and shrubs, principally cultivars, some native species.

NEW JERSEY

Fairweather Gardens
P.O. Box 330
Greenwich, NJ 08323
Retail/mail order. Unusual species and cultivars, many natives.

Princeton Nurseries
P.O. Box 191
Princeton, NJ 08540
Wholesale only. Major supplier of cultivars and native trees and shrubs.

NEW YORK

Panfield Nursery
322 Southdown Rd.
Huntington, NY 11743
Retail/wholesale. Nursery-propagated, mostly native trees, shrubs and wildflowers.

St. Lawrence Nursery
Rte. 2
Potsdam, NY 13676
Retail/mail order. Nut and fruit trees, some selected from native species.

Trees, Inc.
P.O. Box 579
East Hampton, NY 11937
Wholesale. Specializes in rescuing and relocating large trees.

NORTH CAROLINA

Agura Nurseries, Inc.
7000 Canada Rd.
Tuckasegee, NC 28783-9704
Wholesale only. Nursery-propagated, exclusively native trees and shrubs.

Appalachian Trees
P.O. Box 92
Glendale Springs, NC 28629
Wholesale only. Nursery-propagated cultivars and native trees and shrubs.

Arrowhead Nursery
5030 Watia Rd.
Bryson City, NC 28713-9683
Mail order. Trees and shrubs adapted to the Southeast, some native species. Catalog $1.

Camellia Forest Nursery
125 Carolina Forest
Chapel Hill, NC 27516
Retail/mail order. Nursery-propagated, principally cultivars, some native trees and shrubs. Catalog $1.

Fern Valley Farms, Inc.
Rte. 4, US 421 Service Rd. East
Yadkinville, NC 27055
Retail/wholesale/no mail order. Nursery-propagated, exclusively native trees and shrubs.

Gardens of the Blue Ridge
P.O. Box 10
Pineola, NC 28662
Retail/mail order. Nursery-propagated, exclusively native trees, shrubs, grasses and wildflowers. Seeds of native grasses and wildflowers. Catalog $3.

Lamtree Farm
Rte. 1, Box 162
Warrensville, NC 28693
Retail/wholesale/mail order. Nursery-propagated, mostly native trees and shrubs. Catalog $2.

Moser Growers
Rte. 1, Box 269
Whittier, NC 28789
Wholesale only. Nursery-propagated, principally cultivars, some native trees and shrubs.

Niche Gardens
1111 Dawson Rd.
Chapel Hill, NC 27516-8576
Retail/mail order. Nursery-propagated, mostly native trees, shrubs, grasses and wildflowers. Also wildflower seeds. Catalog $3.

A Source for Seed & Special Plants
Rte. 68, Box 301
Tuckasegee, NC 28783
Retail/wholesale/mail order. Nursery-propagated, exclusively native trees, shrubs, cacti, succulents, grasses and wildflowers. Seeds of individual wildflower species. Price list $1.

OHIO

Lake County Nursery
5052 South Ridge Rd.
Perry, OH 44081
Wholesale only. Nursery-propagated trees, shrubs and wildflowers. Principally cultivars, some native species.

Mellingers, Inc.
2310 West South Range Rd.
North Lima, OH 44452
Retail/mail order. Wide variety of species plus garden and landscape supplies. Inquire for cost of catalog.

OKLAHOMA

Greenleaf Nursery
Rte. 1, Box 163
Park Hill, OK 74451
Wholesale only. Major producer of many varieties of native and exotic trees and shrubs.

Midwestern Nurseries, Inc.
P.O. Box 768
Tahlequah, OK 74464
Wholesale only. Major producer of many cultivars and species of native trees and shrubs.

OREGON

(At least one Oregon mail-order nursery produces many tree and shrub species native to the East.)

Forestfarm
990 Tetherow Rd.
Williams, OR 97544
Retail/wholesale/mail order. Nursery-propagated liners (small plants) of trees and shrubs, plus wildflowers and perennials. Many species native to states other than Oregon. Catalog $3.

PENNSYLVANIA

Amenity Plant Products
RD #5, Box 265
Mt. Pleasant, PA 15666
Mail order. Seeds and plants of wildflowers and native shrubs and trees. Catalog $1.

Appalachian Gardens
Box 82
Waynesboro, PA 17268
Retail/mail order. Native species and cultivars of trees and shrubs.

Applachian Wildflower Nursery
Rte. 1, Box 275-A, Honey Creek Rd.
Reedsville, PA 17084
Retail/mail order. Nursery-propagated trees, shrubs and wildflowers. Native species and choice cultivars. Wildflower seeds. Catalog $1.25.

Carino Nurseries
P.O. Box 538
Indiana, PA 15701
Retail/wholesale/mail order. Nursery-propagated trees and shrubs, seedlings and larger plants. Many native species. Free price list.

Ernst Crownvetch Farms
RD #5, Box 806
Meadville, PA 16335
Retail/wholesale/no mail order. Trees and shrubs, ground covers, wildflowers and grasses. Wildflower and grass seeds. Some species collected from the wild.

Flickinger's Nursery
P.O. Box 245
Sagamore, PA 16250
Wholesale only. Nursery-propagated trees for sizable plantings. Mostly native coniferous species, some hybrid cultivars.

Highland Gardens
423 S. 18th St.
Camp Hill, PA 17011
Wholesale only. Nursery-propagated trees, shrubs, cacti, succulents, grasses and wildflowers. Mostly cultivars, some native species. Also seeds of wildflowers and grasses.

Johnston Nurseries
Rte. 1, Box 100
Creekside, PA 15732
Wholesale/mail order. Nursery-propagated trees and shrubs. Mostly cultivars, some native species. Free price list.

Musser Forests Inc.
P.O. Box 340, Rte. 119 North
Indiana, PA 15701-0340
Retail/wholesale/mail order. Specializes in bulk quantities. Nursery-propagated, mostly native trees and shrubs, some cultivars. Free price list.

Natural Landscapes
354 N. Jennersville Rd.
West Grove, PA 19390
Wholesale only. Nursery-propagated trees, shrubs and wildflowers. Mostly native species, a few cultivars.

Rarafolia
Rte. 2, Box 404
Kintnersville, PA 18930
Retail/mail order. Many cultivars and native tree and shrub species.

Strathmeyer Forest, Inc.
255 Zeigler Rd.
Dover, PA 17315
Wholesale/mail order. Nursery-propagated, exclusively native trees and shrubs. Free price list.

Sylva Native Nursery and Seed Company
RD 2, Box 1033
New Freedom, PA 17349
Wholesale only. Nursery-propagated, exclusively native trees, shrubs, grasses and wildflowers. Seeds of wildflowers and grasses, some wild-collected.

Tree Transfers
537 Elkins Ave.
Elkins Park, PA 19117
Specialists in planting and moving very large specimen trees, also rescuers of native trees and large shrubs.

Windrose, Ltd.
1093 Ackermanville Rd.
Pen Argyl, PA 18072-9670
Retail/mail order. Native and exotic hardy trees. Good source for oaks, hickories and other hardwoods. Catalog free with large SASE.

SOUTH CAROLINA

Busby Nursery
4219 Liberty Hwy.
Anderson, SC 29621
Retail only. Nursery-propagated general stock, some native trees and shrubs.

Nurseries Caroliniana
100 East Hugh St.
North Augusta, SC 29841
Retail only. Nursery-propagated general stock, including many native tree and shrub species.

Oak Hill Farm
204 Pressly St.
Clover, SC 29710-1233
Retail/wholesale/mail order. Nursery-propagated trees and shrubs, mostly native species, some cultivars. Free price list.

Sterling Garden Center
P.O. Box 5996
Columbia, SC 29250
Retail only. Nursery-propagated general stock, including native trees, shrubs and wildflowers.

Wayside Gardens
P.O. Box 1
Hodges, SC 29695-0001
Mail order only. Large selection of mostly exotic species, also cultivars selected from native trees and shrubs. Catalog $1.

Woodlanders, Inc.
1128 Colleton Ave.
Aiken, SC 29801
Retail/mail order. Nursery-propagated trees and shrubs, cacti, succulents, grasses and wildflowers. Most species are native to USDA hardiness zones 7 to 9. Also offers cultivars developed from native species. Catalog $2.

SOUTH DAKOTA

Rethke Nursery
P.O. Box 82
Milbank, SD 57252-0082
Wholesale only. Nursery-propagated trees, shrubs, cacti and succulents. Mostly cultivars, some native species.

TENNESSEE

Appalachee Nursery
Rte. 1, Box 1333
Turtletown, TN 37391
Wholesale only. Nursery-propagated, exclusively native trees and shrubs.

Beaver Creek Nursery
7526 Pelleaux Rd.
Knoxville, TN 37938
Retail/mail order. Cultivars and native trees and shrubs. Catalog $1.

Native Gardens
Columbine Farm, Rte. 1, Box 494
Greenback, TN 37742
Retail/mail order. Nursery-propagated, exclusively native trees, shrubs, cacti, succulents, grasses and wildflowers. Seeds of individual species, some wild-collected. Catalog $1.

Natural Gardens
113 Jasper Ln.
Oak Ridge, TN 37830
Retail/mail order. Nursery-propagated, mostly native trees, shrubs and wildflowers.
Catalog $1.

Owen Farms
Rte. 3, Box 158-A
Ripley, TN 38063
Retail/mail order. General nursery stock, some native tree and shrub species.
Catalog $2.

Sunlight Gardens, Inc.
Rte. 1, Box 600A
Andersonville, TN 37705
Retail/wholesale/mail order. Also wholesale. Nursery-propagated, exclusively native trees, shrubs, grasses and wildflowers. Seeds of individual species, some wild-collected.
Catalog $2.

Trees by Touliatos
2020 Brooks Rd.
Memphis, TN 38116
Retail/wholesale/no mail order. Nursery-propagated native trees and shrubs and choice cultivars.

TEXAS

(Texas has so many climates and ecosystems that it is important to patronize local nurseries to find plants suited to your soils and growing conditions. Many nurseries besides the four listed here sell native trees and shrubs adapted to the humid areas of East Texas covered by this book.)

Barber Nursery
13118 Patano Dr.
Houston, TX 77065
Retail/no mail order. Nursery-propagated seedlings of native trees and shrubs, some cultivars. Free price list.

(The Nursery at) Dallas Nature Center
7575 Wheatland Rd. West
Dallas, TX 75249
Retail/mail order. Nursery-propagated native trees, shrubs, cacti, succulents, grasses and wildflowers. Seeds of native grasses and wildflowers. Free price list.

Lowery Nursery
2323 Sleepy Hollow Rd.
Conroe, TX 77385
Retail/mail order. Nursery-propagated southwestern native trees, shrubs and wildflowers, plus some cultivars selected from wild species. Free price list.

Madrone Nursery
2318 Hilliard Rd.
San Marcos, TX 78666
Retail; a specialist in Texas native species.

VIRGINIA

Joseph Brown Seeds
HC 1, Box 495
Gloucester Point, VA 23062
Retail/wholesale/mail order. Nursery-propagated trees, shrubs, grasses and wildflowers. Mostly native species, some cultivars. Seeds of individual species.
Catalog $1.

Edible Landscaping
P.O. Box 77
Afton, VA 22920
Retail/mail order. Native fruit and nut trees plus other edible plants.

Ingleside Plantation Nurseries
P.O. Box 1038
Oak Grove, VA 22443
Wholesale only. Nursery-propagated trees and shrubs, principally cultivars, some native species.

Virginia Wilde Farms
Rte. 2, Box 1512
Hanover, VA 23069
Retail/wholesale/mail order. Nursery-propagated, mostly native trees, shrubs, grasses and wildflowers. Seeds of wildflowers, some wild-collected. Catalog $2.

WEST VIRGINIA

Sunshine Farm & Gardens
Renick, WV 24966
Retail/wholesale/mail order. Native and exotic trees and other plants.

WISCONSIN

Country Wetlands Nursery
P.O. Box 126
Muskego, WI 53150
Retail/mail order. Nursery-propagated native trees, shrubs, cacti, succulents, grasses and wildflowers. A few cultivars. Seeds of wildflowers and prairie grasses. Catalog $2.

Little Valley Farm
Rte. 3, Box 544
Spring Green, WI 53588
Retail/mail order. Nursery-propagated, exclusively native trees, shrubs, grasses and wildflowers. Seeds of prairie wildflowers and grasses, some wild-collected. Free price list with SASE.

Lonergan Nursery
3048 Paradise Dr.
West Bend, WI 53095
Retail/wholesale/no mail order. Nursery-propagated, exclusively native prairie trees, shrubs, grasses and wildflowers.

Reeseville Ridge Nursery
P.O. Box 171
Reeseville, WI 53579
Retail/wholesale/no mail order. Nursery-propagated trees and shrubs. Cultivars and native species.

Retzer Nature Center
W284 S1530 Rd. DT
Waukesha, WI 53188
Retail/wholesale/no mail order. Nursery-propagated, mostly native trees, shrubs, cacti, succulents, grasses and wildflowers. Seeds of prairie wildflowers and grasses, some wild-collected.

West Wisconsin Nursery
Rte. 4, Box 141
Sparta, WI 54656
Wholesale/mail order. Nursery-propagated trees and shrubs. Mostly native species, some cultivars. Free price list.

CANADA

Because of freight charges, gardeners in the United States customarily order only seedlings or "liners" from Canadian nurseries, often in large quantities for reforestation, reclamation and windbreaks. Plants shipped to the United States must be inspected and be accompanied by a phytosanitary certificate to comply with the regulations of the USDA Animal and Plant Health Inspection Service.

MANITOBA

Kackenhof Nurseries, Ltd.
Box 2000
St. Norbert, MB, Canada R3V 1L2
Retail/wholesale/bulk-quantity mail orders to Canada and the U.S. Specializes in native trees and in moving sizable specimens. Free catalog.

Morden Nurseries
Box 1270
Morden, MB, Canada R0G 1J0
Wholesale/retail/mail order to Canada and the U.S. Hardy prairie stock. Free price list.

ONTARIO

Blondeel Nursery
Rte. 1
Straffordville, ON, Canada N0J 1Y0
Wholesale/mail order. Cultivars and native species of trees and shrubs.

Braun Nurseries
RR #2
Mount Hope, ON, Canada L0R 1W0
Wholesale only, to Canada and the U.S. Large caliper trees in wire baskets. Some native species.

Connon Nurseries
383 Dundas St. East
P.O. Box 1218
Waterdown, ON, Canada, L0R 2H0
Retail/wholesale/no mail order. Unusual and hard-to-find species, including some native trees. Large landscape material as well.

Downham Nursery, Inc.
626 Victoria St.
Strathroy, ON, Canada N7G 3C1
Wholesale only, to Canada and the U.S. Major grower of general nursery stock, including some native tree species.

Golden Bough Tree Farm
Marlbank, ON, Canada, K0K 2L0
Mail orders only, to Canada and the U.S. Hardy fruit and nut trees, rare conifers and deciduous trees, some native species. Catalog $1.

Grimo Nut Nursery
979 Lakeshore Rd., RR 3
Niagara-on-the-Lake, ON
Canada, L0S 1J0
Retail/wholesale/mail order, to Canada and the U.S. Grafted nut trees and selected minor fruits. A few native species. Catalog $1.

Hortico, Inc.
723 Robson Rd., RR #1
Waterdown, ON, Canada L0R 2H0
Wholesale/retail by appointment/mail order. Mostly exotic species but some native trees and shrubs. Free catalog.

Langendoen Nurseries, Inc.
32 Runcorn St.
St. Catharines, ON, Canada L2M 1N8
Wholesale only. Inquire about shipping to the U.S. Trees and shrubs, including some native species.

Maple Leaf Nurseries, Ltd.
1535 4th. Ave. Cont'd, RR #3
St. Catharines, ON, Canada L2R 6P9
Wholesale only, to Canada and the U.S. Evergreens, shade trees, lining-out stock, including some native species.

Niagara Holland Nurseries, Ltd.
850 Lakeshore Rd., RR #3
Niagara-on-the-Lake, ON
Canada L0S 1J0
Wholesale only, to Canada and the U.S. Trees and shrubs, sales sizes and liners. Some native tree species.

M. Putzer Hornby Nursery Ltd.
7314 Sixth Line
Hornby, ON, Canada L0P 1E0
Wholesale only, to Canada and the U.S. Trees and shrubs, some native species.

Sheridan Nurseries Ltd.
RR #4, 10th Line
Georgetown, ON, Canada, L7G 4S7
Retail/wholesale to Canada and the U.S. No mail order. Own a chain of garden centers in Ontario and Quebec. Extensive selection of nursery stock, including some native tree species.

Keith Somers Trees
10 Tillson Ave.
Tillsonburg, ON, Canada N4G 2Z6
Retail/mail order, to Canada and the U.S. Shade trees of all sizes. Nut trees. Large selection of native tree and shrub species. Catalog $2.

Van Dongen's Tree Farm
RR #1
Hornby, ON, Canada L0P 1E0
Retail/wholesale/no mail order. Large trees and shrubs, some native species. Tree-planting service.

V. Kraus Nurseries, Inc.
P.O. Box 180
Carlisle, ON, Canada, L0R 1H0
Primarily wholesale. Bulk mail orders to Canada and the U.S. Bare-root ornamental and fruit trees, a few native species. Catalog $2.

Winkelmolen Nursery Ltd.
148 Lynden Rd., RR #1
Lynden, ON, Canada L0R 1T0
Wholesale only, to Canada and the U.S. Mostly bare-root trees, some native species.

W. Richardson Farms, Ltd.
Box 310
Pontypool, ON, Canada, L0A 1K0
Retail/wholesale/bulk mail order, to Canada and the U.S. Tree seedlings, some native species. Free catalog.

QUEBEC

Cramer Nursery, Inc.
1101 Don Quichotte
Ile-Perrot, QC, Canada J7V 5V6
Retail/wholesale/no mail order. Garden center offers large-specimen evergreen and deciduous trees, some native species.

Y. Yvon Auclair et Fils Enr.
1386 Ozias-Leduc
Mont. Ste.-Hilaire, QC,
Canada J3G 4S6
Retail/wholesale/no mail order. Trees, shrubs and evergreens, some native species.

SASKATCHEWAN

Boughen Nurseries, Inc.
Box 1955
Nipawin, SK, Canada S0E 1E0
Retail/wholesale/mail order to Canada and the U.S. Hardy northern-grown deciduous trees and shrubs, some native species. Free price list.

John's Nursery and Market Gardens Ltd.
Box 24
Henribourg, SK, Canada S0J 1C0
Retail/wholesale/no mail order. Colorado spruce, deciduous trees, some native species.

PUBLIC AND PRIVATE NATURAL HERITAGE CONSERVATION AGENCIES AND ORGANIZATIONS

These groups may provide information on natural areas and preserves where native trees can be seen.

ALABAMA
Department of Conservation and Natural Resources
State Lands Division
Folsom Administration Building
64 North Union St., Room 752
Montgomery, AL 36130
(205) 242-3007

ARKANSAS
Arkansas Natural Heritage Commission
Suite 200, 225 East Markham
Little Rock, AR 72201
(501) 324-9332

CONNECTICUT
Connecticut Natural Diversity Database
Natural Resources Center
Department of Environmental Protection
State Office Building, Room 553
165 Capital Ave.
Hartford, CT 06106
(203) 424-3540

DELAWARE
Delaware Natural Heritage Inventory
Division of Parks and Recreation
89 Kings Hwy.
Dover, DE 19903
(302) 739-5285

FLORIDA
Florida Natural Areas Inventory
1018 Thomasville Rd., Suite 200C
Tallahassee, FL 32303
(904) 224-8207

GEORGIA
Georgia Natural Heritage Program
Department of Natural Resources
2117 U.S. Hwy. 278, SE
Social Circle, GA 30279
(706) 557-3032

ILLINOIS
Division of Natural Heritage
Illinois Department of Conservation
524 South Second St.
Lincoln Tower Plaza
Springfield, IL 62701-1787
(217) 785-8774

INDIANA
Indiana Division of Nature Preserves
402 West Washington, Room W267
Indianapolis, IN 46204
(317) 232-4052

IOWA
Bureau of Preserves & Ecological Services
Iowa Department of Natural Resources
Wallace State Office Building
900 East Grand Ave.
Des Moines, IA 50319
(515) 281-8967

KANSAS
Kansas Natural Heritage Inventory
Kansas Biological Survey
2041 Constant Ave.
Lawrence, KS 66047-2906
(913) 864-3453

KENTUCKY
Kentucky State Nature Preserves Commission
407 Broadway
Frankfort, KY 40601
(502) 564-2886

LOUISIANA
Louisiana Natural Heritage Program
Louisiana Department of Wildlife & Fisheries
P.O. Box 98000
Baton Rouge, LA 70898-9000
(504) 765-2821

MAINE
Maine Natural Areas Program
Office of Community Development
State House Station 130
Augusta, ME 04333
(207) 624-6800

MARYLAND
Maryland Natural Heritage Program
Department of Natural Resources
E-1 Tawes Building
Annapolis, MD 21401
(410) 974-2870

MASSACHUSETTS
Massachusetts Natural Heritage & Endangered Species Program
Division of Fisheries & Wildlife
100 Cambridge St.
Boston, MA 02202
(617) 727-9194

MICHIGAN
Natural Heritage Program
Michigan Department of Natural Resources
Box 30028
Lansing, MI 48909
(517) 373-1263

MINNESOTA
Scientific and Natural Areas Program
Natural Heritage Program and County Biological Survey Program
Minnesota Department of Natural Resources
Box 7, 500 Lafayette Rd.
St. Paul, MN 55155-4007
(612) 297-2357

MISSISSIPPI
Mississippi Natural Heritage Program
State Museum of Natural Science
Department of Wildlife, Fish & Parks
111 North Jefferson St.
Jackson, MS 39201
(601) 354-7303

MISSOURI

Natural History Division
Missouri Department of Conservation
2901 West Truman Blvd.
Jefferson City, MO 65109-0580
(314) 751-4115

NEBRASKA

Nebraska Natural Heritage Database
Nebraska Game & Parks Commission
2200 North 33rd St.
Lincoln, NE 68503
(402) 471-5469

NEW HAMPSHIRE

New Hampshire Natural Heritage Inventory
Department of Resources and Economic Development
P.O. Box 856
Concord, NH 03302-0856
(603) 271-3623

NEW JERSEY

New Jersey Natural Heritage Program
Office of Natural Lands Management
22 South Clinton Ave., CN 404
Trenton, NJ 08625
(609) 984-1339

NEW YORK

New York State Department of Environmental Conservation
Natural Heritage Program
700 Troy-Schenectady Rd.
Latham, NY 12110-2400
(518) 783-3932

NORTH CAROLINA

North Carolina Natural Heritage Program
P.O. Box 27687
Raleigh, NC 27611-7687
(919) 733-7701

NORTH DAKOTA

North Dakota Natural Heritage Inventory
604 East Blvd., Liberty Memorial Building
Bismarck, ND 58505
(701) 224-4892

OHIO

Ohio Department of Natural Resources
Division of Natural Areas & Preserves
1889 Fountain Square Ct.
Columbus, Ohio 43224
(614) 265-6453

OKLAHOMA

Oklahoma Natural Heritage Inventory
Oklahoma Biological Survey
2001 Priestly Ave., Bldg. 605
Norman, OK 73019-0543
(405) 325-1985

PENNSYLVANIA

Pennsylvania Natural Diversity Inventory
Pennsylvania Department of Natural Resources
Bureau of Forestry
P.O. Box 1467
Harrisburg, PA 17105-8552
(717) 783-0388

RHODE ISLAND

Rhode Island Natural Heritage Program
Department of Environmental Management
83 Park St.
Providence, RI 02903
(401) 277-2776

SOUTH CAROLINA

South Carolina Wildlife and Marine Resources Department
Nongame and Heritage Trust Section
P.O. Box 167
Columbia, SC 29202
(803) 734-3893

SOUTH DAKOTA

South Dakota Natural Heritage Program
South Dakota Department of Game, Fish and Parks
523 East Capitol Ave.
Pierre, SD 57501-3182
(605) 773-4345

TENNESSEE

Ecological Conservation Division
Tennessee Department of Environment and Conservation
401 Church St., 8th Floor Tower
Nashville, TN 37243-0447
(615) 532-0431

TEXAS

Texas Endangered Resources Branch
Texas Parks and Wildlife Department
3000 South IH 35, Suite 1000
Austin, TX 78704
(512) 448-4311

VERMONT

Vermont Nongame and Natural Heritage Program
Center Building
103 South Main St.
Waterbury, VT 05671-0501
(802) 244-7340

VIRGINIA

Virginia Department of Conservation and Recreation
Division of Natural Heritage
Main Street Station
1500 East Main St., Suite 312
Richmond, VA 23219
(804) 786-7951

WEST VIRGINIA

West Virginia Natural Heritage Program
P.O. Box 67
Elkins, WV 26241
(304) 637-0245

WISCONSIN

Wisconsin Department of Natural Resources
Bureau of Endangered Resources
Box 7921
Madison, WI 53707
(608) 267-7479

UNITED STATES GOVERNMENT AGENCIES

Bureau of Land Management
U.S. Department of the Interior
1849 C St., NW, Suite 5600
Washington, DC 20240
(202) 208-5717
Administers public lands (primarily in western states) for recreation, fish and wildlife, grazing, timber, minerals, and development

Environmental Protection Agency
401 M St., SW, Suite 1200-W
Washington, DC 20460
(202) 382-2090

National Park Service
Interior Building, P.O. Box 37127
Washington, DC 20013
(202) 208-6843
Administers parks and monuments, manages landmark programs for natural and historic properties, coordinates Wild and Scenic Rivers System and National Trail System.

National Weather Service
General Information
(301) 713-0622
Maintains data on prevailing winds and annual rainfall for regions throughout the country.

U.S. Department of Agriculture
Forest Service, Urban & Community Forestry
210 14th St., SW
Washington, DC 20250
(202) 205-9694

U.S. Department of Agriculture
Soil Conservation Service
Public Information Division
P.O. Box 2890
Washington, DC 20013
(202) 447-4543

U.S. Fish and Wildlife Service
1849 C St., NW
Washington, DC 20240
(202) 208-5634
Manages a system of wildlife refuges to conserve a diversity of natural resources. Administers the Endangered Species Act.

U.S. Geological Survey
National Center
Reston, VA 22092
(703) 648-4000
Publishes and distributes topographic maps and reports on nation's land, water and mineral resources.

U.S. National Biological Service
U.S Dept. of Interior
1849 C St., NW
Washington, DC 20240
(202) 482-5707

UNITED STATES TRADE, PROFESSIONAL AND CITIZENS' ORGANIZATIONS

American Association of Botanical Gardens and Arboreta
786 Church Rd.
Wayne, PA 19087
(215) 688-1120
Can provide information on the botanical garden or arboretum nearest you.

American Association of Nurserymen
1250 I St., NW, Suite 500
Washington, DC 20005
(202) 789-2900

American Chestnut Foundation
469 Main St.
P.O. Box 4044
Bennington, VT 05201-4044
(802) 447-0110
Principal research organization in the campaign against chestnut blight.

American Forest Foundation
1250 Connecticut Ave., NW, Suite 320
Washington, DC 20036
(202) 463-2455
Supports charitable education and research projects for the American Tree Farm system. Offers environmental education curricula and training programs.

American Forests
1515 P St., NW
Washington, DC 20005
(202) 667-3300
Nation's oldest citizen conservation organization for trees and forests. Seeks to create an enlightened public appreciation of forests, soil, water, wildlife, and the part they play in the social and economic life of the nation.

American Land Conservancy
44 Montgomery St., Suite 4165
San Francisco, CA 94104
(415) 403-3850
Seeks to preserve land for several uses in the public interest, including the preservation of native plant and animal life and biotic communities.

American Nature Study Society
5881 Cold Brook Rd.
Homer, NY 13077
(607) 749-3655
Conducts environmental meetings and field excursions and assists in training lay leaders for nature study.

American Society of Landscape Architects
4401 Connecticut Ave., NW
Washington, DC 20008
(202) 686-ASLA
Can provide listings of large-scale tree-planting projects by individuals or community groups.

American Wildlands
6551 South Revere Pkwy., Suite 160
Englewood, CO 80111
(303) 649-9020
National conservation organization dedicated to the responsible management and protection of wilderness, forests, wetlands, free-flowing rivers, watersheds and wildlife.

Ancient Forest International
P.O. Box 1850
Redway, CA 95560
(707) 923-3015
Dedicated to preserving, studying and increasing awareness of the earth's few remaining intact temperate forest ecosystems.

Association of Consulting Foresters of America, Inc.
5410 Grosvenor Ave., Suite 205
Bethesda, MD 20814-2194
(301) 530-6795
Administers education program and enforces code of ethics for private consulting foresters.

Audubon Naturalist Society of the Central Atlantic States, Inc.
8940 Jones Mill Rd.
Chevy Chase, MD 20815
(301) 652-9188
One of the original Audubon Societies, organized for environmental, conservation and natural science education in the greater Washington, D.C., area.

Center for Plant Conservation, Inc.
P.O. Box 299
St. Louis, MO 63166
(314) 577-9450
Supported by botanical gardens and arboreta dedicated to the conservation and study of rare or endangered plant species. Maintains the national collection of endangered plants.

Craighead Wildlife-Wildlands Institute
5200 Upper Miller Creek Rd.
Missoula, MT 59803
(406) 251-3867
Pursues long-term research on key components of flora and fauna in critical wilderness areas.

Defenders of Wildlife
1244 19th St., NW
Washington, DC 20036
(202) 659-9510
Advocates action on endangered species, habitat protection, predator protection and wildlife appreciation.

The Ecological Society of America
2010 Mass. Ave., NW, Suite 420
Washington, DC 20036
(202) 833-8773
Professional society of ecologists, encourages study of organisms in relation to their environment.

Famous and Historic Trees
8555 Plummer Rd.
Jacksonville, FL 32219
(800) 320-8733
Offers educational programs, from the significance of a single tree to entire groves and forests.

Holly Society of America, Inc.
11118 West Murdock
Wichita, KS 67212
(310) 825-8133
Collects and disseminates information about the hollies and their culture, promotes research on hollies and hybridization.

International Oak Society
P.O. Box 310
Pen Argyl, PA 18072-0310
(610) 588-1037
Promotes worldwide study and cultivation of oaks. Conducts a seed exchange.

International Society of Arboriculture
P.O. Box GG
Savoy, IL 61874
(217) 355-9411
Publishes educational brochures and training manuals for professionals. Can supply the names of arborist members in your area.

National Arbor Day Foundation
211 North 12th St.
Lincoln, NE 69508
(402) 474-5655
Sponsors of "Tree City USA."

National Arborist Association
P.O. Box 1094
Amherst, NH 03031-1094
(603) 673-3311
Maintains membership list and can supply names of members in your area.

National Audubon Society
700 Broadway
New York, NY 10003-9501
(212) 797-3000
Citizen-based research and action organization to protect air, land, water and habitat resources.

National Tree Trust
1455 Pennsylvania Ave., Suite 250
Washington, DC 20004
(202) 628-TREE

National Wildflower Research Center
4801 LaCrosse Blvd.
Austin, TX 78739
(512) 292-4100
Source of information on prairie, meadow, wetland, and woodland wildflowers to complement native trees and shrubs.

National Woodland Owners Association
374 Maple Ave. East, Suite 210
Vienna, VA 22180
(703) 255-2700
Woodland owners united to foster good stewardship of non-industrial private forest lands.

Natural Areas Association
108 Fox St.
Mukwonago, WI 53149
(414) 363-5500
Works on identification, preservation, protection, management and research of natural areas.

The Nature Conservancy
1815 North Lynn St.
Arlington, VA 22209
(703) 841-5300
Seeks to identify and preserve natural lands and wildlife. Manages over 1,600 nature sanctuaries nationwide.

New England Wildflower Society, Inc.
180 Hemenway Rd.
Framingham, MA 01701-2699
(617) 237-4924
Long-established organization of volunteers who promote conservation of temperate North American flora. Active in education and legislation. Their "Garden in the Woods" has persuaded many people to use wild plants in home landscapes.

North American Fruit Explorers (NAFEX)
Rte. 1, Box 94
Chapin, IL 62628
(217) 245-7589
A network of individuals in the United States and Canada devoted to the cultivation of fruit and nut varieties.

North American Plant Preservation Council
Rte. 5
Renwick, WV 24966
(304) 497-3163
Maintains a database of outstanding American and Canadian plant collections. Publishes directory.

PlantAmnesty
906 NW 87th St.
Seattle, WA 98117
(206) 783-9813
An organization dedicated to promoting proper tree care and pruning of trees and shrubs.

Save America's Forests
4 Library Ct., SE
Washington, DC 20003
(202) 544-9219
National coalition working for strong forest-protection legislation.

Sierra Club
730 Polk St.
San Francisco, CA 94109
(415) 776-2211
A powerful voice for the protection and enjoyment of our ecosystem.

Society of American Foresters
5400 Grosvenor Ln.
Bethesda, MD 20814
(301) 897-8720
Advances the science, technology and practice of professional forestry.

Soil and Water Conservation Society
7515 NE Ankeny Rd.
Ankeny, IA 50021-9764
(515) 289-1227
Multidisciplinary organization promoting the art and science of good land and water use worldwide.

Tall Timbers Research, Inc.
Rte. 1, Box 678
Tallahassee, FL 32312-9712
(904) 893-4153
Studies the role of fire in maintaining natural forest ecosystems and promotes controlled burning to conserve native species.

Treepeople
12601 Mulholland Dr.
Beverly Hills, CA 90210
(818) 753-4600
Promotes improving our environment with trees, through their planting and maintenance.

The Trust for Public Land
116 New Montgomery St., 4th Floor
San Francisco, CA 94105
(415) 495-4014
Helps public agencies and communities acquire land of recreational, ecological and cultural value; pioneers in researching environmentally sound land use.

Wilderness Society
900 17th St., NW
Washington, DC 20006-2596
(202) 833-2300
Devoted to protecting wilderness areas and wildlife, especially America's prime forests, rivers and shorelands, and fostering an American land ethic.

Wilderness Watch
P.O. Box 782
Sturgeon Bay, WI 54235
(414) 743-1238
An organization of scientists and other citizens concerned with promoting the sustained use of America's sylvan lands.

Wildlife Habitat Enhancement Council
1010 Wayne Ave., Suite 1240
Silver Spring, MD 20190
(301) 588-8994
A cooperative effort of conservation agencies and corporations to enhance land held by businesses for the benefit of animals, fish and plants.

CANADIAN NATIONAL SERVICES

Agriculture Canada
Plant Research Center
Building 99
Ottawa, ON, Canada K1A OC6
(613) 996-1665

Canadian Rare Plant Project
Canadian Museum of Nature
P.O. Box 3443, Station D
Ottawa, ON, Canada K1P 6P4
(613) 990-6449

Environment Canada
Ottawa, ON, Canada K1A 0H3
(819) 953-1411
Renewable resources: land water, wildlife, plants; international trade in endangered species.

Forestry Canada
351 St. Joseph Blvd.
Place Vincent Massey
Hull, QC, Canada, K1A 1G5
(819) 997-1107

Secretariat, Canadian Council on Ecological Areas
Environment Canada
Ottawa, ON, Canada K1A OH3
(819) 953-1444

CANADIAN FOUNDATIONS AND ASSOCIATIONS

Algonquin Wildlands League
160 Bloor St. East, Suite 1335
Toronto, ON, Canada M4W 1B9
(416) 324-9760
Educates public in protecting parks in Ontario, especially those with significant wilderness character.

Canadian Forestry Association
185 Somerset St., West, Suite 203
Ottawa, ON, Canada K2P OJ2
(613) 232-1815
Promotes conservation and sustainable development of Canada's forests and related resources.

Canadian Institute of Forestry
151 Slater St., Suite 1005
Ottawa, ON, Canada K1P 5H3
(613) 234-2242
Professional foresters and forest scientists working to improve forestry practices.

Canadian Nature Federation
453 Sussex Dr.
Ottawa, ON, Canada K1N 6Z4
(613) 238-6154
Promotes awareness and enjoyment of nature and conservation of the environment.

Canadian Ornamental Plant Association
652 Aberdeen Ave.
North Bay, ON, Canada P1B 7H9
(705) 495-2563

Canadian Parks and Wilderness Society
160 Bloor St., East, Suite 1335
Toronto, ON, Canada M4W 1B9
(416) 972-0868
Canadian citizens dedicated to the establishment and sound management of national and provincial parks.

Canadian Wildflower Society
90 Wolfrey Ave.
Toronto, ON, Canada M4K 1K8
(416) 466-6428
Promotes the study, conservation and cultivation of North American wild flora.

The Conservation Council of Ontario
489 College St., Suite 506
Toronto, ON, Canada M6G 1A5
(416) 969-9637

Federation of Ontario Naturalists
355 Lesmill Rd.
Don Mills, ON, Canada M3B 2W8
(416) 444-8419
Protects and increases awareness of Ontario's natural areas and wildlife. Nearly 80 federated clubs.

Nature Conservancy of Canada
794A Broadview Ave.
Toronto, ON, Canada M4K 2P7
(416) 469-1701
Acquires, preserves and supports ecologically significant land areas, with the cooperation of industry, conservation, governmental groups and individuals.

Ontario Forestry Association
150 Consumers Rd., Suite 509
Willowdale, ON, Canada M2J 1P9
(416) 493-4565
Promotes protection and utilization of Ontario's forest resources.

Ontario Shade Tree Council
5 Shoreham Dr.
North York, ON, Canada M3N 1S4
(416) 661-6600

Wildlife Habitat Canada
1704 Carling Ave., Suite 301
Ottawa, ON, Canada K2A 1C7
(613) 722-2090

PROVINCIAL ENVIRONMENTAL AGENCIES AND FOUNDATIONS

MANITOBA

Manitoba Natural Resources
314 Legislative Building
Winnipeg, MB, Canada R3C 0V8
(204) 945-3730

Manitoba Naturalists Society
302-128 James Ave.
Winnipeg, MB, Canada R3B 0N8
(204) 943-9029

NEW BRUNSWICK

Department of Natural Resources
Box 6000
Fredericton, NB, Canada E3B 5H1
(506) 453-2510

NEWFOUNDLAND

Department of Environment and Lands
Parks Division
Box 4750
St. John's, NF, Canada A1C 5T7
(709) 729-6974

Department of Tourism & Culture
P.O. Box 8700
St. John's, NF, Canada A1B 4J6
(709) 729-0659

NOVA SCOTIA

Department of Natural Resources
P.O. Box 698
Halifax, NS, Canada B3J 2T9
(902) 424-5935

Nova Scotia Forestry Association
P.O. Box 1113
Truro, NS, Canada B2N 5G9
(902) 893-4653

Nova Scotia Museum
1747 Summer St.
Halifax, NS, Canada B3H 3A6
(902) 424-6478

ONTARIO

Parks and Policy, Heritage Branch
Ministry of Natural Resources
90 Sheppard Ave. East
North York, ON, Canada M3N 3A1
(819) 953-1444

PRINCE EDWARD ISLAND

Department of the Environment
P.O. Box 2000
Charlottetown, PE, Canada C1A 7N8
(902) 368-5340

Island Nature Trust
Box 265
Charlottetown, PE, Canada C1A 7K4
(902) 892-7513

QUEBEC

Department of Recreation, Fish & Game
Place de la Capital 150 East
St. Cyrille Blvd.
Quebec City, QC, Canada G1R 4Y1
(418) 643-6527

Direction des Réserves Ecologique et Sites Naturels
Environment-Quebec
3900, Rue Marly
Ste.-Foy, QC, Canada G1X 4E4
(418) 644-3358

Quebec Forestry Association
(Association Forestière Quebecoise, Inc.)
175 Rue Saint-Jean, 4e étage
Quebec City, QC, Canada G1R 1N4
(418) 529-2991

SASKATCHEWAN

Saskatchewan Environment
3085 Albert St.
Regina, SK, Canada S4S OB1
(306) 787-6133

Saskatchewan Natural History Society
Box 4348
Regina, SK, Canada S4P 3W6
(306) 780-9273
Publishes a journal of natural history of the region and special publications on the flora and fauna of Saskatchewan and neighboring provinces.

Saskatchewan Natural Resources
5211 Albert St.
Regina, SK, Canada S4S 5W6
(306) 587-2930

BIBLIOGRAPHY

And Recommended Reading

American Association of Nurserymen. *State Association Listing.* Washington, DC: 1993.

American Forests. *National Register of Big Trees*, 1994 Edition. Washington, DC: American Forests, 1994.

Bailey, L. H. *The Standard Cyclopedia of Horticulture*, Second Edition. New York: The Macmillan Co., 1917.

Bailey, Liberty Hyde, and Ethel Zoe Bailey. *Hortus Third.* Revised and Expanded by the Staff of the Liberty Hyde Bailey Hortorium. New York: Macmillan Publishing Co., 1976.

Bacon, Sir Francis, Lord Verulam. *Sylva Sylvarum: A Naturall Historie in Ten Centuries.* London: William Lee, 1627.

Baron, Robert C., Editor. *The Garden and Farm Books of Thomas Jefferson.* Golden, CO: Fulcrum, Inc., 1987.

Barton, Barbara J. *Taylor's Guide to Specialty Nurseries.* Boston and New York: Houghton Mifflin Co., 1993.

Boutcher, William. *A Treatise on Forest-Trees.* Edinburgh: R. Fleming, 1775.

Braun, E. Lucy. *The Woody Plants of Ohio* (Facsimile of the 1961 Edition). New York: Hafner Press, 1969.

Britton, Nathaniel Lord. *Manual of the Flora of the Northern States and Canada.* New York: Henry Holt and Co., 1907.

Britton, Nathaniel Lord, and Addison Brown. *An Illustrated Flora of the Northern United States, Canada and the British Possesions.* New York: Charles Scribner's Sons, 1913.

Brooks, A. B. *West Virginia Trees.* Parsons, WV: McClain Printing Co., Reprinted 1976 from West Virginia University Agricultural Experiment Station Bulletin 175, 1920.

Brown, Clair A. *Louisiana Trees and Shrubs.* Baton Rouge: Louisiana Forestry Commission, 1945.

Brown, Claud L., and L. Katherine Kirkman. *Trees of Georgia and Adjacent States.* Portland, OR: Timber Press, 1990.

Brown, D. J. *The Trees of North America.* New York: Harper & Brothers, 1846.

Brown, H. P. *Trees of New York State; Native and Naturalized.* Syracuse, NY: Technical Publication No. 15, The New York State College of Forestry, 1921.

Brown, Russell G., and Melvin L. Brown. *Woody Plants of Maryland.* Baltimore, MD: Port City Press, 1972.

Brown, Wilson. *Reading the Woods: Seeing More in Nature's Familiar Faces.* Harrisburg, PA: Stackpole Books, 1969.

Bryant, Arthur, Sr. *Forest Trees for Shelter, Ornament, and Profit.* New York: Henry T. Williams, Publisher, 1871.

Brzuszek, Robert F. *Native Trees for Urban Landscapes in the Gulf South.* Picayune, MS: The Crosby Arboretum, 1993.

Burns, G. P., and C. H. Otis. *The Handbook of Vermont Trees.* Rutland, VT: Charles E. Tuttle Co., 1979.

Campbell, Robert R. Personal communication: endangered species concepts. Canadian Wildlife Service, 1993.

Canada Department of Northern Affairs and National Resources, Forestry Branch. *Native Trees of Canada*, Fifth Edition. Ottawa: Bulletin No. 61, Edmond Cloutier, 1956.

Clarke, John. *A Treatise on the Mulberry Tree and Silkworm.* Philadelphia: Thomas, Cowperthwait & Co., 1839.

Coker, William Chambers, and Henry Roland Totten. *Trees of the Southeastern States.* Chapel Hill, NC: University of North Carolina Press, 1937.

Cole, Rex Vicat. *The Artistic Anatomy of Trees.* London: Seeley, Service & Co., Ltd., 1915.

Common Trees of South Carolina. Columbia, SC: The State Co., 1944.

Craighead, F. C. *Insect Enemies of Eastern Forests.* Washington, DC: Miscellaneous Publication No. 657, USDA, 1950.

Dame, Lorin L., and Henry Brooks. *Handbook of the Trees of New England.* New York: Dover Publications, 1972, from the original, 1901.

Daubenmire, R. F. *Plants and Environment: A Textbook of Plant Autecology.* New York: John Wilet & Sons, Inc., 1959.

Davis, Richard C., Editor. *Encyclopedia of American Forest and Conservation History.* New York: Macmillan Publishing Co., 1983.

Davison, Verne E. *Attracting Birds: from the Prairies to the Atlantic.* New York: Thomas Y. Crowell Co., Inc., 1967.

de Forest, Elizabeth Kellam. *The Gardens and Grounds at Mount Vernon: How Washington Planned and Planted Them.* Mount Vernon, VA: The Mount Vernon Ladies' Association of the Union, 1982.

de Klemm, Cyrille. *Wild Plant Conservation and the Law.* Cambridge, UK: IUCN Environmental Policy and Law Paper Number 24, IUCN Publications, 1990.

Deam, Charles C. *Trees of Indiana*, Second Revised Edition. Fort Wayne, IN: Fort Wayne Printing Co., 1931.

Dean, Blanche Evans. *Trees and Shrubs of the Southeast.* Birmingham, AL: Birmingham Audubon Society Press, 1988.

Dirr, Michael A. *Manual of Woody Landscape Plants: Their Identification, Ornamental Characteristics, Culture, Propagation, and Uses*, Third Edition. Champaign, IL: Stipes Publishing Co., 1983.

Dix, Mary Ellen, et al., Technical Coordinators. *Common Insect Pests of Trees in the Great Plains.* Lincoln, Nebraska: Great Plains Agricultural Council Publication No. 119, Nebraska Cooperative Extension Service (ND).

Downing, A. J. *A Treatise on the Theory and Practice of Landscape Gardening.* New York: George P. Putnam, 1849.

Duncan, Wilbur H. *Trees of the Southeastern United States.* Athens, GA: The University of Georgia Press, 1988.

Dwelley, Marilyn. *Trees and Shrubs of New England.* Camden, ME: Down East Books, 1980.

Eastman, John. *The Book of Forest and Thicket.* Harrisburg, PA: Stackpole Books, 1992.

Elias, Thomas S. *The Complete Trees of North America.* New York: Gramcrcy Publishing Co., 1987.

Elton, Charles S. *The Ecology of Invasions by Animals and Plants.* London: Methuen and Co., Ltd., 1958.

Evelyn, John. *Silva: or, a Discourse of Forest Trees and the Propagation of Timber in His Majesty's Dominions.* London: The Royal Society, 1729.

Fernald, Merritt Lyndon. *Gray's Manual of Botany*, Eighth (Centennial) Edition, Corrected Printing. New York: Van Nostrand Reinhold Co., 1970.

Flagg, Wilson. *A Year Among the Trees; or, The Woods and By-Ways of New England*. Boston: Educational Publishing Co., 1890.

Flint, Harrison L. *Landscape Plants for Eastern North America Exclusive of Florida and the Immediate Gulf Coast*. New York: John Wiley and Sons, 1983.

Foster, John H. *Trees and Shrubs of New Hampshire*. Concord, NH: Society for the Protection of New Hampshire Forests, 1951.

Fowells, H. A. *Silvics of Forest Trees of the United States*. Washington, DC: Agriculture Handbook No. 271, Forest Service, USDA, 1965.

Gallagher, Arlene, et al. *Directory of Natural Area Programs*. Mukwonago, WI: Natural Areas Association, 1993.

Gerhold, Henry D., et al., Editors. *Street Tree Factsheets*. University Park, PA: Penn State College of Agricultural Sciences, 1993.

Gibson, Henry H. *American Forest Trees*. Chicago: Hardwood Record, The Regan Printing House, 1913.

Gleason, Henry Allen, and Arthur Cronquist. *Manual of Vascular Plants of Northeastern United States and Adjacent Canada*. Princeton, NJ: D. Van Nostrand Co., Inc., 1963.

Godfrey, Robert K. *Trees, Shrubs, and Woody Vines of Northern Florida and Adjacent Georgia and Alabama*. Athens, GA: University of Georgia Press, 1988.

Gordon, Rue E., Editor. *1993 Conservation Directory*. Washington, DC: National Wildlife Federation, 1993.

Green, Charlotte Hilton. *Trees of the South*. Chapel Hill, NC: The University of North Carolina Press, 1939.

A Guide to Common Insects and Diseases of Forest Trees in the Northeastern United States. Broomall, PA: Forest Service, USDA, 1979.

Gupton, Oscar W., and Fred C. Swope. *Trees and Shrubs of Virginia*. Charlottesville, VA: University Press of Virginia, 1981.

Guries, Raymond P. Personal communication: elm disease research. University of Wisconsin-Madison, 1993.

Harlow, William M. *Trees of the Eastern United States and Canada*. New York: McGraw-Hill Book Co., Inc., 1942.

Harlow, William M., and Ellwood S. Harrar. *Textbook of Dendrology Covering the Important Forest Trees of the United States and Canada*. New York: McGraw-Hill Book Co., Inc., 1941.

Harrar, Ellwood S., and J. George Harrar. *Guide to Southern Trees*. New York: Dover Publications, Inc., 1962, from the original, 1946.

Haworth, Paul Leland. *George Washington: Farmer*. Indianapolis: The Bobbs-Merrill Co., Publishers, 1915.

Hepting, George H. *Diseases of Forest and Shade Trees of the United States*. Washington, DC: Agriculture Handbook No. 386, Forest Service, USDA, 1971.

Hightshoe, Gary L. *Native Trees, Shrubs, and Vines for Urban and Rural America*. New York: Van Nostrand Reinhold Co., 1988.

Holmes, J. S. *Common Forest Trees of North Carolina*. Chapel Hill, NC: North Carolina Geological and Economic Survey, 1922.

Horn, Henry S. *The Adaptive Geometry of Trees*. Princeton, NJ: Princeton University Press, 1971.

Hosie, R. C. *Native Trees of Canada*. Don Mills, Ontario: Fitzhenry & Whiteside Limited, 1979.

Hough, Romeyn Beck. *Handbook of the Trees of the Northern States and Canada East of the Rocky Mountains*. New York: The Macmillan Co., 1947.

Hunter, Carl G. *Trees, Shrubs, and Vines of Arkansas*. Little Rock: The Ozark Society Foundation, 1989.

Hyland, Fay, and Ferdinand H. Steinmetz. *The Woody Plants of Maine*. Orono, ME: University Press, 1944.

Illick, Joseph S. *Pennsylvania Trees*. Pennsylvania Department of Forests and Waters Bulletin 11, 1928.

Jaynes, Richard A., Editor. *Handbook of North American Nut Trees*. Knoxville, TN: The Northern Nut Growers Assoc., 1969.

Johnson, Warren T., and Howard H. Lyon. *Insects that Feed on Trees and Shrubs*. Ithaca, NY: Cornell University Press, 1976.

Krussmann, Gerd. *Manual of Cultivated Broad-Leaved Trees & Shrubs*. Portland, OR: Timber Press, 1986.

Krussmann, Gerd. *Manual of Cultivated Conifers*. Portland, OR: Timber Press, 1985.

Kurz, Herman, and Robert K. Godfrey. *Trees of Northern Florida*. Gainesville, FL: University of Florida Press, 1962.

Leighton, Ann. *American Gardens in the Eighteenth Century, "For Use or for Delight."* Amherst, MA: The University of Massachusetts Press, 1986.

Li, Hui-Lin. *The Origin and Cultivation of Shade and Ornamental Trees*. Philadelphia: University of Pennsylvania Press, 1963.

Li, Hui-Lin. *Trees of Pennsylvania, the Atlantic States, and the Lake States*. Philadelphia: University of Pennsylvania Press, 1972.

Little, Elbert L., Jr. *Atlas of United States Trees, Volume 1. Conifers and Important Hardwoods*. Washington, DC: Miscellaneous Publication No. 1146, Forest Service, USDA, 1971.

Little, Elbert L., Jr. *Atlas of United States Trees, Volume 3. Minor Western Hardwoods*. Washington, DC: Miscellaneous Publication No. 1314, Forest Service, USDA, 1976.

Little, Elbert L., Jr. *Atlas of United States Trees, Volume 4. Minor Eastern Hardwoods*. Washington, DC: Miscellaneous Publication No. 1342, Forest Service, USDA, 1977.

Little, Elbert L., Jr. *Check List of Native and Naturalized Trees of the United States (Including Alaska)*. Washington, DC: Agriculture Handbook No. 41, Forest Service, USDA, 1953.

Martin, Alexander C., et al. *American Wildlife & Plants: A Guide to Wildlife Food Habits*. New York: Dover Publications, 1961.

Mattoon, W. R., and J. M. Beal. *Forest Trees of Mississippi*. State College, MS: Mississippi State College, 1936.

McCoy, Doyle. *Roadside Trees and Shrubs of Oklahoma*. Norman, OK: University of Oklahoma Press, 1981.

Meehan, Thomas. *The American Handbook of Ornamental Trees*. Philadelphia: Lippincott, Grambo, and Co., 1853.

Meier, Lauren, and Betsy Chittenden, Compilers. *Preserving Historic Landscapes: An Annotated Bibliography*. Washington, DC: National Park Service, USDI, 1990.

Michaux, F. Andrew, and Thomas Nuttall. *The North American Sylva*, Vol. I-V. Philadelphia: D. Rice and A.N. Hart, 1857.

Michaux, F. Andrew. *A Treatise on the Resinous Trees of North America*. Paris: D'Hautel, 1819.

Moll, Gary, and Stanley Young. *Growing Greener Cities: A Tree-Planting Handbook*. Los Angeles: Living Planet Press, 1992.

Morin, Nancy R., Convening Editor. *Flora of North America North of Mexico*, Volume 2. New York: Oxford University Press, 1993

Morin, Nancy R., Convening Editor. *Flora of North America North of Mexico*, Volume 3. New York: Oxford University Press (in press).

Morse, Larry. Personal communication: native species concepts. The Nature Conservancy, 1993.
Nowak, David J., and T. Davis Sydnor. *Popularity of Tree Species and Cultivars in the United States*. Radnor, PA: General Technical Report NE-166, Forest Service, USDA, 1992.
Oosting, Henry J. *The Study of Plant Communities*. San Francisco: W. H. Freeman and Co., 1956.
Otis, Charles Herbert. *Michigan Trees*. Ann Arbor, MI: University of Michigan, 1931.
Peattie, Donald Culross. *A Natural History of Trees of Eastern and Central North America*. Boston: Houghton Mifflin Co., 1950.
Peattie, Donald Culross. *A Natural History of Western Trees*. Boston: Houghton Mifflin Co., 1953.
Petrides, George A. *A Field Guide to Eastern Trees*. Boston: Houghton Mifflin Co., 1988.
Pinchot, Gifford. *The Adirondack Spruce*. New York: The Critic Co., 1898.
Pool, Raymond J. *Handbook of Nebraska Trees*, Third Edition, Nebraska Conservation Bulletin No. 32. Lincoln, NE: University of Nebraska, 1951.
Les Principaux Arbres du Quebec. Quebec: Gouvernement du Quebec, Ministère de l'Energie et des Resources, 1982.
Pyle, Robert Michael. *The Audubon Society Field Guide to North American Butterflies*. New York: Alfred A. Knopf, 1981.
Quebec Forests. Quebec: Ministère des Terres et Forêts, Service de l'Information, 1974.
Radford, Albert E., Harry E. Ahles and C. Ritchie Bell. *Manual of the Vascular Flora of the Carolinas*. Chapel Hill, NC: The University of North Carolina Press, 1981.
Randall, Charles Edgar, and Henry Clepper. *Famous and Historic Trees*. Washington, DC: The American Forestry Association, 1977.
Rehder, Alfred. *Manual of Cultivated Trees and Shrubs Hardy in North America*, Second Edition. New York: Macmillan Publishing Co., Inc., 1940.
Richard, J., and Joan E. Heitzman. *Butterflies and Moths of Missouri*. Jefferson City, Missouri: Missouri Department of Conservation, 1987.
Riffle, Jerry W., and Glenn W. Peterson, Technical Coordinators. *Diseases of Trees in the Great Plains*. Fort Collins, CO: General Technical Report RM-129, Forest Service, USDA, 1986.
Rosendahl, Carl Otto. *Trees and Shrubs of the Upper Midwest*. Minneapolis: University of Minnesota Press, 1955.
Rowe, J. S. *Forest Regions of Canada*. Ottawa: Department of the Environment, Canadian Forestry Service Publication No. 1300, 1972.
Rupp, Rebecca. *Red Oaks & Black Birches*. Pownal, VT: Storey Communications, Inc., 1990.
Sargent, Charles Sprague. *Manual of the Trees of North America (Exclusive of Mexico)*. Boston and New York: Houghton, Mifflin and Co., 1905.
Sayn-Wittgenstein, L. *Recognition of Tree Species on Air Photographs by Crown Characteristics*. Ottawa, Ontario: Canada Department of Forestry, Technical Note No. 95, 1960.
Schopmeyer, C. S., Technical Coordinator. *Seeds of Woody Plants in the United States*. Washington, DC: Agriculture Handbook No. 450, Forest Service, USDA, 1974
Schwarz, G. Frederick. *Forest Trees and Forest Scenery*. New York: The Grafton Press, 1902.
Seeds: The Yearbook of Agriculture, 1961. Washington, DC: 87th Congress, House Document No. 29, 1961.
Settergren, Carl, and R. E. McDermott. *Trees of Missouri*. Columbia, MO: University of Missouri-Columbia, 1974.
Simmons, James Raymond. *The Historic Trees of Massachusetts*. Boston: Marshall Jones Co., 1919.
Simpson, Benny J. *A Field Guide to Texas Trees*. Austin, TX: Texas Monthly Press, 1988.
Snyder, Leon C. *Trees and Shrubs for Northern Gardens*. Minneapolis: University of Minnesota Press, 1980.
Spurr, Stephen H. *Forest Ecology*. New York: The Ronald Press Co., 1964.
Stephens, H. A. *Trees, Shrubs, and Woody Vines in Kansas*. Lawrence, KS: The University Press of Kansas, 1969.
Stephens, H. A. *Woody Plants of the North Central Plains*. Lawrence, KS: The University Press of Kansas, 1973.
Sternberg, Guy. *Starhill Forest Arboretum Accessions, 1961-1994*. Petersburg, IL (unpublished records).
Taber, William S. *Delaware Trees*. Dover, DE: Publication 6, Delaware State Forestry Department, 1937.
Taylor's Guide to Gardening Techniques. New York: Houghton Mifflin Co., 1991.
Thoreau, Henry David. *Walden*. New York: Thomas Y. Crowell Co., Inc., Apollo Edition, 1966.
Thwaites, Reuben Gold, Editor. *Original Journals of the Lewis and Clark Expedition*. New York: Dodd, Mead & Co., 1904.
Trees: The Yearbook of Agriculture, 1949. Washington, DC: 81st Congress, House Document No. 29, 1949.
Turnbull, Cass. *The Complete Guide to Landscape Design, Renovation, and Maintenance*. White Hall, Virginia: Betterway Publications, Inc., 1991.
Tyrrell, Lucy E. *Old-Growth Forests on National Park Service Lands: NPS Views and Information*. Madison, WI: Great Lakes Cooperative Park Studies Unit, University of Wisconsin-Madison, 1991.
USDA Plant Hardiness Zone Map. Washington, DC: Miscellaneous Publication No. 1475, Agricultural Research Service, USDA, 1990.
USDA Soil Conservation Service, Plant Materials Centers. Personal communications, 1993-1994.
van der Linden, Peter, and Donald R. Farrar. *Forest and Shade Trees of Iowa*. Ames, IA: Iowa State University, 1984.
Van Dersal, William R. *Native Woody Plants of the United States: Their Erosion-Control and Wildlife Values*. Washington, DC: Miscellaneous Publication No. 303, Soil Conservation Service, USDA, 1938.
Van Doren, Mark, Editor. *Travels of William Bartram*. New York: Dover Publications, 1955.
Vines, Robert A. *Trees, Shrubs, and Woody Vines of the Southwest*. Austin, TX: University of Texas Press, 1960.
Walker, Laurence C. *Forests: A Naturalist's Guide to Trees and Forest Ecology*. New York: John Wiley & Sons, Inc., 1990.
Wandell, Willet N., Project Leader. *Handbook of Landscape Tree Cultivars*. Gladstone, IL: East Prairie Publishing Co., 1989.
Wandell, Willet N. *Hardiness of Landscape Tree Cultivars*. Gladstone, IL: East Prairie Publishing Co., 1993.
Wharton, Mary E., and Roger W. Barbour. *Trees & Shrubs of Kentucky*. Lexington, KY: The Univ. Press of Kentucky, 1973.
Wilson, Brayton F. *The Growing Tree*. Amherst, MA: The University of Massachusetts Press, 1984.

INDEX

Boldface page numbers refer to tree and leaf silhouettes.

USDA HARDINESS ZONE MAP

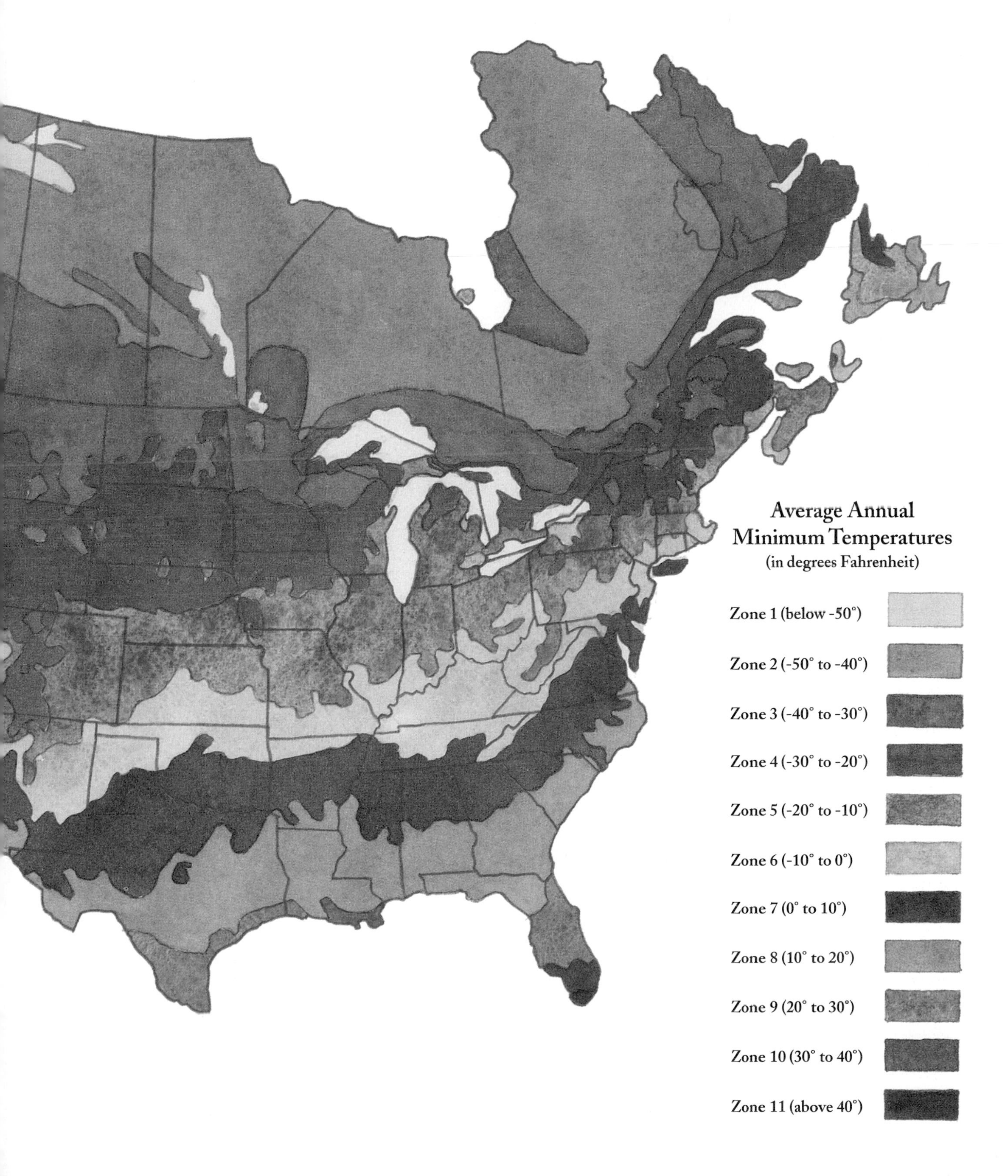

PHOTOGRAPHY & ILLUSTRATION CREDITS

All photographs taken by Guy and Edie Sternberg except as follows:

Front Cover: Larry Lefever/Grant Heilman Photography, Inc.
page 8-9: Derek Fell
page 12-13: Jeff Foott/Bruce Coleman Inc.
page 14: (top) Richard W. Brown; (bottom) Derek Fell
page 18: Derek Fell
page 21: Derek Fell
page 22-23: Larry Lefever/Grant Heilman Photography, Inc.
page 24:(bottom) Derek Fell
page 28-29: Larry Lefever/Grant Heilman Photography, Inc.
page 38: Derek Fell
page 40: Lefever/Grushow/Grant Heilman Photography, Inc.
page 45: Derek Fell
page 51: (top) Derek Fell; (bottom) Jane Grushow/Grant Heilman Photography, Inc.
page 52: Derek Fell
page 53: Roy Klehm
page 55: (bottom) Derek Fell
page 57: Richard W. Brown
page 58: Derek Fell
page 59: Derek Fell
page 60-61: Richard W. Brown
page 70: Derek Fell
page 87: (bottom) Jim Wilson
page 92-93: Larry Lefever/Grant Heilman Photography, Inc.
page 97: (bottom) Albin P. Dearing V/The Davey Tree Expert Company
page 101: (bottom) Derek Fell
page 109: McJunkin Photography
page 116: Derek Fell
page 118: Loran C. Anderson
page 119: (top) Jim Wilson; (bottom) Gil Nelson
page 120: Jerry Pavia
page 126: Jim Strawser/Grant Heilman Photography, Inc.
page 127: Jane Wilson
page 128: Derek Fell
page 131: Larry Lefever/Grant Heilman Photography, Inc.
page 137: Richard W. Brown
page 140: Derek Fell
page 143: (top) Derek Fell
page 147: Derek Fell
page 148: Derek Fell
page 149: (right) Derek Fell
page 150: McJunkin Photography
page 151: (left) Jim Wilson
page 154: Albin P. Dearing V/The Davey Tree Expert Company
page 159: Derek Fell
page 160: (bottom) Jim Wilson
page 162: Jim Wilson
page 164: Derek Fell
page 165: (bottom) Derek Fell
page 169: Andy Wasowski
page 170: Jim Wilson
page 176: Derek Fell
page 180: Derek Fell
page 183: Larry Lefever/Grant Heilman Photography, Inc.
page 187: Michael Thompson
page 188-189: Grant Heilman/Grant Heilman Photography, Inc.
page 190: Grant Heilman/Grant Heilman Photography, Inc.
page 191: Grant Heilman Photography, Inc.
page 196: Derek Fell
page 209: Derek Fell
page 212: (bottom) Derek Fell
page 218: Albin P. Dearing V/The Davey Tree Expert Company
page 221: (top) Saxon Holt
page 224: Robert Carr/Bruce Coleman Inc.
page 226: (top) Derek Fell
page 238: Jerry Pavia
page 241: Derek Fell
page 244: Bailey Nurseries, Inc.
page 245: Derek Fell
page 247: Saxon Holt
page 249: Grant Heilman/Grant Heilman Photography, Inc.
page 253: Grant Heilman/Grant Heilman Photography, Inc.
Back Cover: (background) Richard W. Brown; (author photograph) McJunkin Photography
Tree & Leaf Silhouettes (pages 31-35): Illustrations by Adelaide Murphy
USDA Zone Map (page 287): Illustration by Jean Carlson Masseau